The ERC Family Money Book

1984

by
The ERC Editorial Staff

EXECUTIVE REPORTS CORPORATION

Englewood Cliffs, New Jersey 07632

This publication is designed to provide accurate and authoritative information in regard to the subject matter covered. It is sold with the understanding that the publisher is not engaged in rendering legal, accounting or other professional service. If legal advice or other expert assistance is required, the service of a competent professional person should be sought.

. . From a Declaration of Principles jointly adopted by a Committee of the American Bar Association and a Committee of Publishers and Associations.

Opinions and recommendations given herein are based on research believed to be accurate and reliable but recognized as not infallible. It should be emphasized that the investments mentioned in this book were chosen only to demonstrate a given point or points. Readers must necessarily act at their own risk. No material in this book is given as a recommendation, offer or solicitation for purchase or sale of any security or property. Author may or may not have an interest in any investment medium or media mentioned herein.

© **Copyright MCMLXXXIII**
EXECUTIVE REPORT CORPORATION
Englewood Cliffs, N.J.

All rights reserved. No part of this publication may be reproduced in any form, or by any means, without permission in writing from the publisher. Printed in U.S.A.

Library of Congress Catalogue Card Number: 83-16466

WHAT THIS BOOK WILL DO FOR YOU

Your all-new, up-to-the-minute ERC Family Money Book helps you attain money and security goals you may have thought were beyond your reach. Specifically, it shows you—

(l) How to Build Wealth

With the Family Money Book, you will find out how with less than $1,000 you can get in on Wall Street action, the gold market or Government bonds, and how systematic, low-cost plans can put you on the road to accumulating real wealth. You'll even discover how to take a shot at a fortune in oil & gas for just a little more than it costs to tune up your car. Collectibles aren't just for the wealthy. Your hobby or even a collection of what you thought was household junk can be turned into profits.

Your new ERC Family Money Book shows how the concept of leverage—using other people's money instead of your own—can multiply profits in stocks, bonds, real estate, and commodities. The Money Book points up those armchair strategies that can get you in on lucrative industries (and tax breaks) with a minimum of time, money and risk. We also highlight the latest in sophisticated wealth-building techniques—such as "put bonds", option writing, high-yield Ginnie Mae bonds—as well as offbeat wealth-builders such as precious metals, strategic metals, diamonds and penny stock. The most conservative wealth-builders are also covered—how to turn U.S. Savings Bonds into tax-exempts, how to get a big dollar edge with Treasury bills, and how to kick up your effective yield with special securities that yield income that's fully or partially exempt from tax.

(2) How to Save Big Tax Dollars

You can save hundreds—maybe even thousands—of tax dollars by making tax-wise personal, business, and investment decisions during the year. The first eleven Chapters of your ERC Family Money Book are jammed with tax-saving strategies for you to use right now. You also save tax dollars by using the scores of legitimate tax-saving devices available to you on your return. Chapter Twelve is devoted to such last-minute tax-saving moves. The Money Book spells out the best income-splitting strategies that use tax-savings to finance important family goals. Even your home can be an important source of tax deductions (as well as tax-sheltered profits if and when you sell).

(3) How to Make the Most of Your Money for a Better Standard of Living

Your new ERC Family Money Book pinpoints how you can squeeze extra spending power out of your earnings, how to increase take-home pay without a raise, and painless ways to control personal and family expenses. It includes eighteen ways to get credit, the cheapest ways to borrow for your family needs, and how to protect your rights as a borrower and consumer. There's a special concentration on how to plug up the family's big money drainers—for example, how to slash tens of thousands of dollars off home mortgage interest costs, how to shave a couple of percentage points off credit-card interest, and how to have a high-class vacation without a financial hang-over. We also show you how to slash the skyrocketing cost of a child's education—how the U.S. Government (and other private and public groups) will pitch in with direct aid or low-cost loans, how to fund a big chunk of college costs with tax savings, and how your business or professional practice can deduct what it sets aside for your child's future.

There are hundreds of books that deal with parts of these three key money goals. But they can't—and shouldn't—be dealt with separately. Each is really just one component of the overall goal of attaining financial security. You can't build wealth without capital. And to increase your capital you need to control living costs without cutting your living standard, and cut your tax bill without cutting legal corners.

Here's where your ERC Family Money Book is unique. It literally puts it all together. It shows how today's best cost-cutting, tax-saving, and wealth-building methods can and should go hand-in-hand.

Your ERC Family Money Book is unique in another important way. Each of its wealth-building, money-saving, or tax-saving ideas can be read on its own . You won't have to wade through an entire chapter to understand an idea. You go right to the information you want, grasp the concept in a few minutes, and understand precisely what you should do and how you should do it.

It's a one-source reference and answer guide to your most important money problems.

IMPORTANT: Successful investment and tax-saving techniques depend upon teamwork between knowledgeable taxpayers and competent tax and investment advisers. There's no single investment or tax-shelter strategy that fits every situation and every individual. So make sure the techniques you plan to use are the right ones for you in light of your own overall strategy and your short- and long-term personal objectives. You can best accomplish this by working closely with professional advisers.

The ERC Editorial Staff

Table of Contents

ERC FAMILY MONEY BOOK

Page

Chapter 1—Money-Saving Ways To Buy, Own, And Sell Your Home

Food For Thought for Reluctant Buyers	101
HOW MUCH HOME CAN YOU AFFORD TO BUY?	102
Monthly Mortgage Payment Table	103
DOES IT PAY TO USE A REAL ESTATE BROKER?	104
HOW TO SAVE MONEY BUYING A HOME	105
Homebuyer Checklist For New Homes	107
Two Special Forms Of Ownership—Cooperatives And Condominiums	108
Co-op Ownership	109
Condominium Ownership	109
HOW TO TIE DOWN A HOME WITHOUT SADDLING YOURSELF WITH PROBLEMS	110
HOW TO GET CASH TO BUY A HOME	110
FOURTEEN WAYS TO FINANCE YOUR HOME	110
(1) Fixed Rate Loan	110
(2) Flexible Rate Mortgages	111
(3) Graduated-Payment Mortgages (GPMs)	112
(4) The Growing Equity Mortgage	112
(5) FHA-Insured Mortgage	113
(6) VA-Backed Mortgage	113
(7) FmHA Home Loans	114
(8) The Assumable Mortgage	114
(9) "Buy-Down" Plans	114
(10) Shared Appreciation Mortgage	115
(11) Shared Equity Plan	115
(12) Seller-Held Second Mortgages and "Wraps"	115
(13) "Zero Interest" Mortgage	116
(14) Rent With An "Option To Buy"	116
HOW TO BOOST YOUR CHANCES OF GETTING A HOME LOAN FROM A BANK	116
HOW CLOSING COSTS CAN YIELD TAX BREAKS	117

TABLE OF CONTENTS

	Page
How To Save Money Owning A Home	118
MAJOR MONEY-SAVING MOVE—PREPAYING YOUR MORTGAGE	118
ONE SOURCE OF PREPAYMENT CASH—YOUR LIFE INSURANCE	120
MONEY-SAVING WAYS TO IMPROVE YOUR HOME	121
REMODELING—IMPROVEMENTS THAT BOOST HOME VALUE	124
HOW TO GET A TAX CREDIT FOR SAVING ENERGY	127
HOW TO GET DEDUCTIONS FOR HOME IMPROVEMENTS	128
HOW SPECIAL TAX BREAKS KEEP YOUR HOMESELLING PROFITS INTACT	128
The "Tax-Free Rollover"	128
Once-In-A-Lifetime $125,000 Exclusion	130
Special Tax Break For Job-Connected Sales	131
Does It Pay To Act As Your Own Real Estate Broker?	131
Be Prepared To Bargain	132
Special Situation—A Vacation Home	133

Chapter 2—Top Profit Opportunities In Real Estate: How To Find, Finance And Buy Them

Twelve Top Real Estate Opportunities	202
OPPORTUNITY #1—HOW TO BUILD A SHOESTRING FORTUNE IN RAW LAND	202
OPPORTUNITY #2—HOW TO CASH IN ON LAND SITES OTHER INVESTORS OVERLOOK	205
OPPORTUNITY #3—HOW TO MAKE MONEY IN OLDER APARTMENT HOUSES	206
OPPORTUNITY #4—BUYING SINGLE-FAMILY HOMES FOR INVESTMENT PROFITS	208
OPPORTUNITY #5—HOW INVESTORS CAN GET BIG PAYOFFS BY CONVERTING "WHITE ELEPHANT PROPERTIES"	210
OPPORTUNITY #6—ABANDONED GAS STATIONS CAN PUMP NEW LIFE—AND PROFITS—INTO YOUR REAL ESTATE PORTFOLIO	212
OPPORTUNITY #7—HOW CONDOMINIUM CONVERSIONS CAN BE YOUR KEY TO A REAL ESTATE FORTUNE	213
OPPORTUNITY #8—CONDO AND CO-OP CONVERSION STRATEGY CREATES NEW PROFITS FOR INVESTORS	214
OPPORTUNITY #9—PROFESSIONAL CONDOMINIUMS MAY BE GOOD PROFIT-BUILDING MEDICINE	215
OPPORTUNITY #10—MINIWAREHOUSES—A WAY TO STORE UP PROFITS IN INCOME-PRODUCING PROPERTIES	216

TABLE OF CONTENTS

Page

OPPORTUNITY #11—REAL ESTATE PROFITS IN SAFE-DEPOSIT CENTERS 217
OPPORTUNITY #12—PRIVATE "MAILBOX" CENTERS—A LOW COST WAY TO REAP BIG PROFITS FROM COMMERCIAL PROPERTIES 218
13 KEY WAYS TO BUY REAL ESTATE WITH LITTLE OR NO MONEY DOWN 219
    How New Types of Mortgages Can Give You the Leverage You Need 220
HOW TO GET THE TOP LEVERAGE YOU NEED USING SPECIAL MORTGAGE INSURANCE 220
HOW THE FEDERAL GOVERNMENT CAN HELP YOU GET FAVORABLE FINANCING TERMS 221
    How a Special Government Program Can Be a Two-Way Winner for Real Estate Investors 222
    High-Leverage Opportunity For Investors In New Housing 223
HOW TO SLASH THE AMOUNT OF OUT-OF-POCKET CASH YOU NEED BY USING SECOND MORTGAGES 224
    Use the Seller as the Second-Mortgage Lender 225
    Discounting a Mortgage—Another Way to Convince a Seller to Take Back a Second Mortgage 225
HOW BALLOON MORTGAGES WORK 226
HOW TO BUY INCOME PROPERTY WITHOUT LAYING OUT A PENNY OF CASH 227
HOW YOU CAN BUY THE PROPERTY YOU WANT AT BETTER TERMS WITH A WRAPAROUND MORTGAGE 228
    Caution—Creative Financing Can Cause Due-On-Sale Problems 229
HOW TO PYRAMID YOUR WAY TO A REAL ESTATE FORTUNE 230
HOW TO FIGURE YOUR FINANCING NEEDS 231
    Constant Monthly Payments for Principal and Interest Mortgage Table 232
HOW TO USE TWO TRIED AND TESTED SHORTCUTS TO FIND BARGAIN INCOME PROPERTIES 233
NEGOTIATION TECHNIQUES—HOW TO BUY PROPERTY YOU WANT ON THE BEST POSSIBLE TERMS 235
    How Your Initial Offer Can Get You the Property At a Bargain Price 235
    How to Convince a Property Owner to Sell to You At Below Market Prices 237
    How to Buy Property With As Little Out-Of-Pocket Cash As Possible 237
HOW TO CASH IN ON TAX-SHELTERED OPPORTUNITIES IN REAL ESTATE 238

TABLE OF CONTENTS

	Page
Depreciation Deductions	239
Accelerated Cost Recovery Table	240
Low-Taxed Capital Gain Profits	241
Tax-Free Exchanges	242
How To Get 100% Cash From a Real Estate Deal and Still Defer Tax on Most of Your Profit	242
How Rehabilitating Historic Structures Offers Unique Tax Shelter Opportunity	243

Chapter 3—Popular Money-Makers: Stocks, Bonds And Government Issues

THE BASICS ON BUILDING WEALTH THROUGH STOCKS AND BONDS	301
How to Pick the Right Broker	301
How to Read the Stock Market Tables in Your Newspaper	302
Key Terms You Should Know When Following the Stock Market	303
How to Know What Stocks to Buy	305
How You Can Find Growth Stocks	307
Is Investing in the Stock Market a Hedge Against Inflation?	308
STOCK MARKET TECHNIQUES FOR THE NEW INVESTOR	308
How Dividend Reinvestment Plans Offer Unique Investment Opportunity	308
Special Tax Break for Utility Stocks	309
How to Get in on the Market on a Shoestring	311
How You Can Invest in the Stock Market for as Little as $25 a Month	312
How Dollar Cost Averaging Boosts Your Odds Of Making Money In the Stock Market	314
HOW TO TAKE ADVANTAGE OF MUTUAL FUNDS	315
Load vs. No-Load Funds	316
Open-End vs. Closed-End Funds	317
SOPHISTICATED STOCK MARKET TECHNIQUES	317
How to Buy Stocks and Bonds on Margin	317
How To Take Advantage of Short Sales	319
How to Reap Profits From Stock Options	320
TOP TAX-SAVING STRATEGIES	321
How to Buy Stock That Pays Tax-Free Dividends	322
How to Fingerprint Stock for Tax Purposes	323
How to Make Sure You Nail Down Your Tax loss When Selling Stock	324

	Page
How to Use Short Sales and Put Options to Your Year-End Tax Advantage	325
How To Match Up Your Gains and Losses	326
HOW TO TAKE ADVANTAGE OF CORPORATE BONDS	326
How To Convert Bonds Into Stock	329
MUNICIPAL BONDS GIVE YOU A BIG TAX EDGE	330
How One Kind of Municipal Bond Can Produce a Tax-Sheltered Nest Egg	331
NEW CONCEPT IN TAX-FREE MUNICIPAL BONDS PROTECTS YOU AGAINST A RISE IN INTEREST RATES	332
How to Get a Special Edge by Swapping Municipals	333
Another Kind of Municipal Bond Escapes All Income Taxes	334
SAFETY FIRST: U. S. GOVERNMENT ISSUES	334
New Look to Safe-As-Fort Knox Investment	334
How To Turn U.S. Savings Bonds Into Tax-Exempts	336
Treasury Bills Have a Built-In Advantage	336
How to Buy Treasury Bills by Mail	337
NEW, LOW-RISK WAYS TO EARN MONEY ON YOUR NEST-EGG DOLLARS	338
Money Market Funds	338
HOW TO LOCK IN PROFITS WITH A CERTIFICATE OF DEPOSIT	339
Buying the 'Right Kind' of CD Can Make a Big Tax Difference	339
HOW TO EARN HIGH INTEREST FROM A SOLID INVESTMENT	340
How Some Government-Backed Bonds Can Pay Off In Tax-Free Income	341

Chapter 4—Today's Top Tax Sheltered Investments

HOW THE TAX LAW PROVIDES THE FUEL TO MAKE TAX-SHELTERED INVESTMENTS WORK	401
HOW LEVERAGE HELPS CREATE MULTIPLE WRITEOFFS	403
WHY A LIMITED PARTNERSHIP IS THE MOST COMMON TAX SHELTER INVESTMENT VEHICLE	404
How To Protect Yourself When You Buy Into A Limited Partnership	405
HOW THE RIGHT REAL ESTATE DEAL CAN OFFER A GOOD RETURN—AND TOP TAX SHELTER	407
How A Sale-Leaseback Deal Can Offer Pure Writeoff Up Front, With A Chance At Big Profits Later On	407
How Shopping Center Deal May Ring Up Tax-Sheltered Profits	408
HOW OIL AND GAS VENTURES OFFER TAX SHELTER WRITEOFFS AND TAX-SHELTERED INCOME	409

Page

How to Invest in Oil and Gas Drilling Operations 410
How An Oil and Gas Deal Can Give You Big Tax Writeoffs............ 411
How Oil and Gas Deals Yield Tax-Sheltered Income 412
HOW A GOLD DEAL CAN PAY OFF IN PROFITS AND TAX
    BENEFITS 413
    INVESTING IN CABLE TV AND GETTING TAX WRITEOFFS:
        IS IT FOR YOU? 415
THE RESEARCH AND DEVELOPMENT TAX SHELTER—A NEW
    TYPE OF SHELTER FOR THE TECHNOLOGICAL AGE 416
HERE'S AN INNOVATIVE TAX SHELTER—BILLBOARDS 417
HOW THE RIGHT CATTLE DEAL CAN ROUND UP TAX
    WRITEOFFS AND TAX-SHELTERED PROFITS 419
HOW AN EQUIPMENT LEASING DEAL CAN PAY OFF 420
HOW THE RIGHT FARMING TAX SHELTER CAN YIELD TOP TAX
    BENEFITS 421
MONEY MAY NOT GROW ON TREES—BUT THERE MAY BE TAX
    SHELTER IN TIMBER 423
THE OTHER SIDE OF THE TAX SHELTER COIN—THE TAX RISKS....... 425

Chapter 5—Offbeat and Speculative Money-Making Opportunities

HOW TO GET A CHANCE AT AN OIL STRIKE ON A $75
    INVESTMENT 501
HOW YOU CAN MAKE MONEY WITH COLLECTIBLES 503
    What Are Collectibles?... 503
    Comic Books.. 504
    How To Make Money In Baseball Cards 505
    Collector's Plates 505
    Summing Up.. 507
"WORTHLESS" STOCKS OR BONDS MAY STILL HAVE VALUE......... 507
HOW TO BUY GOLD AND OTHER PRECIOUS METALS 508
    Buy Gold Without Running The Risk Of Theft 508
    Diamonds And Precious Stones...................................... 510
    A Guaranteed Re-Purchase Agreement 510
THE MARKET IN STRATEGIC METALS 511
    Alternative Avenues 513
MAKING MONEY IN COMMODITIES 514
    Becoming A "Position" Trader....................................... 514
    Two Typical Position Traders 515
    Let a Specialist Handle Your Trades................................. 516
THERE'S MONEY TO BE MADE IN PENNY STOCKS—IF YOU CAN
    STAND THE RISK 516

	Page
The Market in Penny Stocks	516
The Pitfalls in Penny Stock	517
Selling Your Penny Stock	519

Chapter 6—How To Get The Most Mileage From Your Hard-Earned Dollars

HOW TO SET FINANCIAL GOALS FOR YOUR FAMILY'S FUTURE	601
HOW TO FIGURE OUT WHAT YOU'RE WORTH	602
Worksheet for Figuring Your Net Worth	603
HOW TO SET UP A BUDGET THAT PUTS YOU IN CONTROL OF YOUR POCKETBOOK	604
Worksheet for Figuring Income and Expenses	605
How To Boost Your Take-Home Pay Without Getting a Raise	607
HOW TO TELL WHEN TO THROW AWAY YOUR CREDIT CARDS	607
How Much You Can Afford to Pay on Installments	608
How to Map Out Strategies for Buying on Credit	608
HOW TO GET THE MOST FROM YOUR MONEY WHEN YOU BUY ANYTHING	609
How to Read the Legal Clauses in Consumer Credit Contracts	609
PRODUCT WARRANTIES—WHAT THEY MEAN AND HOW THEY CAN HELP YOU	611
How to Protect Yourself From Poor Workmanship	613
How to Protect Your Claim When a Product Goes Sour	613
What to Do When Things Go Wrong	614
Don't Wait—Arbitrate	615
How to Press Your Complaint and Come Out A Winner	616
HOW TO BEAT THE SKYROCKETING COST OF HIGHER EDUCATION	617
National Direct Student Loan Program—What It Means to Your Financial Picture	618
HOW TO GET COLLEGE MONEY THROUGH THE GUARANTEED STUDENT LOAN PROGRAM	618
NEW SOURCE OF COLLEGE AID: THE PARENTS' LOAN PROGRAM	620
RESERVE OFFICERS' TRAINING CORPS (ROTC) SCHOLARSHIPS	620
Rewarding Your Child's Scholastic Ability	621
Important Sources of College Aid Might Be Right Under Your Nose	622
There's More Than One Way to Keep a College Education Down to Earth	623
HOW TO TURN A HIGH-COST VACATION INTO A LOW-COST GET-AWAY	624

TABLE OF CONTENTS

Page

    How To Get Your Vacation Off to a Flying Start 626
    How to Buy a Packaged Plan Without Getting Wrapped Up In
        Hidden Costs 627
    How To Apply For Your Passport..................................... 628
HOW YOU CAN TAKE THE VACATION TRIP OF A LIFETIME—
EACH AND EVERY YEAR 629
    Looking for an Off-Beat Vacation? Try Swapping Your Home........... 630

Chapter 7—How To Get Credit Cheaply And Use It Wisely

HOW TO ESTABLISH A GOOD CREDIT RATING 701
HOW TO MAKE THE MOST OF YOUR RIGHTS AS A BORROWER
OR CREDIT APPLICANT 702
EIGHTEEN WAYS TO GET CREDIT 703
    Credit Source #1—The Unsecured Personal Loan..................... 703
    Credit Source #2—Overdraft Privileges 704
    Credit Source #3—Passbook or CD Loan 704
    Credit Source #4—Collateralized Loans.............................. 704
    Credit Source #5—Bank Credit Cards 704
    Credit Source #6—Credit Union Loans 705
HOW TO BORROW FROM THE COMPANY STORE..................... 705
    Credit Source #7—Employer Loan With Interest 705
    Credit Source #8—Interest-Free Loans............................... 706
    Credit Source #9—Homebuyer's Plan 706
    Credit Source #10—Retirement Plan Loans.......................... 706
    Credit Source #11—Retirement Plan Investment Loans 707
HOW YOUR HOME CAN HELP YOU GET CREDIT 707
    Credit Source #12—Refinancing Your First Mortgage 707
    Credit Source #13—Take Out a Second Mortgage 708
    Credit Source #14—Home Equity Loan............................. 708
OTHER SOURCES OF CREDIT 708
    Credit Source #15—Life Insurance As Collateral 708
    Credit Source #16—Credit Card Advances 709
    Credit Source #17—Store Cards.................................... 709
    Credit Source #18—Auto Loans.................................... 709
HOW TO CUT YOUR COST FOR BORROWING MONEY 710
HOW TO FIGURE YOUR COST FOR BORROWING 711
TAX ANGLES IN CREDIT 712
    Investment Interest Limits.. 712
    Use Of Loan To Buy Tax-Exempts 712
    Paying Interest On a Loan You Renew 713
    Loan For Your Child 714

Chapter 8—How Income Splitting Keeps More Money In The Family

HOW TO CUT RED TAPE—AND FAMILY INCOME TAXES—WHEN
    MAKING GIFTS TO YOUR CHILDREN 801
    The Tax-Wise Way to Give Income Property to a Child 801
    How To Make Sure You Cut Taxes When You Set Up A Bank
        Account For Your Child 803
HOW YOU CAN HELP FINANCE YOUR CHILD'S COLLEGE
    EDUCATION—TAX FREE 804
    Tax Scholarship Plan 804
HOW TO LOCK IN A LOW-TAXED CAPITAL-GAIN PROFIT WHEN
    YOU SET UP A TAX SCHOLARSHIP PLAN 805
    Special Trust Setup Lowers Family Taxes Without Cutting You Off
        From Your Money 807
HOW THE RIGHT STOCK GIFT CAN MEAN TAX SAVINGS FOR
    YOU AND YOUR CHILD 807
FIVE TAX-WISE WAYS TO HELP YOUR SON OR DAUGHTER BUY
    A HOME 809
HOW A FAMILY MEMBER'S STOCK LOSSES CAN TURN INTO
    TAX-FREE INCOME FOR YOU 811
HOW PUTTING YOUR SPOUSE ON THE PAYROLL CAN HELP YOU
    PICK UP THOUSANDS OF DOLLARS IN EXTRA DEDUCTIONS 812
    How You Can Build A Tax-Free College Fund By Putting Your
        Children On The Payroll 813
HOW TO GET A BUSINESS DEDUCTION FOR WHAT YOU PUT
    ASIDE FOR YOUR FAMILY'S FUTURE 814
HOW YOU SHOULD HANDLE YOUR CHILDREN'S BUSINESS
    FINANCES FOR MAXIMUM FAMILY TAX PROTECTION 815
HOW TO CONVERT ORDINARY INCOME FROM YOUR
    CORPORATION INTO TAX-SHELTERED CAPITAL GAIN 817
HOW THE FAMILY PARTNERSHIP CAN MEAN MORE AFTER-TAX
    DOLLARS FOR YOUR FAMILY 819
HOW AN S CORPORATION GIVES YOU AN EASY WAY TO SPLIT
    INCOME WITH FAMILY MEMBERS 820
HOW TO EARN A STEADY RETURN FROM YOUR COMPANY,
    KEEP ITS OWNERSHIP IN THE FAMILY, AND SAVE TAXES
    AS WELL 822
HOW TO TRANSFER OWNERSHIP OF YOUR COMPANY TO YOUR
    CHILDREN IN RETURN FOR TAX-SHELTERED DOLLARS 823

Chapter 9—How To Cut Your Insurance Costs

HOW LIFE INSURANCE CAN GIVE YOUR FAMILY THE MONEY IT
    NEEDS WHEN IT'S NEEDED MOST 901

   Page

    How To Figure Out The Amount Of Coverage You Need 901
HOW TO GET THE MOST PROTECTION FOR YOUR INSURANCE
    DOLLAR.. 903
    How One Type Of Life Policy Gives You More Than Pure
        Protection.. 904
    Other Whole Life Variations 906
HOW YOUR COMPANY CAN HELP YOU KEEP INSURANCE COSTS
    AT ROCK BOTTOM.. 907
    The Big Bargain In Insurance—Company-Paid Group Term.............. 907
    How the Company Can Keep Paying Your Insurance After You
        Retire... 908
    How You Can Get Whole Life Insurance Coverage And Have Your
        Company Pick Up The Bill 909
    How Your Company Can Give You Top-Dollar Protection And Get
        A Money-Back Guarantee....................................... 910
HOW TO TAKE ADVANTAGE OF THE INCOME TAX BREAKS FOR
    LIFE INSURANCE 911
HOW THE LIBERALIZED ESTATE-AND-GIFT TAX RULES AFFECT
    LIFE INSURANCE SETUPS.. 913
KEEP ESTATE TAXES AT ROCK BOTTOM BY GIVING AWAY
    YOUR GROUP-TERM INSURANCE POLICY....................... 914
HOW TO PROTECT YOUR HEALTH—AND YOUR WEALTH 915
    Be Sure Your Extra Health Insurance Premiums Are Really Buying
        More Protection.. 917
    You Can Turn Nondeductible Medical Expenses Into Deductible
        Business Expenses.. 917
HOW TO PROTECT YOUR MOST VALUABLE ASSET 919
    You May Be Paying The Home Insurance Premiums—But Are You
        Protected? 920
HOW TO BUY AUTO INSURANCE PROTECTION 922
    Other Types of Auto Insurance 923
    How To Cut The Cost Of Auto Insurance 924

Chapter 10—How To Build Wealth For A Financial Secure Future

    Who is Going To Foot The Bill for Your Retirement Income?........... 1001
THE BEST TAX-SHELTERED WAY TO BUILD A RETIREMENT
    NEST EGG.. 1001
HOW A PENSION PLAN ALLOWS YOU TO FORETELL YOUR
    RETIREMENT FUTURE.. 1002
    How The Tax Law Treats Your Pension Income 1004

TABLE OF CONTENTS

Page

HOW PROFIT SHARING PLANS LET YOU CASH IN ON YOUR EMPLOYER'S SUCCESS	1005
HOW TO HANDLE PROFIT SHARING PAYOUTS	1006
How Lump Sum Distributions from Retirement Plans Get Favorable Tax Treatment	1006
Why Spreading Out Your Plan Payout Can Leave You Dollars and Cents Ahead	1007
How A Retiring Employee Can Receive a Payout of Cash Plus An Annuity and Still Get A Big Tax Break	1009
How to Save Tax Dollars by Taking Profit-Sharing Payouts in Company Stock	1009
HOW TO BUILD A TAX SHELTERED NEST EGG WITH AN IRA	1010
How Your Spouse Can Help You Make Bigger IRA Contributions	1013
How the Tax Law Lets You Choose the Way to a Secure Retirement Future	1014
HOW THE BETTER-THAN-EVER KEOGH PLAN SETUP CAN HELP SELF-EMPLOYEDS BUILD A TAX-SHELTERED RETIREMENT FUND	1015
How to Make the Best Tax-Shelter Use of the Most Popular Type of Keogh Plan	1016
Should You Have a Pension-Type Keogh?	1017
What's the Price You Pay For Setting up a Keogh Plan?	1018
How Keogh Plan Payouts Qualify for Generous Tax Treatment	1018
WHAT SOCIAL SECURITY RETIREMENT BENEFITS ARE YOU ENTITLED TO?	1019
At-A-Glance Guide to Your Retirement Benefits Under the Social Security Law	1022
How to Cope With the New Tax on Social Security Benefits	1023
What You Can Do Now to Make Sure You Get All of Your Social Security	1024

Chapter 11—What You Must Do Right Now To Provide For Your Family's Future

AVOIDING PROBATE	1101
HOW TO PREPARE AN INVENTORY OF ASSETS	1102
HOW IS YOUR PROPERTY GOING TO BE DISTRIBUTED?	1102
CONFIDENTIAL ASSET INVENTORY FORM	1103
Other Choices to Make Before You See Your Lawyer	1112
HOW TO PREPARE A LETTER OF INSTRUCTION	1113
(1) Whom to Contact and What to Do Immediately	1113
(2) Other Matters to Take Care of	1113

	Page
(3) A List of Where Everything Is	1113
HOW YOU AND YOUR FAMILY CAN TAKE ADVANTAGE OF TODAY'S LIBERAL ESTATE AND GIFT TAX RULES	1114
The Federal Estate Tax	1114
The Federal Gift Tax	1114
Unified Gift-and-Estate-Tax Credit	1115
Unlimited Marital Deduction	1115
Joint Property with Right of Survivorship	1116
Retirement Plan Distributions	1116

Chapter 12—How To Save Tax Dollars On Your Tax Return

DON'T MISS THE EXTRA DEDUCTION FOR YOUR WORKING SPOUSE	1201
HOW INCOME AVERAGING CAN SAVE YOU BIG TAX DOLLARS ON RISING INCOME	1202
PLAN YOUR 'REFRESHER' COURSES WITH TAX SAVING IN MIND	1204
HOW YOUR HOBBY CAN ALLOW YOU TO DEDUCT OTHERWISE NONDEDUCTIBLE PERSONAL EXPENSES	1205
HOW YOU CAN SALVAGE HUNDREDS—MAYBE THOUSANDS— OF TAX DOLLARS OUT OF HOUSEHOLD EXPENSES	1206
HOW THE CHILD-CARE CREDIT CAN CUT YOUR TAX BILL	1207
DON'T MISS OUT ON ANY OF YOUR PERSONAL EXEMPTIONS	1209
Exemptions For You and Your Spouse	1209
Exemptions For You and Your Dependents	1210
HOW TO CLAIM A FULL DEPENDENCY EXEMPTION FOR A RELATIVE YOU SUPPORT ONLY PARTIALLY	1211
Here Are the Key Requirements	1212
HOW TO GET TWO DEPENDENCY DEDUCTIONS FOR THE PRICE OF ONE	1212
HOW TO BOOST YOUR DEDUCTIONS BY MAKING EVERY YEAR A "RECORD YEAR"	1213
HOW TO COPE WITH THE NEW, TOUGHER RULES FOR DEDUCTING MEDICAL EXPENSES	1215
Nineteen Deductible Medical Expenses You Won't Find In Your Tax Form Instructions	1215
How to Get a Medical Deduction for the Cost of Help Around the House	1217
How You Can Return Home With a Deduction After Long-Distance Medical Travel	1217
How You Can Deduct the Cost of Supporting an Aging Relative	1219
Are You Passing Up Some Charitable Deductions?	1220
How To Deduct the Cost of Going to Church	1220

Chapter 1

Money-Saving Ways To Buy, Own, And Sell Your Home

Buying a home is the single most expensive purchase a family is likely to make. A home involves an obligation that lasts for years, ties up thousands of dollars and creates opportunities for great profit—or expense.

The very word, "home," has acquired complexity. It refers to more than a frame or brick house on some quiet, tree-shaded street. "Home" can mean a cooperative unit in a towering apartment house or condominium townhouse in a sprawling lakeside community. Whether it's 20 years old or newly built to your specifications, your home is more than just shelter. If it's well-located and well-maintained, your home should appreciate in value. Your home also provides "tax shelter" by way of deductions and credits that reduce your Federal income tax year after year. And if and when you sell the home at a profit, you can protect some or all of your gain from tax.

But before discussing home ownership futher, let's consider those people who may be holding off because they are waiting for a better homebuying climate—lower interest rates and lower home prices. Here's some—

Food For Thought for Reluctant Buyers

The only way you'll come out ahead by waiting is if rates drop by a significant amount—say two or three points—or if both rates and prices go down (unlikely). A more realistic possibility: Interest rates may go down, but not by enough to wipe out low-price increases.

> **Example:** Let's suppose today's mortgage rate is 13%, and that it declines to 12% in one year's time. However, that same year sees an average 8% increase in home prices. Here's how this set of facts would affect a family looking at a $60,000 home right now:

	Buy Now	Wait a Year
Home Price	$60,000	$64,800
25% Downpayment	15,000	16,200
30-Year Mortgage	45,000	48,600
	@13%	@12%
Monthly Payments on Principal & Interest	$497.79	$499.90

Even with an interest-rate drop of a full 1%, the family pays $2.11 *more* a month. And they will have to fork over $1,200 more for a down-payment.

Over the long term, home prices have headed in one direction—up—a fact that's reflected in the lament of almost every new homebuyer: "I should have bought last year."

▶ **IF YOU CAN, MAKE THE MOVE:** Some families have won by playing the waiting game, but most people are not as lucky or as good at economic forecasting. If you can swing it, you ought to try buying now.

HOW MUCH HOME CAN YOU AFFORD TO BUY?

You don't get far into any discussion of homebuying before someone mentions a special, time-honored formula for determining how much of your salary you should budget for mortgage payments. Unfortunately, one person tells you the top amount is 25%, another says he heard it is 28% and then someone else says that it's *cost* that matters—never spend more on a home than two and a half times your annual income.

Actually, in matters like this, every man or woman should be his or her own expert. The question to answer is: How much money do you have left each month after meeting all other expenses to spend on shelter? If you haven't run up any credit-card bills, aren't making car payments and have few expensive habits, you could well afford to put 30% or 35% of your monthly salary into mortgage payments, or buy a home that costs three times what you earn.

What matters then, are *monthly payments*—your mortgage payments and home-related bills (or the maintenance costs if you buy a co-op or condo). To get an idea of how much you can set aside for mortgage payments, total up right now all other expenditures you'd expect to make in an average month leaving out rent (or your present mortgage payments if you already own your home). Subtract that total from your monthly take-home pay. Then subtract an estimate for property taxes and insurance. The result: a fairly accurate idea of what you can afford each month.

To learn the amount of money you can borrow with that figure, see the chart we've run on page 103. It shows the monthly payments for loans of various amounts at various interest rates. For example: Suppose you have $700 available for housing. Subtracting, say, $160 a month for property taxes and insurance leaves you with $540. If prevailing mortgage interest rates are 12½%, you can afford a mortgage in the $45,000 to $50,000 range.

To that mortgage amount, add the total cash you can afford to put into a downpayment. The result is the maximum price you can afford to pay for a home.

The downpayment you will need varies from lender to lender—it can be as little as 4% or as much as 30% to 40%. The key element is your ability to make mortgage payments. If your salary and other income is high enough, you'll be able to make a low downpayment. Otherwise, the bigger your downpayment, the lower the mortgage and, consequently, the lower your monthly payments.

HOME OWNERSHIP

MONTHLY MORTGAGE PAYMENTS ON 20-YEAR LOAN

Loan Amount	11%	11½%	12%	12½%	13%	13½%	14%	14½%	15%
$10,000	103.22	106.64	110.11	113.61	117.16	120.74	124.35	128.00	131.68
$15,000	154.83	159.96	165.16	113.61	175.74	181.11	186.53	192.00	197.52
$20,000	206.44	213.29	220.22	227.23	234.31	241.47	248.70	256.00	263.36
$25,000	258.05	266.61	275.28	284.03	292.90	301.84	310.89	320.00	329.20
$30,000	309.65	319.93	330.33	340.84	351.48	362.21	373.06	384.00	395.04
$35,000	361.26	373.25	385.39	397.65	410.06	422.58	435.24	448.00	460.88
$40,000	412.87	426.57	440.44	454.46	468.64	482.95	497.41	512.00	526.72
$45,000	464.48	479.89	495.49	511.26	527.21	543.32	559.59	576.00	592.56
$50,000	516.09	533.21	550.55	568.07	585.79	603.69	621.77	640.00	658.40
$60,000	619.31	639.86	660.66	681.68	702.95	724.42	746.12	768.00	790.08

MONTHLY MORTGAGE PAYMENTS ON 25-YEAR LOAN

Loan Amount	11%	11½%	12%	12½%	13%	13½%	14%	14½%	15%
$10,000	98.01	101.65	105.32	109.03	112.78	116.56	120.38	124.22	128.08
$15,000	147.02	152.47	157.98	163.55	169.17	174.85	180.56	186.32	192.12
$20,000	196.02	203.29	210.64	218.07	225.57	233.13	240.75	248.43	256.17
$25,000	245.03	254.12	263.31	272.59	281.96	291.41	300.95	310.54	320.21
$30,000	294.03	304.94	315.97	327.11	338.36	349.69	361.13	372.65	384.25
$35,000	343.04	355.76	368.63	381.62	394.75	407.98	421.32	434.76	448.30
$40,000	392.04	406.59	421.29	436.14	451.14	466.26	481.51	498.87	512.34
$45,000	441.05	457.41	473.96	490.66	507.53	524.54	541.70	558.97	576.38
$50,000	490.96	508.23	526.62	545.18	563.92	582.82	601.89	621.08	640.42
$60,000	588.07	609.88	631.93	654.21	676.71	699.39	722.26	745.30	768.50

MONTHLY MORTGAGE PAYMENTS ON 30-YEAR LOAN

Loan Amount	11%	11½%	12%	12½%	13%	13½%	14%	14½%	15%
$10,000	95.23	99.03	102.86	106.73	110.62	114.54	118.49	122.46	126.44
$15,000	142.85	148.54	154.29	160.09	165.93	171.81	177.73	183.68	189.67
$20,000	190.46	198.06	205.72	213.45	221.24	229.08	236.97	244.91	252.89
$25,000	238.08	247.57	257.16	266.81	276.55	286.35	296.22	306.14	316.12
$30,000	285.70	297.09	308.59	320.18	331.86	343.62	355.47	367.37	379.34
$35,000	333.31	346.60	360.02	373.54	387.17	400.89	414.71	428.59	442.56
$40,000	380.93	396.12	411.45	426.90	442.48	458.16	473.95	489.82	505.78
$45,000	428.54	445.63	462.88	480.27	497.79	515.43	533.20	551.05	569.00
$50,000	476.16	495.14	514.31	533.63	533.10	572.71	392.44	612.28	632.23
$60,000	571.39	594.17	617.17	640.35	663.72	687.25	710.93	734.73	758.67

▶ **NEXT MOVE:** After these calculations, you are now in a better position to make good use of the real estate classifieds in your local paper. You've flipped through them before, surely, but without any clear picture in mind about what your budget permitted you to buy. Well, now you know what to look for as you study the ads for condos or ranch-style homes.

And if the mortgage companies and savings & loan associations—your chief sources of home loans—are not advertising their rates, you can learn them with a few phone calls. A few minutes spent on such "research" and you can go out househunting with extra authority.

DOES IT PAY TO USE A REAL ESTATE BROKER?

Most buyers of single-family homes do not deal directly with homesellers but work through a real estate broker, or Realtor (if the broker is a member of the National Association of Realtors). The broker who knows the community and the market can certainly save you time and even money. By all means ask around to see if any one broker comes highly recommended.

However, don't assume that a broker's services are "free." The broker's commission—usually 6% of the selling price—is almost always paid by the seller, who has included it in the asking price. Or, to put it another way, *you* pay for the broker's services, in the end.

Q. Can I hire a broker to work for me, the homebuyer?

A. You may be able to. More and more firms are offering "buyer brokerage" as an extra service. They charge either a flat fee or by the hour, and accept no commission from the seller. That arrangement automatically increases your chances of saving money.

Q. In what way?

A. As we said, a regular broker is paid by the seller. Often two brokers are involved—one who lists the home for sale, another who brings in the buyer. In that case, the 6% commission is split between them (providing the listing broker does not have an "exclusive right to sale listing," which means only the listing agency can get the commission). Say you want to buy a home costing $70,000. The commission comes to $4,200. The home is listed by Broker A, but you are shown the listing by Broker B. Ordinarily, each broker would get $2,100 from the seller. But if "Broker B" is a buyer-broker, he or she will not share in the split. In fact, your buyer broker will insist that the owner in this case cut his $70,000 price by $2,100. If you paid, say, $1,000 for his or her services, then using a buyer broker saved you $1,100. And you could save even more if—as can happen—you buy a home listed by your buyer-broker's firm; in that case, the full 6% commission would be deducted from the price.

Q. What if I go directly to an owner without dealing with a broker of any kind? If no commission has to be paid, won't I be able to save more money?

A. Not necessarily. If the seller has already listed the home, the listing broker will be paid the commission, anyway. The one exception is in those cases where the seller has stipulated that there's to be no commission if the broker doesn't bring in the buyer.

If the seller has *not* listed the home with a broker, you *can* save money by haggling (which you must do, whether or not the home is listed). Keep in mind that the seller has probably inflated his asking price by 6%, anyway. So take that 6% off his asking price right away, and negotiate from there.

> ▶ **BUYING TIP:** Almost all listing brokers inflate the true value of a home anywhere from 5% to 10% on the theory that any buyer will want to haggle. You'll be buying a home at a true bargain price only if you get below this "haggling allowance."

HOW TO SAVE MONEY BUYING A HOME

Whether you are househunting with a broker, or on your own, you can avoid making a costly mistake by following the checklist below. It alerts you to matters you must consider, and questions you should ask, as well as preparations you should make before starting:

☐ Wear old clothes to each showing. Be prepared to get down on your hands and knees and crawl about, peering into and under and around. There's no better way to spot those hidden flaws in your "dream home"—termite damage, patchwork repairs, water stains, frayed wiring—that could give you nightmares later. And bring along a flashlight.

☐ Keep a notebook for jotting down likes and dislikes, pluses and minuses of each home. And review the classifieds regularly to get a good idea of the price range for the neighborhood and the property you're about to see.

☐ Inspect the neighborhood as well as the home. The neighborhood may not be for you if two of the three following questions can be answered "Yes": Are there many *For Sale* signs up? Are there many commercial establishments about or being built? Are many of the houses and lawns poorly tended?

☐ Is the house close to public transporation? Shopping? Schools?

☐ What is the condition of the yard? Look past the fact that the lawn has been mowed and raked to note the texture and evenness of the grass. And the shrubbery. Does everything look well watered and cared for? Are there dead limbs in the trees? Can you see yourself paying for landscaping or pruning soon?

☐ Does the basement contain these signs of past—and future—trouble: cracked floor tiles? items stored on wooden blocks? a sump pump? or water stains? If so, you can bet it floods occasionally.

☐ Are the water pipes copper? Copper pipes are the best. Do the pipes show signs of repair and patching?

☐ What's the condition of the fusebox—new? outdated? After seeing a few homes, you can build up a good standard of comparison for this particular trouble spot. Does it look as if the owner has been playing electrician on his own, or has a professional serviceman left his business card glued to the box?

☐ Is the furnace new or old? Is the house centrally air-conditioned? Or does it have window units, instead? If so, is the owner planning to leave these behind?

☐ Has the owner tagged or in some way indicated which fixtures will be left behind?

☐ Has the owner displayed all fuel, utility and repair bills for the past year? Will he or she show them to you if they are not out for inspection?

☐ Are there enough electrical outlets? Or is the owner using many extension cords or multiple plugs?

☐ Did you note the number of appliances and pieces of electronic equipment the owner uses? If you own considerably more, you may require extra outlets—or even rewiring the house—to suit your needs. Is the home worth such added expense?

☐ What about the condition of the fixtures or appliances in the kitchen and bathroom? Of the tile and cabinets? These rooms can be quite expensive to modernize. If considerable renovation or replacement is required, you've got a major bargaining point for a price cut.

☐ Do all doors open smoothly? Extensive, consistent sticking indicates the house is out of plumb, or unevenly aligned on its foundation. A bad sign.

☐ What about storage space? If the house suits you in most respects but lacks adequate storage space, you had better keep looking or brace yourself for some renovation.

☐ Check the general condition of the heating system. What kind of repairs are needed, how old is it, and how long will the system last?

☐ Choose a home that is connected to a public sewer system in preference to one served by a septic tank or a cesspool. Check with the plumber who last serviced the house to determine condition of the plumbing and ask him to test the water pressure.

☐ Check the type and capacity of the hot water tank to determine if there will be sufficient hot water for family needs (30-50 gallon tank is needed for most families). Look for any signs of rust or leaks. Obtain any guarantee held by the present owner, if it is still in effect.

☐ Were the walls of the house insulated with expanding foam that contains toxic urea formaldehyde?

☐ Is the attic well furnished and ventilated? At least six inches of fiberglass batting is needed for the attic, with the vapor barrier on the bottom. An inadequately insulated attic can be a major source of heat loss in the winter. Extra insulation should be installed about the attic door or on top of the trapdoor, but all vents and electrical outlets should be fully exposed. Cross ventilation in the attic is essential to allow any accumulated vapor to escape.

☐ Is the garage attached to the house? An attached garage is another drain on a home's heating and air-conditioning units unless the common wall and the door are additionally insulated.

☐ If the house interests you, go back through it again, making careful note of any flaw—cracks in plaster or glass, water stains, flaking paint, loose downspouts on the raingutter. All these can be used to persuade the owner to reduce the price. Try to return to the property during bad weather, particularly during heavy rain, to see if the roof leaks, how the yard drains and whether the basement floods.

▶ **DON'T TRY TO BE YOUR OWN EXPERT:** There's a limit to the "expertise" you should personally supply when househunting. It is possible to dispense with the services of a real estate broker, but if you lack such training, don't try to be your own lawyer or property inspector or conduct your own title search (if no one has performed that service). Be prepared to pay professionals to perform these services for you. It's dangerous "penny wisdom" to try to save money by not hiring these experts.

Homebuyer Checklist For New Homes

When you buy a *new* home, you deal with a builder or contractor. In some cases, you may select a recently constructed home in a new development. Or the builder may offer you a choice of several models and erect whichever one you choose in a subdivision under development. You may even hire an architect to create your very own custom-built dream home.

In virtually every instance, the new home will cost you *more* than what you would pay for a comparable existing home. However, you should have far fewer maintenance headaches.

Below is a checklist covering the key items you must consider when buying or building a new home. You will stand a better chance of getting your money's worth if you:

☐ Talk to other customers of the builder, contractor or architect. Visit other owners in that new subdivision to learn how they like their new homes. Ask about services and unexpected costs.

☐ Find out what warranties are involved in the purchase of your new home. What about the kitchen equipment? The furnace? Hot-water heater? How long do these warranties last?

☐ Know precisely what you get for your money. Don't go by the appearance of a model home. Ask the builder's salesperson exactly which features are provided with your new house and which are "extras" displayed in the model. Get it in writing.

Any extra features that are to be included in the finished house should also be specified. Don't assume an item is included and later learn it wasn't.

☐ Will the new community have paved streets, water and sewer lines, and sidewalks? Make sure you know whether you or the builder will assume the costs. Find out about charges for water and trash collection.

☐ Does your contract with the builder set forth the total sales price?

☐ Does the contract definitely stipulate the completion date of your new house? Will the builder compensate you for delays?

☐ Check out the zoning uses permitted for the area in which you plan to buy a home. The neighborhood may be zoned for certain commercial uses. Such zoning may eventually lower property values. Ask at the city, county, or township clerk's office about zoning.

☐ If you are building, be sure you check your lot site in advance. Is it the size and setting you signed up for? Find out before the bulldozer and crew arrive.

☐ Visit the construction site regularly while your house is being built.

☐ Before you actually take title to your new house, make a thorough inspection. Check all equipment, windows and doors.

☐ When you take possession, insist upon receiving: (1) warranties from all manufacturers for equipment in the house; (2) certificate of occupancy and (3) certificates from the Health Department clearing the plumbing and sewer installations, plus all applicable certificates of code compliance.

▶ **MONEY-SAVING MOVE:** If you are having your new home built for you, specify in your agreement with the contractor that the building materials are to be paid by you, personally. Then arrange with your contractor to get a list of what he needs and get in touch with the suppliers. This move enables you to deduct all *sales taxes*, which can run into big money, and big tax savings.

Reminder: You can deduct sales tax on big-ticket items (such as building materials) in addition to the automatic deduction for sales taxes based on your income for the year.

▶ **CAUTION:** You *must* pay for the materials, yourself. If you merely reimburse the contractor, you may lose the deduction. Tell your tax expert that two recent cases covering this area are *Bennett*, TC Memo 1983-183, and *Petty*, 77 TC No. 34.

Two Special Forms Of Ownership— Cooperatives And Condominiums

So far we have discussed single-family homes, but there are two other forms of ownership. In some cases, tenants of existing buildings have become owners of their apartments after their building "went co-op" or "went condo." In others, apartment houses (or townhouse developments or vacation-home communities) are built and sold as cooperatives or condominiums. There are similarities between these two forms of ownership—in both cases, for instance, the owners pay monthly maintenance fees for the upkeep of common areas, such as elevators or grounds or lobbies. But the differences are more important.

Co-op Ownership

A cooperative apartment house is one where the tenants buy *shares in the corporation* that got the mortgage on the building; their monthly payments are applied to the mortgage payments and maintenance. Should any tenant default on his obligation and move, his share of the payments is spread out among the other tenants (if another tenant isn't found right away).

There are two money-saving reasons for the urban dweller's continuing interest in cooperative housing:

1. Rather than pay rent, you, the tenant-owner, pay a carrying charge based on the actual cost of operating the property. The landlord's profit is eliminated; so are demands for increased rentals when the usual short-term leases are renewed.

2. Through your ownership of stock in the cooperative corporation, you as a tenant-owner also get tax benefits not available to the ordinary tenant. You can deduct that portion of your monthly payments applied to the cooperative's real estate taxes and mortgage interest. This helps reduce your housing cost. At the same time, part of your payments build up equity in the property.

> ▶ **BUT WATCH THIS:** While you face little risk as a tenant-owner of a cooperative apartment during booming prosperity, a recession or a similar time can cause some of your fellow tenant-owners to default. Getting another shareholder could be difficult. In such times, each person remaining in the project would have to assume a proportionate share of the vacant apartments' maintenance and mortgage payments.

Condominium Ownership

The condominium is a form of outright ownership of real property, quite different from a cooperative. Each condominium apartment is *owned* by the individual occupant. The title to each unit may be separately transferred and insured. Together with other apartment owners, the condominium tenant is *co-owner* of the common elements such as land, foundations, main walls, halls, lobby, stairs, corridors, elevators, roof, lawn, parking lot, trees, and the like.

The condominium apartment has advantages similar to that of a co-op's. For example, maintenance responsibilities such as heating, outside cleaning, and lawn tending are shared and delegated to skilled employees. And the condominium owner gains an income tax deduction for mortgage interest and property taxes.

> ▶ **MAJOR DIFFERENCES:** In a condominium, each person actually owns his unit, so he can get a mortgage on it to suit his needs. Getting a loan on a co-op is generally more expensive. In a condominium, if an owner defaults, the others are not responsible for his mortgage payments. In a cooperative, the others must take over his obligations.

The condo concept has become increasingly popular over the years because of these differences.

HOW TO TIE DOWN A HOME WITHOUT SADDLING YOURSELF WITH PROBLEMS

When you've found your dream home, you will be required to make a deposit on it—usually called a "binder" or "earnest money"—and sign a sales contract. The deposit you make is forfeited by you if you don't carry out the contract.

▶ **CAUTION:** No matter how much you may like a property, beware of automatically putting down a deposit or signing a contract. It pays to have the agreement checked by an attorney. For example, the contract and the binder should contain a "contingency clause" spelling out the fact that your money must be returned if you cannot get financing at certain terms.

Usually the clause reads something like: "This offer contingent upon buyer and property qualifying for a new first mortgage of at least $____ at an interest rate not exceeding __% for at least __years". Otherwise, should your deal fall through because you can't get suitable financing, the seller might not be obligated to return your cash. Another pointer: If you haven't yet had the home checked out by a professional home inspector, then the agreement you sign should also be contingent upon a favorable report from the inspector.

HOW TO GET CASH TO BUY A HOME

Very few people have enough money to pay cash for a home. Most people have to borrow a good part of a home's purchase price. The usual method is to get a home mortgage loan. Here's how it works, in simple terms.

The lender supplies cash to buy the house. You sign a legal document which obligates and binds you to repay the lender by making regular payments, including interest, for a specified number of years. The house and lot are pledged as security and you promise to pay the taxes, keep the house insured and maintain the property in good condition. If you fail to make payments (you default), the lender has the legal right to take over the property and you may lose any equity you have acquired.

FOURTEEN WAYS TO FINANCE YOUR HOME

Financing a home can be almost as complex as finding the right home. There's a bewildering variety of methods to choose from. Here's a simple explanation of fourteen ways you can get home financing—along with advantages and disadvantages for each:

(1) Fixed Rate Loan

This mortgage remains the first choice of around 50% of all homebuyers. It is also the least complicated. How it works: You get a first mortgage from a bank or

Savings & Loan Association (S & L) for 60% to 80% of your purchase price (depending on the lender and your ability to make payments). The mortgage lasts anywhere from 15 to 30 years and is fully paid off at the end of the term. Each mortgage payment is the same dollar amount.

Big advantage: A fixed rate loan offers you certainty and security. You know how much you'll spend on mortgage payments from now until the mortgage is paid off.

Disadvantages: You may lock yourself into a high-interest-rate mortgage. And the longer your mortgage runs, the higher your total bill for interest.

> ▶ **MONEY SAVING MOVES:** Put down as much cash as possible to cut down the amount of the mortgage. If mortgage rates fall substantially during ownership, you may be able to refinance and get a new first mortgage at a lower interest rate. You can also save big money by prepaying your mortgage (see p. 118).

Up until the late 1970's the fixed rate mortgage dominated the market. Then major changes shook the home-financing field. Lenders developed many new types of loans to protect themselves against skyrocketing interest rates. The Supreme Court dealt a big blow to homebuyers by permitting lenders to enforce the "due on sale" clause in many home mortgages. (In simple English, this means a new buyer cannot assume the homeseller's mortgage.) Finally, out of sheer necessity, many homesellers were forced to extend credit to homebuyers by giving either first or second mortgages.

After interest rates took their big dive in the closing months of 1982, things settled down a bit, and homebuyers discovered some good had come out of the upheavals. In particular, there are many new ways to finance a home. One of the following home financing techniques may be "tailor made" for you and your family.

(2) Flexible Rate Mortgages

These loans go by several names—"flexies," "adjustables," "floaters"—but they share one common trait: *No fixed interest rate*. The lender increases or decreases the interest rate periodically, according to the fluctuations of whatever financial index is agreed to by the borrower. Since the flexible is a long-term loan, it is renegotiated periodically and "rolled over" at the new rate, with a new payment.

Simple example: Jones gets a flexible rate mortgage that offers these terms: The first year, he makes mortgage payments based on an interest rate ½ of 1% below today's going mortgage interest rate. A year later (and every year after), payments are adjusted to reflect changes in the mortgage rate—up or down.

There are many variations: Some flexibles provide that mortgage payments won't be adjusted by more than a fixed dollar amount during each adjustment period. Others "cap" the interest-rate changes that can be made during each adjustment period.

Flexible loan advantages: Lenders almost always offer these loans at an initial below-market rate. Interest-rate drops must be reflected, too. There is no fee for renewing a flexible and no penalty for paying one off ahead of time.

Disadvantages: If interest rates head upward after you buy the home, your monthly payments will go up, too. This adds an element of uncertainty to the biggest single component of your budget. Even worse: With some flexible rate mortgages, all of your monthly payments might be allocated to interest in high-cost periods. Result: You don't build equity in your home.

> ▶ **MONEY-SAVING MOVE:** Shop around among lenders before taking out any kind of "flexible." Learn about the various indexes that lenders use to determine rate adjustments and find a lender that uses the least volatile to determine the changes in your interest rate. Learn what's involved when the lender promises you "caps" on interest and payments.

You could get a bargain by taking out a flexible with a below-market rate with frequent adjustments during a time of falling interest—but it's a gamble.

(3) Graduated-Payment Mortgages (GPMs)

The GPM is a great favorite among young homebuyers who expect their income to increase steadily in coming years but who can spend very little on housing at the present. It's a long-term, fixed-rate mortgage, but the actual interest cost is not reflected in its initial payments. For the first year, the monthly payments are unusually low, perhaps $150 below those of a fixed-rate loan for the same amount. The next year, the monthly payment increases and continues to increase each year for the next five to ten years, then it stabilizes for the life of the mortgage. This stabilized amount is higher than the payment on a fixed-rate loan, to make up for the initial difference, but buyers with rising incomes should be able to afford it.

> ▶ **MONEY-SAVING MOVE:** Take out a GPM during a time of high interest rates and take advantage of its extra low payments as long as you can—then pay it off with another loan when rates drop. Or take out a loan that combines the features of the GPM and the flexible (many lenders offer such mortgages). These combination loans operate as GPMs initially, then become flexibles with rates tied to the market.

Homebuyers whose jobs require them to move every few years should find a GPM an economical way to buy a home.

(4) The Growing Equity Mortgage

Sometimes called "the rapid payoff mortgage," the GEM has a fixed interest rate. However, monthly payments increase year by year. This increase may be determined in advance or be tied to a financial index, as in a flexible. Unlike a flexible, though, the GEM is systematically amortized by these increases—every cent of the mortgage payment increase is applied to repaying the principal.

> *Example:* Suppose you get a GEM mortgage for $40,000 at 12%. First year payments for principal and interest are $411 a month. Second year payments are $461 a month—$50 more.

That $50 extra is applied 100% to paying off the mortgage principal. Monthly payments go up by $50 each year. This rapid payoff of principal means that less of the "base" $411 goes for interest (since there's less of a loan outstanding).

> ▶ **MONEY-SAVING RESULT:** A GEM is paid off within something like half the time of a fixed-rate loan, with a considerable saving in interest costs. A 30-year GEM, for instance, may be repaid within 13 to 17 years, depending on the payment increases.

If you like the GEM concept, try to get one where the increases are determined in advance. This type of GEM is more easily budgeted for than one tied to an index.

(5) FHA-Insured Mortgage

This type of loan is obtained from a regular institutional lender, such as a bank or S & L. But the lender is insured against loss on the loan by the Federal Housing Administration (FHA). An FHA loan can be a fixed-rate mortgage or an adjustable rate mortgage.

Advantages: If you have sufficient income to make mortgage payments, you can get a FHA loan for around 95% of a home's cost. And, with a fixed-rate FHA loan, your home may be—

> ▶ **MUCH EASIER TO SELL AT A BIG PROFIT:** FHA loans are assumable (see p. 114). So if interest rates are way above your mortgage interest rate when you sell your home, any buyer who assumes your loan automatically gets a big bargain. As a result, you can charge a premium price for your home.

Disadvantages: *You* pay the premium for the FHA mortgage insurance (½ of 1% of the loan amount). And, generally speaking, it takes a bit longer to get an FHA loan than it does a conventional.

(6) VA-Backed Mortgage

These loans are very similar to FHA-insured loans except that (1) the Government (through the Veterans Administration) insures the lender against loss on only part of the home loan, (2) the loans are available only to veterans with minimum periods of duty during specific periods of time (e.g., during Korean or Vietnam War), and (3) it's possible to get a—

▶ **ZERO DOWNPAYMENT HOME LOAN:** That's right, a qualifying veteran can get a 100% mortgage to buy a home. See your local Veterans Administration office for details on this popular ex-servicemens' benefit.

(7) FmHA Home Loans

The Farmers Home Administration (FmHA) makes home loans available to moderate and low income people. Some loans are made by FmHA itself; others are guaranteed by this agency. The loans are available in "rural" areas that are not part of or associated with a city or a large, urbanized area. For more details, contact your state Farmers Home Administration Office.

(8) The Assumable Mortgage

In simple terms, a mortgage is said to be assumable if a buyer can take over the responsibility of making payments ("assuming" the loan) from the homeseller. If you can assume a home mortgage when you buy a house, you may be able to finance a good part of the cost at a bargain rate.

>   *Example:* Smith bought his home for $70,000 five years ago with a $60,000 mortgage at 9% interest and $10,000 cash. Now Smith sells his home to you for $90,000. There's a $55,000 balance remaining on the mortgage. If you can assume that mortgage (and come up with the $35,000 balance of the purchase price yourself), you can finance the home at a one-third discount off today's mortgage rates. Result: Lower monthly payments and lower interest costs.

Despite recent changes in home financing and in the law on mortgage assumptions, many mortgages are still assumable by credit-worthy buyers.

All loans insured by FHA remain assumable at their original rate. Any credit-worthy buyer can assume a VA-guaranteed mortgage at its original rate. Another possibility: You may be able to get a reduced-rate mortgage through the Federal National Mortgage Agency (FNMA). FNMA is one of the largest purchasers of mortgages originated by banks. It has set up a program, "The Mortgage Solution," that you may find as economical as an assumption: If FNMA owns the mortgage on the home you want to buy, it will in effect give you a new first mortgage at a below-market rate.

Always ask the sellers how they financed their home, and then ask the lender whether it sold their mortgage to Fannie Mae, before you resign yourself to borrowing the full amount you need at market rates.

(9) "Buy-Down" Plans

This method is so called because someone—often a relative of the buyer but sometimes the homeseller or the homebuilder—advances cash needed to pay part of the initial mortgage interest. In short, the interest rate is reduced, or "bought down," so the buyer can qualify for a mortgage. To understand how this works, you must understand that lenders consider a borrower qualified if he or she has the income to meet the first year's mortgage payment.

> **Example:** Buyer needs $60,000 to buy a new home. His income qualifies him for a mortgage at 10%, but Lender is asking 13%. Solution: Builder sets up a three-year buy-down plan; he supplies enough cash to absorb 3% mortgage interest the first year, 2% the second year, and 1% the third and last year.

Buyer can afford a 10% mortgage the first year; so Lender, who will get the full 13% interest, anyway, agrees to the deal. By the fourth year, Buyer is responsible for the full 13%, and by then he can afford it (hopefully).

The buy-down is a good way for a parent to help a child buy a home. But if the buy-down is financed by the seller or homebuilder, it won't be a free lunch: The buy-down amount will be reflected in a higher purchase price.

(10) Shared Appreciation Mortgage

The lender gives the buyer an unusually low-rate mortgage in return for a share (often 30% to 50%) of the profit when the home is sold or transferred (often within a specified number of years).

(11) Shared Equity Plan

Similar to the above but now the monthly costs and the downpayment are split between the buyer and a partner—either an investor, friend or relative. In return for such assistance, the buyer shares any profit from the home sale with the partner. Under some plans, the partner is considered the landlord and the buyer the tenant whose share of the monthly payments is considered rent. The partner gets investor tax breaks from this set-up.

The complexities of these two plans and the possibility of the buyer's having to sell the home at an inconvenient time in a falling market are major drawbacks to "sharing."

(12) Seller-Held Second Mortgages and "Wraps"

Up to 70% of all existing-homes sales made during the early-1980's mortgage interest crunch involved seller-held mortgages.

Here's an example of how it works: You want to buy a home for $70,000. You can make a downpayment of $20,000 and get a first mortgage for $40,000. That leaves you $10,000 short. You ask the seller to "take back a mortgage" for the $10,000 balance. In effect, the seller is accepting your IOU, secured by the home, for part of his selling price.

Wraparounds: In some cases, the seller may have had an older low-interest loan with a due-on-sale clause: had the lender learned of the sale, it could have forced the buyer to refinance the mortgage at market rates, possibly killing the sale. To prevent this from happening, some sellers continued to make monthly payments on their first mortgages even after they had made a second mortgage arrangement with the buyers. This second mortgage is called a "wraparound" because it included (or "wrapped around") the first; and it was often made at a high rate.

Major drawbacks: A "wrap" may create problems about who actually has title to the property and may leave the buyer exposed to having to repay the old mortgage at once if the lender demands it.

(13) "Zero Interest" Mortgage

This type of mortgage is usually offered by builders and occasionally by individual sellers. The buyer makes an unusually large downpayment and then pays off the balance in monthly installments within a few years. Ostensibly, there is no interest charged; however, the Internal Revenue Service will impute up to 10% interest in such cases. Result: The buyer is entitled to deductions for interest, even though no interest is stated.

Builders and sellers offer such financing in desperation and invariably increase their prices accordingly. Such mortgages may not be much of a "bargain" if the price is substantially above what the builder would charge on a regular sale where you get your own financing.

(14) Rent With An "Option To Buy"

This arrangement permits you to move into your home and live there as a "tenant" while you raise financing. Try for an arrangement that permits all, or at least some, of the "rent" to be applied toward the purchase price. And try to lock in a purchase price, too, when you begin your tenancy.

HOW TO BOOST YOUR CHANCES OF GETTING A HOME LOAN FROM A BANK

Homebuyers can generally boost their chances of getting financing at terms they can afford by taking the following steps.

1. *Consolidate all bank accounts*: Consider putting all your funds into the lending institution you've dealt with most and longest. This may enhance your chances of getting a loan at favorable terms at the bank. Naturally, you should make this move right at the start—while you are still househunting. Don't wait until you apply for the loan. If a relative is helping you out with a cash gift, deposit it in an interest-paying account at the bank.

2. *Cut down on debts*: You may be spending too much of your income on items you can do without. If, say, a big portion of your paycheck is going to pay off two cars, then consider selling one car. Take other steps to reduce debts *before* applying for a home loan.

3. *Follow this checklist*: Here are the facts a lender will need to know when you come in to apply for a loan. Saving time these days can often save you money; so make certain you have all this data ready:

☐ The husband's job history, complete with past as well as present employers, his duties and above all his salary.

☐ The wife's employment history and present position. (Note that all banks are required by law to take a working wife's entire salary into account when considering a loan.)

☐ The total amount of cash the family now has on deposit and where.

☐ All additional income that can come the family's way, such as stock dividends, interest on savings accounts, etc.

☐ The value of any real estate you own, including its location, condition, and the length of time owned.

☐ The current depreciated value of the family car, or cars.

☐ The current value of other major possessions.

☐ The face and the cash value of the family's life insurance policies, and the name of the company that wrote them.

☐ The total amount of all outstanding debts, including home mortgage, car payments, credit-card charges, department-store bills, as well as the amounts paid regularly on each.

☐ Personal and credit references, complete with names and addresses, occupations and phone numbers.

4. *Consider getting a longer pay-off time*: The longer your loan, the lower your monthly payments. Say you need to borrow $60,000 at 13%. Your monthly payments on a 20-year mortgage will be $703.20, or $8,438.40 a year. But your monthly payments on a 30-year mortgage—same amount, same interest—will be $663.60 or $7,963.20 annually, a saving of around $475 a year. Of course, your total interest cost is going to be higher over the longer term. Take that into consideration before you decide. If you don't expect to live in this house for very long, the 30-year mortgage could be the better choice.

HOW CLOSING COSTS CAN YIELD TAX BREAKS

When your home purchase is officially "closed"—that is, when you, the buyer, actually take title to the seller's home—you will find yourself responsible for several expenses, or "closing costs." Naturally, you must demand an accounting well in advance so you can have a cashier's check already drawn up for the amount. The bank is required by law to give you an estimate of your closing costs.

At first glance, some closing fees seem like extra expenses and nothing more—but remember this: The total cost of your home now helps determine your taxable profit years later when you sell. And the higher that cost—or, in tax terms, the higher your basis—the *smaller* your taxable gain when you eventually get around to selling.

Most of the increase to your basis comes from improvements made after your purchase. But it can be increased at the time you actually buy the home by your closing costs. Here are some that can reduce your gain when you sell this home:

- Legal Expenses
- Title Search
- Title Insurance
- Survey Expenses
- Appraisal Costs

Q. Well, that's certainly encouraging. But what are the expenses that can become a tax saving for me this year?

A. Here are the three chief ones:

1. You probably will have to pay a part of the *property taxes* for the year of the sale. That's a currently deductible expense.

2. If you owned a home and sold it to buy your new one, and your old mortgage had a *prepayment-penalty clause*, you're going to be out some cash for that, too. Keep the bank's statement showing how much you paid. This is another currently deductible expense.

3. Any "points" you pay your lender are deductible as an interest charge. Your lender may not use the term, "points." Instead, you may be charged a "mortgage origination fee" or something like that—but no matter. If it's a fee paid *for the use of the money*, it's currently deductible, as long as the "points" are paid in cash.

▶ **HANG ON TO YOUR CLOSING STATEMENT:** You'll lose all these money-savers if you can't prove you paid them. In fact, it's a good idea to start a *Home Expense Folder* for expenditures that beef up your basis.

How To Save Money Owning A Home

There are three basic sources of cash savings available to you as a homeowner: (1) Prepaying or re-financing your mortgage; (2) Improving your property to extend its life, increase its value and improve its energy efficiency; and (3) Taking full advantage of the host of tax-slashing opportunities homeowners enjoy—right up through their becoming *homesellers*.

MAJOR MONEY-SAVING MOVE—PREPAYING YOUR MORTGAGE

When you prepay your mortgage, you increase your mortgage payment by a few dollars each month (or as often as you wish) and apply this extra cash to *principal*, not interest. Reducing your principal regularly this way cuts years off your mortgage term and slashes *thousands of dollars* off your total interest bill.

Q. Won't I have to pay a fairly large amount to realize a substantial saving in interest?

A. Not at all. Let's say you decide to prepay your principal right from the start of your mortgage. Depending on the size of your mortgage, you can probably cover the next month's principal by adding anywhere from $10 to $30 to your initial payment.

Here's an amortization chart that breaks down the fixed monthly payment of $506.60 which you would pay on a 30-year mortgage for $45,000, borrowed at 13¼%. (No escrow payments are included under Payment #1.)

Payment	Interest	Principal	Total
#1	$496.88	$ 9.72	$506.60
2	496.77	9.83	506.60
3	496.66	9.94	506.60
4	496.55	10.05	506.60

As you can see, the bulk of these initial payments is devoted to *interest* so you won't have to spend much to make a double payment of *principal*. Let's say you prepay from the start. Your first check, then, will be for $516.43—Payment #1 ($506.60) plus the principal of Payment #2 ($9.83). With that one move, you save $496.77—believe it or not, that's what 13¼% interest on $9.83 comes to compounded over 30 years!

Q. Since I've paid that principal, am I permitted to skip the next month's payment?

A. No, but you have shortened the total life of your mortgage by one month. Your next payment, due the next month, will be Payment #3. And if you wish to continue prepaying, you include the principal for Payment #4 ($10.05) and pay $516.65. And now you save an additional $496.65 in interest. That's $993.32 you've saved in just two months.

If you continue to prepay in this fashion, you would pay off this 30-year mortgage in 15 years and save yourself a total of $68,560.19 in interest!

Q. But I notice that the principal increases each month as the interest drops. How much extra do I pay after, say, three years of prepayments?

A. After three years, your extra principal payment will have grown to $21.68. That's still a manageable amount, but it will continue to increase. If you stop there, you still have saved yourself over $18,000 in interest over the life of your mortgage.

Q. Is this the only way I'm allowed to prepay?

A. No. One of the most manageable prepayment methods is to pay a fixed amount each month, year after year, so you can budget well in advance to get maximum savings. Let's stick with our original figures—$45,000 borrowed at 13¼% for 30 years, with a $506.60 monthly payment. If you regularly add *only* $25 each month—that is, you pay $531.60—you can pay off the mortgage in 20 years and nine months and save $50,282.68 in interest.

▶ **KEY FACT:** Prepayment can begin at any point—it does not have to start with Payment #1.

Q. Don't lenders object to borrowers' prepaying their loans?

A. A few may. That's why you should always check with yours before you begin prepaying. Some mortgages have a penalty clause covering prepayment during the first year. In that case, you can wait until the 13th payment to begin.

By all means, tell your lender what you intend to do at least a month in advance. Always include a note with each prepayment explaining how the amount of your check is to be broken down, and note each prepayment in your own records, too.

The key to getting massive cash savings is *consistency*. It's a good idea to have your own amortization schedule printed out so you can see exactly how much you save with each payment. Financial Publishing Company is one firm that can provide you with a "custom-tailored" computerized schedule of whatever kind of prepayment you choose. For more about its services, write: Dept. P, 82 Brookline Avenue, Boston, Massachusetts 02215.

ONE SOURCE OF PREPAYMENT CASH—YOUR LIFE INSURANCE

Many homeowners can raise cash for systematic prepayment right now by *borrowing on their life insurance policies*.

Check out your policy now to see what interest rate your insurer will charge you. If it's much lower than the interest on your mortgage—and in some states on some policies it may be as low as 8% or even 5%—then you can save yourself a lot of cash *without jeopardizing your protection*.

▶ **TYPICAL SITUATION:** You and your spouse recently got a new 30-year, $50,000 mortgage on your home. The interest rate is 14% and the monthly mortgage payment is $592. The mortgage allows you to make prepayments without penalty after three years. You also just took out a $100,000 ordinary life insurance policy.

Assuming you're 40 years old, your annual insurance premium comes to $2,005 (or $167 a month). You have a right to borrow against the policy at an 8% interest rate.

Usual way: You handle your mortgage and insurance separately, budgeting a total of $759 a month ($592 plus $167) to meet your obligations. In 30 years, you're out of debt—you own your home free and clear.

▶ **BETTER WAY:** You finance your insurance premiums by borrowing on your policy. You use the freed cash to prepay your mortgage. *New result*: You're out of debt in 20 years and 3 months *and you save more than $60,000*. Let's take a look at the details of the setup:

- *Years 1 Through 6:* You do things the usual way—you pay $592 for the mortgage and $167 for the insurance. This is done (1) to build sufficient cash value and dividends in the policy and (2) to meet the—

   ▶ **TAX LAW REQUIREMENTS:** You must pay the full insurance premium for at least four of the first seven years of the policy. Otherwise, you can't take a tax deduction for the interest you'll pay later on when you borrow on the insurance.

- *Years 7 Through 16*: You pay for the insurance by borrowing the amount of the premium from the policy. The insurance dividends pay the interest on the loan. Since you no longer use out-of-pocket cash for your insurance, you can use that money to prepay your mortgage. So you now pay $761 a month on your mortgage (instead of $592). Even though you're paying $2 more than what you were paying per month for both mortgage and insurance you get this happy—

   ▶ **RESULT:** The 30-year mortgage is completely paid off at the end of *16 years*. But, of course, you now have a $20,050 loan against your life insurance, reducing its effective face value to $79,950. You have two choices: (1) You can settle for the reduced value of the policy, and pay only $167 a month from this point on. Or (2) you can repay the loan and bring your insurance back up to $100,000.

If you choose to repay, here's what happens during—

- *Years 17 Through 20 years and 3 months*: You pay $759 a month for the insurance—$167 for current premiums, and $592 to amortize the $20,050 loan.

   ▶ **WINNING PAYOFF:** You still pay more than $750 a month, but you pay it for just 20 years and 3 months. Your savings build to a net of almost $60,224 because of what happens—

- *After 20 Years And Three Months*: You pay only the insurance premium—$167 a month. In other words, you save almost $600, month in and month out from then on.

   ▶ **REMINDER:** The amount you save depends on a number of things: The interest rates (both on the mortgage and on the insurance loans), your age at the time you borrow; how long you intend to borrow; how much mortgage principal is still unpaid; and the amount of insurance you have. But as long as your mortgage interest rate exceeds the interest rate on your life insurance borrowing, this idea can keep *some* dollars in your pocket.

MONEY-SAVING WAYS TO IMPROVE YOUR HOME

Homeowners are always puttering about their "castle," making minor repairs here and touching up there. At times, they have to call in a professional for a major repair job. It's a penny wisdom *not* to hire a skilled carpenter or plumber who comes highly recommended during an emergency. But there are many unskilled tasks that any amateur can do in only a few minutes that can result in dollars saved.

One sure-fire way to conserve cash is to do anything that cuts back your electricity, gas or fuel oil bills. Here are several chores you can perform and some steps you should consider taking:

Caulking all cracks: You can make a significant difference in your energy bills by spending a couple of weekends caulking the cracks in your house. Wherever wood meets brick or two different materials are joined, you can expect seams to show—and leaks of both air and water to develop. Other trouble spots: where pipes and utility outlets are attached; trimming; window and door frames.

Don't go by appearances only. Make probing spot checks with a pencil or screwdriver to see how firm existing caulking actually is. Unusually large gaps should be filled with oakum before you add caulking.

Check out the kind of caulking that you're buying. Read the label on the compound you're getting. Will it take paint? If it won't, expect trouble later when you're having your place painted.

Oil-based caulking compounds are cheaper but have shorter lives than the new ones made of latex, vinyl or silicone.

Caulking should never be done when the temperature is under 50 degrees.

Installing weatherstripping: Weatherstripping comes in sheets or strips of foam, vinyl or felt that can be stapled or nailed or merely stuck in place around windows and doors. Before application, surfaces should be dry, clean and at a moderate temperature. If you have double-hung windows, apply weatherstripping around the entire frame and where one sash meets the other. For casement windows and doors, apply it around the frame and across the threshold.

Installing storm doors and windows: Maybe you should replace the storm doors and windows in your home. Check out the latest models with double-pane glass. Consider replacing entire windows or doors with new insulated models. For instance, if you have jalousie windows or doors, you are saddled with a style that is notoriously inefficient. Maybe you like its looks. But can you afford it any longer?

There are also low-cost plastic storm windows you can install *inside*; these are sheets of clear vinyl that have two drawbacks; they cannot be opened without being dismantled, and the slight ripples in the plastic distort the view. However, if sparingly used, these windows could provide some extra savings without presenting any major problems.

Adding insulation: There's no need for you to insulate every area uniformly; you can get the same value for less money by using less insulation at the proper spots.

For instance, if you live where there are prevailing northwest winds in winter, the south and east walls require less insulation than the north and west ones. Treating all four walls uniformly with heavy-duty insulation would be wasteful.

Key factor: The "R" rating in insulation refers to a material's ability to resist heat flow; the higher the rating, the better the resistance. By law, it must be plainly stated on the packaging. For moderate climates, insulation rated R-19 will be sufficient; extremely cold regions can require R-38. Your contractor and your local utility should tell you what your region's recommended rating is. You'll know then whether your home is over- or under-insulated.

> ▶ **COST-CUTTING BREAK:** Let's say you learn from your contractor that you have R-19 insulation in the attic instead of the R-30 that's recommended. That lack makes your place colder than it should be in winter and hotter in summer. Does that mean you should rip out the R-19 and install R-30? No—there's no need for all that trouble and expense. R ratings are cumulative; you can bring your insulation up to the proper level by adding R-11 type mineral fiber, blankets or loose wool.

Replacing standard light switches with dimmers: Along with lowering the lights to give a room a more restful mood, a dimmer switch can save you as much as $10 a year for each 100-watt bulb affected. Selecting the old-style dimmer, however, will save you nothing; you will lower the lights but not the amount of electricity you use, or the electric bills you pay.

Ask for the latest in solid-state dimmer switches. These actually cut back the amount of juice consumed; the old ones did not but instead dissipated the unused electricity as heat.

If you installed a dimmer a couple of years ago, check it out. If it feels warm, then it's probably not saving you any money when it's in use. Worse—it could be overworked because too much wattage is under its control. Double check a dimmer's wattage rating and never exceed it.

Fluorescent lights require special switches for dimming; specify the kind of bulb involved when you're buying dimmers.

> ▶ **ADDED SAVING:** Replacing a standard light switch with a dimmer is a relatively simple job. You can do it, yourself, if you take the proper precautions and have the knack for such chores.

Check out these long-lasting light bulbs: The latest in long-lasting incandescent and fluorescent bulbs are costly—but experts say your money is well spent. These bulbs last up to five years, and make the most efficient use of electricity; one 44-watt bulb supplies the illumination of an old-fashioned 100-watt one and lasts 10 times as long. This saving will snowball as electric rates rise.

Invest in meters and timers: For as little as $25, you can buy devices that indicate exactly how much energy your home consumes. You can also buy special timers that turn your furnace or air-conditioner on or off when you're away, saving you fuel without causing discomfort.

What about lowering the thermostat? Lowering thermostats at home is one sure way to cut heating bills, but many homeowners who do so feel uncomfortable with chilly rooms and "hot water" that's only tepid. Often they buy portable space heaters and run these so often they save less cash and energy than they intended. What's needed is a portable heater that generates maximum warmth at minimum cost.

One electric heater that apparently fills the bill is the *quartz heater* that generates radiant heat—that is, it warms whatever surface the heat reaches rather than the surrounding air. The room itself won't be warmer but you will be if you are sitting or standing in its range. The most popular model is some two feet high and can sell as low as $40. A quartz heater uses only 1½ kilowatts an hour of electricity, or around 7½¢ worth (figuring 5¢ a kilowatt hour as cost).

> ▶ **STEADY SAVINGS:** With one of these heaters about, you will be less tempted to raise the thermostat, and your savings will mount up. The heater could pay for itself in a couple of months and keep you comfortable all winter long.

Improving your oil furnace: Experts tell us that the latest in oil burners can considerably improve the efficiency of any furnace that's over six years old. The new line is described as "high-speed, flame-retention burners," which means that they create more heat for each gallon of oil consumed.

These burners also deliver more heat to the house and allow less to escape up the flue. The best can run at 80% to 86% efficiency, or as much as 20% better than the older models.

The burners cost from $200 to $350 but save you up to $20 for each $100 spent on heating oil.

> ▶ **ANOTHER SAVING:** Installing one of these burners costs about the same as installing an automatic vent damper to your existing furnace. This damper prevents heat from escaping up the flue when the furnace is off. However, the new high-speed, flame-retention burners already cut back such heat loss because of their design.

If you're thinking of improving your oil furnace, then the economical step to take is to install one of these new burners—you'll still cut back on heat waste and get more efficient fuel consumption, too.

Improving your natural gas furnace: In older gas furnaces, the pilot light is a steady drain on your pocketbook (anywhere from $30 to $60 a year). Installing an automatic spark igniter for $125 to $200 would eliminate that expense (which could become much more costly if and when natural gas prices are decontrolled).

> ▶ **IT ALL ADDS UP:** All of these suggested improvements can create savings for years to come. Some can pay for themselves many times over. And now let's consider another form of home improvement—

REMODELING—IMPROVEMENTS THAT BOOST HOME VALUE

Remodeling can often be an economical way to meet your needs. It's cheaper to modernize your kitchen and add another bedroom to your two-bedroom house than it is to buy a new three-bedroom house with the latest in kitchen fixtures. Remodeling may also be the best way to increase your home's value, if inflation continues to subside. The right kind of home improvement or new addition can pay for itself two or three times over.

Below is a checklist of the more common forms of improvements and remodeling. You or your family will sell the home eventually. If you remodel it extensively to suit your taste, do not expect others to be willing to pay for your precious improvements. You may have a hard time getting your money back. Keep that possibility in mind when you are thinking of:

☐ *Repainting*: A $1,500 paint job can probably increase a home's value by anywhere from $3,000 to $4,000, regardless of the inflation rate—but not if the color scheme is one very few homebuyers favor.

☐ *Landscaping*: You will probably get your money back and then some from resodding your lawn; just beware of indulging yourself in expensive and exotic shrubs and plants. Not every buyer will pay extra for the greenery.

☐ *Modernizing The Kitchen Or Bath*: If you confine your remodeling to new cabinets and fixtures for the kitchen or bathroom you can't go wrong. But if, say, you spend a lot on luxury appliances or a sunken tub in the master bath, you probably won't get back the money you invested.

☐ *Adding Extra Rooms*: If you need that fourth bedroom, build it on to your place—but if your community is one where three bedrooms is the norm, you may be building a sales barrier at the same time.

☐ *Energy Savers*: Modest improvements like those previously discussed are definitely an asset; however professional appraisers say that high-cost installations, like solar-energy panels for heat or hot water, cost too much for their price to be recovered quickly.

☐ *Luxury Improvements*: Swimming pools, saunas, tennis courts, fully equipped game rooms and the like can "personalize" your home right out of the market, if yours is a fairly modest neighborhood.

▶ **KEEP EXTENSIVE RECORDS:** Enter every home improvement you make in a "Home Expenditure Record Book" and hold on to all your bills. This recordkeeping gives you an idea of just how much your home is costing you. Review it to see if it's time to sell. It can show future buyers what you've spent on it to justify your asking price. And, as we'll show, it's essential for tax purposes.

There are lots of builders and remodelers hurting for business and there are lots of skilled workmen available to do all sorts of jobs. You might be delighted by the unusually low bids many of them will make. But don't go by cost, alone.

Go by a remodeler's professional standing. You can tell you're dealing with an experienced firm if it's a member of the National Remodelers Association, the National Home Improvement Council or the National Association of Homebuilders.

And go by reputation. It won't take much to check with your local Better Business Bureau to learn if complaints have been lodged against a specific remodeler.

You can also ask him for bank references and insurance. You can ask whether he's bonded. You can even demand a financial statement. No experienced reliable professional would think that demand is unreasonable. There's a high failure rate in this business. You don't want to find that (1)Your ceiling in your new bedroom addition is leaking and (2)Your contractor can't live up to his warranty because he went bankrupt two weeks ago.

▶ **KEY MOVE:** Even after you've found a firm you trust, never advance it more than a third of the amount you've agreed on. Pay another third after the work is under way and going well. Hold off on the final third until the job is finished. If your contractor insists on more than a third—or payment in full at the start—you could be in for trouble. And have a lawyer check over any contract before you sign it.

Q. Is there a difference between "homebuilders" and "remodelers"?

A. The remodeler is the specialist who's used to working on existing buildings—rewiring, renovating, replacing. If you just want to add a room to your place, a reputable builder could do the job; but if you're going to want floors ripped up or walls knocked down, you will probably want a remodeler. Plenty of homebuilders are jumping at such jobs today. They may be offering you "bargain rates," too. Don't hire a firm just for that reason.

Q. But how can I tell what bid is reasonable?

A. Most communities have professional home inspectors who can tell you what your remodeling should cost. They'll charge you, of course, probably $100 or so—but the cost could be easily offset. You'll get much more than your money's worth if this information helps you weed out the unrealistic, inefficient remodeler.

Q. Are there any steps I can personally take to bring down remodeling costs?

A. Yes, there are, and you can also make remodeler's estimate realistic, as well as reasonable.

• *Deal With The Boss*: If any prices are to be cut, the boss is the one who should do it and the one who can make the offer that will stick.

• *Provide Plenty Of Details*: Bring along house plans, repair bills, even photos—anything that helps the boss know what's in store once that floor is ripped up. That way any potential problem —like your termite scare in '81—can be figured in.

• *Accept Inconvenience*: Considerable savings can be made on an extensive job, say, if you agree in advance to live in confusion for a while. Don't insist that the workmen clean up the place each day, or that one room must be finished before another can be started.

The one inconvenience you must *not* accept is uncertainty: Insist on a completion date and enter it in the contract. By picking one convenient for the contractor, you could save some cash—but insist on a date.

▶ **CASH SAVING MOVE:** Remodeling your present home can well be cheaper than buying another one. Compare the estimates you get with the going home prices and see how they add up. Just remember that home improvement loans usually have higher interest rates and much shorter terms than home mortgages.

FHA's Title I program is a major source of such mortgages; its interest rates are usually 3½% to 4% higher than FHA's home loans. Be advised that any borrower asking for more than $2,500 through FHA will have a lien put on his property.

HOW TO GET A TAX CREDIT FOR SAVING ENERGY

Many of those energy-saving moves we discussed before can do more than cut your monthly bills. You also may get a tax break for making a fuel-saving improvement to your home.

Home-improvement credit: The credit is available for improvements made on principal residences that were built or were substantially completed by April 20, 1977. In other words, you don't get a credit for making energy-saving improvements in a new home or a recently added room or on your vacation home.

▶ **REPEATED TAX BREAK:** You may get the energy-credit break even if you have already taken it once on your *previous* principal residence—buying another home entitles you to another credit.

Dollars-and-cents savings: The credit is 15% of the first $2,000 spent on energy-saving improvements. Maximum credit per residence: $300. Here are some energy conservers that qualify:

- Automatic setback thermostats
- Caulking and weatherstripping
- Devices to modify flue openings
- Furnace ignition (replacing pilot light)
- Furnace replacement burner
- Insulation
- Meters showing cost of energy usage
- Storm or thermal windows or doors

Note that a new furnace or boiler does *not* qualify. Items such as carpeting, lined drapes, fireplace screens, wood paneling and exterior siding also don't qualify, even though they may have an insulating effect.

▶ **WHAT TO DO:** If you intend to make an energy-saving improvement this year, be sure you spend at least $67. *Reason*: You can't claim any credit for a year in which you spend less than $67 on qualifying energy-saving improvements. (This credit is also available for qualified improvements tenants make to their apartments).

HOW TO GET DEDUCTIONS FOR HOME IMPROVEMENTS

The medical-expense deduction is hard to get these days; your expenses are deductible only to the extent they exceed 5% of your adjusted gross income. As a homeowner, though, you may find some *home improvements* counting toward this deduction—if a doctor says they are medically necessary for you or your dependents.

> ▶ **TAX-LAW PRESCRIPTION:** To be deductible, a home improvement must (1) Be prescribed by your physician; (2) Be directly related to medical care; and (3) Exceed any increase in value to your property.

Case in point: The Geralds' 9-year-old daughter suffered from an illness that made it dangerous for her to be exposed to dry, dusty air. Their physician prescribed an air-conditioning unit so that the temperature and humidity of the home could be controlled. And, since it would be psychologically harmful for the child to be confined to just one room, he advised that a central air conditioning unit be installed. The installation cost $2,000 and increased the value of the home $1,000. The $1,000 *difference* is deductible.

Further break: Your annual expenditures for running and maintaining these medical improvements also count toward the medical expense deduction. So does the *entire* cost of upkeep and maintenance even though none or only part of the original cost of the improvement gave you a medical deduction.

> ▶ **WHAT TO DO:** Get a written recommendation for the improvement from your doctor and an estimate of its value from an appraiser.

HOW SPECIAL TAX BREAKS KEEP YOUR HOMESELLING PROFITS INTACT

Valuable as these on-going home-ownership tax savers are, they are minor compared to the tax-saving advantages you get when you *sell your home*.

That's when you learn the real beauty of owning a home as an investment. When you sell your home, you—

1. Can avoid paying current tax on your profit, if you meet certain conditions, regardless of how many homes you buy and sell, and finally,

2. You get a once-in-a-lifetime opportunity to exclude all tax on up to $125,000 in gain!

The "Tax-Free Rollover"

This special tax break is for people who sell one home and buy another. There is no current tax on your home-sale profit if you: (1) Spend at least as much for the replacement home as you got for the old; and (2) Buy the replacement home within two years before or after the sale and use it as your principal residence within that time.

"Home", incidentally, includes co-ops and condos and mobile homes.

Q. Okay, but what if I buy a home that costs less than what I sell for?

A. In that case, then you pay a tax only on the *difference* between the sales price of the old home and the purchase price of the new (assuming the difference is less than your profit).

Q. Am I limited to the number of times I can roll over?

A. No, you can keep postponing the tax as long as you comply with those two requirements. It's one of the major tax-cutting devices around, and it's yours when you become a homeowner.

Q. But what about the expenses I'll run into selling my home? There may be a broker's commission—some "fixing-up costs," too. Won't these reduce the amount I'll have to spend on my replacement home?

A. Yes, they certainly will. The amount you'll have to spend on your replacement home, "the adjusted sales price," is your sales price *less* two big items: (1) *Direct selling costs* (commissions, legal fees, etc.); and (2) *Fixing-up expenses* (painting, papering, replacing gutters, etc.) provided the work is done within 90 days before the sale and paid for within 30 days after.

> ▶ **ADDED BREAK:** Your direct selling costs (other than fixing-up expenses) do more than just help you delay your tax on your profit — they cut back *the amount you could eventually be taxed on*.

Let's say Jones paid $35,000 for his home years ago. His broker tells him he can easily get $60,000 for it if he fixes it up a little. He spends $1,400 doing just that. His broker sells his place within two weeks for $60,000, as promised, and he pays the broker a $3,600 commission.

Now let's look at the result. First, his adjusted sales price—the price he'll have to pay for his new home to get the roll-over break—is only $55,000. That's $60,000 reduced by $3,600 and by $1,400.

And his gain is cut back, too. Instead of $25,000, it's $21,400—the $60,000 selling price reduced by his $35,000 cost and that $3,600 commission.

> ▶ **REMODELING TAX BREAK:** Your basis can include the *cost of capital improvements*—such as those remodeling expenses we have discussed: adding a bedroom or bathroom or replacing your old oil furnace with a new gas one. And when you make such additions to your home, you get something else at the same time.

> ▶ **BUILT-IN TAX SAVER:** Since these improvements directly increase your tax basis in a home, they also *directly decrease* the tax you may ultimately pay when you sell a home and don't replace with another.

The Andersons bought their home in 1955. They paid a total of $30,000 (price plus lawyer's fees, title search, etc.). Over the years, they made a number of improvements to their home: landscaping ($1,000); concrete sidewalk ($1,000); central air conditioning ($2,000); a new bedroom ($12,000); new terrace and carport ($9,000). Total cost: $25,000.

And they can prove every cent because they have recorded these costs in a Home Expenditure Record Book, and kept all their bills.

This year, the Andersons sell their residence for $155,000 and rent an apartment in southern California.

• If they fail to add capital improvements to their basis: Their gain on the home sale is $125,000—the $155,000 sale price, less the original $30,000 basis (tax cost) for the home.

• If they add capital improvements to their basis: Their basis for the home is $55,000 ($30,000 original cost, plus $25,000 in capital improvements). The $155,000 sales price less the $55,000 basis equals $100,000.

And there is a way for the Andersons to avoid tax on that gain—permanently. If they qualify, they can use the—

Once-In-A-Lifetime $125,000 Exclusion

This massive tax break lets you *exclude up to $125,000 in gain—completely tax free*! Since it's an exclusion you can elect only once, you should wait till you've built up a substantial amount of taxable profit—then wipe it out. There are three major conditions you must meet:

1. You must be 55 or over *at the time* you sell—not in the year you sell your house or condo or co-op. There is some leeway in this rule, through. Say you are under 55 but your spouse is 55. If your home is jointly owned and you file a joint return, the sale qualifies.

2. Your home must be *a principal residence*—not a vacation cottage or summer place—and be used as your home for three of the five years before the sale.

3. This is a *once-in-a-lifetime exclusion*. If you use it to shelter only $80,000 of tax-free gain, you can't carry over the unused $45,000 to a later sale.

Q. This is a tremendous tax-saver. But after I use it, have I used up my chances to roll over, too?

A. Not at all. The rollover can be used as often as you qualify for it. As a matter of fact, many homesellers may want to combine both breaks if they have a massive untaxed gain and want to buy a smaller replacement home.

Q. That sounds special. How about an example?

A. All right, let's say you've rolled over several times and deferred tax on your gain each time. Now you get an offer of $180,000 for your present home. If you take it, you'll have an untaxed gain of $150,000. That means if you elect the exclusion, you'll still pay tax on $25,000. However, if you buy another home, the chances are *you won't have any taxable gain*. That's because you can combine the rollover *and* the exclusion.

You elect the $125,000 exclusion which *reduces the amount you have to roll over dollar for dollar*. Instead of having to buy a $180,000 replacement home, you can buy one for $55,000 and the rollover break allows you to escape any current tax on the $25,000—even after getting your once-in-a-lifetime break.

Special Tax Break For Job-Connected Sales

There's a batch of tax breaks awaiting you if you're moving because your job requires you to do so.

Q. You say my moving into a new home must be "job-connected." What if I'm self-employed and have no employer to shift me?

A. If your move is connected with your livelihood in any way, you qualify for the moving-expense deductions. The fact that you're your own boss won't matter.

Here are the five categories of deductible moving expenses:

1. The cost of moving household goods and personal effects.

2. The reasonable travel costs of you and your family. And on these two expenses, there is *no dollar limit*.

On the last three expenses, there's a total limit of $3,000 (but not more than $1,500 for househunting trips and temporary quarters):

3. Costs incurred while house-hunting, providing you are already working at your new location at the time.

4. Temporary expenses (food, lodging) incurred while you were waiting around to move into the new home. *Note*: You can only deduct such costs for up to 30 days—no more.

5. Certain expenses connected with the sale of your former home and the purchase of your new: attorney's fees, "points," commission paid the broker who sold your old place, etc.

Q. Am I entitled to these deductions if I move from an apartment?

A. You're entitled to them if you move from *and* to apartments, houses, co-ops, condominiums or mobile homes.

▶ **KEY TESTS FOR GETTING THE BREAK:** For you to get these five big breaks, your new job must be at least 35 miles further away from your old home than your former job had been. Also, if you're self- employed, you'll get the deduction only if you work at least 78 weeks at the new location within a 24-month period. If you're an employee, you need only work at your new location 39 weeks in the first 12 months. Meet those requirements and you get the break.

Does It Pay To Act As Your Own Real Estate Broker?

Many homesellers try to act as their own real estate broker to save themselves the cost of a commission. Quite a few sellers succeed, too, especially when mortgage money is easily obtained, the homes are in sterling condition, and prices are reasonable. If those conditions prevail when you put your home on the market—and if you are willing to spend the time and take the trouble to be present whenever anyone shows up to inspect your place—then by all means handle your home sale, yourself. You may well wind up keeping the commission a broker will charge.

But before you decide, think back over your days as a homebuyer. Did you use a broker? How helpful was he or she? Could you perform such services for buyers? What unusual problems came up at the last minute? Can similar ones occur now? Would you know how to handle them? You'll be better able to answer the big question, "Should I be my own broker?," by first answering questions such as these.

> ▶ **GETTING A FREE APPRAISAL:** Many brokers will help you price your home correctly, without charge. Check the classified ads to see which ones are offering owners a "free appraisal" or "free home evaluation service," or some such term.

Brokers have their own reasons for giving their professional opinion away, of course: they want to look over properties just coming on the market; and they want to ingratiate themselves with owners, like yourself, in hopes that you may turn to them in a few weeks or months. By all means, take them up on these "appraisals," if you find that no obligation is involved.

Be Prepared To Bargain

Don't expect to get every dollar you're asking for. Selling a home involves considerable haggling. Be prepared to bargain about:

☐ *The Selling Price*: A buyer will expect you to come down a bit from your asking price (5% to 12%). Price your home accordingly.

☐ *"Points" Paid to the Lender*: You may be expected to pay the lender "points" to help your seller get a mortgage ("points" are 1% of the mortgage amount—on a $50,000 loan, a "point" is $500). Agreeing to pay a couple of "points" to reduce your buyer's closing costs can actually cost you less than dropping your price; this move could also save your sale.

☐ *The Broker's Commission*: If you do list with a broker—and most sellers do—haggle over paying 6%, or the "standard fee." There is no law that says a real estate broker must receive 6% of the selling price; but there *are* laws about price fixing for professional services. The Federal Trade Commission has taken some real estate brokers to court over such practices; let your broker know that you realize this. Or you can set conditions upon your paying the broker's commission—agree, say, to a full 6% commission if the sale is made within 60 days.

> ▶ **TROUBLE SPOT:** Before you sign any listing agreement with a broker, have your attorney check it out. You must know the precise conditions under which you must pay a commission.

Here's a brief overview of what "listings" are:

A listing is a contract between a seller and a real estate broker authorizing the broker to act as the seller's agent in the sale of his property. Under the contract, when the broker produces a buyer ready, willing, and able to buy, under the terms specified by the seller in the listing, or other terms to which the seller may later agree, he will pay the broker a stated commission. There are three principal types of listings that you should be familiar with:

Exclusive right to sell listing: A listing given to *one* broker, giving him the *sole* and exclusive right to sell the named property during the listing term and to collect a commission when it is sold, regardless of who sells the property. Even if the seller himself were to sell the property during the listing term, he would still owe the broker a full commission.

Exclusive Agency listing: A listing given to *one* broker exclusively, as above, but with the seller retaining the right to sell the property himself without having to pay a commission.

Open listing: This is a listing that may be given to as many brokers as the seller wishes, with the seller agreeing to pay a commission only to the broker who sells the property. Under an open listing, the seller may sell the property himself, without having to pay a commission.

▶ **MULTIPLE LISTING:** This isn't really a listing but rather a term used to describe an exclusive right to sell listing that the listing broker has agreed to pool with the listings of other brokers (who are co-members of an area multiple listing service) to gain maximum exposure for the property. When one broker lists a property for sale and another broker sells it, the two brokers share the commission.

Special Situation—A Vacation Home

You may own a vacation home—a lakeside cabin or a seashore cottage or a ski lodge—in addition to your regular residence. If so, you are in line for some extra tax breaks, along with extra income.

▶ **HOW TO GET BOTH:** Rent out your vacation home when you and your family aren't using it. Renting your place enables you to turn what would otherwise be nondeductible household expenses into deductible rental expenses. You can use such costs as utilities, insurance, repairs, mortgage interest and property taxes for the rental period to shelter your rental income from tax.

Even better: What's left after these deductions—your cash profit on the rental—may be partially or completely tax-free. *Reason*: You can take advantage of the—

Magic of depreciation: The deductions that offset your rental income aren't limited to your out-of-pocket expenses. You can also deduct what the home cost you (cash downpayment plus mortgage), and any subsequent improvements you've made. This annual depreciation deduction is figured as if the home were declining in value each year due to use, even though it will probably be increasing in value. Since your depreciation deduction doesn't come from a current out-of-pocket expense, your cash profit on the rental may be a lot bigger than your taxable profit. Result: Tax-free income.

Let's say that Miss Lemmon owns a seaside cottage. She rents out the cottage for two months each year at $1,600 a month and uses it personally for another month. Her total annual cash expenses: $1,200 for upkeep and maintenance and $900 for property taxes. The depreciation on the cottage comes to $2,400 a year.

Pre-tax result: Lemmon has an $1,800 cash profit on the rental ($3,200 of rental income less the $800 of upkeep and maintenance and $600 of property taxes attributable to the two-month rental period).

After-tax result: Lemmon only has to pay taxes on $200 of her profit. Reason: From her $3,200 of rental income, she can deduct (1) $800 for upkeep and maintenance for the rental period, (2) $600 for property taxes for the rental period (she can deduct the other $300 as a personal itemized deduction), and (3) $1,600 for depreciation attributable to the rental period.

Chapter 2

Top Profit Opportunities In Real Estate: How To Find, Finance And Buy Them

Over the years, real estate has been one of the most popular wealth builders. *Reason:* It offers a combination of outstanding benefits few other investments can match.

• *Appreciation and inflation protection:* Over the long term, well located, well managed and well maintained property has appreciated at a rate that outpaces the increase in inflation. And this trend isn't likely to be reversed as an expanding population and a growing economy require more single family homes, condominiums, cooperatives, industrial facilities and office buildings (and vacant land to build on).

• *High leverage opportunity:* Leverage basically means using other people's money—instead of your own cash—to make money. Real estate gives you better leverage opportunities than most other investments. You can buy many properties with a low cash downpayment—25%, 10% or even less—and borrow the rest of the purchase price.

• *Equity buildup:* In the usual self-amortizing mortgage, part of each payment is for interest and the remainder reduces the principal (the unpaid balance of the loan). As the investor reduces the loan's balance, he builds up equity in the property without any additional out-of-pocket cash. *Reason:* The mortgage will be paid off by the rent roll. The greater the equity buildup, the more of the property the investor actually owns. And you need not sell the building to tap a growing equity. For example, you can refinance the mortgage and obtain additional cash to buy additional properties.

• *Tax shelter benefits:* Few investments offer as many tax shelter opportunities as real estate. Operating expenses—taxes, insurance, maintenance—are fully deductible, as is the interest paid on funds borrowed to buy the investment. But the biggest source of shelter is the—

> ▶ **DEPRECIATION DEDUCTION:** In most cases, investors buying a building today can depreciate it over 15 years. Depreciation is a major tax break because it's (a) based on the full cost of the building (including borrowed funds), and (b) does not require an ongoing cash outlay. Depreciation deductions result in tax-sheltered cash flow from your real estate.

If you play your cards right, a good part of your gain on a profitable resale will be low-taxed capital gain. In fact, you may even be able to dispose of your real estate without paying a penny of current tax.

Twelve Top Real Estate Opportunities

Many people think that real estate investments are for the rich only. That just isn't so. Real estate is one area where hard work, imagination, and nerve can substitute for a big bankroll. Here's a look at twelve real estate investments particularly suited for the smaller investor.

OPPORTUNITY #1—HOW TO BUILD A SHOESTRING FORTUNE IN RAW LAND

There are plenty of investments in raw land. Good buys come onto the market because owners need cash quickly. Developers may be ready to unload some raw land to raise cash. Farmers may be willing to part with some unproductive tracts of land. And heirs are always selling off land they can't manage themselves.

But how do you go about selecting the right piece of raw land—the one that can lay the groundwork for your personal real estate fortune?

Unlike other types of investments, there are no cut-and-dried valuation systems to use in raw land, and for that reason some investors have stayed away. The fact is that those investors who have been highly successful in raw land do follow a system, though they may be unable to formulate it, or unwilling to divulge it. It is a system that reduces risk and increases the probability of profit in raw land, and one which any investor can follow.

Here, in capsule form, are the main elements of this success formula:

Buy enough land: Experts discount any parcel smaller than ten acres. For really big profit, look for parcels five or ten times that size, or larger. Remember, the commercial, industrial or residential developer will need at least that much to put up a large project. And with a large parcel, the residential or vacation-home developer will be able to spread the cost of the land over more housing units. One large parcel is always a better buy than several smaller parcels. If you're worried about putting all your eggs in one basket, get together with other investors, pool your resources, and buy several large tracts of land.

What kind of land? Here is a rundown of the varieties you'll be most likely to find for sale:

Farm or ranch property: These are prime candidates for long-term investment. Generally, large tracts of land are involved and most of the property is cleared.

Sometimes the property can still be farmed, creating an interim use for the investor. Even if the land can't be farmed profitably, its buildings can often be sold or rented out for residential or other uses.

Property that has become vacant: This can be property that had been a farm, ranch, hotel, summer camp, and so forth. The business may have failed for any number of reasons, so the land is often available at a bargain price. This type of situation is a top opportunity for the investor who can visualize the profit potential of the property.

Raw, unimproved acreage: This can range from raw, virgin forest to desert land. It can front water or be on the side of a mountain. Improvements, if any, are minimal and prices are generally low.

Buy land only if it has a use: It is not enough to buy or option land you believe lies in the "general" path of development and simply wait for the hoped-for dramatic increase in value. The only kind of raw land that appreciates in value is the kind that can be put to use. So in order to determine about how much you should pay, you must decide on what its "best use" (or uses) would be.

Best use is the most profitable use possible for a tract of land. The more profit a developer or builder can realize from your land, the more he'll be willing to pay you for it. The more profitable the use, the more it may pay you to develop the land yourself. Property suited for commercial or industrial development almost always yields the highest investor-dividends; parcels suitable for multi-family projects, single-family home development and recreational development follow in profitability, roughly in that order.

How to establish best use: How do you know if a best use will be feasible, practical, and profitable for the property? This three-part approach should give you the answer. You should separately consider:

- Accessibility of the parcel.
- Utility of the land and area.
- Availability of the land.

How to judge accessibility: Begin with the parcel itself, and proceed outward as follows: Are there public roads that run by the property (or will roads be built in the near future)? How well are they maintained? Are they usable year-round?

How far is it from the property to the nearest vital services and amenities?

How adequate are all the transit systems in the area? What improvements are planned, where will such improvements or expansion be, and how will they be financed? Given the present state of the roads—and projected improvements—is the tract on the verge of coming within acceptable driving distance to the commuter or second home buyer? Keep in mind that if the land can't be reached, it can't be easily sold, or supplied with sewers and utilities.

Utility of the land and the area: First, there are a number of things you should check about the land parcel before investing:

- *Typography*—Is the site level, gently sloping, or steeply sloped? Generally speaking, the steeper the slope, the higher the construction cost, hence the less a developer or builder will pay for the land. A brook or pond on the acreage may enhance its value; a ravine or stony hill will not. Get a topographical or contour map of the area—one is usually available either through the local government or the state highway commission.

- *Soil and drainage*—Is the land rocky, sandy, or mostly clay? Was any of the land reclaimed from swamp? Does it flood when it rains? Finally, what is the land's bearing capacity? Don't be satisfied with graphs and figures; visit the property yourself and get an expert's evaluation of it.

- *Taxes and assessments*—These will represent a sizeable chunk of your carrying costs for raw land. You should secure accurate information on them—including the tax assessment rate and whether it is likely to go up.

- *Zoning and other restrictions*—Make sure the land is properly zoned for the use you have in mind. However, lack of the proper zoning does not mean you should necessarily rule the land out as an investment. You should be looking 3 to 5 years into the future when zoning may have to be changed because of growth and expansion in the area. You'll have to make sure, however, that there is little or no community opposition to zoning changes. In some cases, you may be able to make your purchase contract contingent on a zoning change.

Utility of the area: The following points will give you a bird's eye view of the area's growth and profit potential.

- Population and income: Is there enough employment in the area? What is the economic breakdown of the residents? Is the population shrinking, growing or relatively stable?

- Type of industry: Is local industry severely subject to swings in the business cycle? Does the local industry rely heavily on depleting natural resources? Is the area's industry more or less self-centered, or does it attract related industries?

- Community's attitude toward industry: Does the area attempt to attract new business and industry? Are there any special incentives (such as a low tax rate) to attract new business? Is there any hard evidence that efforts to attract new business are succeeding?

- Financing: Find out from businessmen and brokers the availability of funds from local S & Ls, commercial banks, mortgage lenders, etc. Is financing available for business expansion or home buying?

- Services and amenities: Any manufacturer, homebuilder or developer will want to know about the area's services and amenities; get the facts on educational, religious and health facilities as well as municipal services, such as gas, electricity and water.

- Climate: An area may be fine for recreational use during summer and winter, but not for industrial development if it gets mammoth snowfalls every year. Go back and check temperature extremes, amount of rain and snowfall.

How to check availability of land: This is a package item that covers such considerations as price, financing arrangements, title and how much your carrying charges will be. But it all really boils down to one point: Is the land available to you *at your price?* The fact that it's for sale doesn't necessarily mean that it's available—not as you would define the term. You must be able to aquire it at your price. Here are some tips on how you can do just that.

Use strategy when making your offer: Shoot for 10% or 15% off what you consider is the real worth of the property. This isn't as hard as it sounds. There are all sorts of pressures—personal and financial—that could lead an owner to knock 10% or 15% or even more off what his land's really worth. Taxes could be going up, there could be changes in family status, or sudden cash needs, etc.

Check prices of surrounding parcels: Check not only today's prices but the trend over the last five years. This is a sure way to find out if you're being asked to overpay and if land prices have been driven up unreasonably by unwarranted speculation. Also check the present uses and projected uses for surrounding land. (Will they enhance the value of your land or detract from it?)

Check ownership of land: Availability also refers to title problems. Some of the cheapest land is that which has a slight flaw in the title. Sure, it's cheap to buy—but it may turn out to be expensive to sell—if your future buyer demands a perfect title.

Buy on the way up: Once you've got the facts on accessibility and utility you'll be able to see whether you're buying in the path of development and whether land values are about to take off. Look for new or proposed major developments, like new roads, new housing projects, growing population, new industry.

Establish an interim use: For the average investor, an interim use may be almost as important as finding a property's best potential use.

Wherever possible, buy land that is either still bringing in money or can support a profitable interim use. Such a use can offset your carrying charges while you're waiting for your land's value to appreciate dramatically. You might even clear a steady profit from the interim use every year.

Buy land only if its value can double in three to five years: This is the bottom line in your decision about raw land. Experts counsel you not to buy unless you can reasonably expect a parcel's value to grow 20% each year you hold it. Remember, you'll probably put down a sizable chunk of your investment capital—money which could be earning interest for you. And you've got to recoup your carrying charges (for interest and taxes) and keep ahead of inflation.

Like every rule, this one has exceptions. If your downpayment and carrying charges are especially low, you may need less than a 100% increase in 3-5 years to get your total cash investment back and still make a hefty profit. If you've established a profitable interim use on your land, you'll need less than a 100% increase in value, too.

OPPORTUNITY #2—HOW TO CASH IN ON LAND SITES OTHER INVESTORS OVERLOOK

Many real estate investors walk right past potential profits every day because they've already classified a choice site as *unsuitable*. They never give a thought to how easy it is to turn seemingly *impossible* sites into valuable properties that could put thousands of dollars in their pockets.

How about you? Here are some examples of how some investors have already built fortunes just because they did what others thought impossible.

Inaccessible challenge: One New Jersey investor put up a 22-story high rise on a building site in a prime location. The site was on the side of a 45-degree cliff. A few feet from the street it plunged 133 feet straight down.

Everyone told the investor the whole idea was crazy. But he had confidence in his building judgment and consulted with top architects and structural engineers. Decision: Start building.

▶ **BIG PAYOFF:** Naturally he snapped up the site for a song. Seven months and 9,000 cubic yards of concrete later the foundation was complete: five stories high with its base resting some 100 feet below street level.

Hidden values: One upstate New York real estate investor learned that 91 acres of wooded land owned by the county were up for sale. For years no one in the area ever showed any interest in the site.

Two things attracted him right off: (1) A new thruway was only a few miles away, and (2) A local highway formed one of the boundaries of the property making it accessible. The entire site was thickly covered with aspen trees.

He checked with the U.S. Forest Service and found out the aspen trees make excellent timber. The county was anxious to sell the land and get it on the tax rolls so the price was low. The timber alone was worth almost the price he paid.

Here's his story: "I had planned to use the timber to pay for the property and keep the land for a long-term investment. But one day as I walked through it, I noticed a lot of fresh deer tracks. The caption *Hunter's Paradise* flashed through my mind immediately. I ran an ad. It produced 200 phone calls, 4 offers and a buyer within 10 days. The price was so good I couldn't turn it down. And I also got some good prospects for other properties of mine as well."

▶ **PROFITABLE ADVICE:** There's no such thing as an impossible site or useless land. So take another look around your area. If you see a potential site in a good location, check with the experts to see if it can be developed. This land usually comes cheap.

OPPORTUNITY #3—HOW TO MAKE MONEY IN OLDER APARTMENT HOUSES

The process of rehabilitating old apartment houses to make them livable and valuable again offers great profit potential. Housing shortages in many cities and towns, coupled with ever-increasing populations, make the availability of additional residential quarters imperative.

What will you need to swing it? To get into remodeling on the proper scale, you will require an operating fund of at least $35,000 to $45,000. You should be able to secure financing from your bank or from one of several finance companies.

Keep in mind that it is risky to go about remodeling without a big enough sum to get you going.

▶ **EXPERT'S TIP:** Some investors in remodeling have found it advantageous to form a "pool," drawn from friends and acquaintances with money, into which each member deposits a sum of capital (usually with a guaranteed return).

How do you select a building? If you pick the wrong buildings for remodeling you can't expect to succeed. Here are proven guides to help you choose wisely.

• Location: When planning to remodel an old building, you should take careful note of its location. If it is surrounded by several other old buildings, some of which are in advanced stages of decay, you should immediately cross it off your list. Bear in mind that even a palatial structure in a run-down neighborhood will have limited appeal.

Another consideration is the proximity of shopping centers, stores, laundries, theaters and other such facilities. If the building is reasonably close to these conveniences, its worth is increased and you have a potent selling point. This is not to say that a building farther away from the center of activity is a poor investment, but rather that its value is a little diminished if the residents will have to travel long distances to get their groceries and use other services.

• Price: You should analyze the initial costs in terms of your expected return from the first year or so. Ask yourself: If I make the necessary repairs, will the building bring me a return that more than makes up for the asking price and the cost of the repairs?

It goes almost without saying that you should "shop around" a bit, and make comparisons of necessary expenses before reaching your decision. When you do decide on one or another of the buildings you are considering, you will probably find that easy mortgage terms can be arranged to suit your budget.

Remodeling tips: Here's the five-step formula that one real estate pro uses:

(1) When he begins remodeling, our pro *avoids major structural changes.* He has discovered that if a property requires a complete overhaul, it's usually not worth investing in. Such a building could end up costing you more than you will realize.

(2) He improves the exterior appearance of the building by removing battered shutters, tearing down sagging porches, replacing broken windowpanes, realigning slanted sills, substituting new boards for those that are split or rotten, reshingling and renovating roofs, repainting where necessary and generally making the structure attractive and sound. The value of that first impression can not be minimized.

(3) Because the interior of a building almost always receives more scrutiny than the exterior, the pro's next step is to have his workmen go through the house and look for building flaws. These include such deficiencies as uneven flooring,

slanting walls, cracked plaster, loose boards, weak timbers and metallic supports that have rusted. The crew also looks for peeling wallpaper, broken light sockets, sagging shelves, outmoded furniture and fixtures, cracked tile and linoleum and other such defects.

(4) Interior reconstruction begins with special attention to the kitchen and bathroom areas. The workers remove old stoves, sinks, tubs, plumbing and any other accessories that make the interior seem antiquated and out-of-date. When our pro installs new, shiny fixtures, they more than pay for themselves through the higher sales price that they justify.

(5) Decoration of the property comes next, assuming that the structure is architecturally sound; otherwise the fifth step is the physical rebuilding of the interior. If the building has hardwood floors, the pro has his workers sand and wax them; if the floors are of softwood, he has them varnished or else covered with linoleum and carpeting. New wallpaper is put up and walls and ceilings are repainted in this phase of the operation, and the whole interior is put in apple pie order.

Our real estate expert adds a few *final touches* to the building to enhance its appeal. New brass doorknobs are installed, windows are washed, chrome and porcelain are polished and new mailboxes are substituted for old. It should be noted here that surface appearance counts for a great deal to most prospective lessees, and the more glamorous the apartment house appears, the more likely it is that they will consider renting.

OPPORTUNITY #4—BUYING SINGLE-FAMILY HOMES FOR INVESTMENT PROFITS

Buying single-family homes as income producing properties can be a big, new source of profits for you. Why? High interest rates and hefty sales prices are crowding many would-be buyers out of the market. Nevertheless, many of these families—especially younger couples with (or planning on) children—prefer living in homes rather than in apartments.

If everything works out right, you can buy a home with a low downpayment, rent it out for a few years, watch the property appreciate in value, then sell it at a substantial profit.

▶ **BIG-DOLLAR PAYOFF:** If you buy a home that appreciates in value 10% a year, you may be able to double your cash outlay in, say, five years. Of course, home investments are speculative. And they carry the usual burdens, responsibilities, and headaches of being a landlord. Keep in mind also that your rentals may enable you to just about break even, or maybe make a small profit, each year you hold onto the property.

But cash flow is a secondary consideration in this type of investment. What you look for primarily is the opportunity to take down a large profit in a few years.

Now let's consider what sort of home you should buy, and where, and how much to pay:

Location: Find an inexpensive house in the path of urban growth where jobs are abundant, or where you project that new companies and industries will locate and bring about more employment. Zoning is a vital consideration. Even though two homes may be identical in size, the one in an area zoned for *lower* density will be worth more than the home zoned for higher density.

Price range: Generally speaking, you get your best bargains by buying the cheapest home on the block. *Reason:* The higher-priced neighboring homes will raise the price of your home. And the reverse is also true: If you buy the most expensive home on the block, the neighboring homes will limit the resale price of your home.

More specifically, you should try to buy a home selling in the $70,000 to $80,000 price range. (This is the average price range of existing homes throughout the nation; of course, the range obviously will vary depending on the area you live in). Reasons:

1. The rent you can obtain does not increase in direct proportion to the cost of a house. You may get, say, $450-$500 a month for a $75,000 home, but you may find it difficult to get $800 a month for a $130,000 home. So if you spend more to buy a more expensive house, it doesn't necessarily bring in a proportionately higher rental income.

2. You have a greater market to tap when the time comes to sell. If you buy an $80,000 home that appreciates in value, to say, $115,000 in four years, there will still be a lot of people willing and able to buy it. In contrast, if you buy a $120,000 home that appreciates to $175,000 four years from now, your market of buyers is going to be smaller. The availability of minimum downpayment FHA and VA financing plans in the lower price ranges is an important factor, too. This generally enables an owner to get all-cash, and avoid the need to take back financing himself, when he sells.

Age: If you do not want to spend Saturday mornings at the hardware store or the lumber yard time and time again, then you had better select a home under ten or fifteen years of age. Better still if it's under five years or three years of age. This is because the hot water heater with an average life of about ten years will last a while longer. The dishwasher, disposal, exhaust fan, washer and dryer will not need much maintenance and should serve you and the tenant well.

Type of home: All things being equal, you want to buy the type of home that has the broadest appeal to the greatest number of people. Best bet: Look for a home that has three or four bedrooms, and one-and-a-half or two bathrooms. Look for a home with brick or aluminum siding, which doesn't require repainting every few years. The home should, of course, have adequate heating and cooling. Central air conditioning is a strong selling or renting feature, although air conditioning units placed in strategic locations will also be fine.

▶ **NO SWIMMING POOLS:** Unless you are buying a home that you figure to sell in excess of $100,000, you shouldn't buy a home equipped with a swimming pool.

People who buy homes in the $70,000 to $80,000 price range generally don't expect, or often don't want homes with pools. They prefer not to have the extra work and expense of cleaning and maintaining the pool.

If you build a pool for an investment home you've bought, you won't get the same return on your cash (in terms of rental or sales price) as you would for money spent on, say, improving the kitchen.

Smart move: By all means have the home and its systems checked out by a local home inspection service. The inspection will give you a good idea of the home's condition, and how much you'll have to spend on maintenance and replacement during your ownership period.

Where to look: Check out the classifieds and pay close attention to those "For Sale" ads that can easily be overlooked. The bold, well written ones will probably attract plenty of buyers while the smaller, poorly written ones won't. Wait a few days before responding to the less impressive classifieds; those owners may well be much easier to deal with by then. You could be one of the few buyers who called.

And always keep your ears and eyes open for bargain homes in your area. Sometimes sudden events (death, divorce or unemployment) or natural progression—a couple's children have grown up and moved out, and they no longer need a large home—make homes available at a low price.

OPPORTUNITY #5—HOW INVESTORS CAN GET BIG PAYOFFS BY CONVERTING "WHITE ELEPHANT PROPERTIES"

For really big profits, many investors are converting and rehabilitating old, and sometimes abandoned buildings for entirely new purposes.

A chance for bargains: Investments can be quite low in this area. The owners of these properties are often eager to get rid of "white elephant" properties. The prime ingredients of turning a profit from conversion, besides the basic investment, are imagination, a certain amount of courage and a strong business sense.

Let's take a look at some of the kinds of buildings that offer exceptional opportunities for conversion.

Municipal buildings: Municipal properties, such as abandoned courthouses or fire stations, libraries or jails can make ideal conversion properties. An investor can often buy government owned buildings at a bargain price because the municipal officials are eager to get potential income-producing properties on the tax rolls.

In some cases, municipal authorities are less interested in the price they'll get for their unused properties, and more concerned with the investor's intentions and the property's new use. *Result:* You may actually be able to buy a municipal property for a bargain price if you can show that your rehab plans may upgrade the community.

Example: In one New England community, an investor and a bank both bid on the old town hall. The bank intended to tear the building down and put in a parking lot. The investor planned to rehabilitate the existing structure into a mini-shopping mall with a number of specialty shops. Although the bank's bid was substantially higher, the town sold the property to the investor. *Reason:* His rehabilitation project would save a beloved old building.

Schoolhouses are a good choice: Almost every community now has one or more structurally sound schoolhouses standing vacant. They're often well-located and low-priced, and they can be adapted to a variety of uses. And they are going to be in abundant supply. As the baby boom dies down, communities across the nation are finding themselves saddled with more school buildings than they need.

Investors who buy abandoned school buildings are converting the structures to apartment houses, professional office suites, and shopping complexes. And certain features of school design give an investor extra advantages. One sharp investor we know has converted an abandoned schoolhouse into condominium apartments and used its extra wide hallways for roomy walk-in closets. These proved to be a very appealing amenity that, in part, helped justify the condo's substantial sale price. Landscaping and parking problems are practically solved in advance with many school buildings. Many have settings that are almost ideal for an office park or luxury apartment house.

And space used for *gymnasiums* has proved to be a bonanza for converters. Recreation facilities are considered essential for the success of condos or apartment houses today. One investor turned a gym into a community room. Another divided the former gym into two floors, turning the lower one into storage space for owners. And developers of commercial projects have found gyms ideal for restaurants or malls.

Vacant motion-picture theaters: These have become a fairly common sight on the American scene, and it's a rare community that doesn't have at least one shuttered cinema on one of its main streets. Alert investors have put this opportunity to work for them, and so can you.

Case in point: A theater building in the heart of a town's business section had been vacant for many years. A farsighted investor decided to purchase it for a new business venture. Because of the investor's experience with motels, he knew of the trend towards more in-city facilities of this kind, and he was aware that the town could use one. An inspection of the building revealed that it was structurally sound and ideally suited for conversion to a motel (it was fireproof; had a large unobstructed floor area, and had sufficient interior height for the addition of a second story).

The investor engaged the services of an architect, who drew plans for the conversion of the building into a two-story, 34-room motel with a restaurant, and a cocktail-lounge fronting on the main street of the town. To provide parking facilities, the investor bought three adjacent properties and razed the buildings standing on them.

The investor had no problem with financing; he arranged a loan from the local bank and was able to pay it back in short order. As for utilities, the city administration was most co-operative on the matter of water, power, sewer facilities, parking meters and so forth.

Of course, an enterprise that worked out in one community will not automatically work in every town. Before you decide to convert a theater to an in-city motel, check on zoning ordinances, demand for motel service, competition, building codes and overall costs. If the motel idea looks risky, don't despair; consider instead a supermarket, a bowling alley, a retail outlet for some local manufacturer, a warehouse or a factory.

Again, you should check local zoning ordinances for possible restrictions on certain enterprises and types of buildings. For example, the chances that you will be able to convert the theater to an industrial plant are minimal, since most cinemas are located in commercial districts where factories are prohibited. However, you should still check on the prospect.

OPPORTUNITY #6—ABANDONED GAS STATIONS CAN PUMP NEW LIFE—AND PROFITS—INTO YOUR REAL ESTATE PORTFOLIO

Abandoned gas stations are ideal for conversion into a new, profitable use. Some possibilities: professional office buildings (attorneys, doctors, real estate and insurance brokers, etc.), drug stores, even convenience grocery stores (like Seven-Elevens, Stop and Shops, Quick-Checks, etc.). And these properties are—

▶ **READILY AVAILABLE:** The wave of gas-station closings that swept the nation a few years ago has diminished, but is far from over. Check with real estate brokers in your area to learn what properties in and around your area may be available for conversion to other income properties.

Here are some of the advantages you get when you convert a gas station to a new, and more profitable use:

1. *Excellent location:* These sites are accessible and highly visible (few stations are failing today because the traffic count has turned against them). 2. *Ample parking:* There'll be plenty of space for clients and customers. 3. *Fully equipped utilities:* In most cases, new tenants will have access to more electricity, water and sewer capacity than they'll ever need. 4. *Big cash saving:* It's far cheaper to convert an existing property—especially one equipped and built as a gas station—than it is to build from the ground up.

Here's why: In most cases, you can remodel an existing gas station for about half of what you'd have to spend on putting up a new building. You can easily cover the outside of the building under a veneer of brick, stone or siding. You can add a new roof and change the look of the building at a nominal cost. The same goes with remodeling and repaneling the interior. You should figure that this work should cost somewhere around $20 a square foot (varying, of course with your particular location), and total anywhere from $25,000 to $50,000.

▶ **MONEY-SAVING TIP:** Try to have a tenant lined up before you renovate and remodel. This way, you can promise the prospective tenant a "custom remodeling job."

OPPORTUNITY #7—HOW CONDOMINIUM CONVERSIONS CAN BE YOUR KEY TO A REAL ESTATE FORTUNE

Given the right conditions, the purchase of an existing rental property, with subsequent conversion and sale of the units as condominiums, can and has yielded substantial profits for many investors. In addition, conversion to condominiums has proved to be a top real estate opportunity for owners of rental property. Here are some keys to success in this expanding area:

Your local market: There should be a large demand for homes and apartments. New apartment houses with amenities similar to yours should be renting for about 30% more than your property is presently renting for; new homes should be going for 20—25% more than you're going to charge for your condominiums.

Within that limitation, you should charge a price for each unit that is equal to 100 to 120 times that apartment's monthly rental. If your building is in an especially desirable location, you might be able to get as much as 130 times the monthly rental.

Your present tenants: Ideally, there should be a low turnover among them. You're counting on their liking the place—and on their being able to put up a substantial downpayment.

Key test: Will a substantial number of tenants, say 35% or 40% buy the converted units? If the answer is "Yes", there's a strong indication that the location is right for your price range. In some areas, a specified percentage of tenants *must* agree to buy before you are given permission to convert. And even where you don't have to get the consent of tenants, they're still your prime market. They're in familiar surroundings, can save moving costs, and so on. In addition, you'll cut down the losses from vacancies that result from tenants moving out as you convert.

Your property: The apartments should have features and a floor plan similar to those of a single-family home. Condominium buyers are looking for more than shelter, and will want the kind of features they expect in a one-family home. That's why apartment houses catering to singles and bachelors are not suitable for conversion. They do not offer the space that buyers want. However, a small percentage of bachelor units is not fatal, and can often be advantageous. They can be converted to an extra bedroom, study or family room and be added to an existing unit to make it more appealing to buyers.

Renovations should not be too extensive though, in an older property, they will be inevitable. *Remember:* Your property must be competitive when it goes condominium.

Investor's checklist: Here's a rundown of some of the key steps to take in a successful condominium conversion:

(1) Make sure the property will yield a higher net price as condominiums as opposed to an outright sale.

(2) Determine the costs of marketing (including advertising, promotion, rent loss and sales commissions).

(3) Start your search for suitable financing.

(4) Make sure existing leases don't preclude delivering possession for an extended period of time.

(5) Get competent legal assistance to draft the necessary legal documents, including the master deed, individual deeds, purchase and sales agreements and the condominium by-laws.

(6) Hire a marketing agent to coordinate a preliminary sales plan including assistance in setting up the advertising and promotion budget, training of the sales force, setting up the sales office and model apartments, and preparation of the sales brochures and auxiliary promotion material.

(7) Arrange for the preparation of a formal appraisal and feasibility study. This study should include, at a minimum, the value of your property both as an apartment property and as a completed condominium. It should also indicate the estimated market value of each condominium unit and the probable absorption rate of these units into the market.

(8) Arrange for your interim and permanent financing commitments.

(9) Your marketing agent should be prepared to provide prospective purchasers with cost estimates indicating probable out-of-pocket costs of ownership along with estimated tax savings and equity build-up due to mortgage principal payments and anticipated growth.

(10) Once a sufficient number of binding contracts to purchase have been executed, dedicate the condominium, deed out your initial units and proceed with the marketing of the remaining units.

(11) Finally, check with your tax and accounting advisers and make sure all allowable additions to your basis in the property have been made for expenses connected with the conversion. These additions to basis will decrease the tax bite on your profits.

OPPORTUNITY #8—CONDO AND CO-OP CONVERSION STRATEGY CREATES NEW PROFITS FOR INVESTORS

Savvy real estate people have come across a new way to profit from the interest in condominims and co-ops. Investors can profit from condos and co-ops, by—

▶ **BUYING UNITS IN BULK:** Investors buy several condominium or co-op units—five, ten or even more—and *rent* them to tenants. It's like buying a small apartment complex, except they own a parcel of apartments located in a large apartment development.

Let's say you invest in several units in this way. Like any landlord, you pocket income sheltered by depreciation deductions. Then when the time comes to cash in on your investment, you will find that it is much easier to sell your individual units than it would be to sell an entire apartment building. *Reason:* There are many more buyers for *individual* condo or co-op units than there are buyers for a whole apartment building.

> ▶ **HOW TO NAIL DOWN A BARGAIN PRICE:** Buy apartments in a large high-rise or garden-apartment complex that has been purchased by a converter specialist. Make your move as soon as possible after the converter has bought the property.

Why this move pays off: The converter has made large cash commitments: cash for the seller of the property, more cash for improvements to make the units salable, and still more cash to carry the property while the building is completely converted and all apartments sold.

In short, the converter needs working capital—and in a hurry.

You offer to buy a number of the converter's units—*for cash.* In return you bargain for a substantial discount off market prices—say *20%-25%*.

The typical investor in this field finances part of the purchase with a short-term personal loan. Your rental income should cover the financing and any other expenses. You can expect only a modest return.

Rapid profits are the key: Investors who buy condo and co-op units in bulk get in and out of their investments in two or three years. If you buy units at a substantial discount off true market value, you don't need extraordinary appreciation in value to take in a big profit.

For example, suppose you buy two units with a fair market value of $120,000 ($60,000 each). You buy them for $96,000 (a 20% discount). You lay out $48,000 cash and finance the rest. Suppose the units appreciate to $140,000 in two years. If you can sell the units at that price, you would have a pre-tax profit of $44,000—a 91.6% return on $48,000!

Word of caution: Your profit depends on whether the conversion project as a whole is a commercial success. If it is, you are carried along with it and make a big profit. If it's not, you may have a hard time selling your units.

OPPORTUNITY #9—PROFESSIONAL CONDOMINIUMS MAY BE GOOD PROFIT-BUILDING MEDICINE

The condominium concept, which has gained acceptance nationwide among homebuyers, is now being successfully applied in many different commercial and industrial applications. One you should look into is the—

> ▶ **PROFESSIONAL CONDOMINIUM:** You build or rehabilitate a structure tailored to the needs of doctors, dentists, or various other professionals. You then sell off the offices you've created as condominiums to individual practitioners.

How to sell space to professionals: Your most persuasive arguments when selling professionals on condominium offices comes from pointing out the advantages and the inflation hedge. First and foremost, the condominium is an office from which to conduct a practice, but it is also a valuable piece of investment real estate. The professional's mortgage payments constantly build up his equity, while he is also being provided with valuable deductions which shelter his income from tax. And the biggest payoff for a professional will come when it's time for him to sell his practice. He'll be in a position to get top dollar, since he's not only selling his intangible good will, but a valuable piece of real estate as well.

The tax advantages: When a professional buys a condominium office, monthly payments, real estate taxes, and other such costs will probably run higher than rental payments on a similiar office. But because of the tax savings a professional gets when he owns a condominium office, his monthly payments may actually be lower in terms of after tax dollars than if he were to rent.

A professional's deductions come from three sources: (1) mortgage interest; (2) condominium carrying charges and an allocable share of property taxes; and (3) depreciation deductions. The professional can write off that part of his condominium cost allocable to the building and other depreciable improvements over a period of 15 years.

OPPORTUNITY #10—MINIWAREHOUSES—A WAY TO STORE UP PROFITS IN INCOME-PRODUCING PROPERTIES

Demand keeps growing for *miniwarehouses,* the small income-producing property that can provide substantial profits for astute investors. Here are some reasons why:

- Millions of Americans, whether they live in apartments or houses, need extra storage space for recreational vehicles, furniture, and possessions of all sorts.
- Hundreds of thousands of businesspeople and companies need storage space for records or equipment.
- Investors can supply such space—in units of 10' by 10' or 10' by 20'—in a secure, compact but economically constructed one-story building that's like a series of single-car garages set side by side—the *miniwarehouse.*

▶ **BIG PROFITS:** Investors can average a 20% return in well located, sensibly constructed miniwarehouses. Units that cost as little as $7 to $10 a sq. foot to build can rent for as much as 50¢ a sq. foot per month. When kept to a tightly managed, "no-frills" operation, these structures can bring in a healthy cash flow and provide all the standard tax advantages of commercial real estate.

Keeping costs low: Miniwarehouses can be built comparatively cheaply. Cinderblock construction is perfectly acceptable; it can be painted in bright colors and requires virtually no maintenance.

Units need neither windows nor insulation. Doors should be the standard overhead model used on garages, but they need not be the most elaborate model available; a door will get very little use since the average customer rarely visits the unit more often than once a month. Experts in the field recommend using the least expensive model that is (a) secure and (b) watertight.

> ▶ **SMART STRATEGY:** Movable partitions can be used to divide interior space. While these cost more than walls, they allow an investor to shift the design according to the market—creating 10′ by 20′ units if demand for those is high; dividing large units into 10′ by 10′ ones if those become popular. Miniwarehouse experts suggest devoting 15% of the space to units 5′ by 6′.

Picking the right site: An investor should expect to draw about 75% of all customers from within a five-mile radius and pick a site accordingly. A market survey will be needed to answer such questions as: How many houses do or do not have basements? How many boats and recreational vehicles are owned? How many people live in apartments? In mobile homes? The answers reveal the need for storage space and the kinds of storage space in your community. This market research can also be used by investors to raise financing from lenders.

Commercial tenants may account for up to 30% of the space; so an investor shouldn't concentrate only on spots near residential areas. In fact, commercial tenants are, on the whole, preferable to individual tenants. They tend to be long-term customers. Access to a main highway is essential, but the miniwarehouse need not be seen from the road; a tall sign over the structure or a large sign near the freeway exit can pull in the patrons.

Offering the right amenities: Plenty of open space around the structure can make a miniwarehouse popular with customers. Experts suggest a two-and-a-half acre site as the minimum today and recommend devoting only 50% of it to buildings. Customers will need the extra space to maneuver when they are parking and unloading. Some will be storing recreational vehicles or U-Hauls in their units. Some may own vehicles too large for storing and will want to rent parking space outside. Naturally, they will go to the miniwarehouse with room to spare.

The successful miniwarehouse should also provide:

- An area with running water and a drain, where vehicles can be washed.
- Electric outlets *outside* the units.
- Restrooms—separate restrooms for men and women are preferable, but not necessary.
- Spotlights on the outside of the building controlled by a photo-electric cell.
- A high, secure fence surrounding the entire tract.
- An apartment for a resident manager—preferably a Mom & Pop team.

OPPORTUNITY #11—REAL ESTATE PROFITS IN SAFE-DEPOSIT CENTERS

There's a new investment opportunity in real estate being created by high burglary rates and soaring insurance premiums. It is the *safe-deposit center*, a privately run safety-deposit vault run independently of any bank.

People want to rent space for their valuables in these centers because:

- Quite a few banks don't have any safe-deposit space vacant.
- Those banks that do have safe-deposit boxes available do not have boxes large enough to store fur coats or sterling tea sets or paintings.
- Unlike banks, safe-deposit centers allow depositors access to their valuables 24 hours a day, seven days a week.
- The rental costs are more than offset in most cases by the big savings depositors make in reduced insurance premiums for their valuables.

▶ **BIG PAYOFF:** These centers have already proved a good deal for many investors. For example, in one major city a center with 3,700 boxes was rented out within 10 months.

What depositors want: Space, security and convenience are the three items depositors look for—and they are willing to pay well for it, too. In one big city, a box 3 by 10 by 24 inches goes for $180 a year. One 15 by 10 by 24 inches goes for $800. In one Northeast suburb, boxes 32 by 32 by 24 inches rent for as much as $3,000 a year.

A typical safe deposit center includes 24-hour air-conditioning, uniformed guards and rooms with a full-length mirror where a woman can try on her fur coat or jewelry. Conference rooms and "coupon booths," similar to space in a bank's vault, are also expected, so be sure to offer them. You should also give depositors the choice of at least 10 box sizes.

Opportunities for investors: A successful, well-run safe-deposit center can ensure an investor a solid, steady stream of income. In addition, it can supply tax shelter for investors. But note that this isn't a low-cost investment opportunity: Investors should raise at least one year's operating expenses to assure working capital in advance. A 2,000-box center, with its thick walls, steel vault and electronic security gear, can cost anywhere from $400,000 to $1.2 million.

OPPORTUNITY #12—PRIVATE "MAILBOX" CENTERS—A LOW COST WAY TO REAP BIG PROFITS FROM COMMERCIAL PROPERTIES

You can make big money by buying sites or buildings that can be used for *private post offices*—small buildings where the public rents individual mailboxes.

These "centers" are catching on fast because they fill a growing need. U.S. post offices are running out of space just when more people are wanting to rent mailboxes. A center is strictly a "no-frills" operation, since all the public wants is a place to pick up its mail. And this means you can make a top profit at a minimum cost. A sorting room, a lobby and four walls of boxes—those are the "facilities" required.

This growing demand gives an investor at least three ways to earn big profits:

- You can lease a commercial property you own (or buy) to someone who will use it as a private mailbox center;
- You can convert all or part of a property you own (or rent) to a mailbox center and operate the business yourself.
- You can buy or rent a property for conversion to a mailbox center.

Another advantage of a mailbox center is that you might be able to acquire property at—

▶ **A BARGAIN PRICE:** You don't need very much space to operate a mailbox center. So you might be able to buy an oddly shaped vacant lot or an undersized storefront at a bargain price.

Profit potential: Some operators are reported to net 30% to 40% of the gross before taxes. One investor with only 312 boxes reportedly grosses $42,000 a year. He opened just a few years ago with a $5,000 investment.

Another operator said his business doubled in a year; customers are people who travel or people who are opening new businesses and like to have their mail addressed to "Suite No." such and such at the address of the mailbox center.

Few management problems: Because of its simplicity, this is one business that can prosper under absentee ownership. A dependable manager or assistant manager would be a former postal worker who is conscientious and knows the system. And it's not hard to find part-time or moonlighting postal clerks to sort mail and serve customers. This makes the business perfect for many real estate investors.

13 KEY WAYS TO BUY REAL ESTATE WITH LITTLE OR NO MONEY DOWN

Leverage—using other people's money to make money—is the fuel that real estate runs on. It helps you buy more property than you could on an all-cash basis and it increases your tax-sheltering depreciation deductions. It also helps you make more money. That's because, as a general rule, a leveraged property should always throw off more in cash than you're paying to carry the loan.

Most people are already familiar with the simple conventional mortgages available from institutional lenders. Generally, these mortgages are paid off over a 15 to 30 year period at a fixed interest rate. Each payment goes in part to pay the interest charged on the loan and part to pay off the loan principal itself (the interest portion is very high in the early years and declines with each payment). At the end of the mortgage period, the loan will be fully amortized, or paid off. Depending on the quality of the property, and its nature (residential, commercial or industrial) institutional lenders will lend you anywhere from 60% or 75% of the property's purchase price on conventional (uninsured) loans.

But that's only the beginning. There are many other leverage techniques that reduce the amount of cash you have to lay out to buy real estate. Here's a look at thirteen of the most commonly used alternatives and supplements to conventional mortgages that can boost your leveraging power on a real estate investment to 80%, 90%—even 100%—of the property's value.

How New Types of Mortgages Can Give You the Leverage You Need

Alternative mortgage instruments (or AMIs, for short) have been developed by lending institutions as tools to cope with rapidly changing interest rates. One of these new mortgages may bail out your deal if standard mortgages aren't available.

Financing Method #1—Variable rate mortgage (VRM). The rate of interest is tied to a given reference rate and fluctuates accordingly. A variation of the standard VRM permits the maturity of the loan to vary in response to changing interest rate levels.

Financing Method #2—Graduated payment mortgage (GPM). This plan requires small payments at the beginning of the loan and increasingly larger payments as the loan is repaid. The rate at which the payments will rise is specified in the GPM, for example, 5%. Because of the low payments at the beginning of the loan, the outstanding balance for the first few years will be greater than the beginning balance of the loan. This type of mortgage may be good for investors who won't have sufficient income to meet high mortgage payments in the early years.

Financing Method #3—Price level adjusted mortgage (PLAM). This mortgage provides for increases or decreases in the loan's outstanding balance based upon a price level index. Lenders use the PLAM as a hedge against inflation.

Financing Method #4—Canadian rollover mortgage (CRO). The CRO is paid back over a long period of time, but the interest rate is automatically renegotiated at the end of each established period (generally five years).

HOW TO GET THE TOP LEVERAGE YOU NEED USING SPECIAL MORTGAGE INSURANCE

Through a combination of a first and second mortgage, an investor can often buy a property and only have to lay out as little as 20% of the purchase price in cash. But you may be able to obtain 80% financing without resorting to a second mortgage at all.

▶ **FINANCING METHOD #5—INSURED MORTGAGES:** Private insurance companies will insure the top 10%, 15% or even 20% of a mortgage on income producing property. Such insurance—available only through banks and other lending institutions—is called *commercial loan insurance*. When the vital top percentage of the mortgage is guaranteed in this way, a lender may increase first mortgage financing to 80%.

Example: You want to buy a commercial property priced at $500,000. You'd like to put down $100,000 and finance the rest. However, the lender says his top mortgage is only $325,000. Commercial loan insurance may be the answer.

How it works: You take out commercial loan insurance for the top 20% of a $400,000 loan—$80,000 of coverage. The insurance protects the lender from loss up to that amount. The lender is thus at risk in the first year of the loan for only $320,000 (less than the amount he was willing to lend without insurance) though he actually advances $400,000.

The cost: The cost of commercial loan insurance depends on the type of property involved and varies from company to company. You may choose to pay a single premium covering the full term of the insurance—say five years. Or you can spread out the cost with an annual payment plan.

Tax angle: Commercial loan insurance is a deductible business expense. However, if you pay the premium in one lump sum, you cannot deduct the full premium that first year. You must spread the deduction over the number of years covered by the insurance. Under an annual payment plan, each of your premium payments is deductible when paid.

It may seem simpler to get a second mortgage for the additional financing you need. But this might not always be possible—or the best way to do things. For one thing, you may not be able to get a second mortgage. Furthermore, a second mortgage places a much greater debt-service burden on the property and may reduce your cash flow to a trickle.

For example, if you get a 25-year first mortgage for $325,000 at say 13%, and a 5-year second mortgage for $75,000 at 15% (if not more) your payments will be very high until the second mortgage is paid off. In contrast, if you get a 25-year first mortgage for the full $400,000, your mortgage payments will be much lower those first five years. Consequently, you'll have a much bigger cash flow.

Of course, if you do get a second mortgage, your monthly payments will shrink substantially after five years when the second mortgage is paid off. But until that happens, you may be left with a negligible cash flow after making your mortgage payments. And, most real estate investors want a substantial cash flow from a piece of property—right from day one. And that's exactly what you get when you arrange for a single, long-term mortgage obligation requiring constant and level payments.

The premium payments on commercial loan insurance will reduce your cash flow somewhat. But, keep in mind that you'll be making them for a limited period of time only—say five years—not for the full term of the mortgage. After the mortgage principal has been paid down to what the lender considers a reasonable level, you won't have to carry the insurance any more.

HOW THE FEDERAL GOVERNMENT CAN HELP YOU GET FAVORABLE FINANCING TERMS

The Federal Housing Administration is an important force in multi-family housing. It does not make loans itself; rather it *insures* institutional lenders against loss on loans to build, buy, or rehabilitate residential rental properties. FHA loans offer three major advantages:

(1) *No personal liability:* You are not personally liable for repayment on an FHA-insured multi-family loan (the property acts as security).

(2) *Loans are assumable:* The FHA loan you take out to buy a property can be assumed by a future buyer. This is a major advantage for both buyer and seller.

(3) *Long repayment times:* FHA multi-family loans can run as long as 35 or 40 years. Result: Lower debt service and better chances for good cash flow.

While there are many different FHA loan programs, two offer particularly attractive terms to investors. Let's take a look, beginning with—

How a Special Government Program Can Be a Two-Way Winner for Real Estate Investors

There's one FHA program tailor-made for investors in existing apartment buildings.

▶ **FINANCING METHOD #6—SECTION 223(f):** Under this program, the FHA will insure mortgage loans to buy existing apartment houses. The major feature: A low 15% down payment. In other words, the mortgage can be up to 85% of the property's appraised value. And the mortgage can be paid off over 35 years.

Types of property eligible for Sec. 223(f) loans: You can get a loan on properties that: (1) are existing residential rental buildings; (2) have at least five rental units (there's no maximum); and (3) are at least three years old. So you can use Section 223(f) to buy anything from a small five-unit rental project to a giant apartment house complex.

Financing terms: As we've said the mortgage can be up to 85% of the property's value. However, the mortgage can't exceed a specified amount per family unit. These per-unit limits are available at your local FHA office.

Big benefits for owners: Section 223(f) can also be a life-saver for investors who bought property through a combination of first and second (or even third) mortgages. Because of changing financial conditions that make payments on the combined mortgages too big a burden, or because of other circumstances, an investor may want to—or have to—refinance his mortgage(s).

▶ **SPECIAL REFINANCING HELP:** Section 223(f) has special provisions designed to aid investors who seek refinancing. Here's an example of how Section 223(f) works in this type of situation:

Smith sells his apartment house to Green for $750,000. Terms: $100,000 cash; Green assumes a first mortgage of $500,000; and gives Smith a second mortgage of $150,000 to cover the balance of the purchase price. The second mortgage is for five years. Green agrees to pay 15% a year interest, and $4,000 a year on principal. At the end of the fifth year, Green must pay the entire $130,000 balance due on principal.

When the fifth year rolls around, Green may run into a number of problems:

(1) Green doesn't have enough cash on hand to pay off the $130,000 balance.

(2) Smith doesn't want to renew the loan, or will renew only on terms that Green can't live with. For example, Smith may want to raise the interest rate and demand annual payments on principal of $15,000.

(3) Private lenders are charging extremely high interest rates and want large annual payments on principal.

(4) Green can't get a new conventional first mortgage big enough to repay the existing first and second mortgages.

The way out: Green can get a new first mortgage to refinance the property under Section 223(f). In addition to the limitations mentioned earlier (the mortgage can't exceed 85% of property's appraised value or a specified amount per family unit), there is another limitation when refinancing is involved. The mortgage can't exceed the greater of (a) 70% of the FHA-appraised value of the building or (b) the cost of refinancing the existing indebtedness.

In our example, Green may be able to get a first mortgage of $630,000—more than enough to pay off both existing mortgages.

Keep in mind that this program is not limited to investors who need refinancing help because they are having financial problems. Many investors with first and second mortgages use Section 223(f) simply to improve their financial situation and their investment yield.

How? Since a Section 223(f) mortgage to refinance property can run as long as 35 years, investors with a second or third mortgage can turn a short-term obligation into a long-term obligation.

Result: The monthly principal and interest payments will be smaller than with the existing financing. So the investor's annual return goes up. In addition, once he refinances, the investor doesn't have to worry about a second mortgage coming due soon and scrambling to refinance at that time.

High-Leverage Opportunity For Investors In New Housing

Financing Method #7—Section 221(d)(4): This program allows you to build a moderate-income multi-family project with as little as 10% down. And it's not just for multi-million dollar deals. A project with as few as five units can qualify.

FHA bases its maximum loan amount on the lowest of three figures:

Limit (1): The number of units in a project times a specific dollar amount for each type of unit. The per-unit allowance is high enough that this standard is rarely the lowest of the three.

Limit (2): 90% of the economic value of the property.

Limit (3): 90% of replacement cost (i.e., the cost of construction). Replacement cost includes the land, proposed improvements, utilities on the land, architect's fees, taxes, interest during construction plus a unique—

▶ **BUILT-IN PROFIT FACTOR:** FHA gives builders and sponsors a special profit-and-risk allowance of 10% of the replacement costs (minus the land). This allowance is commonly referred to as the BSPRA.

The 10% BSPRA is one of the most attractive elements of this program. But you can get it only if Limit (3)—the 90% of replacement costs—is used to determine the top mortgage amount. So you have to try and make sure that Limits (1) and (2) are higher than Limit (3).

As we said, Limit (1), the per-unit allowance, is generally no problem. But limit (2), 90% of economic value, can pose difficulties. But if your rent projections are high enough—and you can convince the FHA they're realistic—economic value will nearly always be either equal to replacement cost, or slightly higher.

Result: You use 90% of replacement cost as your mortgage limit—and you get the benefit of the 10% BSPRA.

Bear in mind that just because Section 221(d)(4) is a program for moderate income projects doesn't mean that they have to be built in the inner city, or in poor or deteriorating neighborhoods. In fact, Section 221(d)(4) buildings have been erected in fairly expensive parts of Manhattan.

One more condition: Because Sec. 221(d)(4) offers a mortgage term of up to forty years, FHA expects that your rents will be lower than the going rates—maybe about 15% or 20% lower. But because of the lower mortgage payments you make due to the long payout period, you can afford to charge a lower rent, and still have a nice building in a neighborhood where values are stable or rising.

HOW TO SLASH THE AMOUNT OF OUT-OF-POCKET CASH YOU NEED BY USING SECOND MORTGAGES

Although the amount that can be borrowed on real estate with a first mortgage is greater than most other investments, the amount of out-of-pocket cash required may still be substantial. Many investors can't, or are unwilling to, invest the cash required. Solution: they use—

▶ **FINANCING METHOD #8—SECOND MORTGAGE:** As its name implies, a second mortgage is second in priority of claim against the property. The property itself generally is the security for the loan. But if the holder of the first mortgage forecloses, it is entitled to recover the entire balance on the first mortgage, plus the expenses of foreclosure. The holder of the second mortgage gets what's left over, if anything.

This added risk to the second mortgage lender means it will cost you more—you'll pay high interest on the borrowed money.

Sources of second mortgages: Many institutional lenders who make first mortgage loans are generally forbidden by law to make second mortgages, so you'll have to look elsewhere for your second mortgage financing. Commercial lenders *can* make second mortgages but their rates may be up to double the rate on first mortgages. That's why you're much better off when you—

Use the Seller as the Second-Mortgage Lender

Why are sellers willing to take back second mortgages? In most cases, that's the only way they can make the sale and get the profit they want. Usually, a seller still gets a substantial amount of cash up front (from the first mortgage proceeds and the buyer's cash downpayment). You—the buyer—get the property you want with a minimum of cash out-of-pocket.

What about sellers who are reluctant to lock themselves into long-term investments like second mortgages? The solution may be—

▶ **GAP FINANCING:** The seller takes back a second mortgage that lasts only until you can find a financing deal you can live with. The mortgage runs, say, one or two years. You can arrange the deal so that you make interest only-payments or part interest and part principal payments. Either way, at the end of that term you pay the seller back the principal. The terms of the mortgage (the amount, the interest, the time period), including terms on which you *must* accept outside financing, will all be set out in the mortgage instrument.

With gap financing, you show the seller that he can avoid locking himself into a long-term mortgage. And you get the time you need to find financing you like—without laying out extra cash from your pocket.

Discounting a Mortgage—Another Way to Convince a Seller to Take Back a Second Mortgage

You're trying to persuade the seller to take back a second mortgage on the property. But he's not buying. He doesn't want the worry and aggravation of making sure he gets paid on the second mortgage. But most of all, he wants cash, and he wants it now—he doesn't want to wait the three, five or ten years.

Well don't give up yet. You have one more option which may do the trick.

▶ **FINANCING METHOD #9—DISCOUNTING THE MORTGAGE:** There are many mortgage brokers, both private and commercial, who buy second mortgages. The seller can take back a second mortgage, and sell it to a broker at a discount, and get back most of his money in as little as a few weeks.

Result: You get the property you want at a minimum out-ot-pocket cost. And the seller gets the cash that he wants, without the possible problems involved with holding a second mortgage.

The amount of the discount depends on a number of factors, e.g., the term of the mortgage, the interest rate charged compared to the market's interest rate, and the security for the mortgage. You and the seller will have to check with several discount brokers in order to get the best deal.

HOW BALLOON MORTGAGES WORK

Conventional mortgages are fully paid off at the end of a relatively long term (15 to 30 years). But some lenders don't want to lock themselves into a long term loan, especially if they think interest rates will rise. They may insist on a shorter term loan, say for five years. This will enable the lender to renegotiate and get a higher interest rate if the market warrants it. Since most investors can't pay off the loan principal over such a short period, these mortgages carry a—

> ▶ **BALLOON:** The mortgage is only partially paid off during its term. At the end of the term, a large payment for the balance of the loan principal ("the balloon") is due. If you can't pay off the balloon, you have to get a new mortgage.

Financing Method #10—Balloon Mortgages: The most common type of balloon is the easiest to understand. Suppose you get a $50,000 loan at 12%. For five years, principal and interest payments are based on a 25-year amortization schedule. The last payment—the "balloon"—is for the remaining balance at the end of five years. There are numerous variations on the balloon theme. Here's a look at four of them (in each example, we assume that the mortgage is for $50,000 and a term of 5 years).

Type One—Interest payments only: Here the borrower pays interest only—on the full amount of the mortgage—each year. At the end of the five years the entire $50,000 is due.

Type Two—Constant principal payments, interest on declining balance: The borrower agrees to pay, say $3,000 each year toward principal, plus 12% interest on the declining balance. This would mean a $9,000 payment the first year ($3,000 principal, plus $6,000 interest) and a $8,640 payment the second year ($3,000 principal plus $5,640 interest) and so forth. The "balloon" at the end of the fifth year is $35,000.

Type Three—Principal and interest on declining balance basis: Here the amount paid on principal is expressed in percentage terms and is paid—as the interest is—on the declining balance of the mortgage principal. For instance, the terms may provide for 12% interest, and 5% principal payments, both on the declining balance of the loan. On a $50,000 mortgage, this would mean first year payments of $6,000 for interest, plus $2,500 principal. Second-year payments would be $5,700 for interest (12% of $47,500) plus $2,375 for principal (5% of $47,500). At the end of the fifth year, there is a "balloon" of $38,689.

Type Four—Constant payments, with interest on declining balance: Stated interest on the $50,000, 5-year balloon mortgage is, say 12%, figured on the declining balance of the loan. But the terms call for a yearly payment of $8,000, the excess over 12% to be applied toward principal. Since the amount of interest steadily declines as the mortgage is being paid off, the amount of amortization increases with each payment. In our example, the $8,000 payment in the first year would be allocated to $6,000 for interest and $2,000 for principal. In the second year, the $8,000 payment would be apportioned to $5,760 for interest (12% on $48,000) plus $2,240 for principal.

Reminder: You have to pay off the "balloon" at the end of the mortgage term, or get another mortgage for the balloon amount. If money is tight, you may have to pay a higher interest rate. Even worse, you may be unable to get another mortgage and thus be forced to dispose of your property. So here's—

▶ **WHAT TO DO:** Try to get as long a mortgage term as possible. Assuming the balloon is a second mortgage, the longer maturity may enable you to reduce your first mortgage substantially before the "balloon" on the second comes due. Your increased equity in the property will considerably improve your chances of getting favorable refinancing terms. If the balloon is a first mortgage, the longer payout period will allow you to reduce the amount—the balloon—you eventually will owe, making it easier to pay off or refinance.

HOW TO BUY INCOME PROPERTY WITHOUT LAYING OUT A PENNY OF CASH

Here's one financing technique that lets you get *100% financing* for a real estate deal. Essentially, you have to persuade the seller to take back a second mortgage that covers the difference between your first mortgage and the property's purchase price. To do this, you offer property you already own as additional security for the second mortgage.

▶ **FINANCING METHOD #11—BLANKET MORTGAGE:** When more than one property is used as security for a mortgage, you have a blanket mortgage. The properties involved don't have to be similar, and there's no limit on how many can be included. This technique could enable you to get 100% leverage.

Example: You want to buy Smith's apartment house for $450,000. You can get 75% financing from a commercial lender—that is, a first mortgage for $337,500. But you want to "mortgage out"—that is, you want to buy the building without making any downpayment at all.

You ask Smith to take back a second mortgage on the building for the remaining $112,500. But Smith is unwilling to take a straight second mortgage—he wants more security.

▶ **BLANKET MORTGAGE SOLUTION:** You offer to include as part of the security for the mortgage some raw land you own, worth about $75,000. This gives Smith added security. He accepts the deal and takes back a second mortgage. Results?

• You get just what you wanted—an income property with no money down. You also get some use out of raw land (for which you have no immediate plans) while you wait for its value to go up. When the second mortgage is paid off, you will once again own the land free and clear.

• Smith has sold his apartment building as he wanted to do. He gets a big chunk of his sales price in cash (from the proceeds of the first mortgage). And he'll be collecting interest for several years on a well-secured loan.

Drawback: The biggest disadvantage to this technique is that you place other property in jeopardy should your new property falter. So, above all, make sure that the property you buy is worth enough to pay off all the mortgages if the worst happens and there is a foreclosure.

Will the second mortgage prevent you from selling the raw land, if you get a good offer on it and have to move quickly? Not necessarily. You can insert a clause in the mortgage providing for prepayment without penalty. Or you can have the seller agree to release the additional property from the blanket mortgage when (1) a certain percentage of the loan is paid off, (2) upon payment of a specific amount of cash, or (3) other property of equivalent value is substituted for it. Of course, you're not limited to just using raw land as additional security for a blanket mortgage. You can use income property as well, such as apartment buildings, office buildings, etc.

How about 100% first mortgage financing? The seller is by no means your only source for 100% financing using the blanket mortgage technique. A regular institutional lender *may* go along with a blanket mortgage also. If you put up valuable additional property as security, the lender may give you a big enough first mortgage so that you don't have to resort to a second mortgage at all.

HOW YOU CAN BUY THE PROPERTY YOU WANT AT BETTER TERMS WITH A WRAPAROUND MORTGAGE

Here's one financing technique that can help you buy the property you want on even better terms than you're likely to get with typical seller-held second mortgages.

▶ **FINANCING METHOD #12—WRAPAROUND MORTGAGES:** A wraparound mortgage is a kind of second mortgage that covers both the existing financing (between the seller and his lender) and the amount of the new loan. The first mortgage is not paid off; it remains superior to the wraparound. All mortgage payments are made to the wraparound lender (in many cases, the seller). He, in turn, makes the necessary payments on the existing mortgage—and keeps the balance of your payments to him as payment on his second mortgage.

How you benefit: First of all, you can obtain financing you couldn't find elsewhere. And wraparound terms generally give you a greater initial cash flow than you'd get with a combination of first and second mortgages.

Example: You want to buy Mr. Green's office building for $300,000. The property has a $150,000 mortgage at 9% which you will assume. You can put up $65,000 cash, but you can't get a second mortgage for the $85,000 balance. Green isn't willing to hold a $85,000 second mortgage unless you make it more worthwhile. A wrap-around mortgage could be the answer in this situation.

▶ **HOW IT WORKS:** Green gives you a mortgage for $235,000 (the $300,000 sales price less your $65,000 downpayment). $150,000 will literally "wrap around" the existing mortgage. The remaining $85,000 supplies the cash you need to put the deal together. You make your payments to Green on the entire $235,000 at 13%. As Green receives your payments, he continues to pay off his 9% first mortgage (which is still his responsibility) and pockets the remainder.

Result: You're able to get property you want—and you do it with nearly 80% financing.

What about the seller: In our example, Green gets a higher yield on his money than he would otherwise. He's lending you $85,000, but he's collecting interest on $235,000. He therefore gets a bonus—as he pays off his $150,000 mortgage at 9%, he collects interest on it at 13%.

Better terms for you: Since the seller gets a higher yield, you may be able to bargain for a lower interest rate than the going conventional rate. The seller may also be willing to extend the payment time to run beyond the maturity of the first mortgage, cutting down the amount of the payments you'll have to make. You may be able to structure your wraparound so the mortgage payments come to substantially less than what you would pay if you simply assumed the existing mortgage (at its low rate) and obtained a second mortgage. Of course, you make payments over a longer period of time. But if you're interested in greater cash flow from an income property, the wraparound can help considerably by leveling out and lowering your annual financing costs. Additional benefit: Since you deal directly with the seller, you save on points.

Caution—Creative Financing Can Cause Due-On-Sale Problems

A due-on-sale clause in a mortgage basically provides that a mortgage lender has the right to demand immediate payment of a mortgage's balance if the borrower sells or transfers the mortgaged property. Although commonly known as a "non-assumption" clause, the due-on-sale clause covers many situations other than when the mortgage on a property is assumed. And many of these situations covered involve creative financing techniques.

For example, a due-on-sale clause may be triggered when a wraparound mortgage setup is used. It can also be triggered in a blanket mortgage situation, if the buyer happens to use previously-mortgaged property as additional security to get 100% financing.

So before you buy property using a creative financing technique, make sure your lawyer checks the language of the outstanding mortgages on the property or properties involved in the deal.

HOW TO PYRAMID YOUR WAY TO A REAL ESTATE FORTUNE

Financing method #13 is pyramiding, a technique that lets you use one successful real estate investment to raise the seed money to invest in another—perhaps bigger—real estate investment. And the next can do the same for the next—and so on up the ladder to a real estate fortune.

When you own successful investment property, the combined forces of appreciation, reduction of mortgage principal and tax-free cash flow cause an increase in your equity in the property. After a number of years, you may find that your investment property is worth twice what you paid for it (if not more). This allows you to borrow against the property, or refinance it, in order to raise funds needed to buy another piece of real estate.

This equity-buildup-and-refinancing cycle can be used over and over again until your relatively modest investment pyramids into real estate properties worth a small fortune.

> **Example:** You bought some rental property for $150,000. Thanks to increased values, it's now worth $250,000 and you've paid off $50,000 of the original $100,000 mortgage. The property is a good income producer and you want to hang on to it, but another good income-producing property is offered to you and you're anxious to buy. What's the best way to put that appreciation in value to work for you without selling and paying a big tax?
>
> ▶ **WHAT TO DO:** The answer may be to refinance. You'll have enough left after you pay off the old mortgage to buy the property you want. Since refinancing is not a taxable event, you don't share any of the proceeds with Uncle Sam. Whatever you get on the mortgage is fully available to you.

How refinancing might work: You get a new mortgage loan of $150,000 (60% of your property's $250,000 value). You use $50,000 to pay off the balance on your original loan. You have $100,000 tax-free dollars left for a downpayment on the property you want to buy. You can buy a property costing anywhere between $300,000 and $400,000. Your return from the new property (after interest and amortization) should be more than the extra interest you pay on the $150,000 mortgage on the old property.

Result: You pyramid your income without any cash outlay on your part. And thanks to depreciation deductions on the second property, a big chunk of this income is tax-free. Added break: Your payments on principal from rental income provide a steady equity buildup—and possibly lead to another refinancing and another purchase.

> ▶ **FORTUNE-BUILDING CYCLE:** This technique has been a key factor in making many real estate fortunes. *Reason:* It can be be used repeatedly to create a tax-free cycle that pyramids a single investment into a large real estate portfolio.

HOW TO FIGURE YOUR FINANCING NEEDS WHEN BUYING INCOME PROPERTY

The bottom financing line for any real estate investor is something called the Annual Constant. This is the amount, expressed in convenient percentage terms, that you can pay each year for financing (principal and interest) and still maintain the cash return you require.

Simplified Example: You are part of a group of investors with some $200,000 to invest in an apartment building. All investors agree that the group should buy the building only if it can yield a 10% pre-tax cash return.

Here's how the figures look initially:

Cost of building	$700,000
Equity investment	200,000
Mortgage required	500,000
Present gross income (rent roll)	$135,000
Minus operating expenses, allowance for vacancies & delinquencies	40,000
Net operating income	$ 95,000
minus required 10% return on equity	20,000
Amount available for debt service	$ 75,000

To find the Annual Constant, divide the amount available for debt service by the required mortgage. In our example, this would be $75,000 divided by $500,000. The result is an Annual Constant of 15%. This is the maximum percentage of the loan you can pay each year and still keep your 10% return intact.

How To Use The Annual Constant: Let's say the prevalent mortgage-interest rate in your area for income producing property is 14%. Refer to the mortgage amortization table at page 232. You'll find, for example, that a monthly payment of $12.04 per thousand borrowed will amortize a loan in 25 years. In percentage terms, this means .01204% of the loan must be paid each month to retire the debt. The Annual Constant is thus 14.45% (.01204 times 12).

Assuming you can get these terms you would pay 14.45% of the loan amount each year. This is below *your* Annual Constant of 15%. Thus you can see at a glance that the financing is viable.

What if interest rates are higher—say at the 14.75% level? Referring again to your mortgage-amortization chart, you'll find that a 30-year mortgage at 14.75%, if available, would still satisfy your investment requirements. At those terms, the constant for this financing setup would be 14.93%, just under your maximum Annual Constant of 15%. If you can't get a 30-year or longer payout, the deal is not viable unless it is restructured.

Another possibility: Show your figures to the seller of the property. Tell him that you (or any other buyer who needs financing) won't have enough financial incentive to buy the property—unless he lowers the price, or helps you out with the financing.

Constant Monthly Payments for Principal and Interest

Following are the approximate monthly payments for principal and interest necessary to pay off a $1,000 loan in full at (a) interest rates from 10% to 20% inclusive, with ¼ of 1% increments, for (b) terms of 10 years, 15 years, 20 years, 25 years and 30 years.

Percent	\	Mortgage Term	\	\	\
	10	15	20	25	30
10	13.21	10.75	9.65	9.09	8.78
10¼	13.35	10.90	9.82	9.26	8.96
10½	13.49	11.05	9.98	9.44	9.15
10¾	13.63	11.21	10.15	9.62	9.33
11%	13.78	11.37	10.32	9.80	9.52
11¼	13.92	11.52	10.49	9.98	9.71
11½	14.06	11.68	10.66	10.16	9.90
11¾	14.20	11.84	10.84	10.35	10.09
12	14.35	12.00	11.01	10.53	10.29
12¼	14.49	12.16	11.19	10.72	10.48
12½	14.64	12.33	11.36	10.90	10.67
12¾	14.78	12.49	11.54	11.09	10.87
13	14.93	12.65	11.72	11.28	11.06
13¼	15.08	12.82	11.89	11.47	11.26
13½	15.23	12.98	12.07	11.66	11.45
13¾	15.38	13.15	12.25	11.85	11.65
14	15.53	13.32	12.44	12.04	11.85
14¼	15.68	13.49	12.62	12.23	12.05
14½	15.83	13.66	12.80	12.42	12.25
14¾	15.98	13.83	12.98	12.61	12.44
15	16.13	14.00	13.17	12.81	12.64
15¼	16.29	14.17	13.35	13.00	12.84
15½	16.44	14.34	13.54	13.20	13.05
15¾	16.60	14.51	13.73	13.39	13.25
16	16.75	14.69	13.91	13.59	13.45
16¼	16.91	14.86	14.10	13.79	13.65
16½	17.06	15.04	14.29	13.98	13.85
16¾	17.22	15.21	14.48	14.18	14.05
17	17.38	15.39	14.67	14.38	14.26
17¼	17.54	15.57	14.86	14.58	14.46
17½	17.70	15.75	15.05	14.78	14.66
17¾	17.86	15.92	15.24	14.97	14.87
18	18.02	16.10	15.43	15.17	15.07
18¼	18.18	16.28	15.63	15.37	15.28
18½	18.34	16.47	15.82	15.57	15.48
18¾	18.50	16.65	16.01	15.78	15.68
19	18.67	16.83	16.21	15.98	15.89
19¼	18.83	17.01	16.40	16.18	16.09
19½	19.00	17.19	16.60	16.38	16.30
19¾	19.16	17.38	16.79	16.58	16.50
20	19.33	17.56	16.99	16.78	16.71

HOW TO USE TWO TRIED AND TESTED SHORTCUTS TO FIND BARGAIN INCOME PROPERTIES

When looking to buy an income property, you naturally hope to find a bargain—one you can buy for less than the market price. How do you spot bargain property? Some real estate experts use two rules of thumb—the gross and net income multipliers—to determine quickly and easily if a property is selling above, at, or below the prevailing area price for such a property. These are only guidelines, not formal appraisals, but they enable you to see right off the bat if a property is worth looking into from the price viewpoint. The first guideline is the—

> ▶ **GROSS INCOME MULTIPLIER:** The gross income is what the property would bring in if it were fully occupied for a whole year (without deducting expenses). Let's say you determine the Gross Income Multiplier for your area to be 6. If a property's gross income is $40,000, you know it should sell for around $240,000. If you can get it for $220,000 you may have found a bargain.

How do you determine the Gross Multiplier for your area? Follow these four steps:

(1) Select the most common type of income property sold in your area. Base your selection on: a specific neighborhood, type of construction, and rental arrangements (furnished/unfurnished, owner-heated/tenant-heated, etc.).

(2) Choose ten typical recent sales of this common type of income property.

(3) For each property chosen, divide the sales price by the total annual income.

(4) Average the results for the ten properties. This figure is your base Gross Multiplier.

> **Example:** The typical multi-family rental property in your area is an attached building, four-story walkup, heated by the owner, consisting of three- and four-room unfurnished apartments of moderate size. The average number of rental units is about ten. Such a typical building generates an annual gross income of about $36,000. It will generally sell for around $288,000. The base Gross Multiplier for this area is therefore 8 ($288,000 divided by $36,000).

> ▶ **NO APPLES AND ORANGES:** The properties you use in your analysis must be as similar as possible. If there is more than one distinct property type in your area, group them separately and work out separate multipliers for each type.

Adjusting the multiplier: Establishing the base Multiplier for your area is only the first step in locating bargain income properties. Certain key variables can be used to adjust the multiplier from one building to another—thus enabling you to spot the real bargains right away. Real estate experts recommend looking at—

- *Furnishing:* If the apartments in a building are furnished, take 1/2 to 1 point off the Gross multiplier. The furnishings generate income in excess of what the building would normally rent for. But they will have to be replaced periodically at your expense. The building, therefore, is not worth as much—on a Gross Multiplier basis—as it would be furnished. *Reason:* You're multiplying an income that is ballooned by the furnishings.

- *Heating:* If the tenant pays for the heat, you can add a point to the base Multiplier. You're multiplying an income from which you do not have to deduct fuel costs.

- *Age:* If your base property is a 40-year-old building and the property you're considering is relatively new, you can add 1/2 to 1 point to the Multiplier. You will have less loss of income due to repairs and maintenance.

- *Construction:* If your base property is brick and the property you're looking at is of frame construction, take a point off. Frame buildings require more maintenance and they have to be painted from time to time. On the other hand, if the property is of superior construction, you can add 1/2 to 1 point to your base.

Know your area: The Gross Multiplier will vary from one area to another, so you must know where one leaves off and another begins. An area's base will be affected by tax rates, desirability of the neighborhood and general condition of property in the neighborhood. The Gross Multiplier may change when any of these factors change—for example, if taxes are raised in an area.

A second rule of thumb for seeing if an income property is priced right is the—

▶ **NET MULTIPLIER:** In general, well-maintained, well-located income property should sell at ten times the net. The net income is the amount left after paying the operating expenses but before accounting for financing, management fees, items such as vacancy and repair allowances, and the investor's return.

Example: You're interested in an apartment building with a gross income of $30,000. You apply the area's Gross Multiplier of 8 and determine that the price should be around $240,000. Now you do a little more figuring, starting with the gross and deducting taxes, utilities, insurance, janitor, etc. (You don't yet have enough information to deduct for vacancies, repairs or management.) You arrive at a net income figure of $22,500 and multiply by ten. You now estimate the building should be selling for about $225,000.

Result: By applying both rules of thumb, you have arrived at a price range of between $225,000 and $240,000. If the property is selling below this level, you may have found a bargain.

▶ **FINAL WORD:** These rules are just quick guidelines. Any property worth purchasing will require more detailed analysis.

NEGOTIATION TECHNIQUES—HOW TO BUY PROPERTY YOU WANT ON THE BEST POSSIBLE TERMS

After a lot of searching, researching and comparing, you find the real estate property you want. You have a pretty good idea how much it is worth, how much cash you can put up to pay for it, and how much financing you will need.

The next step is negotiating with the seller. You want to buy at the lowest price, with as little cash out of pocket as possible and with low-interest financing you can pay off over a long period of time. Of course, the seller has ideas of his own: Generally, he wants to sell at the highest price and get as much cash up-front as possible.

In the following pages, you'll see some time-tested negotiating tips and techniques that you—the buyer—can use when bargaining with a property-owner. Of course, there are no hard and fast rules about negotiating over real estate—or any other type of property for that matter. Just as each piece of real estate is unique, each property-owner and sales situation have their own peculiarities—and they all call for adjustments in negotiation techniques.

> ▶ **KEY POINT:** Sometimes, it helps to have a third party, such as your attorney, do the bargaining for you. Since the attorney is less personally involved and more objective, the negotiation process can go more smoothly. Just make sure that your attorney knows how much you want the property. Otherwise, your attorney's conservative attitude may cost you the deal in some cases.

How Your Initial Offer Can Get You the Property At a Bargain Price

Before you make an initial offer for the property—whether orally or in writing—keep in mind this unwritten rule: Haggling and bargaining are a customary and expected part of the negotiating process. Most buyers and sellers intuitively are aware of this rule.

A seller invariably will ask for a sales price in excess of what he expects to get. You, on the other hand, will—and almost are expected to—make an initial offer of less than what you are really willing to pay.

Because of this unwritten rule, there are very few instances when you should agree to the seller's asking price right off the bat. As we said, the asking price generally has a built-in margin for compromise. *Exceptions:* There are certain times when you might agree to the seller's original asking price. For example: (1) After having done your research, you know that the property owner is selling the property at a bargain rate: If you don't grab it at that price, someone else will; or (2) The property owner has told you that he will not compromise—and you have found out through the grapevine that he means it. Nevertheless, the property is so good an investment that, even at the original asking price, you shouldn't pass it up.

Don't "low ball": There's another unwritten rule to keep in mind when negotiating over property. Don't meet the seller's asking price with an outrageously low figure. Say the asking price is $750,000 and you offer $150,000 for it. There is a slight chance that the seller might agree. But that's not very likely. At best, what probably will happen is that the seller will not take you and your offer seriously, and will not even make a counter-offer. In that case, all you've done is waste your and the seller's time, and are no closer to purchasing the property. At worst, the seller will be insulted and angered by your offer, and will refuse to deal with you. He'll figure that if you are going to play games at the very beginning, you're not the kind of person he wants to do business with since you probably will not bargain in good faith. So, by trying to "low ball" the seller, you may lose the opportunity to purchase the property altogether.

Be reasonable: Unless you have solid information that a property owner is under some pressure to get rid of the property, (e.g., he needs cash fast, he's behind on mortgage payments, he's leaving the city/state/country) it is unlikely that you can "steal" the property. Therefore, you should approach the negotiating process with the idea of being reasonable.

You want to—and should—look for a little edge in price, financing terms and the like. But remember that after more than a little time and effort, you have selected this particular piece of real estate as the best value around. Don't let greed stand in the way of common sense. (Of course, this doesn't mean you should overpay for the property.) In the negotiating process, the seller generally will make a counter-offer to your initial offer. However, if a seller immediately jumps at your initial offer, you might want to give a little thought before committing yourself to a firm written offer that you may be unable to back out of. Why? You might think that since you have the chance to purchase the property at a bargain rate, you should jump on it. And it may be true that the seller is agreeing because he needs the money quickly, or is tired of keeping the property on the market. On the other hand, maybe there is something wrong with the property (the tenants, structural problems, an upcoming political decision that could affect the property's value) that you failed to detect. In any case, it is something you should keep in mind before making a major investment.

Two other negotiating tips: When you make an offer—especially if it's in writing—make sure to include a "time limit" after which the offer expires. This serves two purposes: First, it helps keep the ball rolling. The seller will be pressured to at least make a counter-offer within a reasonable period of time. And second, it prevents the seller from being able to shop around after your offer, and try to jack up the sales price by playing one buyer against another. Once your offer expires, the seller can't use it as leverage to boost the sales price.

Also, when you make an offer to buy the property, have the offer include some items that you really don't care about. *Reason:* These items can be used as bargaining chips—you will give in on these items if the seller makes concessions in the sale price or on other terms.

For example, you offer $350,000 to buy an apartment building; your offer is for the land, building, the furnishings and other pieces of equipment used in the building (e.g., washing machines, dryers). In fact, you intend to refurnish and redecorate the apartment once you buy it (the seller doesn't know that), and you really don't want the equipment or the furnishings. You can "give in" on these items in order to have the seller knock several thousand dollars off of the sales price.

How to Convince a Property Owner to Sell to You At Below Market Prices

Real estate pros have developed several arguments to persuade a property owner to sell at the lowest possible price. These techniques are especially useful if you are thinking about investing in residential rental property.

1. Age and condition of building: The price of an older building can be reduced to its lowest possible point by stressing its age, and the likelihood of repairs (which the owner may have held off making) which you're likely to incur.

2. Income of building: An owner often tries to justify his price on the basis that rentals can be raised. You can counter with several arguments: (a) if rents could be higher, then why hasn't owner raised them; (b) if you as the new owner do raise rents, then you run the risk of vacancies, which can be time-consuming and costly; and (c) assuming you bear the expense and risk of making selective improvements that warrant realistic rent increases, then you should be rewarded, not the seller.

3. Neighborhood drawbacks: These can range from the lack of new construction or renovation in the locality to shopping distances and lack of public transportation.

4. Financing drawbacks: The seller's price may be based on a net income figure achievable only because his mortgage, written long ago, carried a low interest rate. (Or the seller may have paid off his mortgage already, not uncommon in the case of original owners of older multiple dwellings.) Remind the seller that when you—or any other buyer, for that matter—buy the property, the necessary mortgage money will mean higher interest costs, which in turn will mean less in pocket. Point out to the seller that he'll get no takers if his price is too high to yield a buyer a decent net return.

As a final step, consider giving the seller an oversized (more than 1% or 2% of the purchase price) binder check (to be placed in an escrow account) along with your offer. The psychological impact on the seller is obvious.

How to Buy Property With As Little Out-Of-Pocket Cash As Possible

Although price is undoubtedly a crucial element in the buying decision, there is more to the *cost* of the property than just the selling price itself. When you invest, you generally buy the property with a combination of out-of-pocket cash and financing—a first mortgage or a combination of first and second mortgages.

All things being equal, the less out-of-pocket cash you need to purchase a piece of real estate, the better off you are. In addition, the longer you have to pay off a mortgage, the better off you are (your monthly debt service payments are less). With these factors in mind, it is sometimes cheaper to pay a higher price for a property you want if you can get concessions from the seller in the areas of cash downpayment and the length of the mortgage he will take back.

Example: Mr. Smith wanted to buy an apartment house from Mr. Green. Green was asking for $144,000, approximately its current worth. There was an assumable first mortgage of $114,000 on the building held by Bank. And it was understood that Green would have to take back a second mortgage to make the deal. Here's how Smith structured four successive offers to Green, until they reached a compromise that satisfied both parties.

First Offer: $132,000

Cash down	$ 12,000
First mortgage .....(30 year)	114,000
Second mortgage ...(5 year)	6,000

Second Offer: $135,000

Cash down	$ 10,000
First mortgage .....(30 year)	114,000
Second mortgage ...(8 year)	11,000

Third Offer: $138,000

Cash down	$ 9,000
First mortgage .....(30 year)	114,000
Second mortgage ..(12 year)	15,000

Fourth (Accepted) Offer: $140,000

Cash down	$ 8,000
First mortgage .....(30 year)	114,000
Second mortgage ..(15 year)	18,000

What Smith achieved: He felt *price* was particularly important to Green (as it is with most sellers). But each time he increased the price he was willing to pay for the property, he reduced his cash downpayment. This reduction achieved two things: (a) It minimized his cash risk factor; and (b) it increased the amount of leverage.

Also, each time Smith advanced the price, he increased the amount of the second mortgage, and also the number of years to pay it off, thereby reducing his carrying charges. In addition, the final second mortgage agreed to was only partially amortizing (to further cut down on monthly payments) and would leave a "balloon" payment to be made at the end of 15 years (funds to come from future refinancing).

HOW TO CASH IN ON TAX-SHELTERED OPPORTUNITIES IN REAL ESTATE

Real estate investors today enjoy a uniquely favorable tax position. The favorable tax treatment begins the day you buy income property and continues each year you hold it. And when you sell real estate, your profits qualify for the most liberal tax treatment possible. Here's an overview of the special advantages that make real estate work as today's top tax shelter investment.

Depreciation Deductions

Depreciation deductions enable you to write off the cost of a building even while the property itself is increasing in value—as is so often the case today. And you're entitled to these deductions on the full cost of the building even though you may have put up a minimal amount of cash. In other words, you create a big tax shelter for your dollars mostly with someone else's cash.

Say you buy a building for $500,000, and finance $400,000 of the cost with a mortgage loan. Although you've put in only $100,000 of your own cash, your depreciation deduction is figured on the full $500,000 purchase price.

Your cost (basis) includes the mortgage (not just your equity), whether you assume the mortgage or merely purchase subject to the mortgage

Although it's unlikely that you will be able to finance the entire purchase price, if you do, you can take a depreciation deduction on the full $500,000, even though you haven't put up a penny of your own cash. (**Note:** You can also include in basis an allocable share of charges such as attorneys' fees, title charges, brokers' commissions, tax stamps, option payments, appraisal costs, surveys, and cost of acquiring outstanding leases.)

There are two big reasons why depreciation makes real estate a top tax-saver:

1. Since depreciation is a deduction from otherwise taxable income but does not require an ongoing cash outlay, as most expense deductions do, the result is tax-free cash. Even when you're amortizing a mortgage (the cash outlay for amortization is not deductible), the depreciation deduction may be large enough to blanket the amortization and part of the remaining income, resulting in tax-free cash. The amortization payment, since it reduces the mortgage, goes to build up equity in the property.

2. With depreciation and the ability to deduct amounts in excess of your equity, economically profitable real estate operations can produce substantial tax losses. Thus, you may be able to shelter from income tax the economic profit of your real estate operation AND even shelter some of your other income—like salary and dividends—from tax.

Property placed in service before 1981 must be depreciated over its useful life (20-35 years). However, most property acquired after 1980 is eligible for—

> ▶ **ACCELERATED COST RECOVERY:** Under this system (called ACRS), all income producing property (new, used, commercial, industrial or residential) is written off over 15 years. What's more, you can recover your cost using either straight line or an accelerated method (175% declining balance).
>
> *Example:* In January of this year, Mr. Smith buys a new $1,000,000 office building. Here's how his depreciation choices affect his first-year deduction:

ACRS with straight line: Smith's depreciation deduction for his first year is $66,667 ($1,000,000 divided by 15).

ACRS with accelerated depreciation: Smith's first-year depreciation will be $120,000.

▶ **HOW TO COMPUTE YOUR DEDUCTION:** It's easy to figure out your depreciation deduction with ACRS. You simply refer to the Government's tables (reproduced below). All you have to do is find the column for the month in which you place the building into service and read down. It's as easy as that. Each number in the column is a percentage to be applied to the original (unadjusted) tax basis of the building.

How to handle straight-line depreciation: You can elect to write off a building over 15 years using straight-line. For buildings placed in service in January of a year, each year's depreciation deduction is 6.66%. (1/15th). For properties placed in service during the year, the first year's depreciation deduction is based on the number of months the property was in service that year.

Example: Mr. Martin buys an apartment house for $330,000 in May of this year. The purchase price allocable to the depreciable building is $300,000.

If Martin elected to use straight-line over 15 years, his first-year depreciation deduction would be $13,320 (8/12th of 6.66% times $300,000). His second year's deduction would be $19,980 (6.66%).

Accelerated Cost Recovery Tables for All Real Estate Except Low-Income Housing
(based on calendar year taxpayers)

For Year #	Jan.	Feb.	Mar.	Apr.	May	Jun.	Jul.	Aug.	Sep.	Oct.	Nov.	Dec.
1	12%	11%	10%	9%	8%	7%	6%	5%	4%	3%	2%	1%
2	10	10	11	11	11	11	11	11	11	11	11	12
3	9	9	9	9	10	10	10	10	10	10	10	10
4	8	8	8	8	8	8	9	9	9	9	9	9
5	7	7	7	7	7	7	8	8	8	8	8	8
6	6	6	6	6	7	7	7	7	7	7	7	7
7	6	6	6	6	6	6	6	6	6	6	6	6
8	6	6	6	6	6	6	5	6	6	6	6	6
9	6	6	6	6	5	6	5	5	5	6	6	6
10	5	6	5	6	5	5	5	5	5	5	6	5
11	5	5	5	5	5	5	5	5	5	5	5	5
12	5	5	5	5	5	5	5	5	5	5	5	5
13	5	5	5	5	5	5	5	5	5	5	5	5
14	5	5	5	5	5	5	5	5	5	5	5	5
15	5	5	5	5	5	5	5	5	5	5	5	5
16	-	-	1	1	2	2	3	3	4	4	4	5

*Use the column for the month in which the property is placed in service.

Important note: Under ACRS, you disregard salvage value. This is true whether you use the accelerated cost recovery method, or elect to recover your cost using the straight-line method.

Low-Taxed Capital Gain Profits.

Your writeoff for depreciation (or cost recovery) will eventually start to run out. So you may decide to sell your property. If you make a profit (your proceeds exceed your adjusted basis in the property) on the sale—which is likely—you will discover the "hidden" tax shelter of real estate: conversion of high-taxed ordinary income into low-taxed capital gain.

> **Example:** Mr. Brown builds a new apartment house with a basis of $500,000. Using straight line, Brown has an annual depreciation deduction of $33,333 ($500,000 divided by 15). After ten years, his adjusted basis in the property is $166,667 (original basis less $333,333 total depreciation taken). Brown sells the building for $900,000. He has a $733,333 gain (proceeds less adjusted basis), all of which is long-term capital gain.
>
> ▶ **INCOME CONVERSION:** Mr. Brown has converted $333,333 of ordinary income into $333,333 of tax-sheltered capital gain. *Reason:* Brown's $333,333 of depreciation deductions shelter an equal amount of ordinary income. The $333,333 of depreciation deductions also reduces Brown's basis by $333,333. So when he sells the building, his gain is larger by that amount. However the $333,333 is brought back into income as capital gain. In other words, it is taxed at 40% of the rate that applies to the income that was already sheltered by the depreciation deductions.

How the "recapture" rules work: The ACRS recapture rules for property placed in service after 1980 are almost the same as the recapture rules that apply to buildings placed in service before 1981. If you use the straight-line method, all of your gain will be capital gain when you sell (regardless of whether the building is a residential or a nonresidential property). And if you use an accelerated method for residential property, some of the gain may be taxed ("recaptured") as ordinary income. The ACRS rule is the same as the one for pre-1981 property. The amount recaptured is the excess of the total deductions taken over the deductions that would have been allowable if the straight-line method had been used.

But if you take accelerated depreciation on *nonresidential* property, the ACRS recapture rules are a bit tougher than they are for pre-1981 property: Your gain will be recaptured to the full extent of the recovery taken (*including* straight line). If you use accelerated depreciation on commercial or industrial property placed in service before 1981, only the excess of total depreciation taken over straight line is recaptured.

> ▶ **WHAT TO DO:** If you buy commercial property as an investment, it may pay to forego the accelerated method and stick with straight line. But be sure to check the angles with a tax adviser before you decide on a method.

Tax-Free Exchanges

Real estate investors can take advantage of one tax-saving move almost no other kind of investor can make. It's called the tax-free swap.

If you want another investor's property and he's willing to swap it for one you own—and these are *"like-kind" properties*—then chances are good you can each get what you want without paying any tax. Given the right setup, a tax-free swap of real estate not only eliminates current tax on the gain but it can sometimes be used to set up depreciation deductions.

> ▶ **STILL ANOTHER TAX BREAK:** Tax-free swaps are an important exception to the tough recapture of depreciation rules. Thus, there's no recapture on a tax-free swap except to the extent gain is recognized—if you received "boot" in the exchange. Hence, if there's no gain recognized there's no recapture.

The definition of "like kind"—property held for productive use in trade or business, or for investment—leaves you plenty of latitude, too.

You can exchange trade or business property for investment property, or the reverse. "Like kind" refers to the nature or character of the property, not its grade or quality. The Regulations list these as examples of "like-kind" exchanges: improved real estate for unimproved real estate; city real estate for a ranch or farm; a leasehold interest of 30 years or more in real estate for other real estate. In addition, courts have held that the following constitute nontaxable exchanges: lots held for investment for land and building held for investment; exchange of multi-family rental buildings held for investment for a ranch held for investment.

But note that the Government has said that raw land and a building to be newly constructed (as opposed to a building plus land) do not constitute "like kind" property [Rev. Rul.67-255, 1967-2 CB 270].

> ▶ **WATCH THIS:** You can't work a tax-free exchange with stock in trade, or real estate held for sale to customers in the ordinary course of business. This applies to both properties in the exchange. In other words, both the old property, and the new one acquired in the exchange, must be held for investment, or for use in a trade or business.

How To Get 100% Cash From a Real Estate Deal and Still Defer Tax on Most of Your Profit

All things being equal most people prefer to sell real estate on an all-cash basis. But sometimes, a straight all-cash sale isn't possible. You may have to take back a mortgage when you sell your real estate. Fortunately, the tax law gives you a break in this situation: You can report your gain from the sale on the *installment method.*

Thus, if you sell your real estate and get 25% cash now, and take back a three-year note for the balance, you pay tax this year on only 25% of your gain. The balance of your tax is deferred and is payable over the next three years, as you receive payment.

Is there any way you can get all or most of your cash up front—even though your buyer can make only a small downpayment—and still keep the installment sale break?

Yes. There is a way to have your cake and eat it, too. You might call it a—

▶ **TAX-FREE TECHNIQUE:** You get, say, 25% cash when you sell your real estate. You also take back a note for the 75% balance of your selling price, secured by a mortgage, to be paid off over five or ten years. Then you take out a loan at a bank and pledge the note and mortgage as security for the loan.

Net effect: Between the buyer's downpayment and the money you borrow, you can get cash for your equity in the year you sell. And you lock in three key tax breaks:

(**1**) *You get tax-free cash:* What you borrow is tax-free.

(**2**) *You defer the tax:* Your tax on three quarters of the gain is deferred until the following years, as the buyer makes payments. And there's the chance—

(**3**) *You cut the tax:* By using installment reporting, you may actually pay less tax on the gain. Reason: Spreading the gain over several years often keeps you in a lower bracket than if you receive a lump-sum payment in one year.

The pledge of the note and mortgage as security for your personal loan is not considered a sale. But this is where the deal is most vulnerable to Government attack. The personal loan must be separate and distinct from the installment sale. Your payments to the third party creditor (the bank) cannot be tied to the buyer's payments to you. Nor is it a pledge if you are simply a guarantor of the installments to the lender. Keep in mind that you can't sell or discount the note. If you do, you'll have a tax disaster.

▶ **IMPORTANT:** Avoiding current tax on an installment sale is tricky where you borrow on the notes from an installment sale. A pledge in name must be a pledge in fact. The terms of the pledge agreement must make clear that the notes are not being sold. The burden of proof is on you. So make the language of the agreement reflect that you have made a pledge and not a sale. Professional tax advice is recommended here.

How Rehabilitating Historic Structures Offers Unique Tax Shelter Opportunity

Rehabilitating historic properties has become an attractive tax shelter idea. In 1982 and 1983, investors in about 4,500 such buildings qualified for generous tax credits and deductions. The chief tax shelter attraction is a—

▶ **25% TAX CREDIT:** An investor is entitled to a tax credit equal to 25% of qualifying rehabilitation expenses. Typically, these expenses account for a major portion of total project cost.

Example: In January, a group of five investors buys an historic property for $300,000 ($150,000 for land, balance for the building). They spend $500,000 rehabilitating the property for use as commercial office space. The investors make a downpayment of $300,000 ($60,000 from each) and finance the $500,000 balance with a loan. The rehabilitation is completed and the offices are rented by year end.

The investors are entitled to an investment tax credit of $125,000 (25% of the $500,000 rehabilitation cost). That works out to $25,000 for each investor. Since a dollar of credit reduces tax liability by a dollar, each investor gets back $25,000 of his $60,000 cash investment when he pays his tax bill. Taking the credit into account, each investor has, in effect, made only a $35,000 downpayment.

Basic requirements: Four key conditions must be met to claim the rehabilitation credit for historic structures:

1. The building must be listed in the National Register of Historic Places, or located in an historic district and certified by the Secretary of the Interior as significant to the district.

2. At least 75% of the existing external walls must be retained.

3. The rehabilitation must be "substantial." That means expenditures within a 24- or 36-month period ending with or within the tax year must exceed the greater of the building's adjusted basis or $5,000. And the rehabilitation must be approved by the Department of the Interior.

4. You must use straight-line cost recovery on the rehabilitation cost.

The rehabilitated building can be used for commercial, industrial, or residential-rental purposes. However, rehabilitation of a residence used for personal purposes does not qualify.

The credit is strictly for restoring buildings. Adding a new wing to a structure does not qualify, and neither does the addition of building-related facilities, such as a new parking lot.

Effective for property placed in service after 1982, an historic structure's basis is reduced by one-half the 25% tax credit claimed.

Result: The investors can depreciate $587,500 ($650,000 building and rehabilitation cost less one half the $125,000 credit). Assuming straight-line depreciation is used for both the building shell and the cost of rehabilitation, the annual ACRS deduction is $39,167 for 15 years.

You can also rehabilitate a building that is not an historic structure, and still qualify for a rehabilitation tax credit. But it is a smaller credit. The credit is equal to 15% of the cost of the rehabilitation expenses if the building is at least 30 years old when the rehabilitation commences. The credit is 20% if the building is at least 40 years old. To qualify for the 15% or 20% tax credit, you must meet the same conditions listed above for historic structures (except for the first test, which qualifies a building as historic). And you don't have to obtain certification of the rehabilitation, either.

▶ **MAJOR DIFFERENCE:** If you rehabilitate a non-historic building, you must reduce your tax basis—for all purposes, including depreciation—by the *full* amount of the credit claimed. The tax basis of an historic building is reduced by only half the credit claimed. And your non-historic building must be rehabilitated only for commercial or industrial purposes. Unlike historic buildings, you get no credit if you rehabilitate a building for residential rental use.

Chapter 3

Popular Money-Makers: Stocks, Bonds And Government Issues

Some people think the financial pages of the newspaper are the domain of the rich and powerful. But that's just not true. Astute individuals have realized all along that they can take a share of the pie—stocks, bonds, even Government issues.

That's why this Chapter is so helpful. It covers a broad spectrum of opportunities—from the speculative (for example, high-tech growth stocks) to the conservative (such as U.S. Savings Bonds). You can find the offbeat and special-situation opportunities (such as penny stocks) in Chapter Five.

Finally, we'll spotlight special techniques—such as buying stock on margin—that can help maximize profits.

THE BASICS ON BUILDING WEALTH THROUGH STOCKS AND BONDS

The stock market is a fascinating place—and it is also a confusing one. There is a lot for the novice investor to learn. One of the first questions often asked is—

How to Pick the Right Broker

No matter what sort of stock you want to invest in, one of your first moves should be to find a good broker. Word of caution: Registered representatives of brokerage houses make their living from the commissions earned when you buy or sell. In other words, an unscrupulous broker may "churn" an account—buy and sell shares unnecessarily to earn more commission income. So when you are looking for a good broker, above all, you want a broker you can trust.

Where to start: There are two good places to begin: (1) Your friends or family may be able to recommend a good broker. And if they can't steer you toward one, they may be able to steer you away from one. You might also want to ask the family physician or dentist. Doctors have a reputation—at least partially deserved—for being shrewd investors. (2) Ask your accountant or attorney to recommend a broker. They've probably run across one they consider trustworthy in the course of their dealings.

▶ **SHOP AROUND:** Don't commit yourself to the first broker that you talk to. Call a few and find out what their fees are. Brokerage rates aren't fixed, so you may find a great difference in price between one broker and another.

If you can't find a broker through referrals—or you can't find one that meets your approval—here's—

▶ **WHAT TO DO:** You can obtain a free pamphlet from the Wall Street Journal that lists over 300 top firms. Write to: Investors Service Bureau Directory, 11 Wall Street, New York, N.Y. 10005. Of course, you can always consult your yellow pages. Or simply walk into a brokerage house off the street and you will be assigned to a registered representative.

We suggest you give a broker the Family Money Book interview which consists of five simple questions.

1. What are your credentials? For example, you'll want to know how many years the broker has been in the business, other firms he or she has worked for, and so on.

2. How many clients do you serve? Naturally, you'll want special attention from your broker. You do not want him or her to label you a low priority.

3. Do you rely on your firm's recommendations or do you suggest stocks on your own? In some cases, you are doing more than looking for a good broker; you are looking for a good brokerage house.

4. If you do pick your own stocks, what are your sources? Novice investors may feel more comfortable going with the firm's recommendations.

5. What is your overall investment strategy? Find out whether the broker advocates an aggressive or conservative approach to stock investments. If you don't agree, there's a good chance he is not the right broker for you.

The interview should give you a good handle on whether you and the broker are on the same wavelength. If you don't feel comfortable with the broker assigned to you, ask to speak with someone else.

If you feel you are qualified to do your own investment research, you should consider—

▶ **DISCOUNT BROKERS:** Discount brokerage houses will do your buying and selling at lower rates—frequently much lower—than the regular brokerage houses. The drawback: The discounters don't offer many of the services of the regular firms—for instance, investment counseling and up-to-the-minute reports. They merely execute your order. Two discounters are Charles Schwab & Co. and Quick & Reilly. You can obtain their toll-free telephone number in your area by dialing toll-free information (800-555-1212).

How to Read the Stock Market Tables in Your Newspaper

The stock tables, a source of valuable information on stocks, appear regularly in the newspapers. These entries may seem confusing at first, but learning how to read the tables won't take long. And knowing how can provide individuals with the knowledge needed to make intelligent investment decisions. Here's a sample entry taken from a listing on the New York Stock Exchange.

52 High	Weeks Low	Stock	Div.	Yld %	P-E Ratio	Sales 100s	High	Low	Close	Net Chg.
62	41¼	XYZ	1.40	3.3	11	867	43½	42½	42½	−1

This entry provides you with a lot of information about XYZ Corp.'s stock. Starting at the far left, here's what you can learn:

The first two columns are the highest and the lowest price paid for a share of XYZ stock in the past 52 weeks; prices are given in dollars and fractions of dollars.

The next three columns deal with the stock's return: its *annual* dividend per share ($1.40), the yield (dividend divided by current price, or 3.3%), and its price-earnings ratio (11—that is, 11:1 is the ratio of the stock's price to its earnings).

The remaining columns show how the stock has been selling: 86,700 shares of XYZ were traded the day before; the highest price paid was 43½ and the lowest was 42½, which also happened to be the last price paid that day; XYZ was off a point ("minus 1") from its closing price the day before yesterday.

Key Terms You Should Know When Following the Stock Market

Wall Street seems to have a language of its own. Here is a glossary that will help you to understand some of the more common terms:

Bear market: A declining market (so called because a bear is supposed to squeeze its victims).

Bull market: A rising market (no one is quite sure why the bull was picked—but a bull market means good news).

Convertible: A bond, debenture or preferred share of stock which may be exchanged by the owner for common stock or another security, usually of the same company.

Cumulative preferred: A stock having a provision that if one or more dividends are omitted, the omitted dividends must be paid *before* dividends may be paid on the company's common stock.

Diversification: Spreading investments among different companies in different fields—a standard practice among many investors.

Ex-dividend: A synonym for "without dividend." Buyers of a stock selling ex-dividend will *not* receive the stock's recently declared dividend because they will not be recorded on the books of the company's eligible shareholders. Your stock will almost always be worth less if sold "ex-dividend."

Face value: The value of a bond that appears on the face of the bond, unless the value is otherwise specified by the issuing company. Face value is ordinarily the amount the issuing company promises to pay at maturity.

Growth stock: Stock of a company with a record of growth in earnings at a relatively rapid rate.

Institutional investor: An organization whose primary purpose is to invest its own assets or those held in trust by it for others. Includes pension funds, investment companies, insurance companies, universities and banks.

Margin: The partial amount paid by the customer who uses the broker's credit to buy a security or commodity. Under Federal Reserve regulations, the initial margin required in the past 20 years has ranged from 40% of the purchase price, all the way to 100%.

Market order: An order to buy or sell a stated amount of a security at the most advantageous price obtainable.

Odd-lot: An amount of stock that's less than the established 100-share unit of trading (also see "round lot").

Over-the-counter: A market for securities made up of securities dealers who may or may not be members of a securities exchange.

Penny stocks: Low-priced issues—often highly speculative—selling at less than $1 a share.

Point: In the cases of shares of stock, a point means $1. For example, if General Motors advances three points, each share has risen $3. Or, if it advances ⅛ it went up 12½¢. In the case of bonds, a point means $10.

Preferred stock: A class of stock with a claim on the company's earnings; dividends are paid on preferred stock before they are paid on common.

Price-earnings ratio: The current market price of a share of stock divided by earnings per share for a 12-month period. For example, a stock selling for $100 a share and earning $5 a share is said to be selling at a price-earnings ratio of 20 to 1.

Round lot: A unit of trading or a multiple thereof. The unit of trading is generally 100 shares in stocks and $1,000 par value in the case of bonds. In some inactive stocks, the unit of trading is 10 shares.

Short sale: A sale you make when you believe a stock you do *not* own will eventually decline. *Example:* You instruct your broker to sell short 100 shares of ABC. Your broker borrows the stock so he can deliver the 100 shares to the buyer. Sooner or later you must buy the stock to cover your short sale. If you're able to buy ABC at a lower price than you sold it for—the difference is your profit. If you have to pay more, then you take a loss.

Sinking fund: Money regularly set aside by a company to redeem its bonds, debentures or preferred stock from time to time as specified in its charter.

Split: The division of the outstanding shares of a corporation into a larger number of shares. A 3-for-1 split by a company with 1 million shares outstanding results in 3 million shares outstanding. Each holder of 100 shares before the 3-for-1 split would have 300 shares.

Stop order: An order to buy at a price above or sell at a price below the current market. Stop buy orders are generally used to limit loss or protect unrealized profits on a short sale (see above).

Take-over: The acquiring of one corporation by another—usually in a friendly merger but sometimes marked by a "proxy fight." In "unfriendly" take-over attempts, the potential buying company may offer stockholders a price well above current market values.

How to Know What Stocks to Buy

There is no magic formula to determine what stocks to buy. If you were expecting one—preferably in ten words or less—you are going to be disappointed. However, if you are interested in what some of the key stock indicators are and what they may mean—

> ▶ **READ ON:** We're going to give you a quick overview of some of the factors that should be considered when you purchase stock. Undoubtedly, you will hear your broker mention these terms from time to time. As a matter of fact, the analysis of these indicators is best left to experts such as your broker—and even he can't guarantee an accurate reading. But at least you'll have a working knowledge of why some stocks are recommended and others are not.

With that in mind, let's take a look at the key indicators. There are literally dozens of them, but we'll confine ourselves here to a few of the basic ones. Most of them are available in a company's annual report, which you can get free of charge by writing to the company.

Of course, a certain amount of what is contained in the report will be puffery. One area you should concentrate on is the—

Profit and loss statement: This is the bottom line. The P&L statement sums up the amount of money that goes into a corporation versus the amount of money that goes out. Pay particular attention to the management analysis of the P&L statement to see where the company is heading.

Book value: The book value is the total assets of the company less its total liabilities divided by the shares outstanding. When a stock is selling below book value, it is generally an indication that the company is floundering or undervalued. If a company is prospering, the stock may well be selling above book value.

Moving average: This is a do-it-yourself indicator of a stock's trend. How it works: Say you want to compute a ten-day moving average (for investments over the short haul). Add up the closing price of the stock for the last ten days and divide by ten. Then add the price for the eleventh day, subtract the first, and so on. If a stock starts to rise above a declining moving average, it could indicate a trend.

> **Example 1:** The closing prices for XYZ stock is 4, 4¼, 4½, 4½, 4, 5, 5¼, 5½, 5½, 5¼ over a 10-day period. That averages out to 4¾. Say XYZ goes to 6¼ on the 11th day. You add in 6¼, and subtract out 4. New Average: 5. This is a solid indication that XYZ is on the rise.

Current ratio: This is simply the ratio of current assets to current liabilities. A ratio of about 2 to 1 is standard for corporations listed on the stock market.

Earnings per share: Earnings per share may be the most vital statistic issued by a corporation. Here's how it is figured: After all the dividends on preferred stocks are paid out, the company divides its remaining income by the amount of outstanding shares. Obviously, you'll need the company's annual report to compute the earnings per share.

> **Example 2:** In 1983, ABC Corp. had $800,000 in net income and 2 million common shares outstanding. Its earnings per share: 40¢. In 1984, ABC still has 2 million shares outstanding, but its net income rises to $900,000. New earnings per share: 45¢.

Result: The increase in earnings per share indicates ABC is a healthy company.

Earnings per share—besides being a barometer in its own right—is used as a basis for other indicators. For example, the—

Dividend payout: This figure is the annual dividends paid divided by the earnings per share. The dividend payout is a percentage figure. To see what we mean, let's go back to Example 2.

Say ABC's dividends paid is 25¢ a share in both 1983 and 1984. So, in 1983, ABC's dividend payout is 62.5% (25¢ ÷ 40¢); in 1984 it is 55.5% (25¢ ÷ 45¢).

In this case, smaller may be better. The reduced dividend payout percentage in 1984 shows ABC is becoming a more secure investment.

Sales per share of stock: Sales per share of stock is easy enough to understand. It is simply the corporation's total sales divided by the number of common shares outstanding.

> **Example 3:** In 1983, DEF, Inc. has $30 million in sales and 2 million shares outstanding. Its sales per share of stocks: $15 per share. In 1984, its sales go up to $40 million. Now its sales per share figure is $20 per share. Steady growth in this indicator is a good sign.

Price/earnings ratio: We've saved the best for last. The P/E ratio is the most commonly used indicator in the stock market. The ratio is figured by dividing the price of the stock by the earnings per share. Generally, a stock's P/E ratio ranges from 5% to 15%.

> **Example 4:** The price of ZBA stock is $5.50 in 1983 and in 1984. Earnings per share is 40¢ in 1983 and 45¢ in 1984. So ZBA's P/E ratio is 13.75% ($5.50 ÷ 40¢) in 1983 and 12.2% ($5.50 ÷ 45¢) in 1984.

P/E ratios tend to be lower in a bull market and higher in a bear market (because the stocks are undervalued). Stocks in the same industry usually have approximately the same ratio. For example, stocks in growth industries—like computers—traditionally have a high P/E ratio.

▶ **THERE ARE NO GUARANTEES:** Hopefully, your eyes haven't glazed over yet. The important thing to remember: None of these barometers is foolproof. They are just indications of which way the wind is blowing.

How You Can Find Growth Stocks

The dream of every investor is to find a growth stock before the market has recognized its potential and before its price is driven up. What is growth stock? Quite simply, it's tomorrow's blue-chip stock. It is stock in a corporation that shows consistent growth, with a chance at tremendous growth. These stocks are an excellent vehicle for investors over the long haul. You may even want to invest a small part of your IRA or Keogh money in growth stocks—buy them now and hold them until retirement.

Typically, a growth stock company does not distribute dividends. Instead it plows them back into its operations. The big payoff is somewhere down the road. In other words, growth stocks are not for get-rich-quick investors.

Once you've invested in a growth stock, you must have the stomach to sit with it—overcome the temptation to sell when the stock is roaring upward, or dump it when the market turns down—as long as your fundamental reasons for buying the stock remain unchanged. This kind of commitment has advantages that are—

▶ **OFTEN OVERLOOKED:** Unless you buy on margin, growth stock doesn't cost you anything while it builds up a big return. You don't have to fork over cash for brokers' commissions (as you normally would when trading stocks) and you don't have to pay tax on any gain before you sell.

Are there any drawbacks to growth stocks? Yes, mainly two. We've already alluded to one: Since the company's money is being recycled in the company, there is little return in the early going. The other is that growth stocks are, quite frankly, hard to find.

Helpful hints: As a general rule, you'll find growth stocks in industries that are connected with high technology. But you'll need more to go on. Here are some of the things an investor should look for:

• A big rise in the company's earnings per share.

• A company that is dominant in its field—be it anything from heavy equipment to jellybeans.

• A company that is part of an emerging field—for example, telecommunications—or is developing significant new products or services.

• Successful management at the top.

Need more help? You would be wise to seek it. *Reason*: Even if a growth stock meets all the criteria above, it still may not be a wise investment choice. For instance, the company's P/E ratio may be very high, indicating that you may be buying the stock too late in the game to expect significant appreciation in value.

▶ **WHAT TO DO:** You can subscribe to a number of investment journals that make recommendations on growth stocks—for example, Growth Stock Outlook or its sister publication, Junior Growth Stock Outlook, which tracks smaller companies. Both are available on a three-month trial basis. For more information, contact Growth Stock Outlook, P.O. Box 9911, Chevy Chase, MD 20815.

Is Investing in the Stock Market a Hedge Against Inflation?

Investment experts (including a great many employed by brokerage houses) want you to believe your stock investments defend you against the ravages of inflation. The theory: Stocks can keep pace with inflation because they represent ownership in real assets. On the other hand, investments with fixed rates—say, Certificates of Deposit—can get outstripped by inflation.

Caution: Generally, this line of reasoning holds true in a time of moderate inflation. But in the late 70's, a big hole was punched in the stock-as-an-inflation-hedge theory by skyrocketing inflation. In periods of high inflation, stocks are not as effective a hedge. There are three primary reasons: (1) Inflation tends to put a damper on corporate profits, and correspondingly, the value of stock. (2) Interest rates soar, which makes high fixed rate investments more attractive. (3) Cash is hard to come by, which drives the price of stock down (and fewer investors have cash to risk).

The one bright spot: Even when inflation is roaring, stocks have one advantage over many other investments: They are easily disposable. All it takes is a telephone call to your broker.

STOCK MARKET TECHNIQUES FOR THE NEW INVESTOR

There are a number of ways a novice investor can accumulate wealth in the stock market without taking big risks, and without committing large chunks of cash. Here are some time-tested strategies that place a high premium on safety, or have special angles, such as convenience, low initial cash requirements, or special tax breaks.

How Dividend Reinvestment Plans Offer Unique Investment Opportunity

Brokers' commission fees are a necessary evil of stock investing (even though you can reduce the cost through a discount broker). But there is a way you can—

▶ **REMOVE THE CURSE:** You can sidestep most of your broker fees by using something called a dividend reinvestment plan.

How it works: Your dividends are automatically reinvested in the company's stock (close to one thousand companies offer such plans). When your dividends are reinvested in the stock, there are no brokerage fees. Many companies also let you invest additional cash at favorable terms—for example, a 5% discount—and still no brokerage fees.

Result: Your initial investment snowballs. You invest in stock, which is reinvested in stock, which in turn is reinvested, and so on. In the meantime you can buy additional shares which, you guessed it, are reinvested in stock. This is known as the power of compounding.

There is also a beneficial side effect to investing in a dividend reinvestment plan. Without really meaning to, you are setting up a—

> ▶ **CHRISTMAS CLUB OF STOCKS:** The dividend reinvestment plan is a form of forced saving. If you take quarterly dividends in cash, you are likely to fritter that money away. With the dividend reinvestment plan, your money is socked away automatically.

Tax angles in dividend reinvestment plans: The tax treatment depends on the nature of the dividend.

• If the dividend is payable in cash, and you choose to reinvest it in stock, you pay tax on the dividend just as if you had received it in cash. Your basis for the shares you purchase is equal to the cash dividend you pay tax on.

> **Example 1:** You bought 100 shares of ABC for $3,600. During the year, you receive $300 in dividends which you reinvest in 8 shares of ABC. Tax result: You have $300 of dividend income, which qualifies for the dividend exclusion ($200 for joint filers, $100 for other people). Your basis in the shares is $300. If you sell the 8 shares of ABC for $400, you will have $100 of short-term capital gain (treated as ordinary income) if you hold the shares less than one year, or $100 of low-taxed long-term capital gain if you hold for at least one year and a day.

• A company may pay a stock dividend to its shareholders—instead of getting cash, you receive more shares. Here, there's no current tax on the stock dividend. Instead, your original cost for the shares is apportioned among the old and the new shares.

> **Example 2:** Same facts as example 1, except that ABC pays a stock dividend. *Result:* You own 108 shares, and each share has a basis of $33.33 ($3,600 original cost, divided by 108 shares). Your holding period for the new shares—for long-or short-term gain purposes—is measured from the time you bought the original shares. So if you bought the original shares more than one year ago, you can sell the new shares immediately and get low taxed long-term capital gain.

Special Tax Break for Utility Stocks

Investors in utility companies may get more than they bargained for. *Reason:* They can exclude from tax the first $750 of dividends per year ($1,500 on a joint return) if the dividends are used to buy stock under a dividend reinvestment program.

This is an exception to the general rule that a stock dividend is taxable as ordinary income if the shareholder has a choice of cash or the stock. So even though you could receive cash, you are not taxed (within the dollar limits) on a distribution of common stock under a qualified dividend reinvestment program set up by an eligible utility.

Not all utilities are eligible: Generally speaking, the break can only be offered by public utilities whose purchases in the last ten years contain a substantial amount of "long-lived" property. And not all dividend reinvestment programs set up by eligible utilities qualify. For example, the price of the new stock must be at least 95% (but no more than 105%) of the stock's fair market value immediately prior to purchase. And the stock must be newly issued common stock designated to qualify for the tax break.

How you benefit: You owe no tax on the reinvested dividends (up to the dollar limits). Your tax basis in the newly acquired stock is zero. So the tax break you get at the time of the reinvestment is reflected in a bigger taxable profit when you later sell the stock. But without the tax break, the dividends would be currently taxed ordinary income: with it, the dividends are taxed as tax-sheltered capital gain (assuming you hold the stock for more than one year before you sell).

Since only 40% of your long-term capital gain is taxable along with your other income, you may wind up ahead of the tax game by taking the stock dividend instead of cash.

> **Example:** XYZ Gas & Electric has a qualified dividend reinvestment plan. It declares a $1,000 dividend on Mr. and Mrs. Able's shares, payable in cash or newly issued common stock.

If they take cash: Assuming that the Able's top dollars are taxed at 40%, taking the cash would net $600 after tax. Invested for one year at an 8% after tax rate, that cash would grow to $648.

If they take stock: If the Ables take $1,000-worth of XYZ stock instead of the cash dividend, their tax basis in the shares is zero. However, if they hold the stock for at least one year before selling, the maximum tax they will pay is 16% (40% of sales proceeds taxed at 40%). Here is how the Ables would make out at various sale prices:

Sale Price	Income Tax	Net Proceeds
$1,200	$192	$1,008
1,000	160	840
800	128	672

Because the proceeds are lightly taxed long-term capital gain, a sale at an economic loss can still yield more than the cash dividend. In other words, the tax break cuts the Ables' downside risk.

Q. Suppose the stock dividend is not held for at least one year before it is sold?

A. The proceeds are all taxed as ordinary income. In fact, if any shares of the utility stock are sold within one year after the dividend reinvestment, the tax break is lost. The proceeds from the sale are taxed as ordinary income (up to the amount originally excluded under the dividend reinvestment break).

Actually, this isn't quite as bad as it sounds. If you sell the stock at or near its price when the dividend was declared, you have, in effect, merely delayed taking a cash dividend. In fact, the delay may result in—

> ▶ **TAX DEFERRAL:** Suppose the Ables took the $1,000 stock dividend in June of last year, and sell the stock in January of this year for $1,000. The proceeds are all ordinary income since the stock wasn't held for one year. However, the Ables succeed in deferring the tax for one full year.

Important: You don't want to invest in utility stocks (or any other investment) purely for tax reasons. While this special break makes the stock of eligible utilities more attractive, you will want to talk things over with your adviser before going ahead.

How to Get in on the Market on a Shoestring

The more, the merrier. If you subscribe to that theory, you may want to look into an investment club. What is an investment club? It is a group of investors who pool their resources together in order to make stock and bond investments.

> ▶ **SAFETY IN NUMBERS:** With an investment club, you are not going one-on-one with the stock market. You have the comfort of knowing the other investors in your club—there are usually around 15 of them—are in the same boat as you. And the amount you contribute to the club—generally on a monthly basis—is minimal (it can be as little as $10 per month; it is rarely above $50).

Of course, in an investment club you tie your fortunes to the rest of the club, for better or for worse. *Result:* It is not surprising that most investment clubs pursue a conservative investment strategy.

Ten key points: Whether you intend to join an investment club that is already in existence or you are looking to start one up, there are ten key points to keep in mind. They can help you make your investment club a success.

1. Keep your club small. Anything over 20 members starts to become unwieldy.

2. Require monthly payments. Contributions should be made on a regular basis.

3. Contribute at least a minimum amount each month. That way you'll spread your risk out over the long run.

4. Reinvest the dividends. You can't make the money without investing money.

5. Aim for diversification. In this respect, your club will act much the way a mutual fund does.

6. Adopt an overall policy. You and the other members of the club will have to arrive at a consensus.

7. Set reasonable goals. Don't expect to get rich quick. *Remember:* This is the safe approach.

8. Provide for contingencies. For example, you should be prepared in case several members drop out.

9. Do your homework. You and the other members must keep on top of trends, P/E ratios and so forth.

10. Get advice. Don't try to do it all on your own—you can consult brokers, attorneys and accountants for all the investment, legal and tax ramifications.

▶ **FOR MORE INFORMATION:** Contact the National Association of Investment Clubs, 1515 East Eleven Mile Rd., Royal Oak, Michigan 48068. They can send you and your club valuable publications explaining how to set up an investment club, including a model portfolio.

How You Can Invest in the Stock Market for as Little as $25 a Month

We've told you how you can play the stock market for a minimal amount by joining an investment club. However, there's another way to take the plunge without throwing in your lot with other club members. This type of operation is commonly called a—

▶ **SYSTEMATIC PURCHASE PLAN:** There are two immediate benefits: (1) You can invest in stock of your choice by making monthly payments of as little as $25. (These payments may actually be less than the price of a single share.) (2) You pay a smaller brokerage fee than if you buy shares in the normal fashion.

Here's how the typical plan works: After contacting a brokerage firm and obtaining an application form, you start your account by sending a minimum investment of $25. The broker uses the money to purchase shares or fractions of shares in a stock or stocks of your choice. From then on, you may invest as frequently as you wish (with the same $25 minimum). It's as simple as that.

Example: Ms. Johnson decides to invest $50 per month in a blue-chip stock. Her broker suggests XYZ, selling at around $75 per share. Ms. Johnson sends her first $50 and goes along with the broker's recommendation of XYZ. The broker then purchases $50 worth (minus brokerage fees) of XYZ stock for a custodial account under Johnson's name.

Result: Ms. Johnson would be credited with about ⅔ of a share of XYZ on her first purchase. (Ordinarily, the broker wouldn't handle an account as small as Johnson's.)

Here are some frequently asked questions—and the answers—about systematic purchase plans.

Q. Are there any limits on the kinds of stocks I can purchase under this plan.

A. No. You can choose from among the stocks listed on New York and American Stock Exchanges, plus the major issues that trade over the counter (OTC).

Q. What happens to dividends paid on the stocks I own?

A. You can have the broker reinvest your dividends in the stock you have selected, or you can have the proceeds mailed to you.

Suggestion: You would probably be better off reinvesting dividends in the early going, when they may amount to only pennies. Later, you can have the dividends mailed to you.

Q. Why can't I just buy $25 worth of stocks each month on my own—why do I need to enroll in this plan?

A. First of all, many brokers will not handle transactions for as little as $25. Secondly, most brokerage houses have a $25 minimum commission charge, so to invest $25 you'd have to pay $50.

In contrast, a systematic purchase plan overcomes these problems and offers three pluses:

(1) You can get "a piece of the action" on Wall Street for a relatively small price.

(2) You can purchase fractions of shares and, thus, buy into companies whose stock sells for $50, $75, or $100 and more per share.

(3) You pay a smaller commission than if you invested on your own through the same broker. (The commission on monthly investments of less than $300 runs around 6%.)

Q. What if I decide to stop investing?

A. There's no requirement that you keep investing in a systematic purchase plan. Here's—

▶ **HOW TO CASH IN:** You can contact the broker and tell him to discontinue your automatic investments. You direct him to send you your stock certificates or the proceeds of the sale of your shares.

How Dollar Cost Averaging Boosts Your Odds Of Making Money In the Stock Market

There's no such thing as a lead-pipe cinch when it comes to investing in the stock market. But there is something that can boost your odds for success if the stock or mutual fund you invest in (and the market in general) heads upward over the long term.

▶ **DOLLAR COST AVERAGING:** Here's what it boils down to: You invest the same amount of money in the same stock (or fund) at regular intervals—say, quarterly or monthly—no matter what the market is doing. You purchase as many shares as you can for that amount.

Say you want to buy XYZ stock and it costs $20 a share. You have $100 to invest.
Result: You buy five shares. If the price drops down to $10, you buy ten shares. And if the price goes up to $25, you purchase only four shares.

What's so earth-shattering about that? Absolutely nothing—it's simple, dull arithmetic. Your purchase of shares at a lower cost (when the stock or the market in general is down) will even out your high-cost per-share purchases. Over the long run, your cost per share should average out below average price per share at the time of each purchase.

Hypothetical example: Ms. Jones wants to invest in Blue Chip Stock. She has $500 for an initial investment and plans on adding $100 every month from then on. Assuming a normal fluctuation in the stock, here's how Jones' investment looks over the next ten years.

Year	Annual Amount of Investments and Reinvestments	Average Price Per Share	Number of Shares Purchased	Average Cost Per Share
1	$ 1,105	$12.07	93.734	$11.79
2	1,239	13.55	91.982	13.47
3	1,273	12.35	102.674	12.40
4	1.304	14.70	90.192	14.46
5	1,318	12.23	107.180	12.30
6	1,331	13.01	103.391	12.87
7	1,373	14.32	96.321	14.25
8	1,421	14.99	95.531	14.87
9	1,454	14.71	98.682	14.73
10	1,528	16.62	92.505	16.52
Totals	$13,346	$13.86	972.192	$13.76

Result: The average price per share is $13.86, compared to an average cost per share of only $13.76. And the figures above reflect a fairly steady market. The difference between the average price per share and the average cost per share will be bigger if there is more fluctuation in the market.

If Jones sold all her Blue Chip Stock at the end of ten years, she'd realize $16,158 (total shares owned times $16.62 per share). Subtracting her total cost of $13,346 leaves her a $2,812 profit before commissions.

In spite of its advantages, dollar-cost averaging is not without its perils. If the stock you pick keeps declining, or if the market has a long term decline, you are throwing good money after bad.

▶ **IMPORTANT:** You cannot get cold feet if you want dollar cost averaging to work. If you discontinue the plan when the value of your shares is less than your cost, you may wind up with a loss. Dollar cost averaging requires stick-to-itiveness on your part.

HOW TO TAKE ADVANTAGE OF MUTUAL FUNDS

You have to crawl before you walk. And many experts advise investors to do the same thing: Before they plunge headlong into the stock market, they should take a relatively safe approach. For example—

▶ **THE MUTUAL FUND WAY:** Mutual funds allow you to invest your hard-earned money in a variety of stocks and bonds. How it works: You purchase shares in a mutual fund—a federally regulated investment company—which in turn buys stocks and bonds. Your investments are chosen by a group of professional advisers. Your minimum initial investment is typically $500 or $1,000 (there are some that allow a minimum of $200) and subsequent investments can be as little as $50.

Result: The amount you are risking is small, but the payoff can be big. Are there any other advantages to mutual funds? There sure are. To name just a few—

• Diversification: Instead of sinking or swimming with a few stocks and bonds, you cut down your risk by spreading out your investment.
• Top-notch management: With a mutual fund, you have access to the same top professionals that larger investors do.
• Convenience: Owning shares in a mutual fund is like doing one-stop shopping. You get the benefit of diversification without having to put up with paperwork hassles.
• Easy investment and divestment: It's generally easy to invest or reinvest in a mutual fund. For example, most funds allow you to purchase shares over the phone. And sell orders can be easily placed, so your cash isn't needlessly tied up if you need it.
• Fund switching: Most funds permit you to transfer from one fund to another within the same family of funds—also by phone. This allows you to assume an aggressive posture while maintaining a low risk. For instance, if the market is

bullish you may want to switch into a growth stock fund; if it is bearish you could choose a diversified fund.

- Smorgasbord of funds: There are many types of investment funds. Some have specific investment purposes: for example, municipal bond funds, money market funds, growth stock funds, etc. Others are speculative: "junk" funds (high-risk bonds), hedge funds (puts and calls), letter stock funds (fledgling companies not registered with the SEC), etc. The most common type is the balanced fund, which is just what it sounds like—the investments are balanced between many different stocks and bonds.

How do you decide what type of mutual fund to invest in? The most important thing to do is to—

> ▶ **SET YOUR GOALS:** You have to decide what you want out of your mutual funds. For example, you might want to concentrate on long-term growth. Then you can pick your fund accordingly. Of course, you should also check out a fund's investment record, management structure and fee structure, etc. before you commit yourself.

In addition to the different types of mutual funds, there are different *kinds* of mutual funds. The most important classifications are load and no-load funds, and open and closed-end funds.

Load vs. No-Load Funds

Load funds are sold to you by a salesperson. You have to pay a sales charge—that's the "load" for this service. No-load funds, on the other hand, have no sales charge. The only cost you incur with a no-load fund is the management fee (you also have to pay management fees with load funds).

The sales charge for a load fund is typically about 8%. That gives the no-load investor an immediate advantage—which is compounded over a number of years.

> **Simple example:** Mr. Smith invests $10,000 in a load fund and Mr. Brown invests $10,000 in a no-load fund. Assume that each fund yields 10% a year. Here's how things work out for—

Mr. Smith: After subtracting his sales charge, Smith has $9,150 working for him. At the end of the first year, Smith's shares are worth $10,065. After ten years they will be worth around $23,730.

Mr. Brown: Smith has the full $10,000 working for him. His shares are worth $11,000 after the first year. After ten years they'll be worth $25,940—$2,210 more than Smith. And that's without adding any more shares.

Of course, this example assumes equal yields. A load fund that outperforms a no-load over the course of a few years may be a better deal. It does illustrate, however, how the no-load investor gets a head start on the load investor.

Open-End vs. Closed-End Funds

Mutual funds are generally open-end funds. They do not have a fixed number of shares. New shares are continuously available to the public. Open-end funds are listed under "Mutual Funds" in your paper's financial pages.

Some mutual funds are closed-end funds. They have a fixed number of shares and invest in both stocks and bonds. If you want to buy shares, you must buy them from someone else, rather than buying from the fund. Some are traded on the New York and American Stock Exchanges; others are offered on the Over-The- Counter Market.

Both types of funds have advantages and disadvantages. For example, a closed-end fund may sell at a discount; open-end funds don't. And commissions are often less than those connected with open end funds. On the other hand, because they have a fixed number of shares, closed-end funds cannot be as aggressive in the market as open end funds can.

Open-end funds are actively pushed by brokers (which may be another reason they are more popular). As we've said, closed end funds are publicly traded. Three such funds: Madison Fund General Public Service, Tri-Continental, Lehman Corporation.

Final word: Before we leave the area of mutual funds, it is important to note that mutual funds can be used for Individual Retirement Accounts, Keogh plans, pension and profit-sharing plans, and periodic purchase plans, to name just a few.

SOPHISTICATED STOCK MARKET TECHNIQUES

Some investors are in the stock market for money—and others are in it for big money. Here are three techniques—buying stock on margin, buying and selling options, and selling short—that involve greater risk, but can yield you greater profits than conventional means.

How to Buy Stocks and Bonds on Margin

Borrowing funds to finance investments is a time-tested strategy. In the stock-and-bond field, it's called—

> ▶ **BUYING ON MARGIN:** Say you want to buy a particular stock. If you buy it on margin, you pay only part of the cost of the stock. Your broker extends you credit for the rest (you have to pay the broker an interest fee on the borrowed funds).

Result: Any profit you make is increased by the amount of stock you bought on margin.

> *Example:* Mr. Able buys 100 shares of ABC stock at $40 a share. So Able puts up $4,000. If ABC goes up to $50 a share, Able has a profit of $1,000. That's not bad.

But let's say that instead of buying 100 shares, Able buys 200 shares of ABC on 50% margin. He puts up the same $4,000 and his broker puts up the other $4,000. When ABC goes up to $50 a share, Able has a $2,000 profit (less interest and commissions)—twice as much as before.

Of course, buying stock on margin has a comparable downside risk. In our example, if ABC stock plummeted to $30 a share, Able would lose $2,000 instead of $1,000.

Q. How much cash do you have to put up?

A. The Federal Reserve Board sets the minimum percentage you must put up out of your own funds. As we go to press, your initial investment must be no less than 50%.

Q. Are there any other requirements?

A. Yes. On the New York Stock Exchange, you must make a minimum deposit of $2,000. And your equity cannot fall below the level of 25% (your brokerage house may set a higher limit).

> ▶ **WARNING:** If your equity falls below the 25% mark, you will get a "margin call" from your broker. You will be required to bring your equity back above 25%. In other words, you have to sink in more cash.

Q. What happens if you fail to meet the margin call?

A. Your broker has the right to sell the stocks in your account to replace the credit he has given you.

Q. Who owns the stock you buy on margin?

A. It's registered in what is called "street name"—in other words, in the name of the brokerage firm. But you will be sent all the dividends you earn.

Q. Can you buy bonds on margin?

A. Yes. And the requirements are lower than the ones for stocks: You only have to put up 30% for corporate bonds (50% is required for convertible bonds) and 8% for Treasury bonds.

> ▶ **SUGGESTION:** If you are interested in purchasing bonds on margin, you may want to buy bonds that will yield enough to cover your interest costs. This is called a "positive carry."

Result: You can factor out interest charges in deciding how long you want to hold onto the bond.

Q. How much interest do you have to pay when you buy on margin?

A. It depends. In the past, the rates have ranged from 6 ½ to 13%. You will find a difference of ½ to 1 ½% between brokers. You'll have to shop around. If you combine all your margin accounts with one broker, you are likely to get a better rate than if you scattered them around.

Reminder: There is a big downside risk to buying on margin. Neophyte investors should tread carefully here.

▶ **CUTTING THE RISK:** You can always place a stop order with your broker. What to do: You instruct your broker to sell when the stock reaches a specified price. That way, you put a ceiling on your loss.

How To Take Advantage of Short Sales

Some investors actually root for a stock to go down. If they have made a "short sale" of the stock, they come out ahead when the price of the stock drops.
Idea in action: You anticipate—based on strong factual research— that the price of a stock is about to fall. So you sell the stock short—you sell it even though you don't own it. So that you can deliver the stock to the buyer, you borrow shares from your broker (who gets them from one of his customers). Eventually, you have to replace the borrowed stock. By then, hopefully, you can buy the shares on the market at a lower price and replace the borrowed shares.

▶ **PAYOFF:** Your profit is the difference between the proceeds from the short sale and what you pay for the replacement shares. So you make money when the stock goes down.

Example: Mr. White strongly feels that XYZ stock is about to drop. He sells short 100 shares at $50 a share. (*Note:* White is required to put up a good faith margin of 50%, to be held by the broker.)

Say White is right about the stock and it drops to $30 a share. White then "covers" (buys replacement stock) his short position by purchasing 100 shares for $3,000. Result: White has a profit of $2,000 (before commissions and interest charges) by selling short.

What happens if the price of XYZ goes up? Then White comes out on the losing end. If the price rises to say, $70 a share, and White covers, he is out $2,000. And, of course, he still has to tack on commissions.

▶ **NOT FOR THE FAINT-HEARTED:** As you can see, selling short is a highly speculative undertaking. Theoretically, the possibility for loss is much larger than that for gain. *Reason:* Your gain is limited because the stock can't drop any lower than zero. On the other hand, your loss is unlimited because there is no ceiling on how high the stock can go.

Important: In order to place a short sell order, two conditions must be present. (1) Obviously, the broker must be able to borrow the stock, and (2) you have to meet the up-tick rule (the latter is required by the New York Stock Exchange and the American Stock Exchange). Simply put, the up-tick rule says the last price of the stock you are selling short must be up from the previous price.

Example: You want to sell short on ABC stock. The stock is now at 25¼, down from the previous price of 25½. *Result:* You can't sell short. However, if the price goes up to, say, 25 ⅜ (from 25¼,) you then can sell short.

Reminder: We can't emphasize enough that selling short is a high-risk venture. If you decide to sell short, you may want to minimize the risk by—

▶ **PLAYING IT SAFE:** Arrange to buy the same stock at a higher price at the same time that you sell short. That way, if the stock does go up, you take some of the sting out of your loss by offsetting it with a gain.

How to Reap Profits From Stock Options

Stock options are one of the top attractions on the market today. An option is a contract to buy or sell a certain stock (typically, 100 shares) at a certain price within a certain time. An option to buy is called a "call"; an option to sell is called a "put." The length of the option can range anywhere from 30 days to one year (the most common length is nine months and ten days).

The inevitable question: What makes stock options so attractive? The answer: With options you get this—

▶ **INVESTMENT EDGE:** (1) When you *write* an option, you can lock in a profit, and (2) when you *buy* an option you have the potential for a big gain, while cutting down the possibility of a loss.

Writing and buying call options are markedly different techniques. Let's take a quick look at a couple of simplied examples. (Assume we're dealing in calls, we'll get to puts later.)

Example 1: Mr. Allen owns 100 shares of ABC stock, which he bought at $50 a share. The stock hasn't moved much in the past few months, so Allen decides to write a call option on it. He places an order through his broker to sell an option of ABC at $50 a share—the exercise or "striking" price—with a premium of $500 ($5 a share). The option is for nine months and ten days.

Here's what happens to Allen if—

ABC goes down or stays the same: The price of the option goes down and it is not exercised (the price is lower than the striking price).

Result: After the option expires, Allen pockets his profit and can sell another option.

ABC goes up: Say that ABC goes up to $55 a share. Allen's buyer can call the option—he can exercise his right to buy the actual shares at 50. Result: Allen pockets $5,500 ($5,000 from the stock sale, plus $500 from selling the call). Or if Allen wants to keep the stock, he can purchase an identical call for, say, $600.

Result: Allen has a $100 loss, but he still owns the stock, now worth $5,500.

NOTE: Allen isn't locked into waiting nine months and ten days to make a move. He can trade the call on the market any time before and cut his loss (or increase his gain).

▶ **SUGGESTION:** When the price of stock goes up the option writer finds himself in a difficult position: He must close out the call at a loss or part with the stock at the exercise price. So investors may be wise to write calls on stocks that show little fluctuation—blue chip stocks, for example.

Naked option writing: A word about this investment technique —it is strictly for experienced investors. When you write a naked option, you write an option against stock you don't own (similar to selling short). If your call is exercised, you have to acquire the stock at a price much higher than the exercise price. So the risk of loss is much greater.

Buying options: This technique is riskier than writing options, but the potential for a big payoff is greater. *Reason:* Leverage. When the underlying stock goes up, the price of the call goes up by more percentage-wise.

Example 2: Mr. Blair thinks that ABC stock is going to make a dramatic rise. So he buys an option on ABC stock at $50 a share for a $500 premium. Here's what happens to Blair if—

ABC goes up: Say ABC rises to $60 a share. The call option goes right along from $5 a share to $10.

Result: Blair sells his contract and realizes a profit of $500 (an increase of 100%). The underlying stock, on the other hand, has increased only 20%.

ABC goes down or stays the same: Suppose ABC slips to $45 a share. In that case, Blair's call options are worthless. Result: He loses the $500 premium he paid.

Puts: Puts are the exact opposite of calls—they give you the right to *sell* 100 shares of stock at a fixed price for a fixed period of time. Puts are generally used for defensive purposes—for example, as a short-term gain to offset a loss. You can also combine puts and calls in a ''straddle,'' but that's better left to the experts.

▶ **WHERE TO TRADE:** You can find calls and puts traded on the Chicago Board Options Exchange—that's where the idea originated. Other exchanges that list options are the American Stock Exchange, the Philadelphia Stock Exchange, the Pacific Stock Exchange, and the Midwest Stock Exchange.

TOP TAX-SAVING STRATEGIES

Making money on Wall Street is only half the battle. The tricky part is keeping what you earn. Here are some techniques that let you take down gains with a minimum of tax erosion.

How to Buy Stock That Pays Tax-Free Dividends

Many investors are interested in stock that produces income. And while getting steady dividend checks every quarter is fine, it would be even better to get dividend checks that are—

> ▶ **TAX-FREE:** A number of publicly-held corporations pay their shareholders dividends that are wholly or partially free of current tax. The special tax treatment gives these stocks a higher after-tax yield when compared with stocks paying taxable dividends. And the higher your tax bracket, the more valuable the tax-free dividends.

> *Example:* Mr. Green buys stock in ABC Corp. for $20 a share. ABC pays a quarterly dividend of 50¢. That's a good return in itself: 10% annually. But suppose ABC's dividend is 100% tax-free. If Green's top dollar of earnings is taxed at a 33% rate, his 10% yield on the ABC stock is equivalent to a taxable yield of 14.9% on another stock. If Green is in the 50% bracket, the taxable equivalent soars to 20%.

Why do ABC's dividends qualify for favorable tax treatment? It's because ABC is not paying true dividends—an actual distribution of earnings and profits. For tax purposes, the ABC "dividends" are a return of capital. Green is simply getting back part of the $20 a share he originally invested. And since Green already paid tax on that $20 it's tax-free to him when he gets it back.

ABC may be a utility company that has to pay increasing gas prices. When the company receives the gas bills, it pays them. However, state legal requirements prevent ABC from immediately passing on the additional costs to the consumer (instead, increases are collected over a 12-month period).

For accounting purposes, these costs are deferred and don't reduce book earnings and profits. For *tax* accounting, they do reduce current earnings.

Result: Distributions to shareholders exceed earnings and profits.

Because the dividends are a partial return of the price Green paid for the stock, they reduce his cost in the stock for tax purposes. So he has a bigger taxable profit (or smaller deductible loss) if and when he sells ABC. If the dividends exceed Mr. Green's tax cost before he sells, they are no longer tax-free. The dividends are treated as tax-sheltered long-term capital gain—just like his profit would be taxed if Green actually sold the stock.

Here is a random sample of some common stocks that paid tax-free dividends in a recent year, with the corporations' respective percentage of dividend dollars that were exempt from tax.

Detroit Edison	63%	Northern Indiana Public Service	65%
Fairchild Industries	100%	Ohio Edison	75%
Long Island Lighting	100%	Pacific Power & Light	45%
Mesa Petroleum	100%	Penn. Power & Light	100%
Middle South Util.	92%	Va. Electric & Power	88.4%

Where do you find stocks paying tax-free dividends? The easiest thing to do is check with your broker (as you may have noticed, these stocks are predominantly utility companies).

> ▶ **KEEP THIS IN MIND:** There is no guarantee that a stock paying tax-free dividends this year will pay tax-free dividends next year. And, of course, the dividend angle is only one factor to consider. If a company's prospects aren't good, you should not invest in it, even if it is paying out a 100% tax-free dividend.

How to Fingerprint Stock for Tax Purposes

Like many investors, you might have bought stock in one corporation at different times and at different prices. The time comes when you decide to sell some of these shares. The amount of your gain or loss—and whether it's short-term or long-term—all depends on which block of shares you sell. So in essence you have the power to choose the tax result you want.

> *Example:* You bought 100 shares of X Corp. stock at 50 two years ago. This year, you bought another 100 shares at 80. X Corp. is now selling at 70, and you want to sell 100 shares. Which shares should you sell?

Answer: It depends on the tax result you want. If you sell the shares you bought two years ago, you'll get a long-term capital gain of $2,000. If you sell the shares you bought this year, you'll get a $1,000 short-term loss.

But here's the catch: To make sure you get the result you want, you must be able to establish the basis of the shares you sell. This means you must be able to properly identify the particular shares when the sale is made. Otherwise, the Government will apply the—

First-in, first-out rule: The first stock you bought will be treated as the first stock you sell. In our example, the Government would say that you sold the stock you bought two years ago and as a result, you have a $2,000 long-term gain. So if it was the short-term loss that suited your picture, you're out of luck.

> ▶ **SIMPLE MOVE:** One relatively easy way to keep track of your shares is to record the stock certificate numbers. Keep a ledger showing the numbers of the certificates you trade. That way, you can establish a long-term or short-term gain (or loss)—whichever suits you.

A word to the wise: Stock certificate numbers aren't the only way to "fingerprint" your stock transactions. You may want to work out your own system. But whatever system you use, make sure the stock you want to sell—the one that gives you the best tax results—is the one that you do in fact sell.

Q. My broker holds on to my stocks for the sake of convenience. The shares are registered in the broker's name, and are intermingled with stocks held for other customers. Is there a way I can identify these stocks to the Government's satisfaction?

A. Yes. Here's—

▶ **WHAT TO DO:** Instruct your broker in writing as to which lot you want to sell. You identify the lot by listing the date on which you bought it and how much you paid for it. Then get the broker to confirm the order in writing.

How to Make Sure You Nail Down Your Tax Loss When Selling Stock

You can't always go with your first instinct—especially where taxes are concerned. For instance, say you hold stock showing a paper loss. Selling the stock and taking the tax loss would help your tax picture. But if you think the stock has a good future, you may like to hold on to it.

Why not do both—sell the stock and nail down the tax loss and then buy it back? You can't because of this—

▶ **KEY TAX RULE:** If the purchase takes place within 30 days before or after the sale, it's a "wash sale." And the tax law says that you are not allowed a currently deductible loss on a wash sale.

However, you can still take down a tax loss without giving up your position in the stock.

▶ **TAX STRATEGY:** Buy replacement stock first, then sell your old stock more than 30 days later. That means doubling your investment outlay for a month. But by "doubling up," any rise in the stock's price will be your gain. And by selling more than 30 days after the purchase, you can deduct any loss on the old stock on your return.

Maybe you don't want to lay out the money right now to double up. So you decide to sell, take your loss and wait 31 days. But soon after you sell, the stock starts to shoot up in value. You decide to buy right away. Of course, you lose the tax loss this year. But you do get some—

▶ **TAX BENEFIT:** The loss from the sale of your old stock is added to the basis of your new stock.

Result: When you sell the new stock at a profit, less of your proceeds will be taxable.

Example: In October, 1982, Mr. Brown buys 100 shares of XYZ at $20 a share. In early November, 1983, Brown sells XYZ for $15 a share. Talk of a takeover of XYZ by another company causes the stock to rise quickly to $18. Brown decides to buy 100 shares in late November at that price. In January, 1984, XYZ is taken over and Brown sells the stock for $25 a share.

Result: Brown has a $500 loss ($5 x 100 shares) on the early November sale. But since he bought XYZ shares within 30 days of the sale at a loss, the loss is not deductible in 1983. The loss is, however, added to his basis in the XYZ stock bought in late November—raising his basis in the stock from $1,800 to $2,300. When Brown sells in January, he has a $700 profit ($2,500 less $1,800), but pays tax on only $200 ($2,500 less $2,300 tax basis).

How to Use Short Sales and Put Options to Your Year-End Tax Advantage

Suppose you want to sell a stock and take your profit before year-end. But, at the same time, you want to postpone the tax on the profit until next year. Is there a way you can accomplish this objective?

Answer: Sure there is. Both short sales and put options can help you lock in your profit in this year *and* delay the tax until next year.

How to use short sales: A short sale simply means selling stock you don't own. Your broker borrows the stock from one of his other customers and delivers it to your buyer. You don't complete the sale, however, until you purchase and deliver enough shares to repay the stock loan. And, more importantly, you don't realize income until you close out the sale by delivering the replacement shares.

A "short sale against the box" is the same as a short sale, with this exception: You already own the stock you're selling and use it to pay back the loan. There's no sleight-of-hand involved.

▶ **TAX MAGIC:** If you want to throw the tax on a December sale into next year, sell short—*but don't close out the sale until January of next year.*

Result: You get the price prevailing at the time of your sale, but you've shifted the taxable profit into next year. What's more, you wind up with the use of the tax dollars for an extra year. Plus you have that much more time to offset the profit with a deductible loss.

Note: You can't use a short sale to convert short-term gain into long-term gain by postponing delivery of the replacement stock. The holding period is determined as of the date the short sale is initiated.

How to use puts: All short sale arrangements share a common drawback: If your stock rises in price after the borrowed shares are sold, you lose out on the price rise. Your gain is fixed at the time of the sale. As an alternative, you might consider—

Put options: You can buy a put option covering stock you already own. The put gives you the right to sell the stock to the "writer" (the person who sold you the option) at a stipulated price within a designated period of time.

Suppose you have a substantial profit on a stock and you want to shift your taxable gain into next year.

▶ **WHAT TO DO:** You can guarantee your present profit by buying a put (an option to sell) on your stock at about its current price, good for a long enough period to carry you into next year. If the stock keeps climbing, don't exercise the put. Instead, sell the stock at a higher price.

How To Match Up Your Gains and Losses

There's more to analyzing your investment position than checking the daily quotations. You have to know how to match up gains against losses to find out what your tax picture will be.

▶ **WHAT TO DO:** To find out how you stand taxwise on your transactions, take the following steps:

▶ **Step 1:** Add up your long-term gains. Then add up your long-term losses (and any long-term loss carryovers). Offset these figures against each other to get your "net long-term gain (or loss)."

▶ **Step 2:** Do the same thing with your short-term gains and short-term losses. The result is your "net short-term gain (or loss)."

▶ **Step 3:** Compare the net long-term total with your net short-term total.

If you have both a long-term and short-term gain, treat each gain separately. All of the net short-term gain is treated as ordinary income. But only 40% of the net long-term gain is treated as ordinary income (the other 60% is tax-free).

If net long-term gain exceeds net short-term loss, the net is long-term gain. Again, only 40% of long-term gain is treated as ordinary income.

If net short-term gain exceeds net long-term loss, the net is short-term gain, which is taxed as ordinary income.

If you have an overall loss, the loss offsets up to $3,000 of ordinary income. You use short-term loss first, then long-term loss. **Note:** It takes $2 of long-term loss to offset $1 of ordinary income. So you'd need $6,000 of long-term loss to offset $3,000 of ordinary income.

▶ **CAPITAL LOSS CARRYOVER:** After offsetting your losses against $3,000 of ordinary income, any remaining loss can be carried forward indefinitely. The loss retains its character—that is short-term loss remains short-term loss, and long-term loss remains long-term loss.

HOW TO TAKE ADVANTAGE OF CORPORATE BONDS

"Promises, promises." Usually, they're not worth much. But in the case of corporate bonds, they can help you build a financially secure future.

▶ **BASIC PRINCIPLE:** When you buy corporate bonds, you are banking on the corporation's promise to pay you a fixed amount of money over the life of the bond. The rate that the corporation promises to pay is the bond's yield. The amount that you pay for the bond is the price.

Another basic principle: As interest rates go, so go the prices of bonds—the other way. In other words, if interest rates go up, bond prices go down; if interest rates go down, prices go up.

Simplified example: In January, Mr. James buys one Solid Inc. bond, paying 8%, for $1,000. By September, interest rates have dropped to 6%.

Result: Because Jones' bond pays a higher relative yield, it's worth about $1,180. Jones can sell the bond at a profit.

The third basic principle: Yield doesn't tell you all you need to know when buying corporate bonds. *Reason:* It doesn't account for a bond purchased at discount. You have to figure in not only your current cash yield on the bond, but also the profit you will make if you hold the bond till maturity. What you need to know in this situation is your yield to maturity. Here's how you arrive at that approximate figure for bonds bought at discount.

$$\frac{\text{Annual interest plus (discount divided by years to maturity)}}{\text{(Current price plus par value) divided by two}}$$

Example: Mr. Arnold buys a 5% bond selling for $750 with a ten-year maturity. The par value (the principal on which interest is paid) is $1,000. Arnold figures his yield to maturity as follows:

$$\frac{50 + 250/10}{(750 + 1{,}000)/2} = \frac{50 \text{ plus } 25}{875} = 8.6\%$$

Result: Though the current yield is only 5%, Arnold's yield to maturity is about 8.6%.

Note: When bonds sell at a substantial discount (here, $250), it increases the yield to maturity. The bigger the discount and the shorter the period to maturity, the higher the yield to maturity. As a general rule, corporate bonds have a higher yield than comparable Government securities such as Treasury bonds.

Those are the basics on corporate bonds. There are probably two more things you should know about right away—how to buy corporate bonds and how you get your interest income.

▶ **HOW TO BUY:** Usually, you buy corporate bonds through a broker and pay a commission of about 1%. If the broker already owns the bonds, you have to pay the so-called "spread"—the difference between the bid and ask prices for the bond. Minimum bond investment is usually $1,000 (although sometimes you can find bonds for $500).

▶ **HOW TO COLLECT:** It depends on whether the bond is a bearer or a registered bond. If it is a bearer bond (it belongs to whoever owns it), you clip a coupon off the bond and cash it in at your bank. If the bond is registered in your name, you get an interest check through the mail. Note: Starting with 1983, all new corporate bonds have been issued in registered form. However, there are still plenty of pre-1983 bearer bonds available.

Types of bonds: There are different types of corporate bonds. Here are three of the most popular:

- First mortgage bonds: The bonds are secured by a mortgage on property owned by the issuing corporation. Since there is a clear-cut claim to corporate assets, first mortgage bonds are generally a safe investment.
- Debentures: The bonds are backed by a general promise of the corporation to pay—in other words, it is simply an I.O.U. But don't be misled: A debenture of a sound corporation is safer than a first mortgage bond of a shaky corporation.
- New issue bonds: New issue bonds are just what they sound like—they are issues available to the public for the first time. What sets new issue bonds apart is that there are—

▶ **NO COMMISSIONS:** You buy new issues through an underwriting syndicate. The underwriter lends the issuing corporation funds and then the underwriter sells the bonds. If you are interested in new issues, you can ask your broker to put you in touch with an underwriter.

Two important questions remain: (1) How do you know which bonds to buy? And (2) when should you buy? The first is relatively easy to answer. There are a number of independent services which provide—

▶ **QUALITY RATINGS:** Two of the most prominent are Moody's and Standard & Poor's (S & P's). The ratings range from triple to A to C. For example, junk bonds—a high speculative investment—are probably rated no more than a BB. Best bet: Begin by looking at bonds with ratings of A and up.

The second question's a lot tougher: Generally, if you feel interest rates are heading down, then you should buy bonds in order to lock in current yields. But if you feel rates will go higher, you want to hold off your purchase and wait for better yields.

▶ **CAUTION:** When interest rates drop, many corporations have the right to "call in" bonds and replace them with new issues (with lower rates). *Solution:* Buy a non-callable bond (e.g., an industrial bond).

How To Convert Bonds Into Stock

If you want to buy corporate bonds that have a built-in "edge" you may be interested in convertible bonds. What is a convertible bond? It has all the features of an ordinary bond: a fixed interest rate and a fixed date when it's paid off. It's a debt of the corporation that issued it (interest must be paid, whether there are earnings or not).

▶ **WHAT IS DIFFERENT:** Convertible bonds can be exchanged for a predetermined amount of common stock of the issuing corporation. And that is your protection.

Example: Mr. Grant pays $1,000 for a convertible bond of XYZ Corp., with a conversion privilege of 50 shares of common stock. This means Grant can convert his bond into 50 shares of XYZ stock—at no extra cost. The stock is selling at $15 when Grant buys the bond. If the stock goes over the $20 mark, Grant comes out ahead. He can convert the bond into common stock or sell the bond at a profit.

Grant is a potential winner when his stock goes up, but he doesn't have a comparable risk when the stock goes down. That's because convertible bonds have this—

▶ **BUILT-IN SAFEGUARD:** When the price of the common stock underlying a convertible drops, the convertible's price may fall—but not as much. *Reason:* Convertible bonds have an intrinsic value as bonds. When the common stock is selling below the conversion price, the bond won't sell for any less than its value as a bond.

On the other hand, when the stock rises above the conversion price, the bond price goes up. Let's go back to Mr. Grant.

Example: Grant bought the bond for $1,000 when the stock price was $15, but the stock has fluctuated since then. First it dropped to $12 (a 20% decrease). The bond did not drop at the same proportionate rate; it fell by considerably less than 20%. Then the stock rose to $25—and the bond shot up to $1,250.

So the convertible can be a two-way winner. There's a brake on losses and the bond picks up if the stock turns around. What's more, there's no tax when you convert bonds into stock.

Convertibles can be a good thing, but of course—as always in the investment world—there are a few drawbacks. Such as—

• For some convertibles, the value of the common stock you get on exchange is so low that it may be years before the conversion privilege is worth anything.

• For others, the price of the common is so high that you may have to pay a premium of 50% or 100% to buy the convertible. In that case, your yield will be low—and if the common stock sinks, you can lose as much as if you owned the common.

MUNICIPAL BONDS GIVE YOU A BIG TAX EDGE

Every investor welcomes the prospect of high return with open arms. But here's something that may be even better—

▶ **TAX-FREE INVESTMENT INCOME:** Most state, county, and municipal bonds pay interest that is free of federal income tax. In addition, if the bond is issued by the state you live in, there isn't any state tax in most instances, either. What's more, in most cases, bonds are a relatively safe investment.

Just glance at this comparison chart to see the power of tax-exempt bonds. It shows you the rate of taxable interest which "traditional" bonds must yield before taxes to equal various tax-exempt bond yields.

Tax Bracket %	8%	9%	10%	11%
	Rates of taxable interest necessary to yield same amount after tax			
38	12.90	14.52	16.13	17.74
45	14.54	16.36	18.18	20.00
50	16.00	18.00	20.00	22.00

Of course, tax-free interest isn't the whole story on municipals. There are a couple of other tax angles to keep in mind.

• *Capital gain:* If you buy a bond at a discount and hold it to maturity (or if you sell the bond at a profit), the gain is taxed as capital gain. If the bond was held more than one year, you have low-taxed long-term capital gain (only 40% of long-term capital gain is subject to tax).

• *Capital loss:* There may be a capital loss when you sell a bond (interest rates may be higher than your bond's rate). As with other assets, the loss is long-term if the bond has been held for more than one year, and short-term if held for a year or less. The capital loss from the sale of a tax-exempt can offset gain from the sale of taxable investment. Or it can offset as much as $3,000 of ordinary income.

• *Zero coupon bonds:* Some municipals are issued at a discount and pay no interest. The difference between the face value (payable at the bond's maturity) and the discount price is equivalent to the interest an ordinary municipal pays. Key advantage: You don't have to reinvest interest payments—it's strictly a "get it and forget it" investment.

• *Investment expenses:* Commissions and brokerage fees you incur buying and selling a tax-exempt are added to your basis (the cost of your investment). That decreases your taxable profit and increases your capital loss when you sell. However, the tax law prevents you from deducting expenses you incur in obtaining tax-free interest. As a result, you lose deductions that stock and corporate bond investors have locked up. Prime examples: Safe deposit and custodian fees, and interest on a debt incurred to buy tax-exempts.

Important: There are other angles to municipal bonds besides taxes. For example, some bonds pay a high interest rate because there's more risk involved. And the value of your bonds can fluctuate as interest rates change. So don't be completely dazzled by a bond's tax-exempt status.

If municipals do fit into your goals, here's—

> ▶ **HOW TO GET THEM:** (1) Through brokers or commercial banks, (2) investment trusts commonly marketed by brokerage firms, or (3) no-load tax-exempt bond funds advertised in the media. They are available in denominations as low as $1,000 (though most are $5,000).

Effective for new issues after July 1, 1983, a municipal bond must be in registered form. In simple terms, you are listed as the owner of record on the books of the bond's issuing agent, and you receive your dividend by way of a check. Bonds issued *before* July 1, 1983 may be bearer bonds: Your name is *not* registered, and interest is payable when coupons, clipped from the bond, are presented for payment at, say, a bank.

How One Kind of Municipal Bond Can Produce a Tax-Sheltered Nest Egg

You may be after more than just tax-free interest. For instance, you may have a specific financial objective in mind—say, building a college fund for your child. There's a particular type of bond that meets this need.

> ▶ **DEEP DISCOUNT MUNICIPALS:** These bonds carry low interest rates and, sell at big discounts. The interest is, of course, tax free. But when the bonds mature at face value, the investor gets something extra—a handsome, built-in profit, taxed at low capital gain rates.

"Wait a minute," you may be saying. "These bonds pay relatively little interest. How can I be better off with less—rather than more—tax-free interest?"

First off, let's make it clear that discount bonds aren't for everybody. But they may fill the bill for someone who wants to build a special family nest egg with a minimum of trouble. You put your money away and it's done—period. Month after month, year after year, your tax-sheltered profit grows.

Secondly, when we say a discount bond has a "low" interest rate, we're talking about the interest rate of the face value—not the actual current yield. This may be a lot higher. *Reason:* With a discount bond, your cash investment is much lower than the face value of the bond. So your real current return is much higher than the stated interest rate. Let's see how the tax benefits of discount bonds can pay off with this—

Typical example: You have a child (or grandchild) who'll be ready for college in 16 years. You want to build a custom-designed fund for his education by buying some discount municipals now and putting them away till maturity.

▶ **WINNING MOVE:** You buy three XYZ municipal bonds. For simplicity, let's say each bond has a stated interest rate of 4%, a face value of $10,000 and sells on the market for $7,000. The bonds mature in 16 years.

How you profit: You get $1,200 a year in interest ($400 interest on each bond). That means you get a current yield of about 5.7% on your total $21,000 investment. And, as with all municipals, you get the benefit of tax-free income: If you're in the 40% tax bracket, a 5.7% tax-free yield is equivalent to a taxable yield of about 9.5%.

How your child profits: You have a $30,000 fund (the maturity value of the three bonds) ready for him when he goes to college. In other words, you've made a $9,000 profit on your investment—without your having to do a thing. This profit is taxable when you cash in the bonds—but at the low capital gain rates.

New Concept in Tax-Free Municipal Bonds Protects You Against a Rise in Interest Rates

You can lock in tax-free interest income over the long haul by buying a long-term municipal bond. The problem is that if interest rates rise before the bond matures, is there a way to get long-term interest and still be sure of getting your investment back if you decide to sell sooner?

▶ **NEW IDEA:** They are called optional-tender bonds or put bonds and mature in up to 30 years. They pay tax-free interest, just like any other bond issued by a state or local government. But put bonds have one feature that sets them apart from other bonds: Beginning at a specified date after the bond is issued, you have the option of 'putting' the bond to the issuer at least once a year and requiring that it redeem the bond at full face value even if the bond is selling at a discount.

Result: Put bonds take the risk out of interest rate fluctuations. They give you a form of price insurance. You know you can get the par value of the bond from the issuer at least once a year. Not only don't you have to worry about interest rate fluctuations, you have the flexibility to take advantage of them.

▶ **IDEA IN ACTION:** If interest rates fall, you sit tight and collect a higher market rate. If they rise, you simply bail out of your investment by putting the bond to the issuer. You then reinvest your money in a newer bond with a higher interest rate.

In other words, a put bond is comparable to a series of short-term municipals, with maturity dates on the put option dates. In fact, the interest rate on a newly issued put bond is set at the same rate as short-term bonds with maturities at the time of the first tender date. That's why put bonds are popular with issuers. They can raise long-term funds at a short or intermediate term interest rate, usually a percentage point or two below the long-term rate.

Are there any disadvantages to put bonds from the buyer's point of view? The issuer of put bonds can call the bonds—redeem them before maturity—if it wishes and may even be required to do so on a regular schedule. The call feature may prevent puts from rising above par value, the way other bonds do when interest rates fall.

▶ **WHAT TO DO:** If you're interested in put bonds, check with your investment adviser. He will be able to point out which bonds offer the put feature—and whether they fit in to your overall strategy.

How to Get a Special Edge by Swapping Municipals

Remember how you used to collect baseball cards and trade them with your friends? Well, you can swap municipal bonds too—albeit there's a lot more at stake. Handle things right and you can get a—

▶ **DOUBLE PAYOFF:** (1) A currently deductible loss that can shelter your other highly taxed income and (2) more tax-free interest from the new municipal bonds you acquire in the swap.

Example: Mr. White has pulled down a $3,100 short-term capital gain from stock sales this year. White bought an Apple City bond years ago for $10,000. The bond's coupon rate is 3 ¾% with a maturity date of 2011. The bond's present value is only $6,900. White sells the Apple City bond and buys a Peach City bond with the same face value, maturing in 2029 and paying 3 ⅞%. The value of this bond is also down to $6,900.

Dollars-and-cents benefit: White has a $3,100 tax loss this year ($10,000 cost less $6,900 present value) that he can use to shelter his $3,100 short-term capital gain from his stock transactions. Assuming for simplicity's sake that White is in the 50% tax bracket, the $3,100 tax loss saves him $1,550 in taxes.

Let's say, just for the sake of our example, that interest rates continue to drop significantly and White sells the Peach City bond next spring for $10,000. Since his tax basis in the bond is $6,900, he has a short-term capital gain of $3,100. And the tax on that is $1,550. So White has postponed his tax for a year. Of course, if White holds on to the new bond for more than one year, his taxable profit on the sale will be long-term capital gain. And assuming White sells for $10,000, his tax will be no more than $620. In the meanwhile, he will be getting—

▶ **MORE TAX-FREE INCOME:** White now pockets $387.50 a year interest (3 ⅞% of $10,000) instead of $375 (3 ¾% of $10,000). But the $12.50 increase isn't the only benefit. What is significant is that White gets the tax writeoff without worsening his investment position—he improves it.

Important: If the bonds you buy are "substantially identical" to the bonds you sell, and the two transactions take place within 30 days of each other, you can't deduct your loss currently under the "wash-sale" rules. What's "substantially identical?" There's no clearcut answer. One brokerage firm suggests that bonds of the same issuer have at least a ½% difference in the yield to maturity and 5 years difference in maturity dates to avoid the wash-sale rules. However, bonds issued by different states or municipalities are not "substantially identical."

Another Kind of Municipal Bond Escapes All Income Taxes

The interest from a municipal bond is free of Federal income tax, but not necessarily free of state and local taxes. You pay state and local taxes if the bond is issued by a state other than your own (and a few states even tax their own bonds).

▶ **BIG EXCEPTION:** Bonds issued by the Commonwealth of Puerto Rico are tax free across the board—no matter where you live. They are specifically exempted by law from Federal tax *and* state and local tax.

With states and localities taking an ever-increasing share of your income, this total tax-free break can be a big plus. If municipal bonds are your cup of tea, Puerto Rican bonds may be well worth looking into.

SAFETY FIRST: U.S. GOVERNMENT ISSUES

The Government issues many different types of I.O.U.s—short-term, intermediate, and long-term. Most people buy two kinds: Series EE Savings Bonds and Treasury Bills. Let's begin with the—

New Look to a Safe-As-Fort Knox Investment

In the past, U.S. Savings Bonds were popular because they were a safe and sound investment. But they began to lag behind other investments—say, money market funds—that had a greater yield. Now however, U.S. Savings Bonds are sporting a—

▶ **NEW LOOK:** Savings Bonds bought after October 31, 1982, have a variable yield feature (much like money market funds or "money market" bank certificates) if held for five years or longer. They will pay the *greater* of (1) 85% of the average interest rate of five-year U.S. Treasury notes and bonds issued during each six-month period the Bond was held, or (2) 7½% compounded semiannually.

Example: Mr. Brown buys a new EE Bond after November, 1982, and cashes it in six years later. If the average rate of five-year Treasury notes and bonds issued during the six years Brown owns his Savings Bond is 10%, then he earns 8½% interest on the Bond (85% of the average yield). But no matter what happens, the EE bond will pay a minimum 7½% interest.

However, if Brown holds the Bond less than five years, its yield is not linked to Treasury notes and bonds. It will yield something less than 7.5% (according to a schedule of graduated yields published by the Government).

New Series EE Bonds are issued at a 50% discount and have a maturity of ten years. For example, $25 cash invested today in a $50 Bond will yield at least $50 in ten years (that's a 7½% rate of growth).

Of course, millions of dollars worth of E and EE Bonds have been issued before November 1, 1982. Do holders of those Bonds get any benefit out of the new rules?

▶ **GOOD NEWS:** If pre-11/82 Bonds are held for five years past November 1, 1982, it's a can't-lose proposition. You pocket the greater of the yield promised when the Bond was issued or the variable investment yield. In other words, an EE Bond bought in October, 1982, will pay no less than 9% (eight-year maturity) and may pay more if 85% of the average rates for Treasury obligations is higher than 9%.

Of course, like Series EE Bonds purchased after November 1, older E and EE Bonds must be held for five years after November 1, 1982, for you to get the choice between the guaranteed and the variable investment yield.

All Savings Bonds sold at a discount, new or old, Series E or EE, have one key attraction from the tax standpoint.

▶ **TAX DEFERRAL:** You don't owe any tax until you cash the Bonds in (unless you elect to pay tax annually on the Bond's increase in value). In fact, you can defer taxes past the maturity date of your Bonds by rolling the proceeds over into Government HH Bonds.

Q. What are series HH Bonds?

A. HH Bonds are straight interest-bearing obligations that pay interest (7½% on new issues) every six months. After November 1, 1982, HH Bonds were only issued in exchange for Series E or EE Bonds. Tax break: You can trade in your EE Bonds for HH's without paying any current tax on the accrued interest from the EE Bonds.

How To Turn U.S. Savings Bonds Into Tax-Exempts

Because of their variable yield feature, U.S. Savings Bonds are a better investment than ever. But there is a way to make them even better. You can get—

▶ **TAX-FREE INTEREST:** Buy the Bonds in your child's name and have the child report the Savings Bond yearly earnings on his or her tax return. *Result:* Your child's personal exemption shelters the income. If he or she has $1,000 or less of investment income, there is no Federal tax to pay. And since it's a U.S. Bond, there is no state or local tax either.

If you bought the Bonds in your own name, you would pay tax on the accrued interest. So the tax savings increases your yield.

General rule: A taxpayer doesn't pay any Federal income tax on EE Bonds until he cashes them in. He then reports as ordinary income the difference between the bonds' discounted purchase price and their present value. But there's this special election: He can choose to report each year's interest as income in the year it accrues.

By having your child make this election, most or all of each year's accrued interest will be free of Federal taxes—just like more expensive tax-exempt state or local bonds. Without the election, your child might have to pay tax on the entire interest accrual since purchase (minus his $1,000 exemption). That could add up to a sizable tax bill since he's likely to have other income by that time, say from a part-time job.

Treasury Bills Have a Built-In Advantage

A Treasury Bill is an I.O.U. backed by the full faith and credit of the United States Government. It's issued in maturities of three, six, and twelve months. T-Bills are sold in minimums of $10,000 and are also available in multiples of $5,000 after that. Treasury Bills are sold at a—

▶ **DISCOUNT RATE:** You purchase a Treasury Bill at a price below its face value. Then you redeem it at face value at maturity. *Result:* When you figure in the value of the discount, the actual return of a T-Bill is higher than the stated value.

Here's how the yield compares with say, a six month Certificate of Deposit. Assume the annual discount rate on a Treasury bill is 9.6%. And the annual yield on a Certificate of Deposit is also 9.6%. Although the percentages may appear to be the same, there is a—

▶ **BIG DIFFERENCE:** The Treasury Bill sells at a discount. Your annual yield on your actual cash investment is actually 10.08%—slightly higher than the CD.

What you actually pay for a T-Bill selling at a 9.6% discount is $9,520. (The Government sends you a check for $480 soon after your purchase.) But when the bill matures, you get a check for the full $10,000 (more on this later).

So you get a return of $480 on an investment of $9,520—which works out to an annual yield of 10.08%.

Big tax advantage too: Treasury Bills are exempt from state and local taxes (Certificates of Deposit are not). That increases the actual yield even more.

Year-end tax move: T-Bills are discount certificates: A check for the difference between the discount purchase price and the face value at maturity is sent to you shortly after the due date. In effect, you receive your interest in advance, but it is not taxed to you until the bill matures. *Result:* Since any six-month T-Bill you buy in the second half of 1984 will not mature until 1985, the interest you earn will not be taxed until 1985.

▶ **MORE INFORMATION, PLEASE:** For more information on currently available Treasury offerings, check your phone book for the telephone number of the Federal Reserve Bank in your area. They'll have a pre-recorded message and another number to contact if you have further questions.

How to Buy Treasury Bills by Mail

You can buy Treasury bills directly from the U.S. Government and pay no commission. You make your purchase by mailing a bid to a Federal Reserve bank or branch.

Auctions that determine the discount rate for 6-month bills are held every Monday (the previous Friday if Monday is a bank holiday). You mail a Federal Reserve noncompetitive tender form (which you can obtain from the Reserve bank) to the bank before the auction, along with a certified personal check or bank check for $10,000.

Or you can send a letter with your check stating: (1) the face amount of the bills you want, and (2) the maturity you want (3, 6, or 12 months). Also, make sure you include your signature and your Social Security number in the letter. Note: On the envelope make sure you print or type TENDER FOR TREASURY BILLS along the bottom.

Treasury bills are discount, not interest-bearing, certificates. So a check for the difference between the purchase price of the bill and the face value at maturity—called a discount check—is sent to you shortly after the issue date.

Q. How can I redeem maturing bills?

A. Four to six weeks after you purchase a bill, a statement of accounts will be mailed to you. This lets you know that the Treasury has established an account in your name. When your bill matures, you automatically receive a check from the Government for the full amount of the bill.

NEW, LOW-RISK WAYS TO EARN MONEY ON YOUR NEST-EGG DOLLARS

There are plenty of wealth-building opportunities besides stocks, bonds, and regular Government issues. Some that are gaining in popularity are money market funds, Certificates of Deposit, ''Ginnie Maes'' and HUD Notes. One common feature to all: A good deal of safety for your nest egg dollars.

Money Market Funds

If you are still keeping most of your money in a savings account, you are losing money. There is an alternative for even the most conservative investors: Money market funds.

What are money market funds? They're akin to mutual funds—you deposit your money with the fund and let the fund's management do the investing for you (they spread the risk around through a number of money market securities). More than anything else, money market funds offer—

▶ **LIQUIDITY:** You can usually write an unlimited amount of checks on your money market balance with no charge involved. The only restriction is that each check must be for a minimum amount (as low as $100). You continue to earn interest on the amount withdrawn until the check clears.

Result: Money market funds give you flexibility other investments—for example, six-month CDs—don't have. You have access to your money and can earn interest at rates comparable to CDs.

For small investors: The initial amount required to invest in a money market fund is generally only $500. And some funds now allow you to make subsequent deposits of as little as $50.

Q. Are there any drawbacks to money market funds?
A. Yes. Unlike your savings account, money market funds are not federally insured. You can overcome this by using a money-market fund that invests 100% in Federal obligations (i.e. Treasury bills, notes and bonds), or a fund that purchases insurance for its shareholders. Finally, you can put your nest-egg cash in a bank money market fund. In response to the popularity of money market funds, the banking industry has come out with its own version of the money market funds. The big selling point: The funds combine high rates with—

▶ **GOVERNMENT INSURANCE:** The bank money market funds pay rates comparable to regular funds and depositors are also covered by federal insurance (up to $100,000 per account). That appeals to investors who like the security of savings accounts and the convenience of dealing with their local bank.

How it works: You have to make a minimum deposit of at least $2,500. As long as you keep your account balance above $2,500, you earn the high interest rate that the bank offers. But if your account drops below $2,500, you earn interest at only the passbook rate (and you may also have to pay a service charge). The banks generally permit you to write up to three checks on your account balance. So you do have liquidity, though not quite as much as the regular money markets.

Convenience: You may find it a lot easier dealing with your local bank than a money market fund located in a distant city. Many banks also allow you to transfer funds automatically to and from other accounts. Other services may be available—for example, cash may be withdrawn from your money market account through a money access center.

▶ **SHOP AROUND:** Take a long look at the services and the interest rate available from a number of banks—not just the ones where you already have accounts. You may be better off going to a bank you have never dealt with before.

HOW TO LOCK IN PROFITS WITH A CERTIFICATE OF DEPOSIT

Bank Certificates of Deposit (CDs) come in all shapes and sizes. For example, some CDs have maturity dates as long as six years; others are as short as seven days ("six-month" CDs—actually, 182 days—are the most popular). Some pay interest from the date of deposit; others pay interest only at maturity.

▶ **PICK AND CHOOSE:** You'll have to find out what kind of CDs your bank offers. Most banks don't carry all the different kinds; almost all have six-month CDs. If you can't find what you want—say, you want a longer or shorter maturity—take your business to a different bank.

Why invest in CDs at all? Generally, they offer three things: (1) a fixed rate over a period of time, (2) a higher interest rate than the passbook rate, and (3) the benefit of federal insurance. In other words with a CD, you lock in your profit—when you buy the CD.

In addition, six-month Certificates of Deposit have recently become more popular with small investors. Why? Because of—

▶ **LOW MINIMUM DEPOSIT REQUIREMENTS:** Previously, the minimum amount required to purchase a six-month CD was $10,000. Now banks are offering them for as little as $2,500.

Warning: If you withdraw your money from a CD before the maturity date, there is a substantial interest penalty.

Buying the 'Right Kind' of CD Can Make a Big Tax Difference

If you purchase a Certificate of Deposit that matures in one year or less, it may make a big difference what kind of CD you buy.

Here's why: Interest on the certificate doesn't become taxable until it's credited to your account. If you can't withdraw the interest until the certificate matures—or you can't withdraw it without incurring a substantial penalty—you owe no tax on the interest until maturity.

>   ***Example:*** A six-month CD purchased less than six months (actually, 182 days) before the end of the year gives you—

>   ▶ **TAX DEFERRAL:** The Certificate matures next year. So, as long as you can't make penalty-free withdrawals of interest prior to maturity, the interest won't be taxed to you until you file your next year's return. This means that you—instead of the Government—have an extra year's use of your tax dollars.

On the other hand, if you buy a CD that is credited, say, monthly, you would have to pay tax on all the interest credited to your account this year.

HOW TO EARN HIGH INTEREST FROM A SPECIAL TYPE OF BOND INVESTMENT

When you hear the name "Ginnie Mae", it may conjure up an image of home-style cooking, rather than high-finance. Well, bonds backed by Ginnie Mae (the Government National Mortgage Association) may be just the right recipe for your needs.

>   ▶ **TWO KEY INGREDIENTS:** (1) Ginnie Mae bonds generally pay a higher yield than other bonds. (2) They are backed by the full faith and credit of the United States Government.

How it works: To raise cash, a bank sells a group of its home mortgages to Ginnie Mae. Ginnie Mae sells a bond backed by a pool of these mortgages to you. As payments are made on the individual home mortgages, they are turned over to Ginnie Mae by the original lender. Ginnie Mae then makes payments to you and other bond-holders.

Besides being backed by the U.S. Government—as opposed to say, corporate bonds—Ginnie Mae bonds have a lot more going for them. For instance:

• Many bonds can be called back by the corporation that issues them in as little as five years. Ginnie Maes are generally guaranteed to last for 10 to 12 years.

• With a corporate bond, you have to wait until the bond matures to have the principal returned to you. No so with Ginnie Maes. You receive a monthly check for interest *and* principal. *Reason:* You are investing in mortgages which are being paid off monthly.

Ginnie Maes are sold in amounts of $25,000 and up. That's pretty steep for the average person. However, if you keep your eyes open, you may be able to—

▶ **CUT THE MINIMUM:** Many of the top brokerage firms offer Ginnie Mae certificates through a trust. (In essence, you share a bond with other people.) The usual asking price: $10,000.

How Some Government-Backed Bonds Can Pay Off In Tax-Free Income

There is a bond that combines the features of municipal and Federal bonds: tax-free income and top safety.

▶ **BASIC FACTS:** State and local housing authorities issue notes (called Project Notes) under the auspices of the U.S. Department of Housing and Urban Development (HUD). Project Notes get the same tax breaks as municipal bonds and are as secure as U.S. Government notes and bonds.

HUD Project Notes are short-term obligations. Maturities range from ninety days to one year. In effect, they are short-term municipals backed by the full faith and credit of the U.S. Government. They are issued to underwriters, who in turn sell to the public.

Tax-free income: Suppose a HUD Project Note carries an interest rate (figured on an annual basis) of 5.4%. That may not sound impressive, but don't forget, this is an after-tax yield. That interest is entirely free of Federal income tax. So a taxpayer in the 50% tax bracket would have to earn a taxable return (on a corporate bond, for instance) of 10.8% to do as well. To top it all off, you may also get a—

▶ **STATE AND LOCAL TAX BREAK:** Project Notes are usually free of taxes imposed by the state (and localities within the state) in which the housing authority is located. So if you buy notes issued by an agency in your state, the interest is exempt from state and local taxes, as well as Federal taxes. What's more, interest on Project Notes issued by agencies in Puerto Rico, the U.S. Virgin Islands or Guam is exempt from the taxes of *any* state or locality, as well as the Federal government.

Guaranteed safety: HUD Project Notes are the binding obligation of the housing authority that issues them. But beyond that, they are guaranteed by the Federal government. If for any reason the local agency can't pay, even if the project goes completely bust, HUD will pay off the note in full—principal and tax-free interest.

▶ **INVESTMENT FACTS:** At issue, Project Notes have a minimum purchase price of $1,000. There is a well-organized secondary market if you want to sell before maturity. (As with other bonds, a Project Note's value depends on fluctuating interest rates.) You can buy HUD Project Notes at leading brokerage houses and commercial banks.

Chapter 4

Today's Top Tax Sheltered Investments

There are many investments that can provide you with tax shelter. For example, municipal bonds pay tax-free interest. This Chapter, however, explains true tax shelters—complex, leveraged investments that can offer the—

▶ **BEST OF BOTH WORLDS:** If everything works out right, the ideal tax shelter can give you (1) an immediate tax loss to shelter your income from tax and (2) the potential for tax-sheltered income later on. And since these investments are heavily leveraged, the return on your actual cash investment can be quite substantial—*if* the deal ends up making money.

Before we go any further, however, let's get one point across: many tax shelters involve a great deal of risk. So whether tax shelters suit you depends on your total tax and financial situation, as well as your personal attitude toward investments and risk taking.

▶ **RULE OF THUMB:** Only investors of high net worth should consider tax shelters. To begin with, most shelters require a substantial cash investment. And since a tax loss really benefits only investors in high tax brackets, only they should take the risk that's part and parcel to investing in a tax shelter. Lower-bracket investors should stick to safer investments, such as insured money market bank accounts, or mutual funds.

If you are going to put money into shelters, proceed with caution. The investment must make economic sense apart from tax savings. If it doesn't, you may lose not only your money but also the tax breaks you had counted on. You must check out every aspect of a deal with a financial adviser, accountant or lawyer before you invest one penny. You must understand the investment and trust the people behind the investment.

This chapter will first take a look at how tax shelters work in general, and the kind of tax breaks a typical shelter can offer. Then we'll examine some of the shelters available today, with emphasis on what to look for in each type of investment.

HOW THE TAX LAW PROVIDES THE FUEL TO MAKE TAX-SHELTERED INVESTMENTS WORK

The "ideal" tax-sheltered investment offers you three separate and distinct advantages: (1) big initial writeoffs, (2) tax-sheltered income, and (3) conversion of ordinary income to capital gain. Here's how each tax advantage works and which tax law provisions make the breaks possible.

Big initial writeoffs: The name of the game is to crowd as many deductions as possible into the early years of the investment when the income is typically low or non-existent. Where deductions exceed income, there's a tax loss. The tax loss in turn shelters the investor's income from other sources (salary and other investments). The tax otherwise payable on that income is deferred until some future time. In effect, the investor gets an interest-free loan from the Government to the extent of the tax dollars saved. The longer the period of deferral, the better.

> **Simplified example:** Mr. Arnold is a high-income executive whose top dollars are taxed at the 50% rate. Let's suppose he has $20,000 of income to spare. With no shelter, Arnold will pay $10,000 in tax on that income (50%) and be left with a $10,000 net. Instead, Mr. Arnold takes the $20,000 and invests it in a limited partnership set up to build and operate an office building.

The building is completed and ready for occupancy in December of this year. There's no rental income for the year, but there are a lot of deductions. The result is a tax loss. Suppose Mr. Arnold's share of the tax loss comes to $40,000.

Result: The $40,000 loss shelters an equal amount of Arnold's income from tax (the $20,000 he put into the deal plus $20,000 more). So he saves—actually defers—$20,000 of tax on that $40,000 of income. Put another way, Arnold still has that $20,000 of income he started with—undiluted by taxes—and that money can be used as Arnold sees fit. In tax shelter parlance, Mr. Arnold is said to have received a "multiple writeoff"—a loss in excess of his cash investment in the deal.

Source of multiple writeoffs: The tax law contains many tax breaks that generate big initial tax writeoffs. Some of the tax breaks apply to all tax shelters in general (as well as businesses and other investments), while other tax breaks are for specific shelters.

- *Depreciation deductions:* In theory, assets used in an investment (buildings, machinery, equipment, trucks, etc.) become obsolete with the passage of time or wear out with use. So the tax law allows the investor to deduct the cost of the assets over a period of years. You are entitled to these deductions even though the assets may actually increase in value over the years.

- *Investment credit:* The investment credit is a dollar-for-dollar reduction in your tax bill and is claimed in the year assets are placed in service. A credit is worth much more than a deduction. For example, a $2,000 credit is worth $4,000 in deductions to a taxpayer in the 50% tax bracket. The investment credit is 6% of the cost of three-year ACRS property (e.g., cars); 10% of the cost of five-year property (machinery and equipment).

- *Intangible drilling costs:* These costs, better known as IDCs, can frequently be a major portion of the cost of a drilling operation. It is the IDC deduction that gives oil and gas investors large first-year writeoffs.

Tax-sheltered income: When a tax shelter investor starts seeing a return on his or her investment, some or all of that return may be tax-free. *Reason:* The investor may be entitled to one or more of the following three tax breaks: (1) depreciation deductions, (2) interest deductions, and (3) depletion. (Depletion is the special tax break for investors in mineral tax shelters. You can deduct a yearly allowance for depleting—literally using up—the investment's mineral reserves.)

Capital gain conversion: When the investment's assets are sold, the investor may be entitled to favorable tax treatment on the profits. If the assets have been held for more than one year at the time of the sale, all or part of the profit is treated as tax-sheltered long-term capital gain.

Result: Only 40% of the profit is subject to tax. (On the other hand, 100% of ordinary income is subject to tax.) In effect, the investor may be able to convert—

▶ **ORDINARY INCOME INTO CAPITAL GAIN:** The tax shelter writeoffs he's enjoyed over the life of the investment have sheltered ordinary income. These writeoffs lower the investor's basis in the asset, which increases the investor's capital gain on the sale. So the investor is paying tax at capital gain rates rather than at ordinary income rates.

Some of the profit from the sale of an investment asset, however, may be ordinary income and not capital gain. *Reason:* The tax law "recaptures" some of the profit and turns it into ordinary income to the extent of certain tax-shelter deductions claimed by the investor (e.g. ACRS deductions claimed on cattle).

▶ **HOW TO CONTINUE TAX DEFERRAL:** Once a shelter begins to "burn out"—income starts to exceed the tax writeoffs—the investor can put the income from the deal in a new tax shelter. *Result:* New big tax breaks that produce a tax loss that provides further tax deferral.

How Leverage Helps Create Multiple Writeoffs

In the general business world, leverage is desirable because it allows you to make money using other people's money. In tax shelters, leverage gives you another bonus; it multiplies deductions and gives you a shot at getting big writeoffs. Example: Tax deductions are based on your "basis" in a purchased asset. Generally, that's your acquisition cost—including funds borrowed to buy the investment—not just the cash you sink into the deal.

Suppose you buy $10,000 of depreciable assets for cash. Your depreciation deductions are based on $10,000. If you buy $100,000 of assets with $90,000 in borrowed funds and $10,000 cash of your own, your depreciation deductions are based on $100,000.

In the old days, this tax rule led to a great deal of abuse. Tax shelter deals were often financed with what are called non-recourse notes. (The borrower is not personally liable for the debt; the lender can only look to the investment assets for repayment.) Since the investor-borrower did not have to worry about repaying the note, investment assets were often over-valued. For example, an asset worth $20,000 would be purchased for $100,000 ($80,000 in non-recourse notes plus $20,000 cash). Result: Tax shelter deals were structured to yield tremendous tax writeoffs—$5 or $10 of tax writeoff for every dollar put up by the investor. But recent tax changes put an end to most of these deals.

▶ **NEW TAX RULES:** The amount of loss from your tax shelter investment that is currently deductible is limited to your "at-risk" amount. Under the tax law, your at-risk amount consists of: (1) the cash you put up; plus (2) the adjusted basis of property you contribute to the deal; plus (3) promissory notes that you are personally liable to repay (so-called recourse notes). Big exception: Real estate is exempt from the at-risk rules. A real estate deal can still be financed with non-recourse notes.

NOTE: The investment credit that can be claimed on the machinery and equipment used in a shelter is also based on your at-risk amount. Exception: The at-risk rules are not applied for investment credit purposes if you get a non-recourse loan from a bank and put up cash for at least 20% of the property's cost.

Important: The at-risk tax rules are extremely complicated and contain many unpleasant surprises for the unwary investor. For example, you may not be considered at risk even though you are personally liable for the note. If you borrow money from a relative and sign a note on which you are personally liable, the tax law says you are not at risk for the loan.

▶ **LEVERAGE REMAINS VALUABLE:** Despite the tax law changes, leverage is still an important ingredient to any tax shelter. And being personally liable on a note does not mean you will have to put another penny into the investment. A successful tax shelter should generate enough income to pay off the note.

WHY A LIMITED PARTNERSHIP IS THE MOST COMMON TAX SHELTER INVESTMENT VEHICLE

The typical investment vehicle for tax shelter deals is the limited partnership. *Reason:* A limited partnership offers a tax shelter investor this—

▶ **DOUBLE BENEFIT:** The investor can enjoy significant tax breaks with the protection of limited liability.

How a limited partnership works: The promoter of the tax shelter deal is named the general partner. He has all management control and full discretionary powers over the investment. The general partner can be held personally liable for all partnership debts. On the other hand, the investors are limited partners. They put up the money, but they cannot take part in the operation of the investment. Limited partners can, however, inspect the books to make sure the general partner is not violating the partnership agreement.

Limited liability: By very definition, limited partners are not personally liable for debts or claims against the partnership. Thus, if the investment goes sour, all the individual limited partner can lose is the amount he has contributed or has agreed to contribute—no matter how large the investment, or how highly leveraged the deal is.

With a limited partnership, you have the opportunity to own a share of a single, large-scale investment that can be potentially more profitable than a small-scale investment. Couldn't you get the same benefit in a corporation? Sure, but you'd lose the major tax advantage that a partnership offers.

▶ **NO DOUBLE TAXATION:** The partnership is merely a conduit for tax purposes. It does not pay tax. So partnership income passes through directly to the partners, who then take their distributive share on their personal income tax returns.

In addition, partnership losses, deductions and credits also pass through directly to the partners, who can use them to offset or shelter both partnership and nonpartnership income. (With a corporation, on the other hand, income is taxed first to the corporation and then to the shareholder. And the corporation, not the shareholders, claims deductions, credits and losses.)

Private or public partnerships? A private placement must be limited to fewer than 35 investors. And, as you would guess, the deal is private—between you, the promoter and the other investors. The advantage of a private placement is that it may be tailored more closely to your needs; the disadvantage is that these deals are open to abuse by promoters.

A public placement, on the other hand, is for 35 or more investors. A public placement must be registered with the Securities and Exchanges Commission, which makes sure the prospectus contains all the factors (positive and negative) that could affect the success of the investment. That does not mean that a public deal is better than a private deal; it just means that all the pertinent facts must be disclosed to you. A public deal will have more money to invest in the project; but the project may not necessarily be tailored to your financial picture.

How to Protect Yourself When You Buy Into A Limited Partnership

The limited partnership may be the best investment vehicle for tax shelter deals, but you pay a price: As a limited partner, you are specifically prohibited from participating in the management of the investment. That makes it imperative that you not put one penny into a tax shelter until you—

▶ **CHECK OUT THE DEAL THOROUGHLY:** You must sit down with your advisers (your financial planner, accountant, lawyer, etc.) and study both the investment itself and the people behind it. If the investment is not properly set up and not properly run, you can lose both your money and your tax breaks.

There are, of course, different questions that must be asked depending on the investment involved (oil and gas, coal, cattle, timber), and we'll get into the details later on. But there are certain basic inquiries that should be made of any tax-sheltered investment.

▶ **STARTING POINT:** Every investment has a basic source of information regarding the deal. In a public tax shelter it is the prospectus; in the privately offered shelter it is the offering memorandum. Read this information very carefully, and check to see if it satisfactorily answers the following questions:

- What is the cost of the investment?
- How many investors will there be?
- What is your cost? How much of that cost is to be in cash up front and how much of a note do you have to give?
- What are the tax benefits involved? Have these tax breaks been verified by an independent tax attorney or accounting firm?
- What is the projected rate of return? When will the investment begin to show a profit?

If the prospectus does not have all the answers to these questions (and any others you may have) go right to the promoter and get the answers from him.

The general partner: This is the person who is in charge of running the investment. As a limited partner, you are forbidden from making management decisions. So the investment's success or failure really rests on his shoulders. Even a great investment will fail if the general partner just cannot cut it.

Here's a rundown of some important questions you should ask of the general partner:

- What experience does the general partner have in this type of investment?
- What is his track record in this investment and other types of investments?
- What is his credit rating? Be sure to check this out closely, since he can be held liable for partnership debts.
- How much money does the general partner have in the deal?
- What fees are to be paid to the general partner?
- What other investments is he currently running? Check to be sure there is no conflict of interest.

HOW THE RIGHT REAL ESTATE DEAL CAN OFFER A GOOD RETURN—AND TOP TAX SHELTER

In the previous Chapter, we dealt with real estate investments that require active investor participation. But many investors do not want to worry about running a real estate property; they would prefer to be armchair investors and leave the management problems to someone else. If that's your preference, you may want to invest in a real estate limited partnership. A successfully run real estate syndicate offers not only profits, but also—

> ▶ **BIG TAX SHELTER:** Unlike all other tax shelters, real estate is not subject to the at-risk rules. So a deal financed with a non-recourse loan (the lender can look only to the property in case of default or foreclosure) can offer you writeoffs in excess of your cash investment. **Important:** The loan must be non-recourse to all partners (including the general partner) and the partnership, or your writeoffs are limited to your cash contribution.

There are many types of real estate deals—new multifamily residential, existing multifamily residential, commercial and industrial, government-assisted housing, rehabilitation projects and even raw land. Each type of investment offers different risks and rewards. A new multifamily residential investment, for example, can offer good tax benefits, potentially good cash flow and appreciation, but the risk is fairly high. Net-leased commercial property, on the other hand, is a lot safer but offers low income initially and high tax benefit.

Here's a look at how some of the more popular types of real estate shelters can go to work for you.

How a Sale-Leaseback Deal Can Offer Pure Writeoff Up Front, With a Chance at Big Profits Later On

Let's say a corporation wants a new retail outlet built to its specifications but does not want to tie up its capital. It buys land for $200,000, and, in 1984, builds a $2,000,000 building and then sells the land and building at cost to a group of investors organized as a limited partnership. The partnership pays $400,000 and gets a 25-year mortgage for the $1,800,000 balance of the purchase price.

The partnership then leases back the property to the corporation for a period of 25 years. The corporation has the right to renew the lease and the right to repurchase the property at specified intervals. The lease is a net lease. In other words, the corporate tenant pays all the operating costs of the building. The net lease payments are large enough to cover the partnership's mortgage payments and supply a small return to the investors.

However, because the partnership owns the property, it is entitled to depreciation deductions from the building. The deductions are usually substantially greater than the taxable cash flow from the property.

▶ **TAX PAYOFF:** Valuable tax writeoffs for the investors. For example, using the straight line method over the 15-year ACRS recovery period, the partnership would have $1,333,333 in depreciation deductions over the first ten years.

These and other deductions can be offset against the investors' other taxable income to the extent they exceed the income from the building. Thus the sale and net leaseback can result in a top after-tax return to the high-bracket investors.

NOTE: The Goverment is quick to challenge sale leaseback deals that provide big tax shelter, but very little in the way of current cash flow. Fortunately, the Courts have taken a liberal view of these deals, and have approved transactions that offer big tax savings now, with the possibility of economic profits years down the road. In fact, the U.S. Supreme Court okayed a sale leaseback that allowed a taxpayer to save $1,500,000 in taxes over ten years [Lyon, 41 AFTR2d 78-1142].

How a Shopping Center Deal May Ring Up Tax-Sheltered Profits

An attractive real estate investment these days is the shopping center. A properly located and properly managed shopping center can offer big tax writeoffs up front and tax-sheltered income later on.

Most shopping centers are designed either as "strip centers" (those rows of stores that line thoroughfares) or shopping "malls." There are three main types of shopping centers.

- The neighborhood center: The chief tenant of a neighorhood center is usually a supermarket, with such stores as a liquor store, laundry and barber shop also commonly included.
- The community center: Its prime shopper attraction is usually a department store or a variety store. In addition to the stores listed for the neighborhood center, a community center may include more service and specialty stores.
- The regional center: Two department stores are common at either end of a regional center. You can also expect to find tenants such as movie theatres, bowling alleys and restaurants.

▶ **STARTING POINT:** No matter what size or shape of shopping center you're considering, its location is critical. The surrounding population must be sufficient to support the center, and the area shouldn't be saturated with other shopping centers. The center must be easily accessible and feed to or front on major traffic arteries.

Tenants: Every successful shopping center must have a "draw"—an anchor store (such as a major department store). An anchor usually demands and gets a long-term lease at a relatively low per-square-foot rate. (It's not uncommon to have an overage rent clause, which allows you to collect more rent if a specified sales volume is reached.)

Rule of Thumb: The rent from the anchor store and the national chain stores should cover your mortgage debt. Your profit comes from the local stores that fill out the shopping center. You give these stores shorter leases, so you can raise the rents fairly frequently. Most shopping center leases call for the tenants to pay most maintenance costs, common area costs, insurance, increases in property taxes, etc.

How to get shelter from shopping centers: If your limited partnership picks the right shopping center and the right management team to run it, here's how a shopping center shelter can pay off.

> **Example:** XYZ Limited Partnership buys a $2 million shopping center by putting down $200,000 and financing the remainder. (The underlying land is leased from its owner.) Mr. White is a limited partner and owns a 10% interest in XYZ (for which he had to put up $20,000 cash).

As the monthly income comes in from the shopping center tenants, XYZ uses almost all of it to fulfill its obligations. XYZ makes payments on the mortgage. In the early years, almost the entire payment is deductible interest. XYZ also sends a check (also deductible) to a management firm that oversees the day-to-day operations of the shopping center, and also pays monthly rent to the land owner. In the early years, after paying all cash expenses, XYZ has little or no income left over for its investors. But it does provide them with—

> ▶ **BIG TAX SHELTER:** Using straight-line depreciation and the ACRS 15-year writeoff period, XYZ's shopping center throws off an annual depreciation deduction of $133,333. White's share of this deduction is $13,333. In White's 50% tax bracket, the writeoff saves him $6,666 in tax dollars. Over a period of five years, there would be $66,667 in writeoff worth $33,333 to White. So he not only recovers his $20,000. but he is actually $13,333 ahead of the game.

This doesn't mean that White has writeoffs every year—and has no taxable income. Many shopping center leases have rent escalators (based on increased sales, or a price index such as the CPI). To the extent that increased rent from tenants outpaces cash expesense, White will have cash income.

HOW OIL AND GAS VENTURES OFFER TAX SHELTER WRITEOFFS AND TAX-SHELTERED INCOME

There are two basic ways to make money on the country's need for oil and gas.
(1) You can invest in an oil income program—the partnership acquires properties that are already producing oil. You don't get up-front tax benefits. But hopefully, you will have a steady stream of partially tax-sheltered income.
(2) You can invest in a drilling operation in the hopes of discovering oil and gas. The risk is high, but so is the profit potential—if you find oil or gas. And, the tax shelter opportunities are much more attractive. That's why we're concentrating on—

How to Invest in Oil and Gas Drilling Operations

There are two types of drilling operations—exploratory and developmental. An exploratory (or wildcat) operation is a search for new oil fields. Only about one in ten exploratory wells ever produce, so it is obviously a very risky venture. A developmental program consists of drilling in previously proven oil fields. Your chances of hitting oil in developmental drilling are pretty good, but that does not mean the drilling will be profitable.

Key Investment Strategy: Spread the risk. The best type of drilling program combines both developmental and exploratory drilling. Developmental drilling can provide you with income, while exploratory drilling may provide you with the big strike.

Another tip: Look for deals that two or three other oil companies are also investing in. This immediately improves the odds in your favor. It doesn't guarantee that you'll hit it big, but it does increase the odds for your success.

How To Look For a Good Deal: Oil and gas is extremely risky and you stand to lose a substantial amount of money. So you must get satisfactory responses on all the following:

- *The people involved in the operation:* If the geologists, drillers and operators aren't experienced oil and gas professionals, your investment could well be in big trouble. Don't judge the oil professionals strictly by their past performance in finding oil. Success or failure is not measured by the percentage of previous completed and producing wells. Rather, it is measured by the amount of money the investors in those deals actually pocketed, and how long it took before they saw that money.

- *How the deal is structured:* You want things set up so that the people running the program make their money from the discovery of oil and gas. You don't want them to make money right off the top—from the cash you and the other investors put up. Sure, you have to expect that certain costs will come off the top—they have to. But the trick is to get as many dollars as possible into the search for oil.

- *Investment Strategy:* Look for oil and gas deals where the investors pay the cost of finding the oil and the sponsor pays the cost of completing the well. That way, the investors are entitled to big first-year tax writeoffs. And the investors split the income with the sponsor based on how much money each put up.

Let's look at an example. Suppose investors put up $120,000 for two wells. The deal should be set up so that they get a 100% deduction for the intangible drilling costs. Then when the sponsor decides that the wells will be an economic success, he or she puts up the money needed to complete them. That would cost something around $80,000 for the two wells in our example. Since this splits the total costs in a 60-40 ratio—the payout is split exactly the same way: The investors get 60% of the production; the sponsor gets 40%.

▶ **CAUTION:** Stay away from deals where the sponsor gets a percentage of the gross income from the well. Otherwise, the sponsor can pocket a pretty penny even though the investors don't see a nickel out of the well.

Assessment procedures: Many times, the sponsor will need extra money to continue the project. (Drilling may go slower than expected, or the well may cave in.) The sponsor may have the right to turn to the investor-limited partners for the needed money. It is usually in the investors best interests to come up with the money. Otherwise the sponsor may "farm out" the project—bring in other investors to help finance the project. They, in turn, are entitled to a cut of the action.

▶ **INVESTMENT SUGGESTION:** You don't want to be forced into throwing good money after bad. So look for a deal where the assessments are voluntary and a failure to pay the assessment only results in a dilution of your cut of the profits. (Some deals hit investors with severe penalties for not paying the assessment—for example, the loss of the right to participate in revenues.)

Liquidity: You don't want to be stuck with your oil interest forever. Most deals allow you to cash in after three years. But you must be very careful to value your interest properly for sale purposes. The value of your interest includes the deal's proven reserves in addition to what has already been tapped. Be sure the future net worth of these reserves are properly figured.

Once you and your advisers have found an oil and gas deal that shows promise as a money-maker, your next step is to see—

How an Oil and Gas Deal Can Give You Big Tax Writeoffs

One of the principal tax shelter benefits from investing in oil and gas is the large first-year writeoff. Intangible drilling costs, which are deductible when paid, are the main source of the writeoff. These are costs that go into the drilling of an oil or gas well but do not create assets having salvage value after the well is completed. Intangible drilling costs include the fuel, wages, repairs, hauling and supplies used in (1) ground clearing prior to drilling and in the drilling of wells, and (2) in the construction of derricks, tanks, pipelines, and other structures and equipment necessary for drilling. Since these costs are often incurred before the well produces income, an investor usually has a substantial tax loss in the initial year of his investment.

The limited partnership you invest in can earmark part or all of your investment to expenditures for intangible drilling costs (if the principal purpose of the allocation is not tax avoidance). This allows you and the other limited partners to gain the maximum benefit from the writeoff for intangible drilling costs.

If you invest in an oil and gas partnership, you usually make your investment in cash. However, some partnerships leverage the investment. You put up, for example, 20% to 30% of your investment in cash the first year and sign a recourse note (a note on which you are personally liable) for the rest, payable over the next few years. In the all-cash situation, you might expect a first-year tax loss writeoff equal to 60% or 80% of the cash you put up. But in the part-cash, part-note situation, you can expect a first-year writeoff in excess of the 20% to 30% cash you put up.

> **Example:** Mr. Smith buys into a limited partnership that will drill for oil in Texas and Oklahoma. The partnership wants to raise $2,000,000, and the minimum cost to participate per investor is $100,000. Smith pays $25,000 in cash when he agrees to invest and signs a $75,000 promissory note.

To get the cash it needs for drilling, the partnership takes out a loan from a bank secured by the investors' promissory notes. Each investor pays the partnership the balance of his note over a five-year period.

Tax Shelter Result: In a typical arrangement, Smith might get a first-year tax loss writeoff of $37,500. Thus, Smith's writeoff would exceed his first-year cash outlay by $12,500.

How Oil and Gas Deals Yield Tax-Sheltered Income

A large portion of an investor's profits from a successful oil and gas investment (whether it's an oil-income or drilling program) is sheltered from tax. The tax shelter is derived primarily from (1) depletion, (2) depreciation deductions, and (3) long-term capital gain on the sale of the investment.

(1) Depletion: You get a deduction for the depletion of your oil reserves. Your deduction is computed either under the cost depletion method or the percentage depletion method. You must use cost depletion if you drill in a "proven area." For drilling in other than proven areas, either cost or percentage depletion may be used. But you must use whichever method benefits you the most each year.

With cost depletion, your deduction for any given year depends on how much of the potential oil reserves are recovered in that year. Your deduction is computed in two steps: (1) You divide your adjusted basis in the reserves by the estimated number of barrels remaining to be produced, and (2) then multiply that figure by the year's production. When you've recovered all your basis in the well, cost depletion stops.

Percentage depletion allows you to recover your cost of the well by deducting a percentage of your gross income from the well each and every year. This percentage is 15% for 1984 and beyond.

The percentage depletion deduction cannot exceed the lesser of (1) 50% of the taxable income (gross income less allowable deductions other than depletion) from the oil or gas property, or (2) 65% of the investor's taxable income. You can continue to deduct percentage depletion as long as the well continues to produce income and even after you have fully recovered your cost basis. (Note: To the extent your percentage depletion deduction exceeds the adjusted basis of the property, it's treated as a "tax preference" subject to the alternative minimum tax).

There are limits on the amount of oil and gas on which an investor can take percentage depletion. The average daily production limits are 1,000 barrels of oil and 6 million cubic feet of gas. In practice, these limits are very liberal and apply to few tax-shelter investors.

> ▶ **EVEN BETTER:** This daily production limit applies separately to each investor in a partnership, not to each property or each partnership. If, for example, you own a one-tenth interest in a partnership, and the partnership properties have an average daily production of 10,000 barrels, you would suffer no loss in your depletion deduction.

(2) Depreciation: A large part of the tangible costs of the wells goes toward salvageable assets, e.g., derricks, tanks and the like. Such assets can be written off under the Accelerated Cost Recovery System over a very short period of time (usually, five years).

(3) Long-term capital gain: Ordinary income deductions for intangible drilling costs, depletion, and depreciation reduce a partnership's basis in the property (and the investor's basis in his or her partnership interest). This, of course, increases the potential for gain on the sale of the property (or the sale of the investor's partnership interest). But, assuming the one-year holding period requirement is met, this gain is generally taxed as long-term capital gain.

There are two exceptions to this favorable capital gain treatment. The first is that the gain is taxed as ordinary income to the extent of prior depreciation under the usual recapture-of-depreciation rule. The second is a recapture of the gain attributable to the election to deduct intangible drilling costs. The amount subject to recapture is the total amount of the IDC deduction reduced by the amount which would have been deductible had the intangible costs been capitalized and recovered through cost depletion. However, the amount recaptured can't exceed the gain realized or, if no gain was realized, the excess of the transferred property's fair market value over its adjusted basis.

HOW A GOLD DEAL CAN PAY OFF IN PROFITS AND TAX BENEFITS

Gold, a speculative investment, has attracted a lot of investor attention in the past few years. Most people interested in this commodity buy bullion, gold coins, or gold shares (see Chapter Five) and wait for the price of the metal to go up. Naturally, your profit potential would be greater if you acquired gold right from the ground. And that's exactly what you may accomplish by investing in a gold-mining partnership.

How the partnership works: You and other investors buy into a limited partnership. Your potential loss is limited to your investment; the general partner has the gold mining expertise. The partnership owns the mining rights to property with good gold prospects. What you invest goes for start-up costs. Assuming the venture is successful, the partnership agreement requires the partnership to sell off enough gold to pay future mining expenses. The rest of the gold is divided between the investors and the mining contractor (the general partner).

▶ **POTENTIAL PAYOFF:** If things go as planned (and that's always a big "if" in mining ventures), you get a steady stream of gold from the mine. Your only out-of-pocket cost is your initial investment in the partnership.

Result: You can sell your gold immediately (the partnership puts you in touch with a sales agent) and take down your profit. Or you can take a chance and hold on to the gold as a long-term investment (the partnership can also arrange for storage) and gamble on an even bigger profit.

Tax benefits: The tax treatment of the gold the partnership sells is different from tax treatment of the gold that's distributed to the investors. The profit from the gold that's sold is currently taxable, but there may actually be no profit for tax purposes. The partnership shelters the taxable income by subtracting deductions for mining expenses, equipment depreciation and a—

▶ **DEPLETION ALLOWANCE:** There are two ways to figure the depletion allowance for gold. The partnership uses the one that gives you and the other investors the lowest tax.

(1) Percentage depletion: Gold is entitled to a percentage depletion allowance of 15%. This means that 15% of the partnership's gross income from the mine can be deducted each year. And this goes on for as long as the mine continues to produce.

(2) Cost depletion: This allows the partnership to recover its tax basis in the mine (its tax basis is the cost of acquiring the mining rights) as the gold is mined. When the basis is recovered, cost depletion stops.

Key tax angle: There is no current tax on the gold that's distributed to you and the other investors. The partnership's profit on this gold is—

▶ **TAX DEFERRED:** You don't pay any tax on the gold you receive until you sell it. Then you pay tax on the difference between the sales price for the gold and the partnership's tax basis for it.

How is this income taxed? Under a special tax rule, your gold is treated like inventory if you sell it within five years. So, even though you're holding it strictly for investment purposes, the income is taxed as ordinary income. If you sell after five years, the income is treated like income from the sale of other investment property— it's tax-sheltered long-term capital gain.

▶ **CAUTION:** Gold mining is a high-risk enterprise. Unlike other forms of gold investing, you have nothing to show for your money if the venture doesn't pan out. So expert advice is a must, especially for the novice investor.

INVESTING IN CABLE TV AND GETTING TAX WRITEOFFS: IS IT FOR YOU?

Cable TV (CATV) is a growth industry. Industry analysts expect the number of CATV subscribers to increase to 35 million by 1985 and perhaps double that by 1990. What's more, you can pick up tax shelter if you invest in cable.

▶ **TAX-SHELTERED INVESTMENT IN CATV:** You invest in a limited partnership that acquires existing CATV systems. Through a combination of various tax breaks, you can recover a large portion of your investment through tax savings. Net effect: You get a chance to participate in the CATV boom—at a very low after-tax cost.

You may be a subscriber to a CATV system yourself. But, for the uninitiated, here's a quick capsule of—

How CATV works: The programs shown on a CATV system may originate in the system's own studios or they may come to the system through a coded signal received from a satellite transmission. In any case, the programs are then sent out to subscribers through a coaxial cable rather than over the air. The cable typically carries as many as 70 different channels and may have the ability to carry signals both *to* and *from* the subscriber's TV set. For the cable hookup, the subscriber pays the cable system a monthly charge (usually a basic fee plus additional fees for optional "premium" channels).

How to invest: You buy into a limited partnership that buys one or more existing CATV systems, financing part of the purchase price. The systems are operated for the partnership by CATV professionals. The revenues from CATV subscriptions may allow the partnership to make periodic cash distributions to the partners. But the partnership's primary goals will probably be (1) appreciation in the value of the systems, looking toward future sales, and (2)—

▶ **TAX SHELTER BENEFITS:** The partnership will operate at a loss for tax purposes—at least in the first few years. Each partner will be able to deduct his share of the partnership's annual loss on his return. The tax savings from the losses reduce the amount an investor is actually risking in the deal. After just one or two years of tax savings, a high income investor in CATV may only be out-of-pocket 50¢ for every $1 he originally invested.

The losses generated by a CATV partnership come from four basic sources:

Operating expenses: The partnership pays management fees to the professionals running the systems and reimburses them for the systems' operating expenses. These costs are currently deductible by the partnership.

Depreciation: The assets acquired by any partnership being set up today qualify for the Accelerated Cost Recovery System. *Result:* The partnership can recover its costs (including the financed portion) in only five years for equipment and machinery and 15 years for buildings.

Investment credit: The partnership can claim a 10% investment tax credit on most of its equipment and machinery. But, since most of the equipment and machinery acquired by the partnership is used, the tax benefits will be limited. Under present tax rules, the partnership cannot claim an investment credit for more than $125,000 of used property in any one year.

Amortization: CATV systems are operated under franchises issued by local governments for a fixed period. So part of the partnership's purchase price will be allocable to the value of the franchise. An investment partnership may try to write off this cost over the remaining period of the franchise. However, the Revenue Service's position is that, since the franchise is usually renewed, it generally has an indefinite useful life and can't be amortized. But, in the one case of this kind to come before the Tax Court, the Court permitted amortization [Chronicle Publishing Co., 67 TC 964].

> ▶ **IMPORTANT:** A CATV investment is only as good as the people running things. They should have broad experience in the CATV business and a good track record with prior CATV deals. Check carefully for conflicts of interest. The managing partner is likely to be involved in the cable TV industry on his own. Another point: There won't be a ready market for a limited partnership interest, so CATV will be a long-term investment.

THE RESEARCH AND DEVELOPMENT TAX SHELTER—A NEW TYPE OF SHELTER FOR THE TECHNOLOGICAL AGE

Tremendous technological advances are being made every day. It would be great to get in on the ground floor of a new technological innovation in the hopes of it becoming the seed for a new IBM, Polaroid or Xerox. One way to take a flier in new technology is to buy stock in developing companies. Another way is the—

> ▶ **RESEARCH & DEVELOPMENT SHELTER:** You can become a limited partner in a research and development venture that gives you a direct stake in several new technological developments. Tax shelter incentive: You may be able to get a first-year writeoff equal to, say, 85% or 90% of your cash investment.

Caution is the key word here. You're not really getting in on the ground floor; you're in the basement. And the R&D shelter is one of the riskiest types of shelters. You are, in effect, betting an idea may spawn an IBM; but it may also result in an Edsel.

This is definitely one shelter that you must check out not only with your financial advisers, but also with experts in the technological field involved. The shelter won't be worth a penny unless the technology is valid and the idea or product is marketable. You must see market feasability studies. Even the best idea won't prove profitable if it's obsolete by the time it hits the market, or if the market is overloaded with stiff competition.

> *Simplified example:* ABC Limited Partnership contracts with independent consultants to locate new technological and scientific products that (1) are in the embryonic stage and (2) stand a chance at being successfully developed and profitably mar-

keted. Once a number of these products—say, five—have been found, the investors are brought in. The purchase of a limited partnership interest is paid in cash. *Reason:* Lenders are very wary of extending financing to R&D ventures.

Most of the investor's money is used to pay for research and development of the new products, which includes the cost of maintaining a research team. The actual research and development is performed by outside contractors under the supervision of ABC's general partner. The general partner is also responsible for licensing and marketing any product that may be developed.

Tax writeoff: The tax law allows a business to deduct costs for research and experimentation in the year they are paid or incurred. This is an exception to the general tax rule that requires business start-up expenses to be capitalized and written off over a number of years. The deduction is available to a business whether it conducts the research itself, or pays someone else to do it.

▶ **BIG FIRST-YEAR WRITEOFFS:** Many R&D shelters are structured to give investors the maximum deduction in the first year. One way is to prepay expenses that cover research to be done in the following year. To be deductible, however, such prepayments must be made for a valid business purpose. For example, the research contractor needs the funds to meet obligations for material and personnel.

Looking down the road: If all goes well—and that's an especially big "if" in R&D shelters—the partnership will have a number of new, technologically innovative and marketable products. Of course, it could be quite a while before the product actually becomes profitable. (For example, new medical products must be tested for years before they are made available to the public.) But if the products do succeed and the partnership makes money, here is how the profits may be taxed.

(1) If the partnership markets the products itself, the investors will receive royalty income. (Be sure the royalty is based on a fixed percentage of sales; you don't want a fixed dollar royalty.) Any royalty income is taxable as ordinary income.

(2) If the partnership sells the rights to the product to someone else, the profit can be tax-sheltered long-term capital gain.

▶ **CAUTION:** Sometimes, the sponsor wants to reserve the right to buy out the limited partners. Be very careful of such a clause. Otherwise, you might be bought out for only a small percentage of the true potential value of the product.

HERE'S AN INNOVATIVE TAX SHELTER—BILLBOARDS

Billboards are being sold as tax shelters. Fundamental to the investment is their tax treatment as real estate rather than personal property.

▶ **TAX SHELTER SIGNIFICANCE:** Real estate investments are exempt from the tax law's at-risk rule. So if billboards are considered real estate, then an investment in billboards is also exempt. In other words, an investor can leverage the purchase of billboards with non-recourse financing (no personal liability for the investor) and wind up with deductions in excess of his at-risk amount (the cash downpayment).

Simplified example: In January, ABC Limited Partnership buys a number of billboards for $1 million. Let's assume the limited partner investors put up $100,000. The partnership borrows the $900,000 balance of the purchase price from the seller of the billboards. The loan is non-recourse (in event of default, the seller can look only to the billboards for recovery).

The billboards are located on leased land and are all heavy steel models anchored in deep concrete foundations. The billboards cannot be moved without great expense and difficulty. Income is derived from renting billboard space to corporations and advertising agencies. The way the deal is structured, annual income after cash expenses is insignificant until the beginning of the sixth year.

Tax shelter result: The limited partners wind up with tax loss writeoffs, generated by depreciation deductions. The investors' collective $1 million cost basis for the billboards can be written off over 15 years. If the partnership uses straight line depreciation, the total writeoff over the first five years is $333,333, more than three times the investors' cash at risk.

If the billboards weren't real estate, then the investors' tax losses would be limited to $100,000—their investment at risk.

ABC limited Partnership can avail itself of other tax law provisions that benefit real estate. For example, since the partnership uses straight-line depreciation, all gain upon a later profitable sale is long-term capital gain. In other words, unlike an investment in personal property, there's no recapture of depreciation as ordinary income.

Background: In 1980, the Government ruled that whether billboards are real estate depends on their construction and use. Light duty wood billboards that are easily moved about are personal property. Heavy duty billboards (like the partnership's) that are built to remain in one place, and cannot be moved about without great difficulty are "inherently permanent structures" [Rev. Rul. 80-151, 1980-1 CB 7]. Since the tax regulations say personal property does not include "inherently permanent structures," the billboards can only be one thing—real estate [§1.48-1(c)].

There's yet another source for treating billboards as real estate: Sec. 1033 (g)(3) of the tax law, which allows taxpayers to postpone gain when involuntarily converted property (e.g. destroyed by fire) is replaced with like-kind property. This provision allows taxpayers to elect to treat billboards as real property. The election is effective for all income tax purposes.

▶ **CAUTION:** As with any investment, you don't want to put any money into a billboard shelter unless it makes economic sense. In addition, a tax shelter built on billboards isn't immune from Government challenge. For example, the Government may dispute the billboards' valuation. Obviously, professional advice is a must.

HOW THE RIGHT CATTLE DEAL CAN ROUND UP TAX WRITEOFFS AND TAX-SHELTERED PROFITS

An investor in cattle is at the mercy of general economic conditions, market fluctuations and supply and demand in the industry. But money can be made in cattle deals, and tax benefits offset some of the risk.

There are two basic types of cattle shelters. They each offer—

▶ **DIFFERENT TAX BENEFITS:** (1) A cattle feeding deal consists of buying young cattle, fattening them up and selling them for slaughter within eight months or so. These deals can offer one-year tax deferral. (2) In a cattle breeding deal, you try to build up the herd over a period of years and then sell it off. These deals not only offer tax deferral, but also a shot at long-term capital gain when the herd is sold. We'll concentrate on the cattle breeding shelter since it offers more tax benefits.

The cattle deal's promoter must have experience and past success, of course, but the cattle rancher in the deal is even more important. He has complete control over the cattle, so you must be doubly sure about his expertise. (Be careful if the rancher offers to limit your risk of loss; he'll probably expect up to 50% of any profit from the herd in return.)

Cattle are often sold to investment groups at inflated prices. Be sure to check that what you're being charged reflects the going rates. And be sure to check the costs of feeding the animals. The deal won't show a profit if the feeding costs are astronomical.

Typical cattle shelter in action: Mr. Green buys a herd of cattle for $30,000 this July from a company that specializes in cattle breeding (the company also manages the operation for Green for a flat fee). He makes a $3,000 downpayment and gives a personal note for $27,000, secured by the cattle. The note is a recourse note, so Green is personally liable. Green has to spend another $10,000 this year for operating expenses and carrying charges—cattle feed, breeding and management fees, interest on the note and so forth. Total cash outlay this year: $13,000.

Green's first year writeoff is $25,206. Where does the first-year writeoff come from? A large part ($10,000) comes from deductions for his operating expenses and carrying charges. But Green also gets—

(1) "Expensing" deduction: For 1984, Green can elect to "expense"—deduct immediately—up to $7,500 of his cost for the cattle.

(2) Investment credit: Green can claim an investment credit on the $22,500 non-expensed portion of his cost ($30,000 less $7,500). Green claims a $2,250 credit (10% of $22,500). If Green is in the 50% bracket, that credit is the equivalent of $4,500 in deductions.

(3) Depreciation deductions: Green's depreciation basis in the cattle is $21,375. That his $30,000 cost minus the $7,500 "expensed" portion and minus $1,125 (half the investment credit claimed). His first-year depreciation deduction is $3,206.

Bottom line: Green winds up with $15,206 in first year deductions ($7,500 expensing, plus $4,500 in deduction equivalent from the credit, plus $3,206 in depreciation deductions) in addition to his deductions for operating expenses and carrying charges.

Under the tax law, the credit can only be figured on amounts that an investor has "at risk" (the cash he puts up plus borrowings on which he is personally liable). In other words, if Green had financed his purchase on a nonrecourse basis (Green would not be personally liable on the note), his credit would be limited to 10% of his downpayment, or $300. Because Green is personally liable on the note, he can compute his credit on the downpayment *plus* his note.

More breaks down the road: When you later sell off breeding cattle that you purchased, you qualify for another tax break. The profit from the sale of breeding cattle is generally taxed as favorable long-term capital gain for cattle held 24 months or more. Note that this is longer than the usual one-year holding period for long-term capital gain. (If the cattle are not held for breeding—for example, bull calves sold to cattle feeders—the profit from the sale is ordinary income, no matter how long they have been held.) However, when you sell off the cattle, part of any profit you make on the sale is recaptured as ordinary income to the extent of prior depreciation.

Do you get the same tax breaks for cattle born to the herd? No. These cattle are not eligible for depreciation. On the other hand, of course, there can be no recapture of depreciation either when you sell. So the entire profit from the sale of breeding cattle born to the herd gets capital gain treatment (assuming they have been held for 24 months or more).

HOW AN EQUIPMENT LEASING DEAL CAN PAY OFF

Tax shelter deals are now being set up that allow investors to buy "state of the art" sophisticated equipment used in scientific, medical and industrial applications and lease it to a user.

Result: Assuming the deal is set up properly—a key assumption—you should be able to get an immediate tax writeoff that exceeds your cash investment. In other words, you can shelter from tax the income you invest, plus other taxable income as well. Most important, the right kind of deal should show an eventual profit in addition to tax shelter benefits.

> **Example:** Mr. Smith buys scientific research equipment from XYZ Inc. for $50,000. Smith makes a $5,000 downpayment and gives XYZ five personal notes for $9,000 each, due over the next five years. With assistance from XYZ, Smith locates a user, ABC Inc. ABC signs a five-year lease with Nolan and agrees to pay him $1,500 a year plus a fixed fee each time the equipment is used.

If things turn out as planned, Smith's lease income allows him to pay off the notes and pocket a profit. In any case, he gets—

▶ **MULTIPLE WRITEOFFS:** Under the Accelerated Cost Recovery System, Nolan is entitled to a first-year depreciation deduction of 15% of cost (with deductions of 22%, 21%, 21% and 21% in the following four years), regardless of when during the first year the system is put into service. So his first-year deduction comes to $7,500 (15% of $50,000).

In addition, Smith is entitled to an investment credit—a dollar for dollar reduction in his tax bill. If Smith claimed a 10% credit, he would have to reduce his basis in the equipment—for all purposes, including depreciation. Instead, he claims a reduced 8% credit to avoid reducing his basis. This gives him a credit of $4,000. If he is in the 50% tax bracket, his $4,000 credit is equivalent to an $8,000 deduction.

▶ **TAX SHELTER PAYOFF:** Assuming the lease generates no income before year-end (it will probably generate some income), Smith has a tax loss writeoff of $15,500 for the first year ($7,500 depreciation, plus $8,000 deduction equivalent from the credit). So he can shelter the $5,000 of income he uses for the downpayment plus $10,500 of his other income.

Important question: What are some of the risks in equipment leasing deals?
Answer: One obvious risk is that you are personally liable to the seller on the notes, whether or not the lease turns out to be successful. You must be "at risk" on the notes to get the writeoffs. If the lease income isn't sufficient to pay off the notes, you have to dig down into your own pocket to make up the difference. Of course, the chances of this happening depend largely on whom you are dealing with. So you and your investment adviser will want to look into the background of the seller and his equipment and the prospects for obtaining a profitable lease.
There are tax complications in addition to the at risk rules: For example, there are special rules that come into play if you "net lease" the property (where the user pays all the operating and maintenance expenses). In addition, if the user has a right to buy the property at the end of the lease, the Government could characterize the arrangement as a conditional sale instead of a lease. Because the user would be considered the owner, you would lose the investment credit and your depreciation deductions.

▶ **WHAT TO DO:** Sit down with your investment adviser before you sign up for any equipment leasing venture. He's familiar with your financial situation and can advise you whether equipment leasing is right for you. And he can help you find the deal that will give you the tax benefits you want.

HOW THE RIGHT FARMING TAX SHELTER CAN YIELD TOP TAX BENEFITS

While cattle breeding is a popular farming shelter, some investors also find land and grain farming attractive. These investors get in a syndicate that invests in developing lands which were not previously used, or were only partially used for farming. The syndicate can currently deduct feed, fertilizer and similar supplies in the year used; but it will take a number of years before the land yields its produce.

Result: Tax loss that can shelter the investor's salary and other investment income.

Unfortunately, there are many uncertainties surrounding agricultural farming operations—for example, the weather and market fluctuations. So most farming syndicates do not rely just on the sale of agricultural products for their profits. They also rely on their—

▶ **ACE IN THE HOLE:** The syndicate expects the land itself to appreciate. Farmland usually becomes more valuable as productivity improves. Or the syndicate may be able to make a bigger profit by selling the land for commercial, industrial or residential development.

Let's take a look at one farming deal that offers something most tax shelters don't. With this deal, you have complete control over when the farm income its taxed to you.

Tax shelter in action: Mr. Black invests $10,000 in XYZ Farm Partnership. XYZ leases farm land from owners of farm land. Then it enters into sharecropping agreements with selected farmers. The agreement is also a kind of lease: The farmer farms the land in return for a share of the crops that goes to XYZ. As part of the deal, XYZ pays the farmer's crop expenses—planting, fertilizer, insect control and so forth—incurred during the year.

▶ **TAX WRITEOFF:** The payments for crop expenses and land rentals are fully deductible by XYZ the year they are paid. This produces a tax loss that XYZ can pass through to Black and XYZ's other partner-investors. Black's share of the loss comes to, say, $9,000. So he has $9,000 that he can use to offset his business and investment income.

The following year, the farmers harvest the crops and give XYZ its share of the crops. Ordinarily, this is the time the investors would have to pay tax on their share of partnership profits. But not here. Black can postpone his tax bill indefinitely by taking advantage of two special tax breaks.

Tax break #1: As a general rule, rental income is taxable to a partnership (and thus to its investors) in the year the partnership receives it. But there is an exception to the rule for crop shares.

▶ **NO CURRENT TAX:** A farm landlord (in this case XYZ) owes no tax on crop shares until the shares are sold or otherwise reduced to cash. So the receipt of the crop shares the following year has no tax impact on XYZ and Black.

After receiving the crop shares, XYZ distributes them to Black and the other investors two years later. (XYZ doesn't distribute the actual crops; warehouse receipts are merely credited to Black's partnership account.)

Tax break #2: Let's say Black received $12,000 in cash instead of crops. He would then owe tax on $11,000, the difference between the $12,000 cash and his

$1,000 tax basis for his partnership interest (the $10,000 he invested less the $9,000 tax loss taken the first year). But since Black is being paid in crops instead of cash, there is—

▶ **AGAIN, NO CURRENT TAX:** Property distributed by a partnership is taxed to an investor only when the investor sells it. So the mere fact that XYZ distributes the crop shares to Black should not result in taxable income for him that year.

Net result: Black can hold on to the crop shares and sell them when it suits his tax picture. Then—and only then—will he have to pay tax on the income from his farm investment.

▶ **IMPORTANT:** If you are interested in a farm deal like this, there are two things you should do:

(1) The results we have described here are those expected by the people setting up the farming deal. As always in a tax shelter deal, the Revenue Service may not necessarily be in agreement. So you will want to discuss the tax consequences with your tax adviser before investing. And (2) keep in mind farming is a boom-or-bust business. You will want to be sure that the people managing the deal are experienced and have a good track record. Another reminder: You are investing to make money in farming as well as save taxes.

MONEY MAY NOT GROW ON TREES—BUT THERE MAY BE TAX SHELTER IN TIMBER

Astute investors are taking a look at a very special type of natural resource investment: timber. Reason: Besides offering a shot at good profits, timber is loaded with tax advantages.

How to invest: If you've got your eye on a parcel of timberland, your first step should be to hire an independent timber professional to perform what's called a—

▶ **TIMBER CRUISE:** The expert will give you an accurate idea of how much timber there is of different sorts—and how much it's worth. His report will tell you if the property is a good investment. It will also help you to allocate the property's cost among the land and the timber.

Important: Even if the land is loaded with valuable timber, you must also check to see how accessible the land is. No matter how much timber is on the land, it's not worth investing in if there is no way to ship the timber out to the markets.

If after investigating the deal you decide to invest in timberland and plant trees on the land, the tax breaks begin right away.

▶ **DOUBLE TAX BREAK FOR PLANTING:** You can get a 10% tax credit and a deduction of as much as $10,000 for the cost of planting trees held for the commercial production of timber.

Under prior law, there was no current deduction for the direct costs of planting trees (costs of site preparation, seed or seedlings, labor and tools). Instead, you had to capitalize these expenses and offset them against the income received when you eventually sold the timber (usually 15 years or more after the costs were incurred). In addition, there was no investment credit for these timber costs. Now, however, you are entitled to an investment credit equal to 10% of the first $10,000 of each year's planting costs. You can also elect to write off the first $10,000 of planting costs ratably over a seven-year period.

▶ **TAX SAVINGS:** You can now get an immediate 10% discount on the cost of planting timber. And you no longer have to wait until you sell the timber to recover your costs; you can recoup expenses through deductions in just seven years. If planting costs exceed $10,000 in one year, the excess amount is subject to the old rules (no credit and no cost recovery until the timber is sold). So you may want to spread planting costs over two years if you're up against the $10,000 ceiling.

NOTE: If timberland is sold within 10 years of planting timber, the profit from the sale will be ordinary income to the extent the planting costs were deducted under the seven-year writeoff setup.

More tax breaks: Every penny of operating costs is fully deductible—whether your timber operation is harvesting already grown trees or planting new trees (or both). Currently deductible operating costs include management services, labor costs, fire protection and the like.

Sale of timber: Unlike some other investments (such as cattle or horses), you can pretty much decide when to take your profit from timber. Selling a tree one year earlier or later isn't that significant. In addition, you can get tax-sheltered long-term capital gain treatment on the profit when the timber is sold.

▶ **THREE OPPORTUNITIES FOR CAPITAL GAINS TREATMENT:** You can nail down favorable capital gains treatment on your timber whether you: (1) sell the timber outright, (2) cut the timber yourself, or (3) grant cutting rights and retain an economic interest, such as a royalty.

(1) *Outright sale of standing timber:* The investor gets a capital gain or loss, since timber is a capital asset. Assuming he's held it more than one year, the gain is long term.

(2) *Cutting of timber by owner:* The owner-investor who cuts the timber himself can elect to treat the timber as a Sec. 1231 asset. In other words, gains are capital gains and losses are ordinary losses. Gain is derived when you cut (in effect, it's as if you were selling to yourself). Gain is the difference between the value of the standing timber as of the beginning of the year in which the timber is cut and its cost.

Important: To get capital gain treatment under Sec. 1231, you must have owned the timber more than one year before you cut it.

(3) *Disposal under a cutting contract:* An owner-investor who disposes of his timber under a cutting contract treats his gain or loss as a Sec. 1231 gain or loss if:

(a) He retains an economic interest in the timber.

(b) He has held the timber for more than one year before disposal. *But note this:* the date of disposal is the date the timber is cut (not the date it's sold). However, you can elect to make an earlier payment date the date of disposal.

> ▶ **THINK IT OVER:** Timber is used in many ways, but a major use is for construction. So if there's a construction slowdown (as there was in the past several years), you may have a hard time selling your trees. And of course, any one of a number of natural disasters can reduce your tax shelter to just so much ash. Finally, the tax law is very complex in this area, so you must consult with your tax adviser.

THE OTHER SIDE OF THE TAX SHELTER COIN— THE TAX RISKS

As we've shown you over and over again, a properly run tax shelter can offer you special tax savings. But as a tax shelter investor, you can also be hit with special taxes and tax penalties.

The alternative minimum tax: This tax reduces the effectiveness of some of the special tax breaks available to a tax shelter investor (called tax preference items). This alternative minimum tax is payable only if it exceeds a taxpayer's regular income tax.

> ▶ **HOW THE TAX WORKS:** You add up your "tax preference items" and add that total to your adjusted gross income. You then subtract: (1) special minimum tax deductions, and (2) an exemption amount ($40,000 for joint filers; $30,000 for singles). What's left over is subject to tax at a 20% rate.

Tax preference items: Here are the most important tax preference items subject to the minimum tax:

Real estate accelerated depreciation in excess of straight line;

The untaxed portion of long-term capital gain;

Accelerated depreciation on personal property subject to a net lease;

Percentage depletion in excess of the adjusted basis of the property;

A portion of the IDC deduction for oil and gas;

A portion of certain expensed items (including mining exploration and development costs).

Overvaluation penalties: Sometimes, a tax shelter overvalues its assets in order to get much bigger depreciation deductions and investment credits. A recent change in the tax law, however, imposes a special tax in such situations. There is now an addition to tax when the basis or value of property, held for five years or less, claimed on a return is 150% or more of the correct amount. The penalty is imposed if the overvaluation is without reasonable basis and results in a tax underpayment of at least $1,000. If the valuation claimed is:

• 150% or more but not more than 200% of the correct valuation, the penalty is 10% of the underpayment;
• more than 200% but not more than 250% of correct valuation, the penalty percentage is 20%; or
• more than 200% but not more than 250% of correct valuation, the penalty percentage is 20%; or

• more than 250% of correct valuation, the penalty is 30%.

Understatement penalty: Taxpayers who, without reasonable cause, ''substantially understate'' their income tax liability because of an abusive tax shelter are subject to yet another penalty. The penalty is 10% of the understatement. (And, of course, a taxpayer is not entitled to any tax writeoffs from an abusive tax shelter.)

CHAPTER 5

Offbeat and Speculative Money-Making Opportunities

We should stress right at the start that the money-making opportunities in this chapter are volatile and unpredictable—far more so than conventional wealthbuilders, such as real estate or stocks and bonds. The field of collectibles, in particular, has been a rough rollercoaster ride for plenty of unwary buyers. For instance, about five years ago the market for photographic prints suddenly took off. But then the market took a sickening dip. The value of some prints dropped 50-65% in a short time. And then there are precious metals. Everyone recalls the big silver rollercoaster when the price hit around $50, then fell to below $10 within a matter of months; gold was at $850 an ounce one year and some $400 lower the next; platinum was going for $1,050 an ounce when gold soared, and then was selling for $130 *less* than gold during their mutual descent.

▶ **GROUND RULES:** Invest only as much cash as you are prepared to lose. You should buy only after you've investigated the field and only with an agent or dealer or broker you trust. Beware of buying in a fast-rising market—you can get in at the peak.

If you invest in collectibles, decide early whether you want to build a collection or merely hold on to an object until you can sell it at a huge profit—if you have the latter goal, then beware of becoming so attached to, say, a painting that you miss your market. By all means, know the market—keep abreast of quotations, auctions, etc.—and be prepared to sell fast.

Following these rules can make investing less of a gamble, though you can never remove the element of risk or chance. And speaking of chance, let's begin by considering one opportunity that's really something of a lottery. Fortunately, it's a relatively inexpensive one that's open to all individual investors, large or small.

HOW TO GET A CHANCE AT AN OIL STRIKE ON A $75 INVESTMENT

You can begin a fortune in oil for just $75. That's all it costs to buy a chance in the Government-sponsored "great oil lottery." Technically, it isn't a lottery—but it sounds like a lottery, works like a lottery, and can pay off like a lottery. The odds are against your winning—let's admit that, right off. But plenty of people have won, and won big, too.

▶ **HOW IT WORKS:** The Government is required by law to issue gas and oil leases on public lands under the supervision of the Bureau of Land Management (BLM). Every other month, the Bureau gives anyone—the small investor, as well as the big oil company—the same chance at getting one of these leases by holding a drawing in each of its regional offices.

Q. Do you have to be present at this drawing to get a chance at an oil lease?

A. No, you do not. Most of the business is conducted by mail. If you're interested in this idea, then you should write the BLM office for your region and get its list of available parcels and some of its drawing cards.

Q. What is drawing card used for?

A. That's what you submit for each parcel you're interested in, and that's what you hope will be drawn at random from all the rest in your regional BLM office. You're limited to one drawing card per parcel.

Q. And what entry fee is there for this drawing?

A. It's $75 per drawing card. That's not refundable, by the way.

Q. All right, let's say my drawing card is picked—what then?

A. You have 30 days to make a decision. The ideal situation, of course, is that you've picked a parcel that an oil company is interested in again. (All the parcels offered have been leased before.) You sell the company your lease at a big profit and you're a big winner.

Q. You're not telling me that's a common occurrence?

A. No. But if you're like many "lottery winners," you will not want to just forget about the parcel and take your $75 loss. If your parcel is near a productive oil field, say, you may want to hold on for a while and wait for an offer.

Q. Am I allowed to hold on to this parcel?

A. Yes, you can hold on to it but you must pay rent in advance when you notify the office what you've decided. You pay $1 an acre for the first five years of a lease term; $3 per acre thereafter (the lease terms are for 10 years or as long as oil and gas are produced in paying quantities).

▶ **GOOD NEWS:** Your rental payments for the lease are considered ordinary and necessary expenses paid for the production of income. As such, they are deductible.

In addition, winning a lease automatically shortens the odds on that fortune you're aiming at. *Reason:* Roughly one out of 10 parcels is "hot"—it has potential for gas or oil production. And you can—

▶ **CUT THE ODDS STILL MORE:** Know which tracts to go after. You may want to pick a parcel that meets one or more of these qualifications: (a) Close to recent oil or gas production; (b) Close to active or announced exploratory drilling; or (c) In an area of current leasing and buying activity.

Q. Suppose by some chance I do win a lease and my parcel is one of the few that is "hot." And I have someone come in and do the drilling for me. What tax breaks do I get then?

A. You're entitled to the same tax breaks as any other investor in oil: Writeoffs for intangible drilling costs, percentage depletion deductions and depreciation deductions on any salvageable assets (e.g., derricks, tanks, buildings and the like). [See Chapter Four for details.]

▶ **WHAT TO DO:** Write BLM for a copy of its pamphlet, "The Federal Simultaneous Oil & Gas Leasing System." This publication also contains the addresses of all BLM regional offices. Write: Public Information Center, Bureau of Land Management, U.S. Dept. of the Interior, 18th & C Streets, NW, Washington, DC 20240.

HOW YOU CAN MAKE MONEY WITH COLLECTIBLES

So you finally cleared out the attic after all these years. You got rid of those musty-smelling old comic books and baseball cards you collected when you were a kid. And all of those movie posters Uncle Harry gave you when he worked at the Music Hall—a real fire hazard. But cleaning is cleaning. And the stuff *was* junk. Right? *Wrong*!

A copy of the 1938 *Action* comic book featuring the first appearance of Superman can sell for as much as $15,000 (contingent on the condition of the book). The 1952 Topps Chewing Gum Company Mickey Mantel rookie baseball card is valued at $700 or more. And a Bogart "Casablanca" film poster may soar to $10,000 within the next few years.

Admittedly, these are "dream discoveries." But there's money to be made in this area. Just what are collectibles? Should you invest in them? And if you believe you own something that might be of value, how can you cash in on it?

What Are Collectibles?

Collectibles include a broad range of goods that usually have in common some degree of (1) rarity, (2) scarcity, (3) demand, (4) popularity, (5) craftsmanship, (6) antiquity, (7) aesthetic qualities of beauty and taste, or (8) absolute or classical value to our society and culture.

Collectibles include serious investments such as rare coins, stamps, books, antiques (furniture, dolls, classic cars), art, and oriental rugs and carpets. They also include more faddish, "fun" nostalgia items you might well have packed away in a box in your attic or cellar: toys, Mickey Mouse watches, beer cans, baseball cards, comics, Coke signs, Beatle albums, old *Life* magazines, "Peanuts" memorabilia, war mementos, old radio and cereal giveaways, and the list goes on and on. Let's take a quick look at just a few of the items we already mentioned.

Comic Books

This market has done fairly well independent of economic upward and downward trends.

The rates of increase in value from one year to the next of "hot" comic titles can be surprising. Just a few examples:

- A complete mint condition 21-issue run of *All Winners*, a super-hero title published from 1941-1946, increased in value at a rate of 45% between 1981 and 1982.
- *Daredevil,* another hero book, which first appeared on the stands in 1964, continues to be published with increasing popularity, and soared in value by 50% between 1981 and 1982.
- Among the more recent titles, increases can be staggering! A seven issue run (to date) of *Camelot 3000*, which appeared by direct distribution to comic specialty shops in December 1982, has increased in value by 212% in the space of less than a single year.

How to cash in: The first step in turning your comic throwaways into cash is to purchase a copy of the latest Overstreet *Comic Book Price Guide* (Harmony Books, N.Y., Overstreet Publications, Tenn.). It lists virtually every American comic title to see print, along with significant publication information and the latest collector prices in relation to the conditions of the magazine in your possession. It also describes how to grade, protect, and even sell your books.

The next step, once you've assessed the approximate worth of your find, is to decide how to convert your books into money.

If you're looking for a quick profit, take your books to the nearest comic specialty shop (there are now hundreds across the 50 states) and ask for an offer. By selling all at once to a dealer, you get instant cash, immediate profit, and eliminate the long process of placing ads to dispose of the books.

▶ **CAUTION:** Generally, a dealer will offer a maximum of 50% of a book's value if it is a highly desirable item. Otherwise, the average offer for books is 25%-35% of listed value.

If you're looking for a somewhat higher return, you can "go into business for yourself." You can advertise in any of the trade journals devoted to comic collecting or rent a dealer's table at comic book conventions held in major cities during the year.

If you choose the ad route, you should order copies of some of the advertising magazines for comics merchandise. Take note of how most dealers lay out their ads and go about grading their books. Type up your ad copy, carefully pricing each book (note all noticeable defects, i.e., torn or missing pages, waterstains, etc.) and send it to the magazine. You will find that certain books will sell at once while others will not sell at all. You will then resubmit a revised ad listing your remaining books. Price books according to how fast you want to sell. If you want absolute top dollar, expect a much longer selling time.

How to Make Money in Baseball Cards

Sports memorabilia collecting in general and baseball card collecting in particular has grown by leaps and bounds. As with other collectibles, prices have fluctuated up and down. New card sets have been produced in unprecedented amounts. In short, it's a burgeoning market with many desirable cards despite the speculative factor that still exists on a large scale in the hobby.

How to collect and sell. As with comic books, there are no set rules on baseball cards. It's a hobby into which you can put as much time and money as you wish. The collector's/seller's bible in the card collecting field is *The Sport Americana Baseball Card Price Guide*, co-published by Den's Collectors Den, Laurel, Maryland, and Edgewater Book Company, Inc., Lakewood, Ohio. It lists all series of baseball cards by issue date and number, additional information pertinent to price (such as whether the item is a special issue, etc.), as well as grading conditions, and so on.

Similarly, several avenues are open to you to obtain and sell cards. Current issues may be purchased the traditional way at the local candy, grocery, or drug store. You can purchase complete sets from the many mail order advertisers found in sports media publications; e.g., *The Sporting News, Baseball Digest, Street & Smith's Baseball Yearbook*, and others. However, most serious card collectors obtain older cards from the same outlets where you would *sell* cards: other collectors or dealers, the hobby papers, and/or sports collectibles shows or conventions.

Value. The value of a baseball card is determined by many factors: Age of the card, player portrayed, the number printed (initial scarcity), the attractiveness and popularity of the set in which the card is a part, and perhaps most important, the physical condition of the card.

What if you *haven't* discovered any "throwaways" in the attic and are simply interested in investing in collectibles of both artistic beauty and value? Then you might be interested in—

Collector's Plates

This market involves more than 4.5 million collectors worldwide. What began as a hobby in 1895 (with the issuance of a 50¢ Danish Christmas plate—now valued at $4,000) has become a serious investing medium, and limited-edition plates are now the world's most traded form of art.

People collect for the pride of owning a piece of lasting beauty and/or as a long-term investment. Once a limited edition is closed, it is closed forever. No more plates will ever be made, and the law of supply and demand dictates that if demand grows, the price *must* rise.

Result: Limited-edition collector's plates offer something for everyone...at prices ranging from $17.50 to $325.00 for most items.

What is a limited edition? All true collector's plates are issued in editions limited either by quantity or time. A plate can be limited by:

1. Announced quantity, with each plate numbered.
2. Announced quantity, with plates not numbered.
3. Announced firing periods (plates may or may not be numbered).
4. Year of issue, restricting the quantity to the number produced during the year of issue (plates may or may not be numbered).

Edition size *is* important—but only in relation to market demand. *Active trading*—plates moving from one buyer to another, over and over again—is what influences advances in market value.

What should you look for? As with other collectibles, there is really no way to predict demand or appreciation of a particular plate. However, the Bradford Exchange of Niles Chicago, Illinois, the largest trading center for collector's plates in the world, recommends using an Eight-Point Checklist for the evaluation of a collector's plate. They're listed here in order of importance:

(1) Maker: Does the plate bear a hallmark associated with standards of fine workmanship and continuity of other plate series?

(2) Artistry: Is the plate original art created especially for the collector's plate medium by an artist of note? Is the subject one of broad, but not trite, appeal?

(3) Rarity: Is the edition tightly limited, yet not too limited to create a market? If the edition is closed, are dealers bidding in the secondary market?

(4) Collectibility: Is the plate one, preferably the first, of a collectible periodic series, or is it merely a single issue?

(5) Time of acquisition: Can you get the plate at the right time—at issue—or while the price is still rising?

(6) Sponsorship: Is the plate issued in association with a government or a respected non-profit organization?

(7) Commemorative Importance: Does the plate commemorate a seasonal event or an historic event? Or is it an event in the history of the artist or of the maker?

(8) Material: If the plate is made of ceramic, is it true hard-paste (or hard-fire) porcelain, bone china, or fine china? If made of metal, is it solid gold or silver? If made of glass, is it genuine 24% lead crystal?

Future of the market: Since 1974 the Market Bradex (a stock-market-like system of quotations) for plates has shown an almost uninterrupted climb (though prices on individual issues will, of course, fluctuate). This indicates growing collector confidence and market stability. Exceptional new issues can double or triple price in a matter of months.

The collector (or someone who wishes to sell an issue) can make use of many resources to keep abreast of the market.

Probably the most comprehensive coverage of both new and back-issue trends can be found in the Bradex, the Bradford Exchange's bi-monthly newsletter of quotations. (A one-year subscription is available at no charge from the Bradford Exchange, 9333 Milwaukee Avenue, Niles Chicago, Illinois, 60648. The Bradford Exchange's new computerized trading floor enables collectors to obtain the most up-to-date information and prices over the telephone and to make buy and sell transactions as well. Other sources include announcement advertisements in trade publications, and conventions and trade shows such as the International Plate Collector's Fair. (Information courtesy of The Bradford Exchange, Niles Chicago, Illinois)

Summing Up

Whether you're buying or selling collectibles, there are a few things you should keep in mind. Here are some guidelines:

1. Specialize in one area you like. This will maintain your high level of interest over the next ten years and longer.

2. Buy the best you can afford, even if you must accept limited quantities at first.

3. Confine your purchases to collectibles in excellent condition. These will always enjoy better resale value.

4. Read as much literature as you can on the subject. If you're simply selling a "throw-away," this won't be necessary. But if you are thinking of becoming a serious collector, it's a must.

5. The authenticity of the collectible should be guaranteed against a full cash refund. Even in the world of baseball cards and comics there are reprints and even counterfeits.

6. Buy only from reputable dealers or at reputable auctions.

7. You must hold for the long-term to make money.

8. If you are a novice, purchase and specialize in collectibles of known and proven work with a history of regular price appreciation.

9. Compare prices before you actually invest in an item.

10. At auctions, try to spot the dealers in the crowd. Generally, they bid inconspicuously, but the auctioneer usually knows them. Look for "quick glances" between the auctioneer and his known customer. It may pay to outbid dealers. They are planning to pay wholesale prices.

11. Don't be afraid to go to the top for advice, even if you are a small investor. Such establishments as Sotheby's and Christie's of New York have been known for their extreme courtesy to all clients, big and small. (Christie's has started a quarterly newsletter. Write Christie, Manson & Woods, Int'l., 502 Park Avenue, New York, New York 10022, and ask to be put on their mailing list.)

12. Always arrange and investigate trucking arrangements, insurance, storage areas such as bank vaults or safe-deposit boxes, storage fees, pick-up terms, burglar alarms, and other security precautions, before buying the actual items.

"WORTHLESS" STOCKS OR BONDS MAY STILL HAVE VALUE

Here's a special category of "collectibles" that is truly "offbeat." Indeed, you may have been collecting these items without knowing it. We're referring to those stocks or bonds that your grandfather, say, had carefully stashed away in his trunk and that you just uncovered. You thought they were worthless because you couldn't find the firm listed anywhere. Well, don't toss them out. You may still be able to convert them into cash:

1. The company may have merged with another that is still in business today under its own name. Maybe your relative was never told of the merger—or was told and failed to take the proper action. If so, the surviving company is obligated to you because you own the old certificates, and it owes you all past dividends.

2. The certificate, itself, may be considered a valuable antique. Reason: Antique dealers and interior decorators who specialize in Americana pay high prices for certificates in good condition. Just one example: At one auction, an 1882 $1,000 bond of the Chesapeake, Ohio & Southeastern Railroad, signed by C.P. Huntington, brought $1,000. You might say it hadn't lost any "value" at all in 100 years.

> ▶ **FIRST MOVE:** If your family has any of these old "worthless" certificates, make photocopies of the face of each and take the copies to a local stock broker to be researched. The company may just be thriving under another name. However, if the certificate is worthless as a stock or bond, then check with auction houses or interior decorators about its value as an antique.

HOW TO BUY GOLD AND OTHER PRECIOUS METALS

Precious metals have retained their grip on investors' imaginations despite severe fluctuations in the market. There's something about the words "gold," "silver," or "platinum" that makes them alluring to many people. But beware of investing in precious metals just because they are glamorous. There's money to be made here, of course, but not by those investors who think they've bought a sure thing to begin with.

You should also be aware that you're getting into a hyperactive market with its own logic and rhythm. There is, for instance, a 55-year supply of gold already mined and only a three-year supply of platinum—but gold is priced just below platinum as we go to press. And prices fluctuate with unpredictable political and economic developments both here and abroad.

> ▶ **REMEMBER THIS:** Investing in precious metals, whether in the form of coins or a futures contract generally involves the risk of possession. Some people may want to keep gold coins, say, in their safe deposit box, where they can take them out and look at them. But storage charges and insurance increase their costs. Take these expenses, as well as the risk, into account when you buy. Fortunately, there is a way you can—

Buy Gold Without Running the Risk of Theft

Several firms that deal in gold are offering investors *certificates* instead of coins or bullion. In effect, you can buy—

SPECULATIVE OPPORTUNITIES 509

▶ **A "SHARE" OF THE MARKET:** Let's say you decide to invest $1,500 in gold. You get a certificate stating that you own whatever amount of gold your $1,500 bought at that time. If it was selling at, say, $500 a Troy ounce, you own *three* ounces. Later, if it rises to $1,000 an ounce, your certificate is no longer worth $1,500 but $3,000 (if the price of gold falls to $400 an ounce, then your certificate's worth falls to $1,200).

Your three ounces of gold exist as *part* of a larger unit, combined with the gold of other investors and held in storage by the firm that issues the certificate. In legal terms you are the owner of a "specific but undivided amount" of gold.

One big advantage: A certificate allows you more flexibility than ownership of coins or bullion. Say you bought five gold coins worth $300 each. What happens if you need $500? You would have to sell two coins for $600 and reinvest the extra $100 in something else—you can't sell or buy part of a coin.

A gold certificate eliminates this hassle. You spent your $1,500 on a certificate certifying that you own three ounces of gold, so raising $500 is a matter of instructing the issuer of the certificate to sell off $500-worth of gold. You return your certificate and get a new one, showing your updated balance (your remaining ounces of gold).

▶ **FEWER HEADACHES:** The main feature of a gold certificate is that it is an easier way to obtain ownership of gold. There will still be fees and charges, but, for the most part, they'll be up front and clearly expressed at the time of your purchase.

Your chances of making a profit depends almost entirely on the changes in the value of gold as a commodity. A gold certificate does *not* bear interest or pay dividends. So you must rely on appreciation of the underlying metal for your profits.

▶ **INVESTMENT EDGE:** Shop for a deal that doesn't drain away too many of your investment dollars in the form of commissions and storage fees. Naturally, the more of your money that actually goes to buy gold, the less gold must increase in value for you to turn a profit.

Here's a rundown of some typical investment requirements and costs:

- Minimum Investment: A minimum opening investment of $1,000 to $2,500 is required by most firms. Additional purchases may be made in increments of as little as $100 to $500.
- Commissions: 3% on purchases of $50,000 or less; 2% on purchases of $50- to $100,000; 1% charge when you decide to sell your holdings. If you decide to convert your certificate holdings into gold, there is a 1% charge based upon current market price.
- Storage: There is no charge for storage of the gold during the calendar year of purchase. Starting January 1 of the following year there is a 1-1/2% per annum fee.

▶ **WATCH THIS:** The issuing firms are under no obligation to repurchase your holdings. Although it is unlikely that these firms would (at least in the near future) refuse to pay cash for your certificates, this is a possibility. In such an eventuality you would have to take possession of the actual metal.

Q. Can I invest in something other than gold using this method?

A. Yes—silver and other precious metals can be bought in this manner. These certificate dealers advertise in the business sections of major newspapers.

Q. But say I prefer to buy coins or bullion outright. What expenses are involved then?

A. The commissions are about the same as when buying certificates. However, along with the cost of storing your purchase, you may also be charged a fee for having it assayed. You should also insure your purchase.

Diamonds and Precious Stones

Like precious metals, precious stones are put to industrial as well as luxury uses. The prices on the industrial market are tightly controlled (one giant firm, De Beers Consolidated Mines, Ltd., produces 80% of the world's annual output of diamonds). The luxury jewelry market is fairly stable; values rise steadily over the year and transactions are handled quietly at auctions or with dealers.

One market, though, can be very active: *Investment diamonds*— gems bought for the purpose of re-sale by speculators. In the late 1970's, this market was booming. Firms sprang up that dealt only in investment diamonds. They were staffed by high-pressure salespeople who spent most of their time on the phone, promising buyers that the firm would buy back or re-sell the diamonds for them, if need be, at the purchase price.

In this booming market, the lucky investor was someone who had bought several years ago—someone who, say, paid $1,000 for a one-carat D-flawless, round-cut diamond in the late 1960's. Because he could spare the $1,000 he was in no hurry to sell; he held on to the diamond until the market took off in the 1970's. Finally he sold it for around $60,000 in 1980. The *unluckiest* investor didn't buy until 1980, when the market was big news. He dug down deep to raise $60,000 after a smooth-talking salesman whom he'd never met phoned to assure him there was no risk in buying gems—"The company will help you sell if the market should drop." The market did just that, but the company didn't keep its promise and the salesman stopped answering his phone. Two years ago, that diamond was selling for $13,000.

▶ **BIG CHANGE:** There are fewer firms dealing in investment diamonds now. The gem described above had risen to $23,000 by the middle of 1983. Investors with cash to spare and an eye for bargains have returned to the market. More dealers are delivering on their promise to buy back the gems. And some are offering buyers—

A Guaranteed Re-Purchase Agreement

Dealers are starting to put the offer to re-purchase in writing and making it a part of the sale. One dealer, for instance, registers its re-purchase agreement with the Securities and Exchange Commission and posts a bond backed by an insurance company.

Q. Do such agreements guarantee me a profit?

A. Not at all; the offers usually guarantee that you will get back your purchase price. No allowance is made for inflation—but this is better than nothing. There can be other conditions, too. One dealer, for example, makes its offer for only six months, beginning six years *after* the date of purchase.

Q. Is this kind of agreement available in all states?

A. Not at present. The idea is still a novelty. And then there are so many differences among state laws that diamond brokers could not offer one uniform repurchase agreement that would comply with the requirements of every state. However the leading brokers are continuing to adapt their agreements as needed as they expand their territory.

Q. Is this a field for the small investor to explore?

A. Since the lowest purchase price for such stones is only around $2,000, investment in diamonds could be considered open to small investors. But brokers tell us that they prefer to deal with buyers who have a minimum net worth of $100,000 (or have a net worth of $50,000 and earn at least $50,000 a year).

Q. Do buyers of investment diamonds have to take delivery of their purchase?

A. Yes. The gem comes sealed in plastic. The buyer is responsible for its safety. Incidentally, emeralds, rubies and sapphires can also be purchased in this manner.

▶ **MARKET DRAWBACKS:** Purchasers of precious stones as investments have always been plagued by: (1) The high mark-up of retail prices; (2) The lack of any reliable source of prices; (3) The difficulty of finding a buyer for their gems should they need to sell—fast; and (4) Established dealers who can be trusted to stick with them, in good times and bad.

After the shake-up of a couple of years back, when only the strongest and most reliable survived, this market may be in a better shape. Opportunities for profits may be ready to open up again. Meanwhile check out the possibility of buying shares in a "diamond trust," a mutual fund-like setup that enables one to own units of a diamond collection. This could be a good way to get your feet wet without being in over your head.

THE MARKET IN STRATEGIC METALS

So-called "strategic metals" are complicated and highly speculative. You need large amounts of cash to get started and that cash may be tied up for long periods of time. It's definitely not for the fainthearted or the uninformed. Yet some experts claim that today's strategic metals will be tomorrow's precious metals, as demand increases and supplies dwindle.

What they are: Strategic metals are vital to today's sophisticated technology in fields such as electronics, aerospace, armaments, scientific instruments, machine tools, etc. Some of the 40-odd metals considered to be "strategic" are well--

known (like cobalt, chromium, magnesium, and tungsten), while others are obscure, with strange-sounding names (like cerium, gallium, osmium, tantalum, and rhodium).

What they have in common: Each possesses certain unique characteristics crucial to various aspects of modern high-tech manufacturing. When alloyed with other metals, they produce extreme hardness, say, or the ability to withstand intense heat, resistance to corrosion, or strength combined with light weight.

Some of these metals have no known substitutes and are produced in very small quantities. Their supply, naturally, is limited and may eventually run out. Yet new uses are being found in industry all the time.

Adding to the allure of strategic metals is the fact that many are supplied by areas of the world that are either unstable, politically or economically, or unfriendly to the West. Often these metals are not found in the West at all or are in very short supply. So today's high-tech manufacturing is dependent on potentially unreliable sources for metals that have no substitutes. Any number of events—war, revolution, natural disasters—can undercut the supply.

To add to the air of mystery surrounding strategic metals, they are not traded on any formal commodity exchange. Much of the business is conducted directly between major producers and major consumers of these metals. As with oil, the producer price is often agreed upon among producing nations. Smaller holders must sell and buy at the best price they can—usually through professional strategic metal merchant companies. In times of shortage, the prices on this free market naturally rise above the producer price. In normal times, this price is lower. However, more and more metal is being traded on the free market each year. (With tungsten, for instance, there is no producer price at all.)

How you get involved: Suppose you do have a large chunk of cash to gamble with in strategic metals. You can't just call your broker and order a ton of molybdenum, can you? Probably not.

Strategic metals are generally purchased through companies that have sprung up for this very purpose. These companies will advise you on what metals to buy, acquire them for you, store them in a warehouse located in a country not likely to be the scene of turmoil (Rotterdam is the most frequently used site for strategic metals holdings), and eventually sell your metal for you.

> ▶ **CAUTION:** During the sudden explosion of strategic metals investing in 1981 and 1982, many people lost their shirts on advice given by unscrupulous dealers. So you should deal only with reputed dealers who have an established history of trading. Once you have the names of a few traders to check into, you should write for their material and compare offers.

Can you deal with a regular broker? Maybe. There are a few American brokerage houses that have dabbled in strategic metals investing.

Be careful: Get as much advice as possible. Make a thorough study of both the company itself and the strategic metals involved. The more you know, the better your chances of coming out ahead in this volatile market. Read up on the topic.

Alternative Avenues

Putting all your eggs in one basket in an investment of this type would be foolish. A minimum investment in three different metals could run you $30,000 or more. Those are big numbers. So you may want to look into two alternatives.

(1) Some of the metals companies have set up portfolio funds. You rely on their expertise as they move the fund's money among different metals in varying proportions. If you have the cash, and the inclination to invest in strategic metals, a fund may be the best way to go.

(2) You can invest in stocks of companies that mine these metals. Besides requiring a much smaller cash outlay, this approach to strategic metals has other advantages. Stocks are easier to buy than the actual metals. There are none of the carrying charges associated with holding the metals: storage, insurance, etc. Instead of holding a long-term investment that's costing you money, you may have a shorter term investment with instant liquidity. And many of these companies pay good dividends.

On the down side, you won't see the fantastic price rises in a stock you might see in the metals themselves. A jump in the price of the metal may affect the stock only slightly. There is little of what is known as "pure play" in this market —a company that mines only the metals that you're interested in. So you may be locked in with a lot of other interests that the company has (which can, of course, be good or bad, depending on the overall performance of the company).

There are, however, some examples of pure plays. And there have been cases of spectacular results when the particular metal involved had a boom period.

You must analyze your own investment needs and choose what you feel is the right move for you. Tread very carefully in this specialized, sophisticated market. Talk to your broker and your financial adviser before buying strategic metals.

The following companies are among the biggest in the strategic metals field. You may want to write them for further information. This is by no means a comprehensive list.

>Strategic Metals Corporation
>500 Chesham House
>150 Regent Street
>London W1R 5FA, England

>The Strategic Metal Trust
>48 Athol Street
>Douglas, Isle of Man, British Isles

>Wogen Resources
>17 Devonshire Street
>London W1N 1FS, England

As we went to press, Prudential-Bache offered a scaled-down version of the type of contracts offered by the English trading companies. Examine all the material you are sent, keeping in mind that these people are in the business of selling strategic metals, so they are likely to paint a rosy picture.

MAKING MONEY IN COMMODITIES

Commodities are highly speculative—possibly the most speculative of all the money-makers in this book. The items you trade in are called "futures contracts"—that is, you are obligated to deliver or to receive a specific amount of a commodity at a specific time at the price prevailing at the time. If that price is higher than the one at the time you bought, you can sell your futures contract at a profit. But if it's lower, you must sell it at a loss, and you can lose a lot.

You trade in futures under conditions unique to commodities:

1. You always buy on margin—that is, you immediately put down a fraction of the price you are expected to pay. Say you buy one contract of September wheat at $4 a bushel. A contract contains 5,000 bushels so you owe $20,000 (for simplicity, we will exclude commissions in these examples). But your cash-out-of-pocket can be only $750—tremendous leverage.

2. You almost always serve as a middleman between a producer (a farmer, in this case) who sells to you, and a user (a grain processor) who eventually buys it from you.

3. You rarely take delivery on what you've purchased—before September, you hope to sell your futures contract for, say, $4.50 a bushel, or $22,500, a $2,500 profit on a mere $750 investment. That's a 333% profit.

The above scenario may well turn out exactly as described. But it also may not—September wheat may fall to $3.75 a bushel. You not only lost your chance at a profit, but you find yourself required to put up more cash, if you wish to hang on to the contract. If you do hang on, you could well end up having to sell at $3.50 a bushel, garnering only $16,500 of the $20,000 you owe. Since you are responsible for the full price of your contract ($20,000), you must also come with the additional $3,500. And of course, you lose your $750 original cash investment.

Becoming a "Position" Trader

Most commodity traders—and all beginners—are what is known as "position" traders. They take long (buy) or short (sell) positions in commodities. For the position trader, commodities are a sideline, not a profession. (The professional speculators are known as "scalpers," who operate on the floor of the exchange, daily buying low and selling high; and "spreaders," the most sophisticated of traders, who offset purchases with short sales, and hope to come out ahead.)

> ▶ **WINNING MOVES:** Successful position traders usually limit themselves to three or four commodities and master these markets as well as they can. They don't panic during dips or get excited during rallies. But they limit their losses by selling fast when it looks like the market has turned against them and a margin call is due. They also aren't afraid to let their profits run. And they limit their investment in any one commodity to a third of their capital ($10,000 is acceptable minimum capital for this hyperactive field).

Two Typical Position Traders

Let's take a simplified look at how "Mr. Long" and "Mr. Short" go about making their investments. They've both been watching a mythical commodity—"soy peas"—and have decided that now is the time to move.

Mr. Long thinks the price of soy peas will go up between now and January. So he buys a January soy peas future. In effect, he agrees to take delivery of a standard contract amount of soy peas (5,000 bushels in this case) during the month of January. He would pay today's $5-a-bushel market price for January soy peas—if he accepted delivery. But he intends to sell his contract commitment before then.

Here's where the margin enters the picture. Just how much margin is needed depends on the requirements of the particular broker and on the exchange rules for soy peas.

▶ **HOW IT WORKS:** Mr. Long must deposit the required margin (i.e., cash) with his broker on the day he makes his purchase. If the price of soy peas goes down, Mr. Long may be called on by his broker for more margin money. On the other hand, if the price of soy peas goes up, Mr. Long can draw cash against his paper profit, or he can use his increased "equity" to margin additional trades. He simply leaves enough in his account to maintain the current margin requirement, or liquidates his position altogether and pockets his profit.

Mr. Short disagrees with Mr. Long's thinking; he figures that in January the price of soy peas will be lower than the current $5-per-bushel mark. So he initiates a short sale in order to cash in.

▶ **HOW IT WORKS:** Mr. Short makes a contract to *deliver* soy peas after the first of the year at today's price of $5. He figures that before it's time to deliver, the market price will be below $5 and he'll be able to buy back January soy peas to cover his position. So if the January price is $4 a bushel, Mr. Short will profit a dollar a bushel on his contract—$5,000 altogether.

The same technique is used in the stock market. But the short selling of a commodity is different. Here Mr. Short gets a—

▶ **SPECIAL BREAK:** In commodity markets an investor can sell short *any time*. This is not the case in the securities market where a short sale can be initiated only after the market has moved up or stays unchanged after such a move.

Q. Is Mr. Long likely to end up with the 5,000 bushels in the backyard come January?

A. Not at all. Unless he and Mr. Short want to take possession of the soy peas, they'll close out (offset) their positions before the actual delivery date of the futures contracts. Most investors make this move. Brokers call investors to remind them when a delivery date is approaching.

Q. But suppose I somehow forget to have my broker close out my contract?
A. Taking delivery isn't the end of the world. You get a warehouse receipt—not the physical commodity. And as long as there's a cash market for the commodity, a broker can sell this receipt to someone who wants the actual soy peas—let's hope for at least as much as you paid for it.

Let a Specialist Handle Your Trades

You can either deal with a broker who specializes strictly in commodities, or if you already have an account with a stockbroker, insist that your account be handled by a commodity specialist. *Reason:* Your current representative (who handles your stock transactions) is not necessarily the best choice to handle commodity trades. He's not a specialist. Once you're introduced to a "pro", make sure he's as good as he says. Ask for references and proof of past successes.

> ▶ **TAKE YOUR CHOICE:** The term "commodities" now covers a vast array of trades. In recent years, it has even come to include commercial paper, U.S. Treasury bonds and something called "Value Line futures," where the ratings on a stock market index determine whether you lose or make money. Check with a reputable, established broker about the profits—and risks—awaiting you in commodities.

THERE'S MONEY TO BE MADE IN PENNY STOCKS—IF YOU CAN STAND THE RISK

What do IBM, Xerox, Walt Disney, Tandy (which owns Radio Shack) and McDonald's have in common? At one time, they were all penny stocks. Let's take a look at McDonald's. Suppose you bought that stock at $1.60 in the mid-60's, instead of buying a hamburger and fries once or twice a week. And for argument's sake, let's say you bought 1,000 shares for $1,600. What would you be doing today? The chances are that you would be eating filet mignon on your yacht. Why? That $1600 investment is worth over $735,000 today.

To find out more about penny stocks we went to the pros. This section is largely excerpted from *The Penny Stock News' Investor's Guidebook,* published by Jerome Wenger and written by Carolyn Long.

The Market in Penny Stocks

Penny stocks are traded on the Over-The-Counter market (OTC), and most don't meet the minimum asset and shareholder requirements necessary to be listed on an automated market quotation system. Many penny stocks aren't listed in the daily papers either. Instead, they are quoted in the so-called "pink sheets," published by the National Daily Quotation Service, and available at any broker's office. You can call your broker and get quotes on penny stock just as you can with other types of stock.

What companies issue penny stocks? According to Jerome Wenger, publisher of Penny Stock News of Columbia, Maryland, "They're companies involved in everything from cancer cures to computers, from horsebreeding to jojoba beans. Stock can be issued for as little as a dollar, dime, or a penny."

Why buy penny stocks? "From the speculator's viewpoint," says Wenger "penny stocks offer a way to share in the growth of new industries with a small capital outlay."

One example, although certainly *not* typical: In October, 1980, an energy-related firm came out with an initial issue at 10 cents a share. One minute into the trading session, the price per share jumped to 38 cents. Ten minutes later the price was up to 50 cents, and it closed the day near 75 cents. In its first day of trading, the stock price had appreciated 650 percent, converting a $1,000 investment into $7,500—if it had been sold at the peak that day.

Of course penny stocks can sink like a stone after a brief, meteoric rise.

How to pick a stock. Before you invest: Investigate! While the penny market is clearly a high-risk arena, speculators can minimize the risk by following the market and studying the increasingly available information. "More specifically," says Carolyn Long, an investment writer, "investors should first look for industries with a future, those growing faster than other segments of the economy or those regaining popularity for some reason. Few stocks can beat a downward trend in their industry.

"Medicine, high technology and communications are among the more popular industries, but winners can be found in any field, such as entertainment, waste management, and financial consulting. Diversifying among several industries is a hedge against an unexpected slump in any one area.

"Selecting a few companies in each field may protect the speculator from picking the wrong company in the right industry. No one can accurately predict which particular stock will become the next Tandy or Xerox," adds Carolyn Long.

The Pitfalls in Penny Stock

The traditional ways of tabbing a "mover"—price earning ratios and economic conditions—don't always hold true with penny stocks. That's because of promotion—or "hype" as it's known on Wall Street. This hype can cause a stock to suddenly jump from $2 to $4 for no apparent reason. Here's how it works:

Underwriters or large investors often build up a loyal following through their repeated association with winning stocks. They can generate enormous enthusiasm for new underwritings or other "special situations."

These sponsors are in a position to persuade investors or speculators that their stocks will not only go up, but will probably do better than comparable stocks that don't enjoy such promotion. Unfortunately, promotion is just that. It's not quantifiable or controllable. Even if you get in before the promotion commences, you don't know when it will stop.

How to investigate penny stocks: Read all the newspapers, magazines and advisory services devoted to low-priced stocks that you can, and then subscribe to those of particular interest to you. The following list should get you started.

The Penny Stock News (a 40-page bi-weekly newspaper; $50/year, $85/two years, $15/three month trial; 8930-J Oakland Center, Columbia, MD 21045; phone 301-596-0126 or 800-368-2510) concentrates on stocks selling under $5. It provides in-depth analyses of new issues and established stocks, and offers explanations of stocks showing explosive volume increases, insider trading reports, special industry news, and thousands of up-to-date quotes. Back issues are available.

OTC Review (monthly magazine; $36/year, sample copy $3.50; 110 Pennsylvania Ave., Oreland, PA 19075), the self-described Forbes of the over-the-counter marketplace, is dedicated to "pull-no-punches" objective analysis of a broad cross-section of OTC Stocks.

Low-Priced Stock Digest (monthly newsletter, $38/six issues; 55 E. Afton Ave., Yardley, PA 19067) is a new compendium of tips and investment analyses from other newsletters, presented in short, concise form.

Denver Business World (weekly; $32/year; P.O. Box 313, Englewood, CO 80151) is a business newspaper covering the Denver financial markets, particularly high tech and energy issues.

A word about brokers: Plenty of medium and small-sized brokers deal in penny stock. But many New York Stock Exchange (Big Board) brokers have a policy of not recommending a stock selling under $5.00 on the grounds it is too speculative. These brokers do not want to be accountable for a client's possibly losing money in some obscure company. If someone wants to purchase such a stock, the brokerage firm may require him to sign a standard form indicating that the purchase was an "unsolicited order."

Commissions appear in two different forms, depending on whether a stock purchase or sale is an *agency* or *principal* trade. *Agency* trades occur when your brokerage firm purchases or sells a listed stock for you on a recognized stock exchange, or an OTC stock from another broker-dealer or market maker. The amount of the commission is indicated in the appropriate place on your confirmation slip.

A *principal* trade occurs when you buy or sell an OTC stock which was originally underwritten by your brokerage firm, or in which the firm "makes a market." Here, the brokerage firm either adds a "mark-up" to the price you pay for the stock, or subtracts a "mark-down" from the price you receive for the stock you sell. This type of "commission" appears only in the price per share of the stock you buy or sell.

The brokerage firm has some leeway here. It can charge for either a mark-up or mark-down (not fixed by law). The only qualification is that the charge be "fair and reasonable." However, the National Association of Securities Dealers (NASD), the self-regulating arm of the Over-The-Counter market, offers a guideline of 5% as a justifiable commission for either a buy or sell transaction.

Two final notes: When you buy a *new* stock issue, you pay no commission to the underwriter. When you later sell this stock, you will, of course, be charged a commission or mark-down. Also, when placing small orders it's important to calculate into a stock's upside potential the firm's minimum commission, which can range from $25 to $50 per trade. People have been known to call brokers hoping to buy $40 worth of stock only to learn that the commission on the transaction would exceed the cost of the stock!

Selling Your Penny Stock

Just about every investment adviser agrees that knowing "when to sell" is a far more difficult decision than knowing what to buy. When it comes to penny stocks, like other investments, there are some basics. Here's what Jerome Wenger has to say:

"If a stock decline coincides with deteriorating company developments and/or shows prolonged weakness relative to the general market, get out. If it moves up quickly for no apparent reason and you're afraid the bottom will fall out, sell!"

There is another selling angle which can help you make the right decision—insider selling. Insiders—directors and other key personnel of a company—must report to the Securities and Exchange Commission (Rule 144) their intent to sell restricted stock. Most journals in the penny stock field mention such reports and are a big help. You must then determine why they are selling.

It could be they "promoted" the stock and are getting out high. If that's so, it might be a good idea to follow the leaders and sell.

Or, if you are uncertain about rumors of potential "good things" happening with the company, sell enough to cover your initial investment. After that you can relax because you're playing with the "house's money." You can't lose, and anything you win is gravy.

Some speculators arbitrarily sell when a stock doubles, some sell after they reap a 25% gain, while others sell when they think "all the good news is out." Whatever rule you pick, stick with it to avoid being swept away by the excitement of a hot market.

Final notes: Make sure your stocks are registered in your own name (rather than in street form) so you can receive all the corporate news releases that are mailed to registered shareholders. Be prepared to have some losers along the way. But remember that most successful speculators at one time or another have their share of losers.

The trick is in not confusing luck with wisdom. A trader who makes a series of lucky moves in a bull market and assumes he is a genius who has the game beat is sure to go broke in the long run. *Remember: Success in the penny market is largely the result of careful analysis, evaluation, and intelligent execution.*

Chapter 6

How To Get The Most Mileage From Your Hard-Earned Dollars

The road to financial security begins at home. In other words, putting your own house in order will actually increase the amount of money you have available to spend or invest. That's where this Chapter comes in. For instance, we'll show you how to put together a workable family budget—and how to stick to it. You'll find out how to get real clout in the marketplace and how to finance your child's education without losing your shirt in the process. You'll also learn that there *are* ways to take a vacation that allow you to come home with a few dollars left in your pocket. The bottom line: Making every penny count.

HOW TO SET FINANCIAL GOALS FOR YOUR FAMILY'S FUTURE

So you think you're fit? You work out three times a week and your body is in shape. But what about your personal finances? What kind of shape are they in?

In today's world your financial health is an important part of your general well-being. And like the rest of you, it's something you simply cannot afford to neglect. So let's show you how to do a bit of financial self-diagnosis.

(1) What's your financial weight—how much do your assets less debts come to?

(2) What's eating up your dollars—what are you spending your money on?

(3) Where can you trim some unnecessary fat out of your spending?

(4) What are the goals of your financial fitness program? Once you've established specific goals—and the order of their importance— you can then set about achieving them. This is the real purpose of a budget, to help you—

▶ **PROVIDE FOR THE FUTURE:** A budget makes you think about tomorrow. Are you planning to start up a business? You'll need plenty of cash for that. Is college education ahead for your children? That will take a healthy chunk out of your resources—especially if you wait too long to put money aside.

These are just two of the many short and long-term expenses that could put the crunch on your pocketbook. Planning for retirement, buying a new home, reducing your debts all cost money. Starting to save now means less to worry about later on. How does an organized budget help?

Example: Let's say you have an outstanding debt. Your objective is to reduce the debt by $950 over the course of the year. To stay on schedule you'd have to set aside about $80 a month.

▶ **WHAT TO DO:** Take this $80 right off the top of your earnings immediately and without fail. Just pretend you're making $80 less each month. In effect then, the money doesn't exist—at least for spending purposes.

Planning for an emergency: If you think having cash in reserve is something for only big corporations, think again. Cash reserves—putting money aside for the proverbial rainy day—is an essential element of your budget. *Reason:* No one can predict the future. That's why you need a cushion against the unexpected expenses.

If you are asking how much, an emergency fund equal to at least two or three months of your after-tax salary is a good place to start. Put a small amount from each paycheck aside until your cash reserves equal the necessary figure. Thereafter, the payments can be channeled into long-term savings.

HOW TO FIGURE OUT WHAT YOU'RE WORTH

Why do you really need to know how much you are worth? The answer is quite simple—it's the key to your budgeting success. For example, you may be accumulating too much cash in a zero-interest checking account. Personal property may account for a disproportionately large share of your assets—maybe it's time to stop buying your spouse expensive jewelry every birthday. Perhaps you are going overboard redecorating your home. Worse, some of your assets may be under-utilized.

Example: You own your home free and clear, and its value is five times what you paid for it. If you need funds for an important family goal (e.g., the children's education) you may want to consider borrowing against the value of the home. This is a relatively low-cost way to get funds.

What if the cash value of your life insurance policy is high? You may be able to borrow against that amount at super-low rates (see p. 708). Does your summer house sit empty when it could be attracting renters? Just because you don't use it to its full potential doesn't mean that the house couldn't be productive from a rental income point of view.

On the liability side: If your short-term liabilities (e.g., installment payments) are sopping up too much of your assets, it's time to make a change in your spending habits. Don't wait until you see the red ink.

A net worth statement is also a top-notch way for you to begin the estate-planning process (see Chapter Eleven).

To help you put a dollar figure on your family's assets and liabilities we've included a worksheet. All you have to do is plug in the numbers.

ASSETS—WHAT YOU OWN

CASH: AMOUNT

Checking accounts ....
Savings accounts ....
Cash on hand ....
Money market funds ....
Credit unions ....
Time deposits ....
In a safe ....
Other ....

Cash value of investments:

Stocks ....
Mutual funds ....
Government savings bonds ....
Municipal bonds ....
Corporate bonds ....
Loans extended to others ....
Commodities ....
Other ....

Cash that *could* be withdrawn from:

Retirement plans (pension, profit-sharing, Keogh, etc) ....
IRAs ....
Employee savings plans ....
Other ....

Cash value of business ventures ....
Cash surrender value of insurance policies ....

Real estate:

Market value of home and land ....
Market value of summer home ....
Market value of other real estate ....

Market value of personal property:

Car, boat, trailer, other vehicles ....
Household furnishings ....
Jewelry ....
Furs ....
Antiques, art, coins, other collections ....
Clothing ....
Other ....

   Total Assets: $_____

LIABILITIES—WHAT YOU OWE

Amount owed on home mortgage(s) ....
Installments:

Automobiles ....
Furniture & appliances ....
Credit card debts ....
Bank loans ....

LIABILITIES—WHAT YOU OWE *(Continued)*

CASH:	AMOUNT
Finance Company loans	
Amount owed for taxes	
Any other bill outstanding	
Total Liabilities	$_____
Total Assets..	$_____
Less: Total Liabilities:	$_____
TOTAL NET WORTH	$_____

▶ **WHAT TO DO:** Figuring out how much you are worth is a little like taking a snapshot of your financial situation. You see what you own (your assets)—and on the other side, what you owe (your liabilities). But one snapshot is not enough — taking stock of your financial situation should be done routinely, perhaps every six or nine months, to give you an accurate means of comparison. A series of "pictures" will tell you if you are making headway in your financial plans.

HOW TO SET UP A BUDGET THAT PUTS YOU IN CONTROL OF YOUR POCKETBOOK

Applying a few sound management principles to your money affairs can put you on the track to a higher standard of living. By planning and control, you can eliminate money waste and make your income cover the outgo—with a surplus for future spending.

Your first step in successful money management is to—

(1) Determine how many dollars you will have to spend this year.

(2) Then ask yourself, where is it all going? To answer that, you are going to have to look over last year's figures, using your checkbook stubs, receipts, credit-card statements, tax return, etc.

The purpose of the income statement on page 605 is to help you chart your dollars. Start with your gross salary—if you are a two-earner household include the earnings of both. Then add every item of income you expect this year from *all* sources. (Keep any estimates on the low side.)

End result: The true amount of income you have to spend.

Part two of your money management overhaul is an inventory of your expenses. Fill in the expense statement on page 606. Let it guide you as you pull the figures from last year's checkbook, income tax return and your paid bills and receipts. In some cases you'll have to make estimates and in others you'll have more exact figures. But in either event you should be able to come up with an annual and monthly figure for each expense category.

Getting started: Once you've plugged the numbers into the chart your next step is to budget for your fixed expenses (e.g., installment obligations, insurance). Right now, some of these are annual payments, some quarterly, some bi-monthly, and some monthly. When several of these payments come due in the same month, your checkbook becomes a disaster area.

▶ **WHAT TO DO:** Allocate part of your monthly income to take care of these large expenses. Example: Your annual auto insurance costs $800, payable quarterly ($200 every three months). You should set aside about $66 of each month's income to take care of that large quarterly bill.

How to do it: Many banks offer automatic transfer privileges—by telephone, or by "money machine"—between checking and savings. You deposit your payroll check into your checking, transfer cash to savings, then pull cash back when it's needed (in the meantime, you earn interest). Or you can use a payroll savings plan, if your employer offers it. Upon your authorization, part of your check is deducted and deposited into a savings account.

Whatever the method, this reserve for large bills should be a separate account to avoid confusion with regular savings.

Some payments, of course, come every month, like your gas and electric bill. Some utilities, however, provide a monthly budget plan that equalizes the payments. You might consider signing up for it.

Variable Expenses: If you are like most people, your variable expenses (e.g., clothing, vacations, entertainment, hobbies) eat up an astonishingly high percentage of your income. The most important part of your money-management program will be to place controls on these expenses.

▶ **WHAT TO DO:** The easiest way to control the variables is to establish an allowance for each one in advance and try not to exceed that allowance. Don't make the mistake, however, of arbitrarily taking the knife to a particular classification. Chances are you won't be able to make good on your resolution anyway. Your limits should be within reach. And while establishing an allowance may not work every month, don't despair! In the long run, it will put your expenses into line.

Now, your expenses are accounted for—you've adjusted your payments, put controls on your variables and you've established an emergency fund for contingencies. What about those long-term money goals?

INCOME STATEMENT

Husband's earnings . . . . $
Wife's earnings . . . .
Earnings of other family members. . . . .
Bonuses . . . .
Interest & dividends . . . .
Rent income from property owned . . . .
Royalties. . . . .
Business profits. . . . .
Profits from sales of assets . . . .
Child support, alimony. . . . .
Gifts. . . . .
Other . . . .

Net Annual Spendable Income $_____
Net Monthly Spendable Income $_____

EXPENSES

Rent or mortgage payment... $
Home insurance ....
Heat and electricity...
Water..
Telephone ....
Life insurance ....
Health insurance...
Other insurance..
Installment obligations..
Loan repayments ....
School/college tuition...
Dues ....
Real estate taxes ....
Income taxes (federal, state, local) and Social Security taxes ....
Child care/household help..
Licenses...
Other major items..
Food ....
Clothing...
Household operation:
    furniture..
    repairs..
    laundry ....
    supplies, linen, etc...
Car operation:
    gas & oil ....
    tires ....
    repairs & tuneups ....
Commuting costs:
    tolls ....
    train, bus fares ....
    parking ....
Ordinary medical & drugs (not covered by insurance) ....
Recreation/Hobbies ....
Family vacations ....
Magazines/Newspapers...
Education ....
Personal allowance (i.e., hairdresser).................................
Birthdays & Holidays ....
Charitable contributions...
Smoking & Liquor...
Other items & Miscellaneous ....
Cash reserves and savings..

                        Total for Year $_____
                        Total by Month $_____

Let's assume you've divided up your list into short- medium- and long-term goals. Perhaps a video recorder is your short-range goal. A little farther down the road, a trip to the Orient. In the long-range slot lies a vacation home.

▶ **PAY YOURSELF:** Include a payment to yourself—say 5% to 10% of take-home pay—right along with the rest of your fixed obligations. Put the cash into savings and you'll have a realistic expectation of accomplishing your goals.

How To Boost Your Take-Home Pay Without Getting a Raise

Are you overwithheld on your income taxes? If the answer is "Sure, I get a fat refund check," you haven't done yourself or your budget much of a favor.

▶ **DON'T BANK ON UNCLE SAM:** Getting a big refund can backfire. For one thing, the Government doesn't pay interest on the taxes withheld from your paycheck. For another, it is human nature to blow a big refund on indiscriminate spending.

Result: Overwithholding turns into a real budget buster.
Here's a better idea: See that the amount of tax withheld from your pay closely matches your actual tax liability. If this isn't the case now (you've been getting oversized refunds the past few years), you can turn things around this year by filing a revised Form W-4 (Withholding Allowance Certificate) with your employer.

If you qualify for any of the tax breaks listed below, you can probably increase your withholding allowances and your take-home pay:

- Special deduction for two-earner married couples (see p. 1201).
- Tax credit for child-care expenses (see p. 1207).
- Deduction for job-related moving expenses (see p. 131).
- Tax credit for energy-saving home improvements (see p. 127).
- Deductible amounts to an IRA or retirement plan (see Chapter Ten).
- Estimated decrease in tax through income averaging (see p. 1202).
- Itemized deductions in excess of the standard allowance ($3,200 for marrieds, to $2,300 for singles).
- Losses from sales of investment property, such as stock (see Chapter Three).
- Special withholding allowance (available to any single taxpayer with just one job, and a married person with non-working spouse.)

HOW TO TELL WHEN TO THROW AWAY YOUR CREDIT CARDS

Credit cards have an awesome power to singlehandedly destroy your budget. *Reason*: They are easy to use—and use—and use. Since you're not pulling real dollar bills out of your pocket, the temptation is to view credit cards as a ticket to consumer heaven—you buy today, pay tomorrow! And that's a—

▶ **BIG MISTAKE:** Every time you use a credit card (and don't pay off the statement balance immediately) you are taking out a high-interest installment loan. If you string out payments on an item you should not even have bought with cash you are throwing your budget right out the window. Impulse buying is your budget's worst enemy and credit cards can lead you straight down the road to fiscal undoing.

How Much You Can Afford to Pay on Installments

Rule of thumb: First subtract from your monthly take-home pay all your fixed expenses, i.e., mortgage payment and the like. (For this purpose include food, car or commuting expenses as fixed expenses.) Installment payments (including finance charges) shouldn't exceed 10% to 15% of what's left over. This is a *conservative* approach to installment spending.

Example: Let's say your family has a take-home income of $3,000 a month. Your fixed monthly expenses come to $2,000. *Result*: You'd be in the clear if your monthly installment payments were in the $100-$150 range.

Of course, if you charge a little here and charge a little there, your spending is liable to exceed the 10-15% limit you've set for yourself. To remove that possibility you must—

▶ **KEEP RECORDS:** Treat your credit cards as you do your checkbook. Maintain a running balance of what you charge on each card. (Your best bet is to maintain separate index cards for each credit card noting the date, the purchase amount and the balance on the card.) *Result*: You focus in on exactly how much you owe and when you owe it. (Missing a payment date usually leads to late charges and higher interest payments.)

Now that you've safely hurdled the overspending obstacle, you're ready to make your cards work for—and not against—you.

How to Map Out Strategies for Buying on Credit

• Buy big ticket items—furniture, cars, major appliances—on credit. *Reason*: These are exactly the things that credit was designed for—things you'd have trouble paying off all at once in cash.

Helpful hint: The larger the item you intend to finance, the more important it is to *shop around*. For example, a car dealer may offer you very attractive credit terms. But it won't mean a thing if he also charges you the manufacturer's sticker price.

▶ **WHAT TO DO:** It's always a good idea to find out what the car's invoice price is—the price the factory charged the dealer. You can, of course, ask to see the invoice slip. But you might get further by first taking a look at "The Blue Book", available at bookstores and some newsstands. This book gives you a rundown of the new models and how much the dealers actually spent for them.

• Pay off balances—quickly. If you do use a card for everyday items don't string out payments. Finance and late charges can run up the costs of a low-priced item.
• Keep away from revolving credit cards and bank credit cards as much as possible. Paying by a travel and entertainment card such as American Express forces you to pay off the balance at the end of each month. That should help heighten your fiscal awareness and keep you honest. (If you're not prompt, American Express will tack on late charges and may fail to renew your card at the end of the year.)
• Check billing dates. When you charge, the bill you receive usually gives you between 15 and 25 days from the billing date to pay.

▶ **IDEA IN ACTION:** If you intend to buy something new with a credit card, buy it right after the billing date. *Result*: You'll have use of the item—and your money—for almost two months before you have to pay the bill.

Example: Mr. White decides to buy a tape recorder using XYZ credit card. He gets billed from XYZ on the 15th of each month, and doesn't have to pay for 20 days after that. Mr. White buys the recorder on August 16th. *Result*: White doesn't have to pay on the charge until October 5th. Meanwhile, if White keeps his money in an interest-bearing account, he has picked up an extra few weeks' interest.

HOW TO GET THE MOST FROM YOUR MONEY WHEN YOU BUY ANYTHING

The best way to get your money's worth and avoid unscrupulous or unfair sales tactics is to know your consumer rights.

Deciphering legalese—the verbiage that clouds most contracts—is your first step towards consumer literacy. When it comes to concise, cogent wording, consumer credit contracts are often the worst offenders. That's why we're going to show you—

How to Read the Legal Clauses in Consumer Credit Contracts

The nine clauses below are prime examples of unnecessary complexity in installment loans. For each of them, we've provided a plain English interpretation of the consequences when you sign on the dotted line. If any of these provisions is used against you, you stand to lose a great deal.

(1) Confession of judgment clause: "To secure payment. . . [from me,] . . . I authorize any attorney . . . to appear [for me]...after default in payment hereof and confess a judgment without process in favor of the creditor . . . ."

Plain English: If you ever sue me because I haven't paid, I agree, in advance, that you should win—even if I have a good reason for not paying. In fact, your lawyer can represent me.

(2) Blanket security interest clause: "This note is secured by a security interest in all of . . . [my] personal property . . . now owned and hereafter acquired . . . at [my] residence . . . or at any other location to which the goods may be moved . . . ."

Plain English: If I don't pay, you can take all the household goods I own.

(3) Waiver of state property exemption clause: "[I waive the] homestead exemption and all other exemptions or moratoriums to which the signers or any of them may be entitled under the laws of this or any other state, now in force or hereafter to be passed, as against this debt or any renewal thereof."

Plain English: If I don't pay, you can take away even the personal belongings state law would allow me to keep.

(4) Right to collect deficiency clause: "The Creditor may retain the goods as its property or may sell or otherwise dispose of the item pursuant to the (State) Uniform Commercial Code, whereupon Debtor shall be liable for and shall pay any deficiency on demand."

Plain English: If you repossess what I bought from you and you don't get a good resale price for it, I'll still owe you the difference. So if you take back a perfectly good $500 TV and can get only $150 for it, I lose the TV and still owe you $350.

(5) Waiver of right to privacy clause: "The undersigned . . . waives any right of privacy . . . and agrees that the lender may at its option communicate with any persons whatsoever in relation to the obligation involved, or its delinquency, or in an effort to obtain cooperation or help relative to the collection or payment thereof."

Plain English: If I don't pay, you can tell all my friends and relatives and my boss that I'm a deadbeat.

(6) Attorney's fee clause: "In addition if this agreement is referred to any attorney for collection due to any default . . . Debtor agrees to pay an attorney's fee of 15% of the total of payments then due, plus the court costs."

Plain English: I'll pay for your lawyer if you sue me.

(7) Insecurity clause: "If the Debtor fails to pay any installment . . . [and] the Secured Party shall feel insecure, all sums then owing under said Credit Agreement shall immediately become due and payable without demand or notice."

Plain English: If you start to feel insecure about getting paid back, you can demand that I pay the entire amount at any time.

(8) Acceleration clause: "Default in payment of any installment . . . shall, at the option of the holder thereof, render the entire unpaid principal balance . . . at once due and payable."

Plain English: If I miss a payment, you can make me repay the whole loan immediately.

(9) Wage assignment clause: "For value received [I] hereby assign . . . ten per centum (10%) of all salary, wages, commissions and other compensation for services severally earned or to be earned . . . in the employ of the employer specified . . . until the loan secured hereby and described below shall have been fully discharged . . . [I] . . . authorize . . . my said employer . . . to pay said part of [my] wages . . . to the said Assignee . . ."

Plain English: If I don't pay, just have my boss deduct the money from my paycheck. I won't argue about it—even if I have good reason for not paying.

▶ **AND THESE ARE TYPICAL:** The clauses you just read are typical standard form contract provisions used in states where they're permitted. One or more may be in the contract you sign.

▶ **WHAT TO DO:** Read the contract and ask questions *before* you sign a credit agreement. Keep these clauses in mind when you shop for major items. If you're not sure of what you're agreeing to, don't sign the document. Once you've put your signature on the dotted line, the time for questions—and changes in the contract—will have passed.

PRODUCT WARRANTIES—WHAT THEY MEAN AND HOW THEY CAN HELP YOU

Obviously, credit contracts are just the tip of the consumer misunderstanding iceberg. Product warranties are another fertile source of complaints. *Reason*: Many people are unaware what the warranty covers, how long it covers it, and what rights they have if the manufacturer fails to make a repair under the warranty.

Background: Manufacturers who offer written warranties are required to clearly label them as either "full" or "limited." The difference between the two designations lies in what the maker must do if the product does not perform satisfactorily. (Later on, we'll cover what protection you have if the manufacturer chooses not to affix a written warranty to its product.)

• Full warranty: Under a full warranty the manufacturer must repair or replace a defective product without charge and within a reasonable period of time during the warranty period. And it must give consumers a new product or a refund if the original product hasn't been repaired after several attempts.

▶ **TOO LARGE TO SEND BACK?** If a product is too large or too heavy to reasonably expect you to ship it to the store, it must be repaired or replaced right in your home. You pay nothing for either parts or labor.

You are protected by the "full" warranty even if you are *not* the product's original purchaser.

▶ **BUYER ACTION:** By law, copies of the complete warranty must be available in the store where a warrantied product is offered for sale. If a warranty isn't on the product itself or displayed nearby, ask the manager for a copy.

In general, you can measure the value of a "full" warranty by two things:

(1) Duration: A two year warranty is certainly more valuable than one for, say, 90 days. By the way, a "life-time" guarantee may not be as valuable as you think. *Reason*: The product may be guaranteed for its life—not yours.

(2) Parts covered: A "full" warranty can cover so little of the product as to be practically worthless. For instance, a "full" two year warranty on the casing of a food processor is not very valuable. But one on the motor, container, and blades would be.

• Limited warranty: A manufacturer who uses a "limited" warranty can restrict his liabilities in ways not permitted under a "full" warranty.

Items to look for: A "limited" warranty can require that you return the product to the store for repair. It may cover only the cost of parts, not labor. You may have to pay handling charges. Or you may be entitled to only a pro-rata refund under the warranty. A product could be warranted for home use only. An air conditioner installed in your office might have no coverage. The warranty may not cover you if you are not the original purchaser. And, even if you are, you may be required to return a registration card to the manufacturer to get coverage.

▶ **WHAT TO DO:** Weigh the duration, extent of coverage, and restrictions of a "limited" warranty when you decide to buy a product. Keep in mind that the duration and coverage of a "limited" warranty can make it a better deal than even a "full" warranty.

Now let's talk about what happens if a manufacturer exercises the right *not* to expressly warranty its product. Are you out of luck if the product turns out to be a lemon? Fortunately, the answer is no. *Reason*: You are still protected by an—

▶ **IMPLIED WARRANTY:** Implied warranties are created under state law and exist automatically without being written down. The most common implied warranty—the warranty of merchantability—is a promise that a product is not defective and is fit for ordinary use at the time it is sold.

Example: Three days after you plug it in, your new portable TV goes on the blink. Assuming you haven't misused the set, you have a right to get it repaired or replaced under the implied warranty. *Reason*: The TV wasn't in a merchantable condition when you bought it.

Another type of implied warranty requires that the product be suited for the particular purpose for which it was bought. To prevail under this warranty you must be able to show that the seller had reason to know: (1) that the product will be used for a specific purpose and (2) you as the buyer are relying on his skill or judgment in selecting or furnishing suitable goods.

> *Example:* You fix up old cars as a hobby. You go to Auto Supply Co. for a Model-T carburetor. After it's installed, you find out the carburetor is totally unsuitable. Since you relied on the seller's expertise—and he knew the purpose for which the carburetor was intended—you can bring an action against the company under the implied warranty.

The duration of implied warranties varies from state to state. Some states enforce implied warranties for up to four years.

> ▶ **BE CAREFUL:** A *written* warranty may contain a phrase such as "Implied warranties on this product are limited to three months." If the written warranty itself extends for only three months, this could mean you have no legal recourse should you discover the product is defective after three months.

How to Protect Yourself From Poor Workmanship

One scenario: You're at a flea market and you see a great deal on a power drill. But when you bring it home you realize that it's simply a piece of junk.

If you paid by cash: No matter how you cut it, no matter how well-founded your complaint, it will be tough to get your money back. *Reason:* The merchant may have gone out of business or just not want to help you out. It happens all the time. But now look what happens—

If you paid by credit card: It's a different ballgame. *Reason:* As long as you made a good faith attempt to return the defective merchandise or to convince the merchant to make good on the product, you don't have to pay the charge when it comes due.

There are limitations, however. (1) The purchase price must be more than $50. (2) You must have either bought the item in your home state or within 100 miles of your current address.

How to Protect Your Claim When a Product Goes Sour

By law, the following information must be given to you if a written warranty is provided for a product costing more than $15:

- Who is entitled to the protection.
- Identification of the parts covered by the warranty.
- Indication of what will be done to correct defects or failures (including which items or services will be paid by the warrantor and which expenses must be borne by you).
- The warranty's effective date (unless it is the date of purchase).

● Steps you must follow to get satisfaction (including the company's name and address and a toll-free phone number you can use to get warranty information).

The rest is up to you. For instance, don't throw away the sales receipt. You'll need it to prove the date you purchased the product. A few manufacturers require that a special warranty card be returned to activate the warranty—do it. You might even save the ad that led you to buy the product. It may include guarantees that add ammunition to your complaint. And, obviously, keep the warranty itself in a file for future reference.

Extra protection: If you requested service, write down the dates—and keep a folder of your service receipts. *Reason:* If the warranty period runs out before the product is fixed, you will have proof that the defect was discovered while the warranty was still in effect.

NOTE: Many warranties automatically self-destruct if repairs are made by anyone other than the company or an authorized service center. Moral: Read every word of the warranty carefully.

What to Do When Things Go Wrong

It's a rare person indeed who hasn't fought with a store, credit card company, or bank over a billing error. Computer (or human) mistakes can lead to seemingly endless runarounds that succeed only in elevating your blood pressure—next month the error is still on the bill.

Does that mean you're powerless? Not at all. In fact the law gives you a potent weapon to help you fight back. It's called the Fair Credit Billing Act (FCBA).

The main purpose of the Fair Credit Billing Act is to force companies to resolve quickly consumer complaints about their bills. "Billing errors" may arise in a variety of ways. For example, the clerk may fail to credit a returned purchase, or the computer may bill you for the same item twice, or the store may mail the periodic statement to the wrong address.

> ▶ **CONSUMER ACTION:** Write—don't call—the company at the address given on your bill for billing error notices. Do so no later than 60 days after the initial bill containing the error is recieved.

The letter must include your name, address and your account number. You must also indicate that (1) an error exists on the bill, (2) its amount and (3) why you think the error has been made. (If you send along any documentation, a sales receipt, for example, make sure you retain a copy of it for yourself.) You may want to send the letter "return receipt requested" to ensure that the company received it—and when. In any case keep a copy of the letter for your own records.

What happens next: The store, bank, or credit card company has thirty days to respond to your letter (unless, of course, the error is corrected before then). The dispute must be resolved one way or another within two billing cycles (but no later than 90 days) from the time the notice was received. *Important:* The notification letter you send activates the resolution process and shifts the burden of solving the problem to the creditor. A creditor can't retailiate against you for exercising your rights on a billing error. Once the creditor has your letter, it *cannot*—

- Try to collect the disputed amount or charges (by instituting court action or attachment proceedings, for example).
- Make or threaten adverse credit reports, or report the contested amount as delinquent to a credit bureau. The amount may, however, be reported as disputed.
- Close your account or accelerate the debt.
- Levy finance charges or late penalties on the amount in dispute.

▶ **IF YOU WERE RIGHT:** The store, bank, or credit card company must correct its mistake, make any necessary credits, and send you a correction notice.

This notice may either be sent separately or it may be included with the billing statement that is sent to you during the resolution time period. (If a periodic statement is used, the billing error must be specifically identified.) But—

▶ **IF YOU WERE WRONG:** If the bill turns out to be correct, you will be sent an explanation of why you were wrong and you will get documentary evidence of the indebtedness. You may be required to pay both the minimum payments and finance and other related charges that accumulated during the resolution period on the disputed amount.

A creditor, store, credit card company, or bank that doesn't comply with these procedures is subject to penalties: (1) The creditor cannot collect the amount of the billing error (up to $50), nor the finance charges, even if the billing error turns out to be no error at all. (2) You can bring the creditor to court and sue for actual damages, and twice the amount of any finance charges (not less than $100 or more than $1,000). You may also be able to recover the costs of the court action plus attorney's fees.

Don't Wait—Arbitrate

Many Better Business Bureaus have established arbitration panels that are legally binding in many states. Their function is to serve as mini-courts for victimized consumers who want their problems resolved quickly and cheaply. The panels are composed of impartial volunteer arbitrators who have been through a training course (usually lawyers from the community).

Setting the process in motion: Let's say you and a local business person are at odds. To go the arbitration route, both of you must first agree to abide by the arbitrators' decision, no matter how it turns out. In many states, local courts will enforce the decision if one party to the dispute tries to back out. Check to see if your state is one of the few that will not.

Once you've agreed to the process, a list of potential arbitrators is made available, along with biographies. A panel (sometimes one, usually not more than three) is then picked based on who both of you decide will be fair.

Court on wheels: Arbitration panels are flexible. They can meet almost anywhere, and at any time to accommodate your schedules. And you can present whatever evidence (including witnesses' testimony) to back up your case. If you want to bring a lawyer along, fine, but you really don't need one. As a rule, the costs of an arbitration panel are picked up by the sponsoring Better Business Bureau. But to be on the safe side you should contact your local Bureau just to make sure that this policy hasn't changed.

How to Press Your Complaint and Come Out A Winner

If you've done all you can to have your grievance solved in the normal fashion, and you still have a product or service that's not up to par, you must get tough. It's time to threaten legal action. You don't have to go to law school to sound like a lawyer, and you don't need a law degree to write a so-called "Lawyer's Letter".

Here's the story: A lawyer's letter states your complaint so forcefully that the shopkeeper or manufacturer decides to resolve the problem to your satisfaction. The letter's main purpose is to save you the hassle of a full-fledged law suit when the amount of money involved doesn't warrant one.

To give you an idea of what a "lawyer's letter" should sound like here's a format you could adapt to your own situation.

> To whom it may concern:
>
> 1. [State complaint and steps taken to reach an equitable resolution of the problem. Attach copies of all prior correspondence with the seller and others you may have contacted to intervene on your behalf (*never* send originals).]
>
> 2. As you can see, I have done everything in my power to elicit a response from you and to straighten out this misunderstanding. But you have chosen not to cooperate and I am left with a [state the product or service] that is not satisfactory.
>
> You therefore leave me with no choice. I have forwarded all pertinent information to my attorney who will be in touch with you shortly. I strongly recommend, however, that you settle this problem with me on an informal basis before the attorneys enter the picture. I guarantee you that once that happens the costs of reaching a solution will be much higher than they are now.
>
> Sincerely,

You could of course hire an attorney to write this kind of letter for you (the cost depends on what the complaint is and the caliber of attorney). A law firm's letterhead at the top and a lawyer's signature at the bottom carry weight. But you may be able to get the same results if you write the letter yourself. The trick is to sound like you mean business and will back up your threats with action.

HOW TO BEAT THE SKYROCKETING COST OF HIGHER EDUCATION

A child's college education can cost a fortune. Latest estimates indicate that four years at an Ivy League university will cost upwards of $46,000 in the next few years. Scary isn't it? It doesn't have to be, though, if you start looking around now for creative ways to find enough money to pay the bills.

How much will it really cost? Although tuition is the big ticket element of college costs, there is a lot more that has to be tacked on to arrive at the bottom-line figure. What follows is a list of items that must be taken into consideration:

Tuition	Commuting costs
Room and Board	Allowance for recreation,
Books	and entertainment
Equipment & Supplies	Clothing & Laundry
Student fees	Fraternity or Sorority dues
Lab charges	Personal care and health

Q. Where do we get this information?

A. The colleges themselves usually have literature that you can send away for. Catalogs are readily available from guidance counselors and public libraries. And by all means, talk to other parents who have children in college. They may be the best source of current information.

In this section we'll cover the best ways for you to get dollar help for your child's education:

- Federal aid programs
- Student loans
- ROTC scholarships
- National Merit Scholarships
- Private scholarship opportunities
- Cooperative education program
- Advanced placement and
- Other down-to-earth cost-cutting techniques

Each aid program has different financial need requirements. Some are more stringent than others. One that requires the greatest showing of financial need is the—

National Direct Student Loan Program—
What It Means to Your Financial Picture

The National Direct Student Loan (NDSL) is a low-interest loan from the Federal Government paid directly to the college on behalf of your child.

▶ **LOW-INTEREST LONG-TERM LOAN:** The interest rate on a NDSL is only 5%, and you have ten years to repay it. Payments do not begin until six months after your child either graduates or begins to attend school only half time. You don't pay interest on the loan until payments commence.

How much can you borrow? Amounts that can be borrowed each year for undergraduate study range from $200 to $1,500. The maximum you can borrow for your child's college years is $6,000. For graduate students, the maximum loan is $12,000 (this total includes any amount borrowed to finance undergraduate school).

The first step in obtaining a National Direct Student Loan is to get and complete the required paperwork.

Forms can be obtained from your child's high school or the colleges that he or she will be applying to. Different colleges require different forms, so you must check with each college that is on the child's list. The most common forms are:

- The College Scholarship Service's Financial Aid Form (FAF)
- The American College Testing Program's Family Financial Statement (FFS)
- Application for Federal Financial Aid (AFSA)

Award of Federal money is based on financial need. Need is based on such factors as income, assets, liabilities, number of children in college, family size, and medical expenses.

▶ **IMPORTANT:** Financial aid is often distributed on a first-come-first-served basis, so it's crucial that your child submit the application as early as possible. January 1 is the earliest application date for a given year. And aid from Federal programs does not automatically continue from one year to the next. Your child must *reapply* every year.

HOW TO GET COLLEGE MONEY THROUGH THE GUARANTEED STUDENT LOAN PROGRAM

The Guaranteed Student Loan Program (GSL) is one of the more widely used sources of financial aid.

Here's the story: To help you pay for your child's higher education, a bank, credit union, or savings and loan association will make you a low-interest loan. The loan is insured by a state agency and reinsured by the Federal Government.

If you are a middle-income family you may have read about the recent crackdowns in the GSL. Good news: You haven't been ruled out!

▶ **NEW GSL CRITERIA:** Your child still *automatically qualifies* for the maximum loan if your adjusted gross family income is under $30,000. If family income is over $30,000, your child can still qualify—the difference is that you will have to undergo a "needs analysis" to determine how much money your child is eligible to borrow.

How the needs analysis is carried out: The school your child applies to will calculate need based on the following three factors: 1) the cost of education; 2) other aid your child might be receiving; and 3) expected family contribution. The school will take the sum of the last two factors and subtract it from the cost of education. The remainder represents student need.

The third factor—family contribution—is based on Government tables that take into account family income, family size, and the like. But before we go into greater detail on this, let's take a look at how a needs analysis would be carried out in this—

Example: Mary and John Smith have three dependent children, the oldest of whom will be attending State University in the fall. The cost of a year at State U is $7,000, but part of that cost will be defrayed by a $1,500 scholarship. The Smith's adjusted gross income, based on their Federal tax return, is $36,000.

Needs Analysis

Cost of education		$7,000
Expected family contribution	$3,010*	
Financial aid	$1,500	
	$4,510	
Available resources		-$4,510
Student need		$2,490

*This figure is based on tables compiled for the 1982-1983 academic year.

How the GSL works: Generally, you can borrow up to $2,500 a year for undergraduate work ($5,000 for graduate work). The total amount you're allowed to borrow is $12,500 for undergraduates and $25,000 for graduate students.

The interest rate for the loan is 9% but the Federal Government pays the interest until six months after the child leaves school or drops below half-time status. That's also when loan repayments must commence. Under Federal law, the minimum monthly payment is $50, and the term of the loan can't exceed 10 years. The payment schedule your lender sets up may be shorter term and call for higher monthly payments. *Make sure to discuss the repayment schedule with your lender before you take out the loan.*

Where to apply for a Guaranteed Student Loan. Applications can be obtained from neighborhood lenders or schools. You must complete a portion, and then the school your child will attend fills out the remainder. Once the school has completed its portion, take the application to a lender (a bank, savings and loan institution, or credit union).

▶ **WHAT TO DO:** Go to a lender that you have done business with on a regular basis. Financial institutions do not *have* to lend you money, but a lender that you have an account with is more likely to do so.

NEW SOURCE OF COLLEGE AID: THE PARENTS' LOAN PROGRAM

The Parents' Loan Program (PLUS) is a relatively new way to help finance a child's college costs. Like the Guaranteed Student Loan, the PLUS loan is made by financial institutions, such as banks, savings and loan institutions, or credit unions. Unlike the GSL's however, PLUS loans are—

▶ **AVAILABLE TO ANYONE:** Any parent, regardless of income, is eligible to receive a PLUS loan. You can borrow up to $3,000 a year, up to a total of $15,000 for each child who is enrolled at least half-time and is a dependent undergraduate student. Independent children can take out their own loans of up to $2,500 per year. (However, if these students also have a GSL, the total of both loans cannot exceed $2,500 per year.)

The interest rate for PLUS loans is 12%. Repayment is monthly, and begins 60 days after the loan is made. Graduate and professional students as well as independent undergraduates can defer payment of the principal while they are attending school full time. Interest payments, though, are due after 60 days. Like the GSL's, the precise repayment schedule is up to the individual lender. So be sure to discuss this when applying for the loan.

RESERVE OFFICERS' TRAINING CORPS (ROTC) SCHOLARSHIPS

Scholarships awarded by the Armed Forces ROTC offer big benefits to college students. Army and Air Force scholarship winners receive full tuition and other academic fees at the colleges they choose, plus $100 a month for each month of the college year. Navy and Marine ROTC scholarships award up to $25,000 in benefits.

▶ **IMPORTANT:** The ROTC scholarships require a commitment that your child ought to consider carefully. *Reason:* Upon graduation from college he or she is required to fulfill a six-year military obligation. Participants will also be required to take certain college courses in addition to their regular workload, or they may be required to select a particular major, or to attend a training program during the summer.

Eligibility: Applicants for scholarships from the Army program (ROTC), Navy and Marine Corps program (NROTC), and Air Force program (AFROTC) must meet the following criteria: be U.S. citizens of at least 17 years of age; be high school graduates or have equivalent credit; Meet certain physical standards; and complete college and commission requirements by a certain age (ranging from 21 to 25, depending on program).

There are additional eligibility criteria that your child might have to fulfill, depending on which of the ROTC programs he or she is interested in applying to.

The four-year scholarships are awarded competitively. An application and often an interview are part of the process. For more information on the specifics of the ROTC scholarships, and to find out whether the colleges your child is interested in have an ROTC program, contact your local recruiter or write to one of the addresses below:

Army ROTC Information Center
Fort Monroe, VA 23651

Navy Opportunity Information Center (05)
P.O. Box 5000
Clifton, NJ 07015

AFROTC Advisory Service
Maxwell Air Force Base
Montgomery, AL 36112

NOTE: The G.I. Bill of Rights also helps *veterans* meet their expenses while attending college. The bill provides a minimum of $342 a month for veterans of the post-Korean conflict period and the Vietnam era.

Rewarding Your Child's Scholastic Ability

If your child is currently in high school and preparing to take the barrage of tests necessary for college admissions, you've probably heard about the—

▶ **NATIONAL MERIT SCHOLARSHIP:** Over 1,500 scholarships are awarded annually, *based solely on merit* (financial need is not taken into account). In addition, thousands of other national merit scholarships take into account both merit *and* financial need.

How to qualify: The initial qualifying test is the PSAT (Preliminary Scholastic Aptitude Test), which is usually scheduled for the fall of your child's junior year in high school. Performance on this test determines who will be a semifinalist.

Semifinalists are given a scholarship application to complete, and then must take the SAT test in their senior year. The score on the SAT determines who is a finalist.

▶ **$1,000 SCHOLARSHIPS:** The National Merit Scholarship Corporation (NMSC) awards approximately 1,800 scholarships each year to finalists, based on academic excellence. Selection is determined primarily by the student's scholarship application. Financial need is *not* a factor in the selection.

If a finalist is not selected to receive a $1,000 scholarship from the NMSC, there are still two more ways that he or she can receive scholarship money:

1. Colleges. The NMSC will release finalists' names to the colleges the students apply to. Many colleges sponsor national awards. If the college your child plans to attend is a sponsor, then he or she could be awarded a scholarship for four years of undergraduate study. Awards typically range from $100 to $1,500 and are based on financial need.

2. Corporations. Many corporations sponsor national merit awards for the children of their employees. If your child is a finalist, and your employer sponsors awards, the NMSC will send the corporation your child's name. Awards are four-year scholarships and are based on financial need.

If your child is a finalist and did not receive scholarship money from any of the above three sources, all is not lost.

▶ **WHAT TO DO:** Be sure to include the fact that your child is a finalist (or, for that matter, a semifinalist) on the applications on other scholarships you are competing for. *Reason:* To be designated a national merit finalist is a mark of academic excellence. It could be a deciding factor in winning other scholarship money.

Important Sources of College Aid Might Be Right Under Your Nose

"If only I had known about these scholarships I would have applied. Why didn't anybody tell me about them?" Unfortunately, this is an all too common complaint. Hundreds of scholarship opportunities exist, but for one reason or another go unused.

Private scholarship sponsors include: Labor unions, corporations (some scholarships are strictly for children of employees, but others may be awarded to outsiders), trade associations, and civic and fraternal organizations that award scholarships to students located in the community.

▶ **WHAT TO DO:** Contact the sponsors as early as possible and ask for an application form and details of necessary qualifications. Important: Watch out for deadlines. Many an applicant has been disappointed because a deadline was inadvertently or carelessly missed.

Merit scholarships: To attract bright students whose families don't qualify for aid normally, colleges and universities offer merit scholarships. *The A's & B's of Merit Scholarships* is one book that lists the schools that offer this type of scholarship.

More common are talent and athletic scholarships. Once again family wealth is not a consideration. The heads of the applicable departments and coaches should be able to give you more information.

Does your child know what career path he or she wants to follow? If so you might be in line for career-related scholarship aids. Various companies and foundations offer them and guidance counselors should have a list of which do and the requirements that must be met.

There's More Than One Way to Keep a College Education Down to Earth

Financial aid and grants are just two means to an end. Don't forget that there are other methods to keep college costs within reason.

• *Advanced placement:* Advanced placement allows students who take college-level courses in high school—and pass competency exams—to receive college credit for them. *Result:* By accumulating enough of these credits the student could chop off a semester or two of college—and the expenses that go along with it. To find out more, ask the high school guidance office or—

▶ **CONTACT THE COLLEGE BOARD:** The Advanced Placement Program is administered through the College Board. Write to CLEP, Box 2815, Princeton, NJ 08541 to find out when exams are given. **Note:** Colleges have differing policies on advanced placement credits.

Also sponsored by the College Board is—

• *The College-Level Examination Program:* Let's say your child is a math wiz. If he or she scores high enough on a CLEP exam many colleges will grant credit in the tested subject. "Placing out" of introductory level college courses has gained in popularity as college expenses have risen.

• *College Cooperative Programs:* Students who qualify for this program alternate periods of study with periods of work in their chosen area of study. Although it may take longer to graduate, tuition costs are distributed over, let's say five years rather than four years. And co-op deals help to spread the burden. The student shares financial responsibility with both his parents and his college.

• *Shopping around:* One of the best, and one of the most sensible ways to trim the fat off a college education is to shop around for a less expensive school. Armed with your list of typical college outlays you should be able to make intelligent comparisons. Important: It's crucial that you match up a child's needs with your own financial requirements. You won't want to choose a school based solely on cost.

▶ **STATE COLLEGE BOOM:** With private college costs going through the roof state colleges are having a resurgence of popularity. If your child lives at home, rather than on campus, the savings should be dramatic. (Even if you're not a resident of the state, the state school will be less costly than a private one.)

• *Private loans:* Commercial lenders, credit unions, employers, civic or religious groups, individual colleges and, as a last resort, finance companies may be able to help you out. As always, try to get the best possible interest rate and don't delay paying the loan off. Ask each lender how much can be borrowed for each child; whether and how the plan can be terminated; whether you can make prepayments; if there are extra charges and whether there are any other restrictions.

• *Income splitting plans:* High bracket parents can divert income to their low bracket children as a means of saving for college. The details on income splitting can be found in Chapter 8.

▶ **INTERESTING IDEA:** Parents' loan programs have been set into motion by a number of organizations nationwide.
What they involve: Repayment schedules are established which are keyed into the family's income and the amount that the family wants to borrow on a per year basis. The annual figure can be adjusted up or down. Payments to the colleges are made through the bank and repayment schedules are quite generous (often up to six years). Many plans include an insurance policy. *Reason:* In case the parent becomes disabled or dies, the student is protected. He or she won't be forced to drop out of college.

Who are these plans for? The middle-class family that has fallen through the cracks of financial aid and has a child who wants to attend a good—but expensive—four year school. Once the bank has approved your credit you're on your way.
Here is a list of plans and their sponsors: The Knight Agency Plan. The Knight Agency, Boston, Massachusetts.
Girard Bank's Educ-check Plan. Girard Bank, 2nd & Chestnut St., Philadelphia, PA 19106.
Parents' Loan Plan of Princeton University. Princeton Parents' Loan Plan, Office of the Controller, P.O. Box 35, Princeton, NJ 08534.

HOW TO TURN A HIGH-COST VACATION INTO A LOW-COST GET-AWAY

Going on vacation doesn't have to be an expensive proposition—if you follow a few simple rules:

- Travel offseason: If you know the right time to go, you can get your vacation at a discount. And there's always an off-season somewhere. For instance, high-season in the Caribbean starts in Mid-December and ends in Mid-April. *Reason:* That's when residents of colder climes want to migrate south. But the weather will generally be just as good (and often better) during the "off-season." And the prices for air fare, hotel rooms, restaurants, etc. will be lower. You'll get better service and you'll have the place to yourself.

- Go where the crowds don't: Most tourists meekly follow fellow vacationers to the most overcrowded and underserviced locations around. And they are guaranteed to be miserable. So stay away from tourist traps and get off the beaten path.

- Always ask for lodging discounts: It's worth the cost of a long-distance phone call to learn about a "Supersaver Discount Weekend" or "Off-Season Specials." Use a motel or hotel chain's toll-free reservation number to make inquiries, too. And pay attention to ads in the travel sections of newspapers for dollar-saving arrangements.

- Play the exchange rate game: Try to visit a country where the cost of living is low and the rate of exchange for the U.S. dollar is high. As we go to press, that means countries like Greece, Mexico, Morocco, Brazil & Yugoslavia. Since this information changes, ask someone at your bank to give you a rundown of the most up-to-date exchange rates for the countries you might like to visit.

- Shop where the locals do: It's fine to window shop on some of the exclusive and high-priced streets around the world. But stick to department stores and out-of-the-way places where the local population do their shopping. Money-saving tip: Many countries have a Value-Added Tax (10% to 18% added automatically to the purchase price). If you spend more than $55 in one store, you can usually get refund forms to present to customs when you depart. Note: Don't pack your gifts; they may be inspected.

- Prepare your own meals: Browsing through another country's supermarkets can be just as interesting as visiting its museums—and it could add up to dollar savings. Preparing your own food can alleviate some of the strain on your pocketbook while you are traveling. In France, for instance, grocery stores are well stocked with ready-to-eat delicacies perfect for on-the-go tourists and picnikers. There's simply no reason that you have to eat in restaurants all the time.

- Check out tourist discounts: Bus, subway and train tickets for unlimited travel can be bought cheaply in many countries. Some foreign restaurants feature specially priced tourist menus or fixed-price menus. So, before you leave for your trip abroad ask the tourist offices of the countries you'll be visiting what special discounts are available.

- Call home collect: To avoid those huge service charges that hotels routinely add to your bill, call collect when you call home. And don't assume that calls from U.S. hotels are any better. They're not. You can wind up spending more than four times as much for a local phone call from your hotel room than from the public phones in the lobby or out in the street.

How To Get Your Vacation Off to a Flying Start

A little knowledge of airline procedures and Civil Aeronautics Board (CAB) regulations will make your plane trip easier and help you get the most for your money.

Before the departure date: Careful comparison shopping can lead to substantial savings in air fare. There may, however, be restrictions, or conditions that you must meet. Deregulation and the multitude of air fares further complicate the picture. Check out these important points about special-rate flights—*before* you make reservations:

• Does the air fare include the types of services that airlines have traditionally provided, such as free baggage handling?

• If you are stranded, will the airline arrange alternate flights? Will it pay for meals or hotel rooms during the wait? Find out what will happen if you decide to switch flights.

• Is there a cut-off date for making and changing reservations without paying more money? And will you lose the benefit of your discount fare?

• Are there any cancellation fees?

On international trips, some airlines will guarantee the special-rate fare. Others reserve the right to collect more money if the fare goes up before the departure date and you have not yet been ticketed.

When making a flight reservation, be sure to review all of the essential information with the agent before you hang up the phone or leave the office. Then—

▶ **DOUBLE CHECK THESE FACTS:** Is your name spelled correctly? Are the flight numbers and travel dates correct? If there is more than one airport at either city, be sure to check which one you'll be using. And don't forget to give the airline your home and work telephone numbers, so they can let you know if there is any change in its schedule.

Left at the gate: It's crucial to know your rights as an air traveler in case your flight is delayed or you are bumped from your flight. *Reason:* You may be entitled to a cash payment—or maybe a free trip or other benefits. According to the CAB you can get dollar compensation if:

(1) An airline overbooks your flight and has to "bump" passengers with confirmed reservations. The airline is required by CAB regulations to ask for volunteers to give up their seats.

(2) There are too few volunteers and you are involuntarily bumped. The airline must immediately give you "denied boarding compensation" of from $37.50 to $200, depending on the price of your ticket. You also retain your ticket, which will get you on an alternate flight.

▶ **IMPORTANT:** No compensation is due you, however, under these circumstances: (1) You are bumped as the result of the substitution of a smaller plane; (2)

The Government requisitions space on your flight; or (3) You are offered a seat on your original flight but in a different section than on your ticket.

You are also out of luck if you have failed to comply with ticketing, check-in or reconfirmation procedures; you are traveling with certain foreign airlines; or you are traveling between foreign cities.

▶ **WHAT TO DO:** Minimize your chances of being bumped by asking what the airline's priorities are for honoring reservations on oversold flights. *Reason:* A few airlines give priority to higher-priced tickets over discount fares. Most, however, bump the last people to arrive at the boarding gate.

Preserve your right to negotiate: If you are bumped and receive "denied boarding compensation," the airline will pay you by check. Once you cash the check, or deposit it in your bank, you will probably lose the right to demand more money from the airline later on. But you don't have to take the check in the first place. If being bumped costs you more money than the airline will pay you at the airport, you may be able to negotiate a higher settlement with the carrier's complaint department. Or, you could take the airline to court.

Remember: The CAB's overbooking regulations spell out the airlines' *minimum* obligation to people they bump involuntarily; you *may* be able to ask for—and get—more.

Cancellations and Delays: If your flight is canceled, some airlines will rebook you on the first available flight to your destination at no additional charge. Finding extra seats may be difficult, however, especially over holidays and other peak travel times.

Lost baggage: In case you and your suitcase fail to rendezvous at your destination, don't panic. The airlines have very sophisticated systems that can track down about 98% of the bags they misplace, and return them to their owners the same day. Still, it is wise to set up a safety net. Pack your carry-on-luggage with the essentials you'll need for at least 24 hours, just in case your bags don't make the connection.

Bonus for the bother: The airlines will usually absorb reasonable expenses you incur while they look for your missing belongings. (What's reasonable, however, is subject to negotiation.)

▶ **WHAT TO DO:** If your bags don't come off the conveyor belt, report this to the airline *before* you leave the airport. You must fill out a form describing the bag, listing its contents, and providing other information for the baggage-tracing staff. Be sure to keep a copy of this form for your records

How to Buy a Packaged Plan Without Getting Wrapped Up In Hidden Costs

A vacation package is one convenient cost cutter offered by travel agents, airlines, tour operators, colleges and special interest groups that is quickly gaining in popularity.

▶ **HOW IT WORKS:** A typical package combines hotel accommodations, transportation, and transfers between airport or railroad station and hotel. Optional features at additional cost may include sightseeing tours, meal plans, upgraded rooms or hotels and car rentals. Some packages may even be structured around particular activities, such as sports or the arts.

Major benefit: A flat low price—a figure usually far below what you'd wind up paying if you bought the travel components separately. But packaged deals aren't perfect. Many contain major restrictions regarding duration of stay and advance payments. Most don't have just one price. And the lowest price (usually in big bold print) may come with strings attached—the price may be available only in the off-season, during the middle of the week, or at the least expensive hotel.

Here are a list of factors to keep in mind as you're leafing through the literature:

- Exactly what the package includes and whether you're interested in all those things
- How many meals are provided, and which ones they are
- Types or classes of hotels offered
- Whether payments are refunded if you bail out of the trip
- Whether the tour operator can cancel if not enough people sign up
- Tour operator ability to change services or schedules

One way to protect yourself: Think about buying some form of trip cancellation insurance. Depending on the policy, you may be fully or at least partially reimbursed if you call the trip off. Your travel agent should be able to steer you towards the right type of policy with the right price tag.

How To Apply For Your Passport

If you want to vacation abroad, you'll need a valid passport. You can pick up applications at the nearest passport office. They can also be obtained at some post offices, courthouses, and county clerks' offices. You must apply in person if: (1) It's your first passport, (2) your current passport is more than eight years old or (3) it was issued before you turned 18. In all other cases you can apply by mail. (If you have to apply in person at the passport office, expect long lines and waits of a few hours.)

What you must submit: Along with the completed application form, you must include proof of U.S. citizenship (a birth certificate or naturalization papers), identification (for instance a driver's license) and two identical recent photographs which measure two inches by two inches and have a plain white background.

Passports now cost $35, but they are good for ten years. Once you've applied, it will generally take from two to four weeks for the passport to arrive.

Q. I'm scheduled to leave the country in a few days and I've completely forgotten about my passport. I think it's lapsed. What can I do?

A. Don't panic. If you are leaving within 48 hours, the Passport Agency will rush through the application while you wait. Condition: You must have valid proof of your departure date (your airline tickets should do).

Of course, one way to avoid the problem is to periodically check the effective date of your passport. If it needs to be renewed you can simply send it to the nearest passport office and they'll issue you a new one. If it has lapsed, however, you'll have to reapply as if it were your first one. Moral of the story: Don't wait until the last minute to get your passport from the Government.

HOW YOU CAN TAKE THE VACATION TRIP OF A LIFETIME—EACH AND EVERY YEAR

Many people may be able to own a piece of luxury vacation property without actually paying luxury prices. There is a fast-growing concept of ownership that enables vacationers to use a ski lodge, lakeside townhouse, or beach cottage, for years to come. Or maybe the use of all three.

> ▶ **TIME-SHARING:** You don't buy property outright. Instead, you buy *time-shares* that entitle you to the use of the lodge, or townhouse or cottage for a specified time each year—for a week, say, every July—at a fraction of the purchase price of the entire unit.

Naturally, time-sharing is not going to suit everyone. But if taking your vacation amid a resort setting means something to you, it can be a special treat for comparatively little money. What's more, a well-designed timeshare program can be a hedge against inflation in resort accommodations.

Q. But what if I don't want to take my vacation at the same place or time every year?

A. Many time-sharing resorts have what they call an "exchange network" that lets members swap their shares for suitable locations or dates. For a fee you can join networks that swap shares among resorts—you vacation on the ski slopes one year, on the beach the next. It depends on what your particular deed or agreement provides.

Q. What would I get for my money if I bought a time-share—say in a lakeside townhouse?

A. It depends on the developer you deal with. Some will sell you a deed that is yours until you sell it again. Some offer what amounts to a long-term lease. And in some time-share resorts you may have a choice of different types of time shares. But you will always be charged an annual maintenance fee.

Q. Does that maintenance fee apply to my expenses during my stay at the townhouse?

A. No it doesn't. The maintenance fee pays for keeping the townhouse and grounds in prime condition for all owners.

Important: Buying time-shares is not just another vacation arrangement. You're not signing up for a cruise or tour. It's a long-term obligation involving property and expenses. So look before you buy. Study the resort and its location carefully. If possible spend some time there and check out the following points:

• Are the buildings of quality construction? Are they kept clean and in good repair?

• Is the furniture durable and easily cleaned?

• Are the appliances backed by adequate warranties and do they meet your standards?

• Are recreation facilities properly maintained?

• Are grounds and building maintenance costs kept down?

• Is management competent?

▶ **WHAT TO DO:** After you've done all your homework and decided that time-sharing suits your pocketbook and your needs, you should see if the developer is a member of the National Timesharing Council (NTC) of the American Land Development Association (ALDA). ALDA is the national trade association for recreation, resort and residential real estate developers and is located at 1000-16th Street, N.W., Suite 604, Washington, D.C. 20036.

Looking for an Off-Beat Vacation? Try Swapping Your Home

Capturing the unique charm and flavor of a foreign country—or even another part of this country—is difficult when surrounded by camera-toting tourists. So instead of staying in an expensive hotel, elbow to elbow with people back home—

▶ **EXCHANGE YOUR HOME:** There are a number of firms that arrange home swaps for those who want a slice of life somewhere else. They match Americans who want temporary homes, in let's say, Europe with Europeans looking for the same thing in the United States. Many agencies will also set up swaps for "let's see America first" travelers.

Added attractions: Basing your vacation out of a temporary home allows you to bring along the whole family—at no extra cost (unlike a hotel or motel). What's more you'll have the comfort, convenience and privacy of a home away from home. Many deals can be structured to provide cars, household help, country club privileges and child care services.

And while you are enjoying the ambience of your new surroundings, someone is watching and taking care of your home.

▶ **INTERESTED?:** More information is available from Vacation Exchange Club, Inc. 12006-111th Ave., Unit 12, Youngtown, Arizona 85363 (602-972-2186).

Chapter 7

How To Get Credit Cheaply And Use It Wisely

Borrowing and using credit is a necessity for almost all of us. You certainly need credit to make large purchases (e.g., a home). You may even need it to take care of temporary cash emergencies. Anyone who needs — or will need — credit must know the essentials: How and where to get it and how to pay the rock-bottom minimum for it. That, in a nutshell, is what this Chapter's all about.

HOW TO ESTABLISH A GOOD CREDIT RATING

Even if you have no present need to borrow money, it's a good idea to establish a credit record. Some preliminary steps are necessary. First, you must have income. Second, you should have checking and savings accounts in your own name—they'll be useful as financial references. Third, you should pay bills—like telephone and utility bills—on time.

▶ **WHERE TO START:** A department store charge account is easier to obtain than a travel and entertainment card or a bank card. Once you have a few store accounts—and pay them promptly—you should be able to get credit cards or even a bank loan.

The credit application: In deciding whether to advance credit to you, a bank, store or other organization offering credit will ask you to fill out an application form. This form gives them information on your employer, your salary and other income, and details about your rent or mortgage payments, bank accounts and other assets and credit you have obtained from other sources. Be sure the information you supply is complete and correct.

Credit bureaus: When you apply for credit, your application is usually referred to a credit bureau. The credit bureau collects information on your credit history from public records, merchants and banks or other organizations who have extended credit to you or with whom you have accounts. They supply their client with information that includes your present and prior employment, earnings, marital history, and repayment patterns on previous loans. If the information supplied by the credit bureau meets whatever guidelines have been established by the lender, credit will be extended to you.

▶ **TIP FOR BORROWERS:** Before you take out a loan, it may be wise for you to obtain a credit report on yourself. You can do this by asking a local store or bank which bureau it uses. Contact the bureau and ask for a copy of your file. They will either mail you a copy of the file or ask you to come in to look at it if you've been turned down for credit, the credit bureau must show you the record free. Otherwise, you'll pay a few dollars.

Advantages: If there's an error on your report, you can have it corrected before you apply for the loan. To trigger a correction, you merely report the error to the credit bureau. They are obliged to reinvestigate and remove from your file any information that is incorrect or cannot be verified.

If the report shows negative, but correct, information, you can increase your chances for getting the loan by telling the loan officer about it and explaining the circumstances surrounding the negative information. For example, "Five years ago when I got out of college, I paid off a car loan late because the company I went to work for folded and I was unemployed for six months." It's better to make a clean breast of such information on your own rather than having the bank officer discover it on a credit report.

HOW TO MAKE THE MOST OF YOUR RIGHTS AS A BORROWER OR CREDIT APPLICANT

Say your application for a credit card or a bank loan has been turned down. The Fair Credit Reporting Act gives you specific rights that may help you rescue the situation. The company denying you credit must tell you which credit bureau supplied the data that caused them to deny you credit. You can get a copy of your credit history at no charge if you request it within thirty days after credit has been denied. If you find information that is incorrect or incomplete, you can require the credit bureau to reinvestigate and furnish a new report to creditors.

▶ **TIME LIMITS:** Negative credit information, like failure to pay a bill, must be removed from your record after seven years. Judgments and lawsuits may remain on file for ten years and bankruptcy may remain for fourteen years.

Costs of credit: Under the Truth in Lending Act, you are entitled to know the cost of credit you obtain. Most important: Your creditors must tell you what annual interest rate you will be paying. Also, a merchant must inform you of the cash price of a purchase and the deferred payment price. Creditors must disclose the amount of downpayment required, whether there is any penalty for prepayment and how the unearned part of the finance charge is calculated. In addition, you are entitled to know what the penalty will be if you pay late or default.

▶ **INSTALLMENT PLANS:** The lender on an installment loan must tell you the number of payments, the amount of each payment, the due dates, and whether there is a balloon payment (a high final payment).

Similar rules apply to a revolving charge account--where you agree to pay a stated amount on your account balance every month and interest on the unpaid balance. You must be told the monthly interest rate and the minimum monthly payment.

Discrimination: Under the Equal Credit Opportunity Act, creditors cannot discriminate against applicants on the basis of sex, marital status, race, color, religion, national origin, or age. Special protections are provided for women. A creditor cannot, for example, ask a woman about the financial status of her husband or ex-husband unless she is relying on income from him to support her application for credit. *Exception:* In community property states (Arizona, California, Idaho, Louisiana, Nevada, New Mexico, Texas and Washington), a woman can be questioned about the financial status of her husband.

EIGHTEEN WAYS TO GET CREDIT

There are many sources of credit. Some are appropriate for long-term needs—like financing a home improvement. Others are appropriate for short-term needs—like taking advantage of a sale item. It's wise to stick to appropriate sources. Otherwise you may find yourself either paying interest on more money than you need over a longer period than necessary or paying (usually higher) short-term interest rates over too long a period. Most important, as a prudent borrower, you'll want to—

> ▶ **SHOP AROUND:** You want to borrow at the least possible cost. And there will probably be a number of sources and ways of borrowing that you can choose from. Considerations of convenience—like the location of the lender and ease of application—should be secondary. Consider all possible sources and select the one that offers the lowest interest rate within the appropriate (short-term or long-term) category.

Perhaps the most common and convenient source of cash is your neighborhood bank or savings and loan. Rates vary depending on the type of loan and they also vary from one savings institution to another—so it pays to shop around. The bank where you have your savings and checking account is the best place to start. Since you're an established customer, it's more likely to be helpful than a bank that doesn't know you.

Here are eighteen other ways to get credit for your financing needs:

Credit Source # 1—The unsecured personal loan: An unsecured personal loan is given to you without collateral. It's an installment loan. That means you pay it off in specified amounts at periodic intervals. Most often you pay an equal amount every month over a period of from twelve to sixty months.

Guarantors: If you do not have an established credit rating, your bank may require that you get a relative or friend to cosign your loan. If the cosigner is a guarantor of payment (the usual case), he or she is as liable on the loan as you are. If the cosigner is a guarantor of collection, the bank must try to collect from you before it can hold the cosigner liable.

Purposes: The bank will ask you why you need a loan. It's best to give a purpose that they are used to, i.e., medical, dental, emergency, funeral or educational expenses or furniture, vacation, auto or home repair.

Credit Source #2—Overdraft privilege: Most banks offer customers an automatic line of credit they can draw upon. It may be activated by the customer drawing a check on his or her regular checking account for an amount that's greater than he or she has on deposit. In other cases the reserve is in a separate account that requires special checks. No interest charge is made until you use the line of credit and the interest stops when you repay the amount withdrawn.

> ▶ **CAUTION:** If you use overdraft checking, make sure that deposits to your checking account go first toward paying off the overdraft. Otherwise you may find deposits building up in the checking account while interest charges tick away on unpaid overdraft balances.

> ▶ **SHORT-TERM ADVANTAGE:** This kind of credit should be used for short-term purposes (bargains or weekend emergencies) and then repaid as soon as possible. Financing long-term debt, e.g., for a college education, or a home improvement, can usually be done at less interest cost through other credit sources.

Credit Source #3—Passbook or CD loan: If you have a savings account or certificate of deposit, the institution where the account is maintained will normally allow you to borrow against the account. As a general rule, you can borrow up to 80% of the face value of a CD and up to 100% of the value of a savings account. Rates are fairly reasonable—usually about 2% above the savings account or CD rate.

Because of the low rates, these loans are preferable to most other kinds of small loans for those who can take advantage of them. *Disadvantage:* You have no access to the savings account or CD funds while the loan is outstanding.

Credit Source #4—Collateralized loans: If you have stocks or bonds, your bank will normally allow you to pledge them as collateral for a loan. The bank will loan you an amount that's equal to a percentage—usually 50-60%—of the market value of the securities.

Credit Source #5—Bank credit cards: Certain credit cards, like MasterCard and Visa, are issued through banks. You can use these cards to pay for goods and services at participating establishments. If you don't pay your monthly bill promptly and in full, there will be an interest charge on the unpaid balance. You can also borrow cash up to a pre-approved limit on many cards. It's a good idea to reserve bank card borrowing for short-term situations. As with bank overdraft privileges, the interest charges on bank card loans tend to be high. It pays to —

> ▶ **SHOP AROUND:** Some banks will rebate a percentage of your annual finance charges and/or waive the annual fee (otherwise $15-$30) if you agree to maintain a certain minimum savings or checking balance.

Credit Source #6—Credit union loans: Credit unions are one of the very best sources for loans. *Reason:* Low operating costs allow credit unions to offer low interest rates. The credit unions we most commonly think of are organized by employees of a business firm or members of a labor union. But other groups—members of a club or lodge, for instance—can also organize credit unions. And many have done so.

What kinds of loans can credit unions make? Small personal loans are a traditional specialty. But credit unions can also make automobile, mortgage and home improvement loans. Although there is no restriction on the amount credit unions can lend to a member, individual credit unions impose maximums on the different types of loans they make.

▶ **ADVANTAGES:** The main advantage of credit unions is that they offer the lowest interest rates around—often ¼ or ½% below bank rates for the same kind of loan. Another plus is that you're dealing with colleagues or friends who are likely to lend a sympathetic ear.

Any disadvantages? A committee of your fellow workers or club members must approve or disapprove your loan application. You may not be anxious to let them know of your financial affairs.

HOW TO BORROW FROM THE COMPANY STORE

Some employers have plans that allow employees to borrow money from the employer either for the purchase of a home or for other reasons. In other cases, employees—usually only top management employees—can borrow from their companies at no interest cost. Another source may be a company's pension or profit sharing plan. An employee may be able to borrow from his own account in the company plan. Or he or she may be able to borrow from the plan itself. Perhaps best of all, low cost loans may be available from an employee's credit union.

▶ **WATCH OUT:** Employees considering a loan from their employers should find out whether they'll be obligated to pay up when (and if) they leave the company. Loans that must be paid off upon departure may be a good idea only for employees planning a career—or at least an extended stay—with the firm.

Credit Source #7—Employer loan with interest: Usually an employer with a formal procedure for making loans to employees will charge the same interest rate as a bank. The usual term of an employer loan is six months to a year. One disadvantage: You may not want to supply the information about your personal finances to your employer that it may require before making a loan. In any case, it is wise to consider the impact of an employer loan on your overall relationship with the employer.

Credit Source #8—Interest-free loans: Major stockholders and others in a position to get a tax-free company loan should probably seize the opportunity. One caveat—

> ▶ **WATCH OUT FOR TAX PITFALLS:** The Revenue Service is not happy with these arrangements. It can challenge an interest-free loan on two grounds: (1) the amount loaned is actually a dividend (if the borrower is also a shareholder) and therefore fully taxable; or (2) the economic benefit obtained from an interest-free loan is taxable income to the borrower.

To head off a challenge on the ground that the loan is actually a dividend, a stockholder-borrower should formalize every detail of the loan transaction. For example, have the loan specifically okayed by the Board of Directors and recorded in the corporate minutes. And have the company's attorney check out the company's charter and applicable state laws. (Some states prohibit lending corporate funds to officers and directors; others require stockholder approval.) In addition, if you are a major stockholder, you can take these—

> ▶ **TAXWISE PRECAUTIONS:** Do everything you can to establish that the loan is bona fide: (1) You should give the company a promissory note with a fixed maturity date. (2) The company's books should reflect the loan as an account receivable. And finally, (3) you should make payments as called for in the note.

Even if the interest-free loan you get from your corporation isn't tagged a dividend, you're not out of the woods. The Government could argue that the economic benefit you derive—that is, the interest you avoid paying—constitutes taxable income to you. Fortunately, the courts have generally disagreed with the Government's position. However, the Government continues to challenge these arrangements.

Credit Source #9—Homebuyer's plan: Some employers offer employees assistance with the purchase of a home. The employer provides a loan and takes back a second mortgage. Usually there is a requirement that the employee have a certain minimum number of years of service with the firm. Another common requirement is that the home be located within a reasonable commuting distance to the place of work.

Although the terms of these plans vary, a typical plan provides up to 25% of the purchase price of a home to an employee who can borrow 65% elsewhere and provide 10% himself.

Credit Source #10—Retirement plan loans: If your retirement plan allows plan loans, they can be a good source of long-term credit. The tax law requires that plan loans (a) bear a reasonable rate of interest, (b) be adequately secured, and (c) be available to all employees on a non-discriminatory basis.

Loans repaid over a period of more than five years are considered taxable distributions from the plan, rather than a tax-free loan transaction. Loans that are required to be repaid within five years are not taxable distributions as long as the loan doesn't exceed the lesser of (1) $50,000, or (2) one half of the employee's vested benefit. (If one-half the employee's vested benefit is less than $10,000, the employee may still borrow up to $10,000 tax-free.)

▶ **SPECIAL BREAK FOR HOME LOANS:** A housing loan is not subject to the five-year rule. In other words, the repayment period can be longer than five years without the loan being tagged a distribution. But note that a housing loan is fully subject to the dollar limits.

What is a housing loan? It's a loan made to enable an employee to buy, build, or substantially rehabilitate housing to be used as a principal residence by either the employee or a member of his or her family.

Credit Source #11—Retirement plan investment loans: These are different from regular retirement plan loans in that they're not based on the borrower's own retirement plan account. They are part of the general investment activities of the plan. In addition to conventional investments, a plan may allow its trustees to invest in obligations of employees—usually secured by home mortgages.

Although these loans are not subject to the same requirements as to amount and duration as regular retirement plan loans, security requirements are apt to be stringent. Reason: The plan is obligated to limit itself to prudent investments. One more thing—these loans are not yet widely available.

HOW YOUR HOME CAN HELP YOU GET CREDIT

If you're like most people, your home is the most valuable asset you own. As such, it can be used as collateral to obtain credit. This can be done by refinancing with a bigger first mortgage. Or, you can take out a second mortgage. But there are some important things to consider before you do either.

Credit Source #12—Refinancing your first mortgage: If you've had a mortgage on your home for some time, chances are the amount of the loan that you've already paid off can be made available to you again. In addition, if the property has increased in value since you bought it, the amount of that increase can usually justify a larger loan. To draw down additional cash you only have to "refinance" your mortgage—that is, take out a new first mortgage—and repay the original loan. The net proceeds (amount of new loan less the old) are yours to do with as you please. You can refinance through the original lender or through a new lender.

What if the mortgage you've got is at a lower interest rate than the current rate for a new mortgage? You should be able to gain some advantage from the bank. They may, for example, waive payment of points on the new mortgage. Alternatively, you may want to keep the low-rate first mortgage and take out a second mortgage on the property.

Purposes: There has been a trend in recent years for homeowners to borrow money for non-home purposes through mortgage financing. This might seem like a good idea—interest rates on home mortgages are lower than on most other kinds of loans. But the problem is that the homeowner may be "borrowing long to buy short." He is using long-term borrowing to pay for short-term purchases or expenses. By spreading interest payments over say twenty years, his total interest cost will be much higher than it would be with a conventional loan (even at a higher rate) repaid over a shorter period.

▶ **WAY OUT:** A homeowner using a refinanced first mortgage or a second mortgage to pay for a short-term expense—say a child's college expenses—should make sure the mortgage agreement allows for penalty-free prepayment of principal. Then he should work out a schedule for himself that calls for prepayments at as fast a rate as possible—and stick to it. Borrowers without the willpower to make significant mortgage prepayments should consider limiting themselves to short-term borrowing to cover short-term expenses.

Credit Source #13—Take out a second mortgage: The same unmortgaged equity in your home that would allow you to refinance can be utilized as collateral for a second mortgage. Usually banks or other lenders will loan up to about half of the amount of the unmortgaged equity. Say you own a house worth $100,000 on which the first mortgage has been paid down to $50,000. You should be able to get a second mortgage for $25,000.

▶ **SHOULD YOU DO IT?** Generally, a second mortgage is a less desirable source of credit than refinancing a first mortgage or taking out a short-term loan. Main reason: rates are high—usually three to five percentage points above rates for first mortgages.

Credit Source #14—Home equity loan: In a variation on the usual second mortgage arrangement, the home equity loan gives a borrower a line of credit (rather than cash in hand) in exchange for a second mortgage. An increasing number of banks and brokerage firms are offering these arrangements. The borrower borrows (up to his credit limit) and repays whenever he wishes. The advantage is flexibility. The borrower is not paying interest on more funds than he needs at a given time. The usual interest rate is about two points over the prime rate plus a two-point origination fee.

OTHER SOURCES OF CREDIT

There are other sources of credit besides your bank and your employer and other items of collateral besides your home. We'll wrap up our examination of ways to get credit by considering life insurance as collateral, credit card advances, and auto loans.

Credit Source #15—Life insurance as collateral: Your insurance policy may be the best source of credit you have. If it's a whole life policy (also called "regular" or "permanent" insurance), it builds up a cash surrender value that you can borrow against. (Note that term insurance does not build this kind of cash value.) Best of all, interest rates are specified in the policy. And they're as low as 8 to 10 percent—even lower on policies that have been in effect for many years.

Any portion of a policy loan that is left unpaid at your death will be deducted from the amount paid to your beneficiary. Suppose you have a $50,000 policy on which a $10,000 loan is outstanding at your death. Your beneficiary will get only $40,000. [See Chapter Nine for more details on life insurance.]

Credit Source #16—Credit card advances: Travel and entertainment cards—American Express, Diners Club and Carte Blanch are the biggest—offer a number of advantages. You can use them to charge a wide variety of goods and services. So you can travel about without carrying a lot of cash. And if you use them to charge tax deductible items, your receipts and your monthly bills can be used to substantiate the deductions.

Cash advances: Most travel and entertainment cards allow you to borrow money—up to a pre-approved credit limit. These credit card loans work in much the same way as loans on a bank card like MasterCard or Visa. Interest rates are high so cash advances should be reserved for short-term needs and paid back as promptly as possible. Note that although there's no interest on charged items if your bill is paid promptly, interest on cash advances starts the day you get the cash.

Credit Source #17—Store cards: Single purpose credit cards allow you to charge purchases with the issuing company. They're offered by many large providers of goods and services—department stores, oil companies and car rental agencies, for example.

> ▶ **INCREASING YOUR CLOUT:** A charge account gives you some extra leverage if your purchases turn out to be unsatisfactory. A department store, for example, is more likely to be helpful about making adjustments or accepting returns for a charge customer with an identifiable record of purchases.

Department stores often have two types of accounts. One charges no interest but requires prompt payment. The other is a revolving account where you pay installments and owe interest on the unpaid balance. (Some stores offer only revolving accounts.) Interest rates are usually high—18% to 20% is typical. So it's a good idea to keep the interest payments down by paying as much as possible each month. If you pay your bill in full within the required period—usually 20-25 days—you avoid interest charges altogether.

Credit Source #18—Auto loans: Auto loans are installment loans with your car pledged as collateral. You'll repay the loan in equal monthly payments of interest and principal over the term of the loan. Loans are available for as short a period as one year or (for new cars) as long as five years. You'll hold down the total amount of interest by making as large a down payment as possible and selecting the shortest repayment period you can manage.

Used Cars: The interest rate lenders charge on used-car loans is higher than for new cars. Also, lenders usually require a larger downpayment (as a percentage of the price) for used cars. If a used car is more than a few years old, you may not be able to get a car loan at all. In that case, you may be able to finance the purchase with a personal loan secured by some other collateral.

this may not always be true. As usual, it's best to check all the rates before you sign up.

Another source: Some chapters of the American Automobile Association offer very favorable interest rates on car loans to their members. So check with your local AAA. If their rates are good enough and you don't already belong, it may be worth taking out a membership.

HOW TO CUT YOUR COST FOR BORROWING MONEY

The best way to keep the cost of interest at a minimum is to shop around for credit. The savings can be substantial. For example: One bank we know of will rebate 3% of your annual credit card interest charge if you make the minimum monthly payments on time. And they'll waive the annual card fee if you maintain a $400 savings account with them.

Here are some additional guidelines to help you cut the cost of borrowing money.

- Interest rates aren't the only factor in determining the cost of borrowing. The size of your loans and the amount of time in which you repay them are equally as important. The cheapest loan is always one where you make as large a down payment as possible and schedule repayment over the shortest possible time.

- In any long-term loan contract, try to include a clause that will allow you to prepay (in full or in part) with no penalty—or with a minimum penalty. *Advantage:* You will be able to save yourself a bundle in interest costs if it turns out that you are able to prepay. If you are not able to prepay but interest rates drop, you may be able to refinance the loan at more favorable rates.

- Don't accelerate repayment of any loans you may have at especially low interest rates. Just keep up the required payments and invest your estra cash at higher rates.

- When you take out a loan, you'll usually be encouraged to take credit life and credit accident insurance. With this insurance, your loan will be paid off by the insurance company if you die or have a disabling accident while the loan is outstanding. It shounds like a good idea but it's not. *Reason:* The insurance is almost always overpriced. Where you have an option— and you usually will— pass it up. **Exception:** Credit insurance may be a good idea for borrowers who are elderly or in ill health.

▶ **CONSOLIDATING YOUR LOANS:** You may have a number of small loans and credit arrangements outstanding. Ask your banker or credit union representative if you qualify for a personal installment loan that would allow you to pay off all the others.

Say you have a fair amount of debt on bank carfs, store charges and overdraft checking that's costing you an average of 18-20% interest. A single installment loan at 12-14% would be a preferable alternative.

HOW TO FIGURE YOUR COST FOR BORROWING

Comparing loan costs is not easy if lenders quote rates in terms of 'add-on' and 'discount' loans. A 10-percent add-on rate, for example, actually works out to 18% on a one-year loan. And a 10% discount loan comes to 19.9%.

Fortunately, the Truth in Lending Act requires lenders to disclose the true interest you pay—the annual percentage rate (APR). The APR is a simple annual rate that relates the finance charge to the amount of credit you get and the amount of time you have the money.

To illustrate the different methods for figuring interest, let's consider three types of loans: simple interest, add-on loan, and discount loan.

Simple interest: If you pay 12% simple interest, you are paying 12¢ a year for each dollar you borrow. Say you borrow $100 at 12% for a year and make no repayment until the end of the year. You would have the use of the whole $100 for the entire year. At the end of the year, you repay $112. You would be paying simple interest of 12%.

Add-on loan: In the case of an add-on loan, the interest charge is added to the amount of the loan at its inception. On a one year $100 loan at 12% add-on interest, you have to repay $112 over the course of the year. That works out to $9.33 a month ($112 divided by 12).

That 12% *appears* to be reasonable. But keep in mind that with 'add-on' interest, you pay interest on the total loan amount for as long as your payments last, even though there is less and less cash available to you as you make payments. Your true annual interest is not 12%. It's over 21%!

Discount loan: With a discounted loan, the bank discounts (deducts) the interest in advance. On a one-year $100 discounted loan at 12% interest, the bank gives you only $88. But you have to repay $100. Each monthly installment is $8.33 ($100 divided by 12). The true annual interest rate is over 24%.

▶ **WHAT TO DO:** Whenever you're confronted with an add-on or discount loan situation, always ask for the equivalent annual percentage rate. Then compare this rate to the rate available from other sources before you buy.

Unpaid balance: Some lenders list interest charges as a percentage of the balance that is unpaid each month. This procedure is common with credit unions, small loan companies, retail merchants and banks (on certain charge plans). The true annual interest can be determined by multiplying the monthly rate by 12. A monthly rate of 1-3a true annual rate of 21%. Where daily interest is stated, multiplying by 365 will yield the annual rate.

TAX ANGLES IN CREDIT

As you might expect, taxes play a part in your use of credit. For one thing, the interest payments you make generally are deductible if you are able to itemize deductions. That can be a big break—especially if you're in a high tax bracket.

> *Example:* You're in the 40% tax bracket. Between your home mortgage payments and other borrowings, you pay out $10,000 in interest this year. Since your $10,000 deduction saves you $4,000 in taxes, your after-tax cost for interest this year is only $6,000.

However, not all interest payments are deductible. Here's a quick look at the rules:

Investment Interest Limits

There's a limit on the amount of interest you can deduct in any one year to buy and carry investments.

Your yearly deduction for interest paid to buy or carry investment property is limited to:

(1) $10,000 (joint returns), PLUS

(2) Your net investment income from *all* sources (dividends, interest income, royalties, and so forth).

As you can see, the rules are fairly generous. And any investment interest that's disallowed as a deduction in one year can be carried over and deducted in following years. Note that investment interest does not include personal interest.

Use of Loan to Buy Tax-Exempts

There's no interest deduction on debt that's incurred or continued to carry tax-exempt securities like municipal bonds. The Government says that the deduction is barred whenever there is a "sufficiently direct relationship" between the indebtedness and the tax-exempts. In fact, the borrowed money doesn't even have to be used to buy tax-exempts for the rule to apply.

Let's look at one taxpayer victory—and one defeat— to see how the courts view the situation:

Taxpayer victory: Mr. Batten and his co-owner entered into a buy-sell agreement in which the survivor would buy the other's stock. When his co-owner died and his obligation under the agreement ripened, he had substantial holdings including $63,000 worth of tax-exempts. Instead of selling the tax-exempts, he borrowed money on an unsecured note to finance the stock purchase. Nevertheless, the Revenue Service disallowed part of the interest on the loan. Was the Revenue Service correct?

Answer: No, says a District Court. There's no direct relationship between the loan and the tax-exempts [Batten, DC Va., 27 AFTR 2d 71-513]. Here are the key factors the Court listed:

(1) The buy-sell agreement was a pre-existing obligation.

(2) He had more than enough other assets which could be used to repay the loan since the tax-exempts amounted to less than 6% of his total assets.

(3) A reasonable person wouldn't sacrifice the tax-exempts to pay off a loan carrying a low interest.

(4) Business reasons were the sole motivation for borrowing to finance the stock purchase.

Now here's a case where the taxpayer wasn't as fortunate:

Taxpayer loser: McDonough owned a large portfolio of securities—stocks, corporate bonds and tax-exempts. In one year, he also took out a short-term bank loan in order to pay taxes. When McDonough deducted the interest paid for buying on margin and the bank loan, the Government objected. It claimed that interest was incurred so McDonough could hold on to his tax-exempts.

Tax Court: McDonough loses. The mere fact that McDonough owned tax-exempts didn't cost him his interest deduction. Rather McDonough lost because he failed to disprove the Government contention that there was a 'sufficiently direct relationship' between the debt and the ownership of the tax-exempts. It was up to McDonough to show the Court his purpose for incurring the debt, and he didn't [McDonough, TC Memo 1977-50].

Paying Interest on a Loan You Renew

Here's something that happens quite frequently. You borrow money from your bank—say, to invest in real estate or securities. When the note comes due, you renew the loan, adding on the interest. When it come time to file your tax return, you deduct the interest. Then comes this—

▶ **TAX SURPRISE:** No interest deduction. *Reason:* A cash-method taxpayer can't take an interest deduction until he actually pays the interest. And a new note is not payment [England, 34 TC 617].

Added twist: Let's say that instead of renewing your note, you borrow from the bank to pay the bank. That is, as soon as the bank receives your check for interest, it advances you an amount equal to your interest payments. Have you paid interest? No, says the Fifth Circuit Court. Payment must be made in cash or its equivalent; an exchange of checks with the bank isn't good enough. [Battelstein, 45 AFTR 2d 80-770].

Is there a way out of this tax dilemma if you're short of funds? There sure is.

▶ **WHAT TO DO:** Borrow from Peter to pay Paul. In other words, borrow the money from someone else or from another bank, and make the payment. That way, you've paid the interest and you get your deduction.

Loan For Your Child

You may be considering loans to help finance your child's college education. Your son or daughter can get a Government-insured low-interest loan—but only up to a certain amount. This may mean another bank loan.

Let's say you pay off the principal and interest on both loans. Are you entitled to interest deductions for these education loans?

> ▶ **A TALE OF TWO LOANS:** Even though you repay the Government-insured loan, you don't get an interest deduction. However, you probably could deduct the interest on the regular bank loan. It depends on who is primarily obligated to pay the debt.

Government loan: Your child is primarily liable on this debt, not you. You neither endorse nor cosign the note. Even if you pay off this loan under an oral agreement with your child, you still cannot deduct the interest. *Reason:* Your position is analogous to that of a guarantor, and a guarantor is only secondarily liable on the debt [Secunda, TC Memo 1977-185].

Bank loan: Since you expect to repay the loan anyway, you'll probably take it out in your name alone. There's no doubt you get the interest deduction. But suppose your child wants a chance to repay the loan. He can either pay you, or he can take out the bank loan in his own name. If he does the borrowing, the bank will require you to cosign the note. If you end up paying the interest, are you entitled to the interest deduction? Yes. By cosigning the note, you're jointly liable and thus entitled to deduct the interest payments [Rev. Rul. 71-179, 1971-1 CB 58].

Chapter 8

How Income Splitting Keeps More Money In The Family

Income splitting is one tax-saving idea almost any family can use. It is also an eminently practical arrangement. For example, most families set money aside for future obligations—sending children through college, or setting up a child in business, for example. What could be more sensible than to give the children cash or property now (with the proper safeguards). The income generated by the gift is taxed to your low-bracket child, not to you. As a result, more dollars are left over for your family's future. The technique works whether you lay aside $500 a year, or $5,000.

In the following pages, you'll see a wide variety of income splitting techniques—simple and complex—that can save you and your family a small fortune in taxes.

HOW TO CUT RED TAPE—AND FAMILY INCOME TAXES— WHEN MAKING GIFTS TO YOUR CHILDREN

The easiest way to cut the family income tax bill is to make outright gifts of property to your children. The gift can be cash, stocks, bonds, even assets such as real estate. However, even in this simplest of all tax-cutting methods, there are a few complications to steer clear of. Let's start with—

The Tax-Wise Way to Give Income Property to A Child

A gift of income-producing property to a child is a two-way winner. Your child builds up a college fund, and you get this—

> ▶ **FAMILY TAX-SAVER:** Since you no longer own the property, you pay no tax on the income it produces. The child who gets the property gets taxed on the income, but at his low-bracket rates. *Result:* Your family keeps more of the income, and Uncle Sam gets less.

The popularity of this income-splitting technique has led all the states to adopt the Uniform Gifts to Minors Act. The Act cuts to a minimum the red tape of giving securities. You make the gift, and name yourself as custodian. The mechanics are simple. For example, suppose you want to give some of your stock or other securities to a child. You merely re-register the securities in the child's name, with the parent as custodian. Generally, the following language may be used: "_____(name of donor/parent) as custodian for _____(name of minor child) under the _____ (State) Uniform Gifts to Minors Act." No other trustees, guardians or court procedures are necessary.

While your child is a minor, you manage the property. You can sell, reinvest and collect income and accumulate it or apply it for the child's benefit. When your child reaches majority (age 21 for Uniform Act purposes in some states, age 18 in others), he or she gets the property outright. No trustees, guardians or courts are involved. And all the while, you're piling up tax savings.

> **Example:** Father owns 150 shares of XYZ, Inc. The stock pays annual dividends totalling $1,600. In Father's 50% bracket, $800 of that is taken by taxes. Father decides to give the stock to 12-year-old Son. He simply re-registers the stock in the name of "Father, as custodian for Son."

Result: Of the $1,600 in dividends, Son can shelter $1,000 with his personal exemption and another $100 with the dividend exclusion. (The zero bracket amount—the standard deduction—can't be used to shelter investment income.) Assuming he has no other income, Son's tax bill on the remaining $500 is $55. That's a family tax saving of $745.

> ▶ **DIVIDEND TAX SHELTER:** Don't pass up the $100 dividend exclusion when you make your gift. Even when you give rental or other income-producing property not covered by the Uniform Act, you get the benefit of the exclusion if you also give securities that yield at least $100 in dividends.

There are things you have to watch, but with a little ingenuity—and with help from a professional tax adviser—you can handle them.

Income tax: Income from the gift spent by the custodian on items you're legally obligated to provide for your minor child are considered taxable income to you.

Let's say Father is the custodian and uses $1,000 of the XYZ dividends to pay part of Son's tuition. In effect, Father is getting an extra $1,000 that he can use to discharge his support obligations to Son. Therefore, the $1,000 is taxable to him and not to Son.

> ▶ **WHAT TO DO:** Whenever possible, pay your child's bills out of your own pocket. By banking or reinvesting the income from the gift, you can avoid income tax while your child's nest egg builds up even more.

Gift tax: Gifts made to a minor under the Uniform Act are subject to gift tax. However, your potential gift tax liability can be eliminated by the $10,000 gift tax exclusion and your unified gift and estate tax credit [see Chapter Eleven for details].

> ▶ **DOUBLE THE GIFT TAX BREAK:** Your spouse also has a unified gift and estate tax credit and an annual gift tax exclusion. By joining together in a gift to your

child (a so-called split gift), you and your spouse double the unified credit and the gift tax exclusion. *Result:* You lower or eliminate the tax bill on your gift.

Estate tax: There is a problem when a parent-custodian makes a gift of securities, names himself custodian and dies before his child reaches majority. In that situation, the courts have said that the gift is included in the parent's taxable estate. *Reason:* A custodian has the power to terminate the custodianship and give the property to the child outright. That means it is still the parent-custodian's property for estate tax purposes (Stuit, 28 AFTR2d 71-6289).

▶ **WHAT TO DO:** Name someone else as custodian. If the gift isn't made jointly, your spouse will do fine. The problem arises only when the giver of the gift is also the custodian. If you're making a gift to your grandchildren, you can name one of their parents as custodian, and get the same tax-saving result.

If you've already made a gift and named yourself custodian, consider resigning and designating a successor. In some states that could involve a court proceeding, but it should be a routine one. In any case, you'll want to discuss the problem with your attorney before you commit yourself.

How to Make Sure You Cut Taxes When You Set Up a Bank Account for Your Child

Let's say you want to set up a savings account for your child in order to provide him or her with a good start in adult life.

At the same time, you do not want the child to have immediate access to the money—you want him or her to grow up first. So you go to your local bank and find out it has two kinds of accounts that will fill the bill.

• Trust account: The account is in your name as "trustee" for the minor child. You can make withdrawals as you see fit, and the account balance automatically goes to the child at your death. You retain clear control of the funds. You can revoke the gift, and pay it out to the child whenever you wish.

• Custodial account: This account complies with the provisions of the Uniform Gifts to Minors Act. The money belongs to the child, but withdrawals can be made by the custodian for the benefit of the child. The money in the account will go directly to the child when he or she reaches majority (usually age 18).

Though each type of account has plusses and minuses, from a tax point of view there is—

▶ **NO CONTEST:** Setting up a custodial account under the Uniform Gifts to Minors Act is a clear tax winner.

Income taxes: You cut the family income tax bill by shifting the interest income out of your bracket into the child's lower bracket. With a trust account the interest will almost always be taxable to you.

▶ **TAX-SAVING TIP:** Be sure to get a Social Security number for your child and give that number to the bank officer when you open the custodial account. Otherwise, the bank will list *your* Social Security number on the account and will report your child's earnings on *your* Form 1099.

HOW YOU CAN HELP FINANCE YOUR CHILD'S COLLEGE EDUCATION—TAX FREE!

You can arrange things now so that your child will have the money required when he or she is ready for college. How? By setting up a "Tax Scholarship Plan"—one that's written right into the tax law.

▶ **HOW IT WORKS:** Transfer enough income-producing property, let's say certificates of deposit, to a short-term payout trust set up for your child. (A short-term trust is one that lasts more than ten years.) Thanks to the tax law, he or she can currently receive $1,000 a year of investment income absolutely tax free. And amounts over that are only lightly taxed.
When your child is ready for college, a good part of the tuition money is available and—best of all—it costs little or nothing in taxes. In fact, you're several thousand dollars ahead of the game.

That's the fast picture. Now let's take a close look at the dollars and cents impact.

Typical situation: Your son Bob, age 6, will be ready for college in 12 years. It could cost you at least $35,000 to put him through a good college. Paying the tuition yourself with after-tax dollars could amount to an almost prohibitive expense. And you ask yourself—"Isn't there a better way to do it?"

▶ **TAX-SAVING ANSWER:** There certainly is. The short-term trust can provide a good part of the cash for Bob's education at rock-bottom tax cost and save you literally thousands of dollars. We call it the—

Tax Scholarship Plan

Transfer enough of your CDs to Bob through a short-term trust—set up by your lawyer to last for the 12 years—to provide him with $1,500 in interest income per year. Now the $1,500 is taken out of your income and becomes Bob's. So, you don't pay any tax on it. What's more, Bob pays practically no tax either since the first $1,000 of Bob's income is tax-free.

Result: Assuming Bob deposits his annual after-tax income in a savings account, he will have close to $18,000 from the trust principal alone when he's

18. And on top of that will be the interest earned on his trust payouts. (Of course, there will be a small tax on this too.)

And from a tax angle: Taking the $1,500 in CD interest out of your income cuts the overall family bill by hundreds of dollars each year.

Added breaks: (1) You get your cash back when Bob goes to college and the trust goes out of business. (2) You can still probably get a dependency deduction for Bob—at least up until the time Bob's in college. *Reason:* As long as Bob keeps saving the trust payouts, the money isn't counted toward his support. So you'll meet the more-than-half support test to win the deduction.

Will there be a gift tax? The answer will be "no" in most cases. When you set up a trust such as we have described, the tax law considers you to have made a gift of the present value of an income interest. For example, a transfer of $11,000 in CDs to a trust that lasts 12 years results in a gift of under $6,000. This gift is completely tax-free. *Reason:* The tax law allows you to give up to $10,000 each year to each child on a gift-tax-free basis. In fact, if your spouse joins in the gift, you can give up to $20,000 to each child each year on a tax-free basis

Even if you transfer larger sums into the trust, chances are good that you won't pay any gift tax. *Reason:* The big unified estate/gift tax credit can be applied dollar-for-dollar against any gift tax bill [see Chapter Eleven for details].

The tax scholarship plan can work even if your child's off to college in a couple of years—it just takes more of your property to fund the trust.

One problem here is that a short-term trust has to last a day longer than 10 years to be effective. So if you set one up for your 18-year-old son, the trust pays his tuition for four years, but you don't get your property back till he's 28. On the other hand, many people don't consider this a problem at all. Their children intend to go to a graduate school, and they'll need Mom and Dad's help for six, seven or eight years, rather than four. Even if your child doesn't go to graduate school, he might still need your financial help after he graduates from college.

> ▶ **IMPORTANT:** If you use the trust income to support a person you are legally obligated to support, the income is considered yours for tax purposes. In other words, the trust income is taxed to you. And courts in some states have held that under some circumstances, parents are obligated to furnish a college education for their child. If that's true in your state, your attorney will be able to determine whether it would jeopardize a short-term trust for your children's education.

HOW TO LOCK IN A LOW-TAXED CAPITAL-GAIN PROFIT WHEN YOU SET UP A TAX SCHOLARSHIP PLAN

Here's a way to obtain the income splitting advantages of a short-term trust and a built-in low-tax capital gain. The net result can be an excellent after-tax return on the property placed in the trust.

How it works: Instead of using cash or stock to fund the trust you use—

▶ **DEEP DISCOUNT CORPORATE BONDS:** Many good quality corporate bonds that were issued years ago when interest rates were low are now available at substantial discounts. Some sell for as little as 50% of their redemption value.

Funding a trust for your child with this type of bond yields: tax-free income for the family; tax-deferred growth for your dollars; and built-in low-taxed profit.

Scholarship plan in action: Mr. Simpson has $10,000 available to build up a college fund for his son Charles, age 7. He buys 20 XYZ Industries bonds in 1984, selling at $500 a bond. The bonds carry a coupon rate of 6% and will be redeemed in 1996 at their face value of $1,000 a bond. He transfers the bonds to an 11-year payout trust set up for Charles.

Result for Charles: The $1,200 annual bond payout is taxable to Charles. But, assuming he has no other income, it is almost tax-free. *Reason*: Charles has a $1,000 personal exemption. Charles will accumulate $13,200 by the time the trust ends—and almost all of it will be tax-free. The annual bond payouts will be reinvested for Charles. If they are put in a high-yield bank time deposit account, there will be a small annual tax on the additional interest income. But if the payouts grow at a modest after-tax rate of 8%, Charles should have around $20,000 at the end of 11 years to help pay for college.

Result for Simpson: While the XYZ bonds yield tax-free income to Mr. Simpson's son, their value builds up on a tax-deferred basis for Mr. Simpson. As the maturity date nears, the bonds steadily increase in market value. When the trust ends, Mr. Simpson gets his bonds back. When the bonds are redeemed in 1996, Simpson takes down a big—

▶ **LOW-TAX PROFIT:** XYZ Industries pays $20,000 cash for the bonds. Subtracting Simpson's cost of $10,000 leaves a profit of $10,000 taxed as long-term capital gain. The tax on the profit is $2,000 (assuming current favorable capital gain tax rates and a 50% tax bracket for Mr. Simpson). So Simpson puts $18,000 in his pocket. In addition, Mr. Simpson will receive $1,200 bond interest for the year he holds the bonds—after the trust ends and before the bonds are redeemed. This is taxable interest income to Mr. Simpson.

Bottom line result: Mr. Simpson and his family net a $21,800 after-tax yield on the $10,000 investment.
Here's how:

(1) Bond payout to Charles for 11 years (disregarding negligible taxes)...	$13,200
(2) Interest income to Mr. Simpson in 12th year (after marginal tax of 50%)	600
(3) Payout to Mr. Simpson at bond maturity (net amount after capital gains tax)..	18,000
	31,800
Less original investment...................................	10,000
Net after-tax return..	$21,800

▶ **IMPORTANT:** You want a quality corporate bond with a redemption date after the termination of the trust. Timing is important in a bond purchase, especially in today's volatile market. So you should consult with a bond specialist as well as with your tax and investment advisers, before making a move.

Special Trust Setup Lowers Family Taxes Without Cutting You Off From Your Money

As we've seen, the ten-year, so-called short-term trust can yield impressive family tax savings. But the traditional ten-year trust does have one big drawback. If a money emergency arises, you're out of luck. You can't get the trust assets back until the ten years are up.

Here's an alternative: You set up a regular ten-year trust for your child but you fund it with only a nominal amount of assets. Then—*and here's the key*—you make an interest-free loan to the trust payable on demand. The trust invests the loan proceeds, and the income from the investments goes to your child.

▶ **PAYOFF:** The income ends up in your child's low tax bracket, just as with the traditional setup. But here you don't tie things up for ten years—you can call in the loan any time you want. So you get the tax savings of a ten-year trust without having to lock up your cash for ten years.

How about gift taxes? The Government contends that there's a taxable gift in this kind of arrangement: When you make an interest-free loan, you're making a gift of what the interest would have been had you charged interest. But two courts have held interest-free loans are also—

▶ **GIFT-TAX FREE:** The Tax Court and the Seventh Circuit Court of Appeals say that you are not taxed on interest that you could have charged—but didn't. And even if there were a taxable gift, there would be no way to value the interest on a demand note [Crown, 67 TC 1050, affirmed USCA, 7th Cir., No. 77-1898].

On the other hand, the Eleventh Circuit has held that there is a taxable gift when a parent makes a no-interest demand loan to a child [Dickman, No.81-5297, 11/1/82]. The issue is before the Supreme Court as we go to press. For most parents, however, the gift-tax issue isn't even relevant. Even if the no-interest loan is subject to a gift tax, the annual gift tax exclusion of $10,000 per donee ($20,000 if the spouse joins in the gift) will probably cover the entire amount.

HOW THE RIGHT STOCK GIFT CAN MEAN TAX SAVINGS FOR YOU AND YOUR CHILD

There's a happy event in your family that calls for a large gift—a marriage, birth, graduation, or the start of a new career for a child. With the right kind of giving, it can be a happy time tax-wise, too.

> *Example:* Your daughter Ellen is getting married this month. As a wedding present, you want to give Ellen 100 shares of Growth stock. You've been buying Growth stock at various times over the years, and have 300 shares. You bought 100 shares at $20 a share, another 100 at $48 a share, and another 100 at $70. Growth stock is now listed at $50 a share.

You want to do the right thing for Ellen, and for yourself. What are the tax consequences of the stock gift, and which block of stock should you give her?

First of all, there won't be any gift tax on your present, because the tax law allows you to give up to $10,000 to each of as many people as you wish, without a gift tax. (If your spouse joins in the gift, the limit is $20,000 per recipient per year.)

Income tax consequences to Ellen: From your daughter's point of view, getting a gift of stock is not a taxable event. However, when she sells the stock, Ellen has to figure out her taxable gain or deductible loss. To do that, she needs to know her tax basis in the stock, and her holding period.

Her tax basis, is what *you* paid for shares you give her. Exception: If you paid more for the stock than its market price on the date of the gift, her basis is the market price at the date of the gift. (However, if she sells for more than the market price on the date of the gift, but less than your cost, she has neither gain nor loss.) For example, say you give her the Growth stock shares you bought for $70 a share. Ellen sells the shares for $20 at a later time. Her basis for figuring her loss is $50 (market value at time of gift), not $70. If she sells for, say, $60, she has neither gain nor loss.

Her holding period, used to figure whether the gain or loss on a later sale is short- or long-term, includes *your* holding period. So if you give Ellen stock you bought seven months ago, and she sells the stock six months after the gift at a gain, her profit is low-taxed long-term capital gain. *Reason*: Ellen's holding period is deemed to be 13 months (yours, plus hers), and that's longer than the one-year holding period required for long-term capital gains.

One exception: If Ellen sells at a *loss* and uses fair market value as of the date of the gift as her tax basis, her holding period runs from the date of the gift (and doesn't include your holding period).

Which block of stock should you give to Ellen? Let's divide your Growth stock holdings into three classes and look at each:

(1) *Your low-cost stock:* This stock is not a very good choice from the tax viewpoint. If you give Ellen 100 shares of Growth stock you bought at $20, and she turns around and immediately sells the shares, then she will owe a fairly large capital gains tax.

Of course, if you plan on selling the shares soon, anyway, then it's better to have the gain taxed in Ellen's low tax bracket, rather than in yours. But, if that's not the case, you should hang on to these shares.

(2) *Your high-cost stock:* It doesn't seem wise to give these. Suppose you give Ellen the 100 shares you bought for $70 a share. They are now worth $50 a share, and may stay at that level for a while. If Ellen sells the shares at $50, there's an economic loss of $2,000—the difference between the $7,000 cost, and the $5,000

sales proceeds. But Ellen has to figure her capital loss using $50 per share as her basis (value at time of gift). *Result*: The $2,000 loss cannot be deducted either by you or by Ellen (her basis is the same as selling price). Nobody benefits from the loss.

▶ **WHAT TO DO:** Sell the shares you bought at $70, yourself. Then give the $5,000 sales proceeds to Ellen. If the prospects for Growth stock are good, have her purchase 100 shares at $50 per share. *Result*: You nail down a $2,000 loss, and Ellen winds up with a cost basis of $5,000 for her shares of Growth stock.

(3) Your medium-cost stock: As another alternative, you can give Ellen your third block of Growth shares, the 100 shares you bought at $48. If Ellen sells the shares for more than $48, she has a small gain to pay tax on. If she sells for $48, she has neither gain nor loss. If she sells for less than $48, she has a deductible loss.

▶ **HOW TO MAKE STOCK GIFT:** Give Ellen the stock certificate, and endorse it over to her. Give her the following information: Your date of purchase; price paid; and broker's commission on the purchase (Ellen can add this to her basis).

To establish that your gift does not exceed the annual per-donee gift tax exclusion, be sure to record the market value of the stock at the time of the gift (average of the high and low at which the stock was sold on that date).

FIVE TAX-WISE WAYS TO HELP YOUR SON OR DAUGHTER BUY A HOME

How can a young couple afford a home—and the monthly mortgage payments—in this day and age? They usually can't. So many young couples ask their parents for assistance. The parents are only too willing to help—but at the same time, they want to make sure that they handle things the—

▶ **TAX-WISE WAY:** You want to make home ownership available to your child—at the lowest possible tax cost to you and your child. In short, you want to avoid gift tax complications and maximize income tax savings. Here are five strategies that help you do just that.

(1) You make a gift of part or all of the cash downpayment. Your child and your child's spouse take out the mortgage and buy the home.

▶ **GIFT TAX-FREE:** You can give your child up to $10,000 a year—$20,000 if your spouse joins in the gift—without paying any gift tax. And the gift tax exclusion is on a per-recipient basis. So if you and your spouse also make a gift to your child's spouse, the total exclusion jumps to $40,000—a tidy, tax-free downpayment.

(2) Your child makes the downpayment and gets the mortgage. But you give him enough in advance so that he can "buy down" the mortgage interest rate.

How it works: Your child gets a standard mortgage at, say, 13½% interest. But his monthly payments for the first year are based on 9½% interest, gradually increasing thereafter until they reach 13½% in the fifth year. Why the low interest payments if it's a 13½% mortgage? Because your money is deposited with the lender and used to make up the difference between the low interest he is paying and the 13½% market rate.

Buy-down benefit: Your child may be able to qualify for an otherwise unobtainable mortgage. *Reason*: In a buy-down, the lender looks at the buyer's ability to make the *first year's* payments. So while your child's income may not be able to support the monthly payments of a 13½% mortgage, he may qualify for a mortgage based on payments at only 9½%.

▶ **INTEREST DEDUCTIONS:** The money deposited with lender is a sort of prepayment of interest—the difference between the low rate paid by your child and 13½%. As the deposit is drawn on to supplement your child's monthly payments, your child should be able to deduct it, along with the interest portion of the monthly payment. So while your child is actually only paying 9½% on his monthly payments the first year, his interest deduction should be based on 13½%.

(3) You make the downpayment, obtain the mortgage and buy the home in your own name. Then you rent the home to your child and also give him an option to buy the home within, say, five years. Your rental income offsets the expense of owning the home. And you get—

▶ **TAX SHELTER:** The rental income is taxable. But, like any landlord, you can deduct your out-of-pocket expenses for upkeep and maintenance—insurance, repair costs and the like. In addition, you are entitled to depreciation deductions based on the full purchase price. *Result*: You may wind up with a tax loss. In other words, your writeoffs may not only shelter your rental income, but some of your other income as well.

More tax shelter: Assuming you eventually sell your home to your child for more than you paid for it, most or all of your profit will be tax-sheltered capital gain—taxed at only 40% of the rate of your regular income.

(4) Your child makes the downpayment and takes out the mortgage. But your child borrows part of the downpayment from you and gives you a personal note in return. The note matures in, say, five years and no payment of principal or interest is required before then.

▶ **WHAT TO DO:** You may want to charge interest. If so, spell out in the terms of the note that no interest payment is required until maturity. That way, you won't owe tax on the interest until the note matures in five years.

Of course, your child can't deduct the interest until he pays it in five years. But, by that time, he will probably be in a higher tax bracket and the deduction will be worth more to him than it is now.

Is there a taxable gift if no interest is charged (or the interest charged is less than the market rate)? The Government may say "yes."(The issue was before the Supreme Court as we went to press.) But, in any case, your gift tax exclusion should provide you with more than enough shelter.

(5) You and your child enter into an "equity sharing" arrangement.

How it works: You put up part of the cash needed for the downpayment and buy an interest in the home. You take title along with your child as a co-owner; each of you pays a proportionate share of the mortgage payments and maintenance and upkeep expenses. Your child pays you rent for his use of your portion of the home.

▶ **TWO-WAY WINNER:** (1) By shifting mortgage payments and expenses to you, your child is able to afford a home he otherwise couldn't. The savings more than compensate for the rent he has to pay. (2) You get the tax-sheltered benefits of owning income real estate—see homebuying idea (3). And if the home goes up in value, you get a share of the profits—at low capital gain rates—when it's sold.

HOW A FAMILY MEMBER'S STOCK LOSSES CAN TURN INTO TAX-FREE INCOME FOR YOU

A tax loss today can sometimes result in tomorrow's tax-free income. Let's say your son owns stock currently showing a paper loss.

▶ **TAX-SAVING MOVE:** When your son decides to sell his stock, you have him sell to you instead of to a stranger. *Reason*: Your son gets the same amount for his stock, but you might be in for—

Tax-free income: When you sell the stock in the future—hopefully at a profit—the profit is tax-free to the extent of your son's loss. Here's why: A taxpayer (your son here) can't deduct losses from sales to so-called tax relatives (like you). But the loss can be used later by the tax relative to offset taxable gain when he sells.

Of course, you're not going to buy stock that isn't a good investment. After all, you can't get tax-free income if you don't sell the stock for more than it cost you. What's more, the tax benefit from the family member's loss is thrown away if you sell at a loss. *Reason*: You can't tack the family member's loss on to yours.

But if you're convinced the stock's prospects will improve, an intra-family sale can make a lot of tax sense.

Idea in action: Randolph Howard has a son, Robert, who's about to enter college. Robert's going to pay his own way through school, and, in January of this year, wanted to sell some stock to raise cash. It's 100 shares of ABC stock that his grandfather left him. The stock has a tax basis of $2,000, and, in January, could have been sold on the open market for $1,500.

Howard, however, scotched the idea. If Robert sold ABC on the open market, the $500 capital loss would be wasted. *Reason*: Robert is going to have very little income for the year, and consequently doesn't need a capital loss deduction.

Because Howard is convinced that ABC stock will increase in value, he suggests a better alternative. On January 12, Robert sells his 100 shares of ABC to his dad for $1,500. Howard's hunch about ABC is right. In November of the same year, ABC recovers and Howard sells the 100 shares and nets $2,100 after commissions. Howard has an economic profit of $600 ($2,100 sales price less $1,500 cost). But his profit for tax purposes (taxed as short-term capital gain since Howard held ABC less than one year) is only $100. *Reason*: Since Robert sold his shares to his father, a relative, he couldn't deduct his $500 capital loss. That disallowed capital loss reduces the gain that Randolph Howard must report on a dollar-for-dollar basis.

HOW PUTTING YOUR SPOUSE ON THE PAYROLL CAN HELP YOU PICK UP THOUSANDS OF DOLLARS IN EXTRA DEDUCTIONS

Making your spouse a regular employee in your office can put you in line for thousands of dollars in extra deductions. All it takes is a simple change in your current payroll setup.

Typical situation: Mr. Brown owns a small business and needs someone to help with the bookkeeping and also fill in when anybody on the staff is out sick or on vacation. Mrs. Brown has often done both duties but she's not actually on the payroll.

However, by not treating her as a bona fide employee, Brown—and his wife—may be missing out on a good chunk of—

> ▶ **TAX-DEDUCTIBLE SAVINGS:** If Mrs. Brown is actually paid as an employee, she can contribute up to $2,000 of her annual earned income to an Individual Retirement Account (IRA) and deduct the contribution. Brown, of course, can do exactly the same. Together, they can put away $4,000 per year.

Key point: If you're self-employed, making your spouse a bona fide employee costs nothing extra. The wages paid to your spouse are exempt from Social Security tax. And although your spouse's wages are taxable, you get an offsetting deduction for wages paid.

The salary stays in the family and the tax-sheltered IRA money goes toward family retirement.

If your company is incorporated, putting your spouse on the payroll may mean higher Social Security taxes, but it also puts you in line for—

> ▶ **ANOTHER TAX SAVER:** A working couple is entitled to a special deduction to offset something called the "marriage penalty." Generally, the joint income of a working couple is taxed more heavily if they are married than if they are not. However,

married couples are allowed a deduction of 10% of the lower-earning spouse's income, up to a maximum deduction of $3,000.

Let's say Mr. Brown pays his wife $10,000 over the course of the year for the work she does (and correspondingly decreases his own salary).

Result: They are entitled to a $1,000 marriage penalty deduction for 1983 without *any* loss in family income.

Key points: Before you act, keep in mind that:
1. Your firm must be incorporated for you to get a marriage penalty deduction; the tax law denies the deduction for amounts paid by a self-employed taxpayer to his working spouse.
2. If the salary you get from your corporation is above the Social Security wage base (it was $35,700 in 1983), you will end up paying higher Social Security taxes by putting your wife on the payroll.

▶ **SILVER LINING:** The tax savings from the IRA and marriage penalty deductions should more than offset the increase in Social Security tax. In addition, putting your spouse on the corporate payroll makes other benefits possible:

Group life insurance: The company can purchase life insurance for your spouse—along with other employees—and it can deduct the premiums. And the premiums covering the first $50,000 of insurance are not income to you or your spouse [see Chapter Nine for details].

Pension and profit-sharing benefits: The corporation gets a full deduction for what it contributes for your spouse each year. And your spouse realizes no income until she actually cashes in on the fund. So her retirement nest egg grows tax-free [see Chapter Ten for details].

Company-paid travel expenses: It's tough to deduct a spouse's expenses on a convention trip. But if she's an employee, all of her convention expenses can be deducted by the company, assuming there's a business purpose for her presence.

How You Can Build A Tax-Free College Fund By Putting Your Children on the Payroll

Your children probably do odd jobs for your business or practice. Make them legitimate employees and have them set aside their wages to pay at least part of their tuition and expenses.

▶ **TAX-FREE COLLEGE FUND:** Currently, each child can earn up to $3,300 a year without owing any Federal income tax. This money can be put into the bank until they are ready for college. Another benefit: Your corporation can deduct the wages it pays to your children.

There's even a way you can have your children increase their take-home pay immediately.

▶ **WHAT TO DO:** Have your children's wages exempted from Federal income tax withholding. All they have to do is write the word "exempt" on line 3 of the Form W-4 that they are required to file with your company or P.C. (their employer). To qualify, they must (1) have had no income tax liability for the prior year, and (2) expect to incur no tax liability for this year. (Note: Social Security tax must still be deducted.)

Of course, everything must be business-like when your children work for you. The wages must be reasonable and paid for actual services. If you don't handle things in a business-like manner, your children may owe tax on their earnings or your corporation could lose its deduction.

Your child is still your dependent: No matter how much your child is paid in wages, you can still claim a $1,000 dependency deduction for your child. *Reason:* Your child is still your dependent as long as you provide more than half of the child's support and he or she either (1) won't reach 19 this year, or (2) is 19 or older but is a full-time student during any five calendar months of the year.

▶ **CAUTION:** You can lose your child as a dependent if he or she spends earnings on support and thereby provides for half of his or her total support. If that's a possibility, make sure your child banks some of the earnings, so you can meet the more-than-half-support test.

HOW TO GET A BUSINESS DEDUCTION FOR WHAT YOU PUT ASIDE FOR YOUR FAMILY'S FUTURE

How would you like to help your son buy a new home or pay for your daughter's college education *and deduct every cent.* Of course you would. And you can do just that with a special income-splitting setup.

▶ **GIFT-LEASEBACK:** You transfer property you use in your business or practice—for example, your office building—to a trust set up for your child. (The transfer is subject to gift taxes, but you and your spouse's gift tax exclusions and credits should cover it.) Then you lease the property from the trust and continue your business as in the past. Each year, the trust distributes the net rent to your child.

Result: You deduct the rent—what you're putting into the trust for your child—as an expense of your business or practice. Your child pays taxes on the payments received from the trust. In effect, a portion of the income from your business or practice (equal to your rent payments less expenses) is shifted out of your high tax bracket and into your child's lower one. So now more of the same dollars of income are left after taxes because they are going to your low-bracket child.

The Government's long-standing position is to oppose this type of setup. Thus, the matter frequently ends up in court.

Circuit Court case: Richard and Roger Quinlivan, brothers and attorneys, transferred their office building to a short-term trust set up for their children at a local bank. They leased the building back for their practice and deducted the rent.

The Goverment said the sole purpose of the gift-leaseback was tax avoidance. Therefore the rent payments were not an "ordinary and necessary business expense" and were not deductible.

▶ **TAXPAYER VICTORY:** The payments are deductible, says the Eighth Circuit Court of Appeals. *Reason*: The rent did serve a business function. The Quinlivans needed the office to practice law and they had to pay rent to get the office [Quinlivan, 44 AFTR 2d 79-5059].

Important: A small change in the facts might have changed the outcome. For example, if the Quinlivans had named themselves trustees, they might have lost their deduciton. So you will want a competent tax adviser at your side all the way. A gift-leaseback can save your family a bundle of tax dollars—just make sure all the i's are dotted and the t's are crossed.

HOW YOU SHOULD HANDLE YOUR CHILDREN'S BUSINESS FINANCES FOR MAXIMUM FAMILY TAX PROTECTION

It's only natural for you to help a son or daughter get a good start in a new business venture.

▶ **TAX STRATEGY:** If the business prospers, you have one kind of tax problem: how to minimize the profit that goes to Uncle Sam in taxes. There are also tax complications if the venture goes under; how you handle things from the very outset can make a great deal of tax difference.

Example: Arthur White owns a dress manufacturing firm. His son, Ed, has been in the family business for several years, but now he wants to strike out on his own. He wants to start his own company, Fashion Enterprises. Although Ed will be sinking his own capital into the new company, he still needs $50,000 cash from Arthur to start his business.

If Ed's new venture succeeds, there's nothing to worry about. But the clothing business is tough—one bad season can wipe a company out. Arthur wants to cut his potential loss to a minimum. Here are four ways White can handle the financing—and how they would affect his out-of-pocket loss if Ed's business goes under:

(1) *He makes a gift:* Arthur gives Ed the $50,000 cash. Now the money is Son's. If he loses it, the tax loss is his—not Arthur's. Since Arthur may have very little income in the year his business goes under, the loss will be almost completely wasted. Even with a loss carryover, it may be years before he will be able to use much of it.

▶ **DOLLAR DISASTER:** Arthur has lost the entire $50,000 with nothing to show for it taxwise. Gift-tax angle: Even if Arthur's spouse joins in the gift, only $20,000 of the $50,000 is completely tax-free. To shelter the other $30,000 from gift taxes, Arthur has to use up some of his unified gift/estate tax credit. So there's less of a credit to shelter Arthur's estate.

(2) *He guarantees a loan:* Arthur guarantees Ed's $50,000 bank loan.

▶ **TAX RESULT:** Unless Ed gives his father a reasonable amount of consideration in return for the guarantee, Arthur's out of luck. When he has to repay the loan and Ed can't reimburse him, Arthur gets no deduction for his loss.

What if Ed pays his father a reasonable amount in return for the guarantee? Arthur's loss is a short-term capital loss, which can shelter up to $3,000 of ordinary income per year—not much consolation.

(3) *He makes a direct loan:* Arthur loans Ed $50,000. Again, Dad's loss is only a short-term capital loss—of limited value.

Another problem: It's up to Dad to prove the loan is worthless and to pinpoint the tax year it became so. Otherwise there's no deduction at all.

(4) From a tax angle, here's the—

▶ **BEST WAY:** Arthur has Ed incorporate his new business as the Fashion Corporation. The corporation elects to be treated as an S corporation—in other words, any profits or losses are passed through to the shareholders (including, of course, Arthur White). Finally, the new corporation issues "Sec. 1244" stock to its shareholders.

Arthur gets 100 shares of Fashion Corp. stock for his $50,000 cash. Use of this type of stock ensures that Arthur White will get an ordinary loss for his capital contribution—if Ed's business goes under.

• S Corporation treatment: A corporation that can elect to be treated as an S corporation pays no federal income taxes, itself. Its taxable income(whether distributed or not) is taxed directly to shareholders. And its losses are also passed through directly to shareholders. Generally, any domestic corporation can elect this special treatment—if it has 35 or fewer shareholders, has no corporations as stockholders and has only one class of stock.

• "Sec. 1244" stock: Stock which is classified as Sec. 1244 stock gives a shareholder maximum tax protection: If he sells the stock at a loss, or the stock becomes worthless, the shareholder gets an *ordinary loss deduction,* which offsets income subject to tax on a dollar for dollar basis. The maximum allowable loss in any one year is $50,000 (it's $100,000 if stock is owned by husband and wife and they file a joint return).

On the other hand, if the stock is sold at a gain, it's treated as capital gain, just like any other profitable stock sale.

"Sec. 1244" stock is stock issued for money or property by a "small business corporation" (in simple terms, one which has less than $1 million in contributions to capital).

Here's how Arthur White makes out with this "best tax arrangement."

If the business goes under: Let's say that Ed's Fashion Corp. goes under in the first year of operation.

Result: Arthur White can claim a $50,000 ordinary loss on his income tax return and thus reduce his total income subject to tax.

If the business thrives and prospers: Let's say that things go well for Ed, and Fashion Corporation does a booming business. White has several options: He can remain a shareholder and earn income from the corporation; he can make a gift of the stock to Ed (over a period of years, so that the annual $10,000 gift-tax exclusion covers each gift); or he can sell the stock to Ed (resulting in low-taxed long-term capital gain, if the stock is held more than one year).

HOW TO CONVERT ORDINARY INCOME FROM YOUR CORPORATION INTO TAX-SHELTERED CAPITAL GAIN

If your family business is incorporated— or you're about to incorporate—you have the opportunity to achieve one of the best kinds of tax-savings. You can convert high-taxed ordinary income into low-taxed capital gains by following a simple blueprint set forth right in the tax law. The technique enables you to unload a substantial portion of stock at capital gain rates— while keeping full, undiluted control over your business.

> **Example:** Years ago, you set up a business venture in corporate name. From the outset, you have owned 55% of the corporation; your wife 20%; and your two children 12½% each. The business generates a substantial income.

Part of this income is distributed as dividends. (There's some intra-family tax-savings here, since the dividends that go to your kids are taxed in their low brackets).The balance of the income has been accumulating; and the corporation has substantial cash on hand.

Problem: How to get this cash out of this corporation without paying a huge tax?

> ▶ **WHAT TO DO:** Have the corporation buy back *all* of your spouse's stock, using some or all of its cash on hand. Finally, see to it that your spouse does not acquire any more stock in the corporation for the next ten years.

Tax-saving result: The gain your wife realizes on the redemption of her stock is *capital gain*—not ordinary income—and you still control the corporation.

Important: Your spouse gets capital gain treatment only if she has held the corporate stock for at least ten years. So if you set up your corporation say, eight years ago, with your spouse as a shareholder, you have to wait two more years for this tax-saver to work. Or, if your spouse doesn't yet own any stock, you can give him or her some now, wait out the ten-year period, then have the corporation redeem the stock.

Q. Why does my spouse have to hold on to the stock for ten years before the stock is redeemed? Why can't he or she redeem after five years, if the stock's value has increased?

A. The redemption must be complete. And it isn't if the stock is redeemed from your spouse within ten years of him or her acquiring it. If your spouse hasn't held the stock for at least ten years, the attribution rules say that stock owned by you and your children is considered owned by your spouse. *Result*: Your spouse will not have completely terminated his or her interest, and the entire amount will be taxable as a dividend.

Just as important: A redemption is complete only if your spouse does not reacquire any of the corporate stock for ten years following the redemption.

Q. Why couldn't I just redeem the stock I own myself?

A. You could, of course, if you meet the ten-year rule. However, it means you must be willing to give up all your interest in the corporation (except as a creditor). This includes such things as being an officer, a director or an employee.

Q. Wouldn't I get capital gain if I simply sold some of my stock to someone else?

A. Sure, you would. But you also dilute your control of the corporation. As a matter of fact, you might have to *give up control* of the corporation.

> ▶ **WATCH THIS:** There is one more requirement. Your spouse must file an agreement to notify the Revenue Service if he or she acquires any of the corporation's stock within ten years from the date of the redemption. What's more, your spouse must file it on a timely return in the year of the redemption or the entire capital gain break is lost. Be sure you talk things over with your tax adviser before you make your move.

Now say it's your children who want to get out of Family Corp. Any difference? No, the same rules apply—they must completely disassociate themselves for 10 years or their redemption proceeds will be tagged with dividend treatment. But what happens if they inherit stock? A prohibited reacquisition? No, there's a—

> ▶ **SPECIAL EXCEPTION:** The tax law explicitly permits a reacquisition by inheritance or bequest. The family isn't expected to give up its business just to honor the 10-year hands-off pledge.

HOW THE FAMILY PARTNERSHIP CAN MEAN MORE AFTER-TAX DOLLARS FOR YOUR FAMILY

Let's say you own income-producing real estate or an unincorporated business. You want to save taxes by splitting the profits with your child each year.

▶ **HOW TO DO IT:** Form a family partnership, and make your children your partners. If things are handled correctly, a family partnership can be a double tax-saver: (1) Some of each year's profits are taxed to your children, so the family's overall income tax bill goes down. (2) The partnership interest you give to your children now won't be part of your taxable estate. So your family's estate tax is less than if the property passed under your will.

You may have to pay a gift tax when you set up a family partnership. However, you can make a $10,000 gift to each of your children every year ($20,000 if your wife joins in the gift), that's exempt from tax. On top of the exemption, you can use part of the generous unified estate and gift tax credit to offset any tax.

But even if there is a tax on the transfer, you may be better off making a gift rather than leaving it in your estate. *Reason:* Part of the property's later appreciation in value—the part attributable to the children's partnership interests—won't be taxable in your estate.

How to set up a family partnership: You'll need written documents and a deed if you're transferring real estate assets to the partnership. Your children will then be given an interest in the partnership. You'll want a written partnership agreement, stating each party's interest in the transferred assets. You can create a partnership by oral agreement, but that may mean trouble with the IRS.

Minor children can be partners, but you must set it up carefully. Unless your children are old enough to handle their own business affairs, you'll have to set up trusts to handle their interest until they reach their majority. You can even be the trustee—but you must keep accounts, books, and records for the children.

▶ **WHAT TO DO:** With minor children as partners, you might be wise to consider a limited partnership. Make your children limited partners with you as the general partner. As general partner, the management of the property remains completely in your control. As limited partners, your children get their share of the profits each year.

How should profits be split? First, you, as the managing partner, must get a reasonable compensation for your services. What's reasonable? What you would pay an outsider to do the same work. Second, what's left over must be allocated according to each partner's interest in the partnership. You and your child will be taxed on your respective shares of the partnership's profits.

Important: Your business must be one in which "capital is a material income-producing factor." If you own rental real estate or a business with inventories, you're okay. But it won't work if you own a personal service business.

HOW AN S CORPORATION GIVES YOU AN EASY WAY TO SPLIT INCOME WITH FAMILY MEMBERS

An incorporated enterprise that elects to be treated as an S corporation gives its shareholders a double benefit: First, shareholders get the limited liability that goes with the corporate form. Second, the shareholders avoid the one big reason why so many people object to the corporate form, namely double taxation—first at the corporate level, and then at the stockholder's level. That's because S corporations get this great tax shelter: Profits and losses, deductions and credits are passed through to the shareholders with no tax at the corporate level.

Question. Can a breadwinner use the S corporation technique to split family investment income and save on taxes? Due to some key tax law changes, the answer may well be "Yes."

In the past, there were two main barriers to using the S election as a family tax-saver:

(1) *Passive income test:* An S corporation election terminated automatically if more than 20% of its gross receipts were from "passive" sources such as royalties, rents, dividends, interest, annuities or gains from stock or securities. Since investment holding companies and real estate corporations derive their income from such passive sources, they could not be S corporations.

> ▶ **PASSIVE INCOME TEST RELAXED:** In general, S corporations are no longer subject to passive income limits. All of their gross receipts can be from investment sources. *Result*: For the first time, investors can incorporate their holdings in S corporations.

Exception: Real estate and investment holding companies that elect S status may still be subject to passive income limits if they were regular corporations at one time. If these companies have accumulated earnings and profits from pre-S years, they are subject to a passive income limit more liberal than the old 20%: Passive income in excess of 25% of gross receipts is subject to a 46% corporate income tax. However, note that the S election terminates if the 25% limit is exceeded and earnings are retained for three consecutive years.

(2) *One class of stock:* An S corporation can have only one class of stock. Under prior law, any difference in voting rights was deemed to create a second class of stock. Thus, a parent who wanted to transfer S corporation stock to his children had to surrender voting rights and possibly voting control.

> ▶ **NON-VOTING STOCK OKAY:** Differences in voting rights no longer create a disqualifying second class of stock. The shares, however, must be identical in every respect other than voting rights. For example, they must carry equal rights in the profits and assets of the corporation.

Result: Parents can shift income by transferring S corporation shares to their children without giving up control of the corporation. The parents continue to make all the investment decisions.

These two changes give owners of investment property a ready means of—

▶ **FAMILY INCOME SPLITTING:** By transferring investment property to an S corporation and making gifts of stock to children, parents can cut both their income and estate tax liabilities.

Lower taxes: There is no corporate tax on the investment income. And since all S corporation income is taxed to shareholders, there are no personal holding company tax problems. Most important, the corporate earnings attributable to the shareholder's children are taxed in their low brackets, instead of in the parent's high tax bracket. Under current law, a child can shelter $1,000 of investment income from tax ($1,100 if the income includes $100 of dividends). Amounts in excess of that amount are taxed to each child at very low tax rates.

What about gift taxes? This shouldn't be a problem. You can keep the value of stock gifts to each child below the $10,000 annual per recipient gift tax exclusion ($20,000 if you and your spouse make the gifts jointly). And by keeping the gifts below the exclusion, you remove assets from your taxable estate with no reduction in your unified estate-and-gift exclusion.

▶ **ANOTHER TAX BREAK:** S corporation income, deduction and credit items are passed through intact to shareholders. For example, the rehab tax credit of an S corporation [see Chapter Two] passes directly to its shareholders who claim it on their own tax returns. (On the other hand, a rehab credit of a regular real estate corporation reduces corporate income tax, but the resulting savings to the corporation is taxable as ordinary income to shareholders when passed through as a dividend.)

Note: The same is true of corporate capital gains. They are also passed through separately to S corporation shareholders.

Ease of transfer: Corporate shares can be transferred with less formality and expense than can title to all or part of investment properties. No formal deeds or recording are required.

How to make an S corporation election: Here's a rundown of the most important rules for getting favorable S corporation treatment:

(1) Not all corporations can make the S election. Generally, the corporation must have no more than 35 shareholders (husband and wife are treated as one shareholder), and only resident individuals, estates, and certain types of trusts can be shareholders. The corporation can't be a member of an affiliated group, and there can be only one class of stock (but, as we've seen, differences in stock voting rights don't create a separate class of stock).

(2) A corporation can make the S election during the first 75 days of a tax year. The election is retroactive to the beginning of that year, and continues in effect until revoked or terminated. An election after 75 days is effective for the next year.

(3) Generally, a new S corporation must use the calendar year as its tax year. Exception: A non-calendar tax year can be used, if a business purpose can be established.

HOW TO EARN A STEADY RETURN FROM YOUR COMPANY, KEEP ITS OWNERSHIP IN THE FAMILY, AND SAVE TAXES AS WELL

The value of your company is growing at a healthy rate, but that very growth has created an estate tax problem (or will if something isn't done). Easily the biggest asset in your estate is the stock of your company. And if the net worth of your company continues to grow at its present pace, an overly large share of your estate will go to the Government in estate tax—despite the liberal estate tax rules.

As you'll see in Chapter Eleven, what you leave your spouse is exempt from estate tax. Starting in 1987, the credit against estate tax for assets left to your children will shelter $600,000. By combining the two breaks, you and your spouse can ultimately leave $1.2 million to your children (assuming a $600,000 estate tax exemption). But your estate may very well exceed that figure.

What you need is something that, for estate tax purposes, freezes the value of your stock at its current value so that it grows no further.

▶ **TAX-FREE TRANSFER:** You can impose an estate tax freeze by recapitalizing your company. A recapitalization allows you to impose a cap on the value of the company stock that's included in your taxable estate. At the same time, it allows you to make a tax-free gift to your children of the future appreciation of the company stock.

Result: You leave your company to your family—without owing a thin dime of estate tax. In addition, you can be assured of a continuing return, while your children are given sufficient incentive to keep the business growing.

Idea in action: Mr. Nolan owns 1,000 shares of XYZ, Inc. voting common stock, all of XYZ's outstanding stock. The current value of the shares is $500,000. Mr. Nolan wants to receive a fixed income from the corporation for his retirement. His children, who have been working for the company for years, are willing to take over management. But they want an equity interest in the business right now. Nolan sets up a recapitalization plan for XYZ. The corporation issues two new types of stock: 1,000 shares of non-voting common and 1,000 shares of voting preferred stock. Nolan exchanges his common stock for the voting preferred. The voting preferred has a fixed value of $500,000 and pays an annual dividend of 8%. Nolan's children receive the new non-voting common stock.

Result: The value of the new common will rise as the value of XYZ, Inc. rises, so all future appreciation in the value of the corporation accrues to the children. On the other hand, the value of Nolan's preferred stock stays fixed at the current $500,000 value. And through his voting rights, Nolan stays in complete control of the corporation. He also has the right to the first $40,000 (8% of $500,000) of XYZ's profits each year.

▶ **ESTATE TAX SHELTER:** Nolan won't have to worry about the value of his taxable interest in XYZ being any larger than what can be sheltered from estate tax. If he dies first, he can leave the preferred stock to Mrs. Nolan and get a marital deduction for the entire value.

Mrs. Nolan will be entitled to $40,000 a year for life. She can pass on the $500,000 of stock to the children tax-free (sheltered by her unified credit). If Mrs. Nolan dies first, Mr. Nolan can leave the $500,000 of stock directly to the children without any estate tax depletion.

How about income taxes? A recapitalization has no income consequences—either to you or your corporation—as long as there is a business purpose behind it. And the Government says that estate planning—the desire to prevent the corporation from being liquidated to pay estate taxes—qualifies as a valid business purpose.

How about gift taxes? The Revenue Service may assign some value to the new common stock. In that case, there would be a taxable gift to the children in the form of the new common they receive. But to the extent the common has value, the preferred has less value. So the owner's estate tax will be reduced.

Caution: Taxpayers who have received preferred stock in a recapitalization may be subject to tax at ordinary income rates if they dispose of the stock. Sec. 306 was designed to prevent a bailout of earnings and profits at capital gain rates where a taxpayer retains stock tied into corporate growth. Sec. 306 would not be a problem in Mr. Nolan's case. *Reason:* He does not intend to sell his preferred stock. And the Sec. 306 taint is erased when the Nolan children inherit the stock with its basis stepped up to date-of-death value.

▶ **FIRST MOVE:** If you are interested in the benefits of freezing your estate by recapitalizing your corporation, talk things over with your professional adviser. A recapitalization is a sophisticated move. And while the tax saving potential may be large, there are too many things that can go wrong if you try to handle it yourself.

HOW TO TRANSFER OWNERSHIP OF YOUR COMPANY TO YOUR CHILDREN IN RETURN FOR TAX-SHELTERED DOLLARS

Sooner or later, it's going to happen. You'll call it quits and turn over the company to your children. When that time comes, you'll want to be paid full value for your interest in the business. At the same time, you want to keep your tax bill to a minimum and avoid any cash problems for your children.

A private letter ruling issued by the Internal Revenue Service describes how one owner-executive solved these very problems. He transferred his company to his child in exchange for a—

▶ **CAPITAL GAIN ANNUITY:** Here's what he did: He had his company buy back all of his stock and pay for the stock with a lifetime annuity. He came out a four-way winner: (1) a good part of each payout he received for his stock was low-taxed capital gain; (2) his income tax bill was cut still further since he received payments over a long period of time; (3) the control of his company passed to his children without any estate and gift tax problems; and (4) a cash crunch was avoided.

Facts of the ruling: Mr. Hughes wanted to retire from his company and turn it over to his son, who is a full-time employee of the company. Over the years, Hughes gave his son stock in the company (a minority interest). The company agreed to redeem all of Mr. Hughes stock in exchange for an equal value lifetime annuity. The redemption agreement specified that Hughes wouldn't be connected with the company in any capacity after the redemption.

Tax result: Part of each monthly payment Hughes receives from the company is a tax-free return of capital, part is ordinary income, and part is low-taxed capital gain. And because the stock and the annuity are of equal value, no gift tax is owed on the transfer of the company to the son. Since the son owns all the outstanding stock after the redemption, he controls the business. And he gains immediate control with company cash doled out in small amounts over Mr. Hughes' lifetime [Ltr.Rul. 8011050, P-H Ltr.Rul. ¶1316(80].

Low-taxed capital gain: Even though Mr. Hughes "sold" his stock to his company, part of what he gets from the sale is capital gain only if he makes a—

▶ **CLEAN BREAK WITH THE COMPANY:** To get capital gain treatment on part of each payout, a shareholder-executive must divest himself of all of his stock in the company. As a general rule, however, a shareholder-executive hasn't divested himself of all his stock if a relative owns stock (the tax law attributes the relative's stock to the executive).

Exception: If an executive stays out of company affairs for at least ten years after the redemption, the relative's stock will not be attributed to him or her.

Tax-sheltered annuity treatment: Having the company pay for the stock with an annuity slashes the executive's tax bill even further. *Reason:* Under the annuity rules, the tax on the sale of the stock is spread out over the annuity period (the executive's life expectancy). Only part of each payment is taxable. (And remember, much of the taxable portion of each payout is low-taxed capital gain.) The remainder of the payment is a tax-free return of capital.

Important: Even if the executive outlives his or her life expectancy, part of the monthly payments remains tax-free. But the taxable part of each payment becomes all ordinary income.

Chapter 9

How To Cut Your Insurance Costs

HOW LIFE INSURANCE CAN GIVE YOUR FAMILY THE MONEY IT NEEDS WHEN IT'S NEEDED MOST

Life insurance has become one of life's basic needs. It's right up there in importance with food, clothing and shelter. Why? Because without adequate coverage, your family may be left without the means to secure these basic needs should you die prematurely.

Life insurance is a must if you have dependents who would be financially insecure if you were to die before accumulating a substantial estate. Ask yourself if your family could get along without your salary or self-employment earnings, and be able to maintain your current standard of living. If not, you need life insurance. If you are among the very few who have enough secure assets (savings accounts, stocks, bonds, real estate) to protect your dependents, or if you have no dependents, you do not need life insurance for family protection. You may want it for other reasons.

Other uses for life insurance: A policy's proceeds can help offset the decrease in a large estate from the estate tax bite. And the proceeds are usually immediately available to the beneficiary, while it might take a year or more to settle and distribute a large estate.

Life insurance can also be a source of additional retirement income. Certain types of policies build up cash values payable at retirement. There are cheaper, and arguably better, ways to save for retirement and other major needs. But for those who find it all but impossible to discipline themselves to save, life insurance can provide a compulsory savings plan.

How to Figure Out the Amount of Coverage You Need

Once you have decided that you need life insurance protection, you are faced with the next logical question. How much? There is no pat answer. How many children do you have? How old are they? Does your spouse work? Does your retirement plan have a death benefit? Do you have employer-paid group term insurance? How much debt do you have? What is your standard of living? How much have you saved or invested? These and many other highly personal and individual factors must be taken into account to answer the seemingly simple question "How much?"

Most people just take a stab at the answer, and buy a nice round figure of insurance coverage. As a result, some buy too much insurance, saddling themselves with high premium payments that could be better invested elsewhere. Others buy too little, leaving dependents unprotected.

With a few fundamental facts and some simple arithmetic, you can arrive at the amount of coverage that will provide adequate protection without unduly draining your resources.

First, figure out how much annual income your family would need to maintain an adequate standard of living. Here's a useful—

> ▶ **RULE OF THUMB:** Your family would need about 75% of your after-tax income. Let's assume your after-tax income is $40,000 per year; as a rough estimate your family income would need about $30,000 per year. But this rule of thumb will vary with your individual situation. For example, you may want to budget $2,000 per year to pay for your children's education.

Now come the adjustments: (1) Subtract from your $32,000 estimate (living expenses, plus fund for education) the amount of Social Security Survivors' Benefits your family would be entitled to receive. The amount of these benefits will vary with the size of your family and your earnings subject to Social Security tax. Your local Social Security office can give you the information needed to estimate how much your family would receive. For our purposes, say that the benefits would total $10,000 per year.

That means that your insurance would have to cover the gap of $22,000 per year.

(2) Divide this $22,000 figure by the rate of interest which you conservatively estimate your family would earn on the insurance proceeds. Keep in mind (1) your family will probably use some of the principal to meet major expenses (2) inflation will take its inevitable toll, and (3) income tax will be owed on the interest earned.

A net interest figure of around 6% seems reasonable, but if inflation picks up or interest rates continue to fall, an adjustment may be necessary.

Dividing $22,000 by .06 gives your approximately $370,000. That's how much your family will need to cover the shortfall, assuming the principal remains intact. Subtract from that all assets you now possess which could produce income for your family—savings accounts, stocks and bonds, real estate, trust funds, etc. (Do not figure in equity in your home unless you want your survivors to sell the home. *Reason:* The equity will not generate any income for them.) If these assets total $70,000, you need $300,000 of life insurance.

(3) Subtract the face value of your employer-paid group-term insurance (say $100,000), and any pension or profit-sharing funds that would go to your survivors in the event of your death (say, $70,000). What's left—$130,000—is the amount of insurance coverage your family will need.

> ▶ **IMPORTANT:** This amount can also be reduced if you intend for the principal of your estate to be amortized and paid out with the interest earned.

HOW TO GET THE MOST PROTECTION FOR YOUR INSURANCE DOLLAR

Mention life insurance to the average person, and his eyes will almost immediately glaze over. Images are conjured up of a mystifying array of policies, options and riders which can be combined in almost endless ways ("tailored to suit your individual needs"). As a result, if you don't know what you need, you may be sold the wrong type of policy.

Life insurance policies can offer protection, savings features, retirement income and many variations and combinations of each feature. But what most families—especially younger families—want and need is *protection*. Protection gives a means of financial stability if the family income-producer dies, and that's what you got with—

> ▶ **TERM INSURANCE:** It is the simplest and least costly type of life insurance available. Since term insurance has no cash value buildup, your premiums pay only for insurance coverage. That's why term insurance costs roughly one-fourth or one-fifth of the same amount of whole life coverage in earlier years. As its name suggests, term insurance provides coverage for only a specific length of time.

Coverage can range from one year to 30 or more years. The premiums are determined by your age and sex. Term insurance costs less when you are younger and gets more expensive as you get older. But since most families need less insurance coverage as the years go on, coverage can be reduced as premiums increase.

If you buy term insurance, your best bet is to get *renewable* term. When the policy expires, it can be renewed (usually until age 65) at a rate determined by your age at the time of renewal. It is renewable even if your health condition has deteriorated in the meantime.

Term insurance is also available with a *conversion* option. This enables you to transfer to a whole life plan at a later date without a medical examination.

The least expensive way to acquire term insurance is usually through a group plan. Many employer-paid plans allow you to purchase additional coverage at favorable rates. Group rates are available through professional associations, and are also offered by mail to credit-card users. Unlike many more complex types of life insurance policies, term insurance prices are easy to compare. Shop around at a few reputable companies (or savings banks if they sell insurance in your state) for the best rate. By paying premiums annually rather than, say quarterly, you will help keep premiums at rock bottom.

Types of Term Insurance: Although there are some variations, term insurance policies usually fit into one of three types:

(1) Annual term: This type of term insurance lasts for only one year. It is usually renewable (if not, steer clear). Each year when you renew the policy, your premium will increase to reflect your increased age. But the money you save on

premiums in earlier years can be used to pay the increased costs as you get older. Or if your insurance needs have lessened—say, your children are grown, you have more saved or your spouse becomes employed—you can decrease your coverage to save premium costs.

(2) Level term: This type is similar to annual term except the policy remains in force for a longer period of time, say, five or ten years. The coverage and the premium payments remain level throughout the term the policy is in force. So the initial annual premiums will be higher than a comparable annual term policy. And the later premiums will be lower. Again, buy only if the policy can be automatically renewed.

(3) Decreasing term: With a decreasing term policy, premiums remain level while the face value of the policy declines. The rate of decline may follow the amortization schedule of a mortgage, or may be at a fixed percentage or dollar value per year. Premiums are lower for this type of term policy because its face value declines as the risk to the insurance company increases. Decreasing term is most often used to enable survivors to pay off a home mortgage or other major debt obligations.

A newer type of level term is known as "deposit" level term. It is so called because a deposit, usually $10 per thousand of face value, is required with the first year's premium. The deposit is returned to the policyholder, with interest, when the policy expires. (The interest is tax-free). But if the policy is cancelled, some or all of the deposit is forfeited.

Deposit term was developed because insurance companies found they were losing money on the high number of policies cancelled in early years—after the company had paid for physical exams, commissions, and administrative costs. By protecting themselves against the risk of early cancellation, the companies hope to keep rates lower.

Should you buy deposit term? If the difference in premiums between a deposit and a level term policy is small, and you think you can get a better after-tax rate of return on your "deposit" elsewhere, probably not. And if there is a chance that you would cancel the policy in its early years—definitely not!

How One Type of Life Policy Gives You More Than Pure Protection

Whole life insurance, also known as ordinary life, permanent life or straight life, is what most people think of when life insurance is mentioned. But whole life is more than pure life insurance—it is life insurance protection that builds up a cash value.

▶ **HOW WHOLE LIFE WORKS:** You pay a level annual premium each year for life. The face amount of coverage also remains level and is payable to your beneficiary when you die. That's how the insurance part of whole life works. But part of each whole life premium accumulates tax-free to build up a cash value. That's the reason whole life premiums are considerably higher than the cost for an equal face amount of term coverage.

This cash value can be used in a number of ways:

• The policy holder can borrow against the cash value at less than generally prevailing interest rates. But there are drawbacks: (1) You are paying for the use of your own money, and (2) your insurance protection is effectively decreased by the amount of any outstanding policy loan.

• The cash value can be used to pay premiums if you are unable to meet a payment deadline.

NOTE: The cash value does *not* increase the amount payable to your beneficiary if you die while the policy is in force. In effect, a larger cash value increases the degree to which you are self-insured. So the cash value buildup decreases the risk of the insurance company.

When you no longer need insurance coverage, you may cancel the whole life policy, and the cash value will be refunded to you. This may not sound bad—you had the insurance protection when you needed it, and when you no longer need it you get part of your premiums refunded. And you would be right except for whole life's—

▶ **MAJOR DRAWBACK:** The investment return on a whole life policy's cash value is usually considerably lower than that of many other sound investments. Critics of whole life have long maintained that most people would do better in the long run by buying term coverage and investing the money saved on the lower premiums.

Point to consider: Saving takes self-discipline that many of us don't have. Well-intentioned people buy term insurance meaning to invest the saved premiums—but never do. For those people, whole life coverage may be exactly what is needed. By paying higher premiums on a regular basis, they are forced to save for the future. On the other hand, people in this category might find the incentive they need to save for the future in this—

▶ **TAX-LAW BREAK:** Individual Retirement Accounts give more incentive to save for the future than anyone should need. First, by saving in an IRA you reduce your income tax liability. Second, your investment grows tax-free until withdrawn. Third, you can choose almost any kind of investment vehicle. (For more information on IRA accounts see Chapter Ten.)

Best advice: If you don't trust yourself to save regularly, even with the advantages of an IRA, buy whole life for its "forced savings" feature.

Popular whole life options: Whole life can be purchased with a variety of riders and options at additional cost.

• Waiver of premium: This option keeps your policy in force if you are unable to pay premiums due to disability.

• Guaranteed insurability option: This allows you to increase your insurance coverage by certain amounts at certain ages no matter what your health condition.

• Accidental death: With this rider, the policy typically pays your beneficiaries two times the face amount of the policy if you die as a result of an accident.

Other Whole Life Variations

Standard whole life coverage requires premiums to be paid for your entire life to keep your insurance coverage in force. Other variations compress the time over which premiums must be paid to get lifetime coverage.

• Limited payment life: On this whole life variation, premiums are paid for 20 or 30 years, or until age 65. Since your coverage under these policies lasts for a lifetime, and premiums are paid for only a specified number of years, annual premium payments are higher than those on a regular whole life policy. Cash values also accumulate at a faster rate.

• Single payment life: This variation is an extreme form of limited payment life. One large premium payment is made at the policy's inception which applies to an entire life's coverage. Single payment life is not recommended for individuals. The premium is usually prohibitive, and the money could usually be put to more productive use in another investment. Single premium life is usually purchased by corporations.

• Endowment policies: These policies are similar to limited payment life, but do not provide insurance protection for a full lifetime. Premiums are paid for a specified number of years or until age 65. Life insurance protection is in force only during the years premiums are being paid. The policy then terminates and the cash value buildup is returned. Endowment policy premiums are higher than limited payment life, and cash values build at an even faster rate. These policies have traditionally been used as investment vehicles, but they suffer from the same drawbacks as regular whole life—low investment return.

Newer variations: In an effort to overcome the criticisms leveled against whole life, insurance companies recently have developed policies designed to be more flexible and to yield a better investment return. These are known by such names as variable life, adjustable life, and flexible premium or universal life. By far the most popular of these is—

> ▶ **UNIVERSAL LIFE:** Stripped to its basics, universal life combines the benefits of term insurance coverage with a money-market fund approach to the policy's cash value. The policyholder can change the face value of the term coverage component and can increase his premium payments, within certain limits, to build up the investment component of the policy. Typically the insurance company guarantees a minimum rate of return on the cash value, but actual return may be higher than the guaranteed amount. The cash value can also be used to pay premiums if the policy holder fails to make them.

Best features: A universal life policy holder has access to the cash value without having to borrow against it and pay interest. The cash value simply can be withdrawn, but there is usually a service fee charged on each withdrawal. As long as the policy meets some technical tax-law requirements, universal life also qualifies for the same favorable tax breaks as whole life insurance: The return on the investment component is not subject to tax when earned—it compounds tax-free until withdrawn, And withdrawals are treated like insurance dividends: They are subject to tax only to the extent they exceed the premiums that have been paid.

HOW YOUR COMPANY CAN HELP YOU KEEP INSURANCE COSTS AT ROCK BOTTOM

Everyone comes out ahead with company-paid life insurance. That's why it's such a popular fringe benefit. Employees get protection for their dependents at minimum cost, and the company gets a tax deduction for the premiums it pays. If you are an incorporated professional or a company owner, you win two ways. Your corporation saves taxes while it picks up the tab for one of your most important personal expenses. You on the other hand, pick up what is, in essence, tax-free income.

Lets take a look at some of the ways that your company can help you keep your life insurance costs down, starting with—

The Big Bargain In Insurance—Company-Paid Group Term

Term insurance is the best individual life insurance buy around. But employer-paid group term may be an even better buy. The premium payments do not come out of your own pocket; what's more, some of the premium payments are—

> ▶ **TAX FREE:** The first $50,000 worth of group-term coverage is tax free to the employee. It's like getting a tax-free raise to pay the premium.

You are taxed only on the value of employer paid coverage in excess of $50,000.

And there are these other advantages:

• Generally, you do not have to pass a medical examination to qualify for coverage.
  • You can usually purchase additional coverage at favorable group rates.
  • Your employer can deduct the premiums it pays as a business expense.

You must report as income only the cost of the coverage in excess of $50,000, less any contributions you have made. This cost is computed by using a Government table. The table on page 908 reflects the latest changes made by the Government in a 1983 proposal. Check with your tax adviser at tax-return time to be sure the changes have been finalized.

Age Bracket of Insured	Monthly Cost per $1,000 of Protection
Under 30	$ .09
30-34	.10
35-39	.13
40-44	.20
45-49	.34
50-54	.57
55-59	.91
60-64	1.44

Example: Mr. Smith is 48 years old, married and has taxable income which places him in the 40% tax bracket. His life is insured under an employer-paid policy for $100,000. Half of that is tax-free because of the exclusion for the premiums paid for the first $50,000 of coverage. The cost of the other $50,000 is computed as follows: $.34 × 50 × 12 = $204 (i.e., monthly cost for age 48, times thousands of dollars in coverage, times months in the year).

Result: Mr. Smith pays only $81.60 ($204 × 40%) in taxes for $100,000 in employer-paid insurance.

If Smith and his employer share in paying the premiums, the taxable cost of his insurance coverage does not include the payments Smith makes. For example, if Smith pays $150 in premiums, his taxable income for the insurance coverage is reduced by $150. The same rule applies even if Smith assigns the insurance policy to his spouse and she pays the premiums for the extra coverage.

Added break: An employee's spouse and children may be included in an employer-paid group-term plan. The cost of the insurance coverage is tax-free to the employee as long as the cost is "incidental" (even if the employee is covered for $50,000 or more). The cost of coverage is incidental if the amount of insurance for the spouse and children does not exceed $2,000 each.

Important: If you are a company owner, you can't set up a group term plan that covers only you and your key people. Generally, the plan must benefit all employees. But the amount of insurance coverage per employee can be based on factors such as salary. So as an owner-employee, it is possible for you to get more insurance coverage than your employees.

How the Company Can Keep Paying Your Insurance After You Retire

Company-paid group-term life insurance has one key drawback: The conventional group insurance plan only covers employees during their working years. You are not covered after you retire. And if you need life insurance then, it will be very expensive—if you can get it at all.

▶ **TAX-FAVORED SOLUTION:** Some companies solve this problem by setting up a "retired lives reserve fund." Here's how it works: Your company makes yearly contributions to a fund during your working years. The amount of the contributions is actuarially determined. At retirement, the fund uses the accumulated contributions to buy term life insurance protection for you during retirement. Premium payments are made by the reserve fund after you retire. Here are the tax advantages:

- None of the accumulated funds are taxable to you when they are used to buy your insurance at retirement.
- The fund grows tax-free.
- The contributions to the fund are fully deductible by your company when they are made. And that is in addition to the deductions your company can take for the premiums it pays under your current group-term insurance.
- All employees need not be covered by this type of plan. The coverage can be limited to one or more *classes* of employees based upon salary, years of service, or position.

How You Can Get Whole Life Insurance Coverage and Have Your Company Pick Up the Bill

If you own your own company, you may want to give some extra insurance coverage to your most important employee—yourself.

▶ **WHAT TO DO:** Have your company buy a whole life insurance policy for you. Tax result: The premiums your company pays are deductible as compensation. Of course, the premiums are also taxable to you. But you'll be receiving dividends from the policy— these are tax-free and will go a long way towards meeting your tax bill.

Any permanent life insurance policy may be used for this setup. However, many companies and employees prefer a "modified ten" policy. Reason: Your company's premiums—and your tax—are relatively low in the policy's early years when you'll be getting little in the way of dividends. The premiums increase later on but so will the dividends needed to pay tax on the premiums.

"Modified ten" in action: Mr. Smith is 40 years old, married, and is in the 50% tax bracket. His company buys a $100,000 modified ten policy for him.

Result: Over a 20-year period Smith's net cost for the insurance is only $11,284 (his income tax on the company-paid premiums minus the tax-free dividends he receives). For that, Smith gets $100,000 of insurance protection for his family—if anything happens to him, his family would get *$100,000 income-tax free.*

▶ **SOMETHING EXTRA:** At the end of 20 years, Smith's policy has a cash value of $38,600—and he's only out-of-pocket $11,284. Smith can cash in the policy and take a lump-sum payment. (There will be a modest income tax bill on Smith's gain when he cashes in the policy.) Or Smith may want to take the cash out in a lifetime annuity—as a supplement to Social Security, his pension and so forth. If he goes the annuity route, only a portion of the amounts he receives each year will be taxable.

How does the company make out? The company's premium for the first year of Smith's policy is $905: This amount gradually increases over the next nine years. In the 11th year and thereafter, the annual premium is a fixed $2,715. Total for the 20 years: $44,345. But, as we said, each year's premium can be deducted by the company. So, assuming the company is in the 46% tax bracket, its after-tax cost over the 20 years is only $23,946.

▶ **IMPORTANT:** This permanent insurance setup is very easy to adopt. It doesn't require prior Government approval or added forms or reports. Of course, you'll want to discuss it with your investment adviser first.

How Your Company Can Give You Top-Dollar Protection and Get a Money-Back Guarantee

There's a setup called split-dollar life insurance that produces this—

▶ **DOUBLE PAYOFF:** (1) Split-dollar gives you what is, in effect, term insurance at a radically reduced cost. (2) It really doesn't cost the company anything, because the company gets its money back. *Reason:* The policy's cash value belongs to the company.

Split-dollar gives the company flexibility. The plan can be set up for the top exec alone, for all executives, for all employees, or for any combination of people the company wants to cover.

What is split-dollar insurance? It's not a special type of policy; it's simply a method of sharing the insurance costs between an employee and his company. As far as the policy is concerned, although ordinary life is almost always used, you can use any policy that has a steadily increasing cash value.

▶ **HOW IT WORKS:** Either you or your company take out cash-value insurance on your life. If you take it out, assign the cash value to the company; if the company takes it out, it retains the cash value. In either case, you name the beneficiaries. Each year, the company pays the portion of the premium equal to that year's increase in the cash value. You pay the difference (if any). The dividends can be used to reduce your premium cost, the company's or both.

Your annual premium costs are little or nothing after a few years. This, of course, depends on a number of factors—your age, the type of policy, and how the dividends are credited. But your average yearly cost of insurance protection starting at 45 can be as little as $2 per $1,000 over a 20-year period.

How much coverage do you really get? First of all, the company has to be repaid for its share of the premium cost, so that part of the proceeds that equal the policy's cash value go to the company. As a result, your net protection goes down as the cash value increases. But even after 20 years (assuming you join the plan at age 45) you're still covered for over half of the face value of the policy.

And there is a way you can keep your insurance protection near the face amount of the policy:

> ▶ **HOW TO DO IT:** Buy term additions. Many split-dollar plans allow some of the dividends to be used for the purchase of annual renewable term insurance equal to the increase in cash value. With the term addition option, the company still recovers its loan—but 100% of the face value of the policy is available to the employee's family.

Do you pay tax on the split-dollar break? Yes. The value of the insurance protection less your share (if any) of the premium is taxable. Figuring the exact amount is complicated, but the life insurance company usually does this for you. You just enter its figure on your tax return.

Another benefit: Unlike many other compensation plans, it is not necessary to get Government approval of your split-dollar setup.

Q. Why wouldn't group-term insurance do just as well as split-dollar? The company pays the premiums with group-term, too.

A. True, your company could buy a group-term policy for you and pay all the premiums. And the premiums would be tax-free to you up to $50,000 of coverage. But in group-term, your company must buy insurance for a group. Split-dollar allows your company to buy insurance for just you—coverage designed specifically to meet your needs. The best move for your company may be to buy both types of insurance.

> ▶ **WHAT TO DO:** If you are interested in split-dollar insurance, see your insurance and tax advisers. Split-dollar does not require a special type of policy; ordinary life insurance is almost always used. But there are all sorts of variations on the way you and your company can share the insurance costs. Your advisers can help you decide which method would be best in your situation.

HOW TO TAKE ADVANTAGE OF THE INCOME TAX BREAKS FOR LIFE INSURANCE

As a general rule, there are no special tax complications to carrying life insurance. In fact, there's a tax break if the policy pays dividends. The dividends are considered a reduction of cost and are not taxable. This holds true whether the dividend is paid in cash or is used to reduce premiums. (Of course, dividends become taxable if they cumulatively exceed premium costs.)

Life insurance turns out to be a real tax winner when the policy proceeds are paid out to the insured's beneficiaries: If the payment is made in form of a lump sum, the entire amount is free of income taxes. However, there are a few exceptions you should be aware of:

- Proceeds are taxable if the policy was transferred for something of value (not, however, if the policy was given as a gift).

- Proceeds payable as alimony are taxable.

- If the proceeds are from a qualified pension or profit-sharing plan, the amount equal to the cash surrender value is taxable as a distribution from the plan.

Q. What if the proceeds of a regular life insurance policy are paid out in installments, or in the form of an annuity?

A. Part of each payment—representing interest earned on the proceeds—is taxable. The balance is tax free.

> ▶ **TAX-FREE BREAK:** If the beneficiary of a life insurance policy is a surviving spouse who elects to receive installment payments under either a life income or a term-of-years plan, up to $1,000 of interest income each year is not subject to income tax.

Important: If a surviving spouse leaves the proceeds with the insurer, and elects to receive payments of interest only, there is no interest exclusion. All payments are fully subject to tax.

Life income option: Under this payment option, the face amount of the policy is divided by the beneficiary's life expectancy. The resulting amount is the part of each annual payment that is a tax-free return of the proceeds of the policy. The remainder of each annual payment is taxable interest.

> ▶ **TAX BONUS:** The tax-free portion of each payment is fixed when the payments begin. So this tax break stays in place even after a beneficiary outlives his or her life expectancy and collects more than the face amount of the policy.

Term-of-years option: If the beneficiary chooses to receive installment payments for a fixed number of years, the amount of each annual payment that is tax-free is found by dividing the face amount of the policy by the number of years that the payments are to last. The balance of each annual payment is taxable interest.

Here's how the tax-free portion of the installment payment is computed in the case of a surviving spouse who is the beneficiary of a $60,000 policy and receives 10 annual installments of $7,000 each:

Amount held by the insurer	$60,000
Period over which the proceeds are to be paid	10 years
Tax-free proration of face value ($60,000 divided by 10)	$ 6,000
Widow's interest exclusion	$ 1,000
Total exclusion	$ 7,000
Annual taxable income from $7,000 payment ($7,000 minus $7,000)	0

What if the surviving spouse has a 20-year life expectancy and elects to take the $60,000 in installment payments of $4,500 a year for life? Here's how to compute the portion of the annual payment on which he or she must pay tax:

Amount held by the insurer (face value)	$60,000
Life expectancy	20 years
Tax-free proration of face value ($60,000 divided by 20)	$ 3,000
Widow's annual interest exclusion	$ 1,000
Total exclusion for widow	$ 4,000
Taxable portion of each installment payment ($4,500 minus $4,000)	$ 500

▶ **TAX-SAVING IDEA:** If the beneficiary isn't a spouse, income tax can be avoided by investing the tax-free insurance proceeds in municipal bonds. Since the interest paid by these bonds is tax free, the beneficiary escapes tax on the payout, and on all of the interest it generates.

This idea would also benefit a higher-tax-bracket surviving spouse whose $1,000 annual interest exclusion isn't enough to shelter the full interest payment.

HOW THE LIBERALIZED ESTATE-AND-GIFT TAX RULES AFFECT LIFE INSURANCE SETUPS

Thanks to some important changes in the tax rules, buying life insurance is a better than ever way to protect your family's future. Reason: If you handle things right, your insurance can also be gift-tax free and estate-tax free.

Here are some of the common ways that you can arrange your insurance strategy, and the tax consequences of each method.

(1) *You own the policy and name your child as the beneficiary:* With this type of insurance setup, you are assured that the proceeds go directly to your child. Obviously, since you purchased and own the policy, you have not made any gift. Naming your child as the beneficiary is not considered a gift of the policy to him or her. Therefore, there is no gift tax due under this arrangement.

Estate tax consequences: Since you own the policy, the proceeds will be included in your estate. True, most small and medium sized estates won't have to pay any estate taxes. But increasing financial prosperity, and inflation, could bring yours over the tax-free threshold.

Instead of your retaining ownership of the policy, there may be a better course of action—

(2) *Transfer the policy to your spouse and name your child as beneficiary:* When you transfer an insurance policy to your wife you are making a gift. But the gift is tax-free because the law now allows an unlimited gift-tax marital deduction. This simply means that you can transfer an unlimited amount of property to

your spouse without having to pay a gift tax. In fact, after you transfer the policy to your spouse, you can generally continue to pay premiums on the policy without worrying about gift or estate tax consequences.

Since you no longer own the policy, its proceeds will not be part of your estate. However, there's one important exception to this rule. The tax law says that an insurance policy given away within three years of death is included in the donor's estate.

▶ **WHAT TO DO:** If you plan on transferring ownership of your policy to your spouse, the sooner you do it, the better. *Reason:* The sooner you make the transfer, the sooner the three-year period will expire.

(3) *You own the policy, and name your spouse the beneficiary:* This may be the most common of all arrangements. And, thanks to some big tax law changes, there are no estate taxes to pay.

▶ **UNLIMITED ESTATE TAX MARITAL DEDUCTION:** The tax law gives estates an unlimited estate tax marital deduction. (The estate tax marital deduction used to be the greater of $250,000 or one-half of your adjusted gross estate.)

Result: Whatever you leave to your spouse, including the proceeds of an insurance policy, is estate tax-free. Although technically, the amount of the proceeds are included in your estate, you are entitled to an offsetting deduction equal to the amount that's left to your spouse.

Best advice: Review your insurance setup—and your entire estate—with your professional adviser. We've covered only the most common types of arrangements. Yours may well differ, or your particular personal situation may require another approach.

KEEP ESTATE TAXES AT ROCK BOTTOM BY GIVING AWAY YOUR GROUP-TERM INSURANCE POLICY

The proceeds from your employer-paid group-term policy are usually subject to estate tax. But if your spouse is the beneficiary, the proceeds qualify for the unlimited estate-tax marital deduction. So the proceeds are effectively estate-tax free. If you set things up right, the proceeds that go to your children can also escape estate tax.

▶ **TAX-SAVING MOVE:** These proceeds will not be taxed if you give up all "incidents of ownership" in the policy at least three years prior to death. If the policy is transferred within three years of death, the proceeds will be included in your taxable estate.

What to do: If you decide to assign a group-term policy, do it as soon as possible. The sooner the transfer is made, the sooner the three-year rule will be satisfied.

> **Example:** Mr. Brown has a $400,000 group-term policy paid for by the company of which he is treasurer. Brown's *children* are the beneficiaries of the policy. Brown assigned ownership of the policy to his wife in 1982. He also has $600,000 in other assets he bequeaths to his wife. Assuming he made no taxable gifts during his lifetime, here is the difference if he dies in 1984 owning the policy versus not owning the policy:

	Owning the policy	VS	Not owning the policy
Gross estate	$1,000,000		$600,000
Less marital deduction	600,000		600,000
Taxable estate	400,000		0
Tentative tax	121,800		0
Less credit	96,300		—
Tax owed	$ 25,500		—0—

Suppose your group-term policy calls for payment of an annual renewal premium. You assign the policy to your spouse more than three years before death, but renewal premiums are made within three years of death. Are the proceeds included in your estate?

Answer: No. But any premium payments made by your employer within three years of death are taxed in your estate.

Contrast this: An insurance policy which provides yearly coverage without the automatic right of renewal cannot be removed from your estate. *Reason:* Each yearly premium for a nonrenewable policy, in effect, pays for a new policy for that year. So there can never be an assignment of that policy more than three years before death. This is another good reason to steer clear of nonrenewable term insurance.

Another point: Be sure to make the gift of the policy absolute and irrevocable. Do not retain any rights in the policy—even the right to choose another beneficiary. The only sure way to handle this is to use a preprinted assignment form from the insurance company that's designed for this purpose. Be sure the insurance company makes the proper endorsements on the policy to indicate the change in ownership. Then complete the transfer by handing the policy and a copy of the assignment form to the new owner.

HOW TO PROTECT YOUR HEALTH—AND YOUR WEALTH

Health care costs continue to rise at an alarming rate. The cost of even routine surgery and a short hospital stay is staggering. To protect yourself in the event of illness you need health insurance. The foundation of your health insurance coverage should be—

▶ **GROUP HEALTH INSURANCE:** Group health coverage is by far the best buy available. Premiums are up to 40% lower than comparable individual coverage. Most employers offer some type of health insurance plan to their employees. Many pay the entire premium—and it's a tax-free fringe benefit to the employee. Some employers share the cost with employees, or pay for basic coverage only. In the latter case, extended coverage is usually available to the company's employees for an additional premium.

Best bet: Purchase whatever coverage is available through your employer's group plan. It's invariably cheaper than individual coverage.

Group health plans are also available through many professional associations, labor unions, and fraternal groups. Basic coverage usually includes:

• Hospital expenses: Covered items generally include the cost of a semi-private hospital room and board, and nursing services, drugs, operating room fees, bandages and dressings, and lab fees associated with a hospital stay. Benefits vary from policy to policy. The covered length of a hospital stay generally ranges from 21 days to one year. The length of coverage is the major factor determining the cost of this type of insurance.

• Surgery: Surgical coverage pays a doctor's fee for covered procedures up to the amount spelled out in the policy. Anesthesia costs are also partially covered under some policies. Some policies' payments are not spelled out—the policy pays a "reasonable" amount for each procedure. While some policies cover only surgery performed in a hospital, others also pay for office surgery.

• Doctor's visits: Physicians' fees for covered hospital visits are paid up to the limit specified in the policy. There is usually a daily limit to these payments, and coverage may be confined to the first part of a hospital stay.

Basic coverage is often quite limited. For example, policies exclude payment for health conditions in existence before the policy was in force; and oral surgery, surgery performed by a podiatrist, cosmetic surgery, and long-term psychiatric hospitalization are generally not covered.

Perhaps the most important form of health insurance is major medical coverage. As its name suggests, it provides coverage in the event of a major illness. Major medical payments take over when basic coverage ends. There is usually a deductible of between $100 and $1,000 for each individual covered (some plans have a combined family deductible). Once the deductible is satisfied the policy pays a percentage of medical costs (usually 80%) up to one limit and 100% of costs thereafter up to the policy's top limit. The insured is responsible for payment of the deductible amount and 20% of the costs up to the first limit which usually ranges from $2,500 to $5,000. The top limit on major medical policies generally ranges from $50,000 to $250,000.

Another type of health insurance is disability coverage, which partially compensates you for lost income due to extended illness. This is available for both long and short terms. These policies pay a percentage of your monthly earnings (usually 60%) up to a specified monthly maximum. Payments under these policies begin after an "elimination period"—usually six months after the disability begins. Disability benefits are paid in addition to what you may receive from Social Security and usually cover less severe disabilities than does Social Security.

Be Sure Your Extra Health Insurance Premiums Are Really Buying More Protection

You may have employee-paid group health insurance which you supplement with one or more individual policies. If you do, there's a good chance that you are paying more than you should for your coverage. That's because most health insurance policies have a—

▶ **COORDINATION OF BENEFITS:** If your policies have overlapping coverage, you will not be able to collect on each, even though you are paying full premiums on each. The primary insurer will pay up to its policy limit and the secondary insurer will be responsible for additional payments if its limit on the covered item is higher. As a result, the premiums you pay on overlapping coverage are wasted.

What to do: Check over your policies, and eliminate any duplicate coverage on the extra plans. Be sure that the supplementary plan does what it is supposed to—give you *extra* coverage for the extra cost.

Another important thing to consider in this regard is duplicated extended benefits under group health plans. Your spouse and dependent minor children are covered under your employer's plan. If your spouse is employed and also has a group plan, check the details of each group plan. Purchase extended coverage selectively. If both plans have prescription drug riders, pay only for the one that gives you the best coverage. If extended hospitalization coverage is available under both plans, choose the plan with the best coverage, and pay only one additional premium.

You Can Turn Nondeductible Medical Expenses Into Deductible Business Expenses

If you own your own company, you have the opportunity to give yourself great health coverage at low after-tax cost. This top fringe benefit is known as a medical reimbursement plan. And due to some recent tax law changes, it's now more attractive than ever.

▶ **HOW IT WORKS:** Your company sets up a plan that pays for your family's medical expenses. The reimbursements are tax-free to you and deductible by the company as a business expense.

What makes medical reimbursement plans so attractive now? The new rules on medical expenses that are now in effect. Before 1983, you may have been making do with just health insurance. And whatever expenses were not reimbursed could be deducted on your tax return to the extent they exceeded 3% of your adjusted gross income.

But in 1983 and later years, medical expenses are deductible only to the extent they exceed 5% of your adjusted gross income. So a bigger part of your unreimbursed expenses—possibly all of them—are nondeductible.

> *Example:* Mr. Green has an adjusted gross income of $70,000 a year. Green's family incurs $3,500 in annual doctor and dentist bills. In prior years, Green could have deducted $1,400 (the excess of 3% of his adjusted gross income). Green can now deduct zero. *Reason:* He has no medical expenses in excess of 5% of his adjusted gross income.

However, if Green's company sets up a medical reimbursement plan, the expenses are—

> ▶ **FULLY DEDUCTIBLE:** Green's company can deduct whatever it pays out for his medical expenses—the entire $3,500. So Green has converted his nondeductible medical expenses into his company's deductible business expense—without costing Green one red cent.

Generally speaking, medical reimbursement plans cannot discriminate in favor of your company's key employees (the five highest-paid officers, more-than-10% shareholders, and the highest-paid 25% of all employees). The plan must meet broad coverage requirements similar to those for qualified pension plans. In general, 70% of all employees must be plan members. And the plan may not provide greater benefits for key employees than the rank-and-file. For example, a plan can't supply benefits in proportion to compensation.

What happens if a plan discriminates? A key employee pays tax on some or all of his benefits, based on a formula. But even if all the benefits are taxable, an employee is no worse off than if he didn't have a medical reimbursement plan.

There is a way, however, that you can set up a medical reimbursement plan for you and your key executives only.

> ▶ **EXCEPTION TO THE RULES:** The anti-discrimination rules apply only to self-insured medical reimbursement plans. A plan funded with outside insurance is exempt from the rules. So your company can buy a comprehensive health insurance policy that covers only the top echelon of the company. The premiums are still tax-free to you and deductible by your company.

You may find out that the cost of an insured medical reimbursement plan is prohibitive, even though you are covering only your key execs. If you have a relatively small work force, you may want to stick with a self-insured plan.

> ▶ **SPECIAL BREAK:** Reimbursements for annual physicals and diagnostic exams are tax-free even if made available to top execs only. For example, the cost of

> routine medical and dental examinations, blood tests and X-rays all qualify under this exemption.

However, medical diagnostic procedures do not include any expenses for the treatment, cure, or testing of a known illness, disability, complaint or specific symptoms of a bodily malfunction. Furthermore, the exception applies only to diagnostic procedures to the company employee. Company-paid examinations and so forth for members of the employee's family are taxable income to the employee.

HOW TO PROTECT YOUR MOST VALUABLE ASSET

Almost no one fails to insure his home—the single most valuable asset for most people. But it is estimated that half of America's homes are underinsured. Most of these homes were adequately insured at one time, but rising construction costs and home values have eroded the coverage. To be sure your home is adequately protected, you need to know some basics about homeowners insurance and about a couple of dangerous pitfalls.

The three most common types of policies are:

(1) *Basic:* This least expensive form covers the holder against personal liability and damage or loss due to fire or lightning, windstorm or hail, explosion, riot or civil commotion, aircraft, smoke, vandalism or malicious mischief, theft and breakage of glass that is part of the building.

(2) *Broad:* This covers all of the perils in the basic policy, but adds several more, such as damage from the weight of snow, sleet and ice, building collapse, and accidental discharges of a broken plumbing system. This is the most common form of homeowner coverage.

(3) *Special:* This is the broadest and most expensive form of homeowner insurance. It covers most perils except earthquakes, landslides, flood, surface water, waves, sewer backup, seepage, war and nuclear radiation.

Each of these policy types provides liability coverage to protect you if someone is injured on your property. The standard liability limit is $25,000, an amount insufficient to protect most homeowners. At least $100,000 of liability coverage is generally recommended. The extra protection you get is well worth the small additional premium involved.

Homeowners with substantial assets should also consider an "umbrella" policy to protect against large liability claims. The premium on an umbrella policy is very low. Payments from the policy pick up where homeowner's liability coverage ends; the policy's limits generally run upwards of one million dollars.

Each standard policy contains limits on payments for losses of certain types of personal property, such as cash, precious metals, jewelry, furs, and silverware. And standard policies generally do not cover art objects, antiques, or business equipment in your home. If you need coverage for these items, you can purchase a "floater" or a rider to your policy.

Some coverage is not generally available. Most insurance companies do not offer theft coverage in designated high crime areas. But Federal Crime Insurance is available through programs funded by the Department of Housing and Urban Development. Similarly, flood insurance is available in certain areas through the Department of Housing and Urban Development's National Flood Insurance Program. Your insurance broker can give you the details on these programs if you need these kinds of protection.

Like auto collision and comprehensive coverage, most homeowner policies contain a deductible. It is usually quite low—you pay, say, the first $100 of each loss before the insurance company becomes liable. A cost cutting technique is to increase the deductible amount to, say, $500, thereby reducing premium cost and increasing the degree to which you are self insured. The important thing is that you are still protected against major disasters.

Homeowner policy premiums do not vary as greatly from one insurer to another as those on auto insurance policies, but it still pays to shop around once you have decided upon the type of coverage you need. Costs will also depend upon such factors as the type of home (wood frame or brick), the area, the distance from a fire hydrant or firehouse, whether the home is equipped with smoke detectors, and, of course, the amount of coverage required.

You May Be Paying the Home Insurance Premiums—But Are You Protected?

When you bought your home you probably insured it for its full value. But even if the home is only a few years old, you are probably under insured if you have not increased your coverage. If your home were totally destroyed you would collect the face value of the policy—not enough to replace your home. But that's only the beginning. If your home is partially damaged you could fall into the—

> ▶ **CO-INSURANCE TRAP:** To receive full payment for partial damages, you must carry insurance equal to at least 80% of the *replacement* cost of the home (excluding the land and foundation). If your coverage is less than 80%, you bear part of the risk of each partial loss—you become a co-insurer with the insurance company. The percentage of the loss that you bear depends on how far below the 80% your total coverage is.
>
> ***Example:*** You bought your house for $48,000 ten years ago and insured it for its full value. The house, now valued at $80,000, is partially damaged by a kitchen fire. The repairs cost $6,000. Since your home is insured for less than 80% of its replacement value ($64,000) you receive only a percentage of the $6,000. You are only insured for 75% of the required amount.

Result: The insurance company pays only 75% of the repair cost—$4,500. The other $1,500 is your responsibility.

▶ **WHAT TO DO:** Purchase inflation protection to protect yourself from this trap. With this feature, the face value of your policy increases by a certain percentage at regular intervals, or is keyed to a construction cost index for your area. This should give you the protection you need, but it's still a good idea to check your policy every year or so to be sure your coverage keeps pace with inflation and increased home values.

Even if your home is insured to its full value, you may run up against the—

▶ **COVERAGE GAP:** Even if your home is insured to its full value, you could still run up against an insurance problem if disaster strikes.

Here's why: In general your homeowners policy will provide coverage on your personal property based on a percentage of your coverage. Most policies protect this property in a total amount equal to 50% of the coverage of the house.

In other words, if your home is insured for $60,000, your personal property is insured for half that amount or $30,000. Is that adequate?

Crucial step: One way to come up with the answer is to *make a detailed inventory*. Then if your possessions have greater value than the 50% figure, you can increase the amount of coverage on unscheduled property or buy a floater policy to cover personal articles.

Making an inventory involves more than just listing possessions. You should also take photographs of each room. These pictures coupled with cancelled checks and bills to verify values are helpful in documenting claims. You may also wish to keep photos or descriptions of smaller possessions such as art, jewelry, or antiques. These are useful in case of theft as well as in loss by fire. Update your inventory periodically—say, every two years. Keep a copy of the inventory and other records in a safe place.

Another smart move is to—

▶ **HIRE A PROFESSIONAL APPRAISER:** Find out what your home is really worth today so you can accurately and adequately increase your insurance. (Just adding $10,000 or $15,000 more coverage probably won't be enough.) An appraiser's fee can run up to a few hundred dollars but, when you consider the thousands of dollars involved it can be one of the wisest investments you can make.

You'll find appraisers in the Yellow Pages. Look for those whose names are followed by "MAI" (Member of the Appraisal Institute) or "SRA" (Senior Residential Appraiser).

▶ **CAUTION:** Homeowner policies do not cover you for the full purchase price of damaged, destroyed or stolen personal possessions. They pay only the depreciated value—cost *less* depreciation. Suggestion: Buy personal property replacement-value coverage. This additional coverage will pay you enough to replace the lost personal items.

HOW TO BUY AUTO INSURANCE PROTECTION

The first question about auto insurance is not "Do I need it?" Your first question should be "What kind?" and your second, "How much?" Make no mistake about the need for auto insurance—even if your state does not require you to carry it.

The most important function of the auto insurance is not to protect you against financial loss if your car is damaged or stolen. Its primary function is to protect you against potentially gigantic liability claims if you are involved in an accident—claims that could wipe out your entire nest egg. This type of auto insurance is—

> ▶ **LIABILITY INSURANCE:** This protects you against claims resulting from an accident for which you are found to be at fault. It compensates injured parties for both personal injury and property damage resulting from an accident.

Auto liability coverage is broken down into two major components: bodily injury and property damage. The bodily injury portion provides one coverage limit for injuries to one person, and a higher limit for injuries to two or more people. Many states require 10/20 coverage. This will pay a single accident victim up to $10,000 for damages resulting from bodily injury, and limits payment to $20,000 if more than one person is injured.

With judgments of hundreds of thousands of dollars now being commonplace (and millions not unheard of), the required minimum liability coverage is insufficient to protect anyone with any assets from financial disaster. Required property damage limits—often as low as $5,000—are also too low to protect you against a major claim.

It will do you little good to have minimum liability coverage when a single misjudgment on your part (or on the part of anyone else who drives your car) can result in a seven-figure judgment against you.

> ▶ **WHAT TO DO:** Do not stint on liability coverage. Carry a minimum of 100/300/25 ($100,000 single bodily injury; $300,000 group bodily injury; $25,000 property damage) coverage. Higher limits are highly advised if you have a substantial amount of assets to protect against the claims of an injured party. Surprisingly, the cost of the additional coverage is not prohibitive—especially in relation to the devastating losses from which you are shielding yourself.

Many states have adopted forms of no-fault insurance. In these states, each insured's company compensates him or her for economic losses resulting from injuries, up to certain limits. An injured party who receives payment for physical injuries cannot sue the driver at fault for damages unless the injuries exceed the no-fault limits. But since these limits are generally extremely low, it is still essential to carry additional liability insurance.

Other Types of Auto Insurance

Collision coverage: If your car is damaged in an accident, collision coverage pays for its repair. Remember, the "other guy" may not be insured—or there may not be another guy. If you sideswipe your garage, for example, there's no one else to collect from. Premium costs are based on factors such as the age, sex, marital status, and driving record of the car's driver, and the type and cost of a car. Rates also vary tremendously according to the area in which you live or drive—urban rates are much higher than rural. (The same holds true for other types of auto insurance.) Insurers rate cars according to the cost of repairs. Collision coverage will cost more on a car that is more costly to repair.

Collision coverage is always sold with a "deductible". The deductible is the amount of repair cost which the owner pays for before the insurance company becomes liable. In some areas the minimum deductible on these policies is $200—the owner pays the first $200 of any repair bill. A higher deductible substantially reduces the premium for collision coverage.

The insurance company pays for repairs above the deductible amount, but with this—

▶ **IMPORTANT LIMIT:** The insurer will not pay for repairs that exceed the car's book value. For example, if repairs to a damaged car will cost $2,000, but the car is worth only $1,500, the insurance company will pay only $1,500 less the applicable deductible.

If you borrow from a bank or finance company to buy a car, the lender requires you to carry collision (and comprehensive) insurance to protect its loan collateral. If the car is totally destroyed, the lender collects the amount outstanding on the loan from the insurer. The balance of the insurance payment goes to you.

Comprehensive coverage: This pays for losses from the theft of a car or from damages as a result of fire, vandalism, falling objects, flood, and the like. Some comprehensive policies also pay for towing charges resulting from an accident or breakdown. There is usually a separate deductible on glass breakage, and premiums can be reduced by a general comprehensive deductible. Premiums can also be saved by limiting comprehensive protection to fire and theft losses.

Like collision coverage, the policy will not pay for repairs in excess of the car's value.

Uninsured motorist coverage: It is estimated that upwards of 20% of today's drivers are uninsured—even where insurance is mandatory. Many of these are the highest-risk and least responsible drivers on the road. Uninsured motorist coverage helps compensate you, your family, and other passengers in your car for damages from injury caused by an uninsured motorist or a hit-and-run driver. You are also covered if you are hit while walking or riding a bicycle. Payments under this type of coverage are usually limited to the minimum mandatory liability coverage required by state law; but in some states higher coverage limits are available.

Medical payment coverage: This provides limited coverage for medical expenses incurred by the car's owner and passengers as a result of an accident, regardless of who is at fault. This also covers family members who are injured while riding in someone else's car, or who are injured by a car while walking. These policies are typically coordinated with other health insurance you may have: payments will meet your other health insurance's deductible and pick up after your other health coverage is exhausted.

How to Cut the Cost of Auto Insurance

There are a couple of things you can do to ease the jolt every time you see your bill for auto insurance. The first is to make sure you are paying the lowest possible rate for your auto coverage. The second is to see that you're not paying for unnecessary coverage. Let's start with—

▶ **COST-CUTTING TACTIC #1:** It pays to shop around for the best deal on auto insurance rates. This may sound like shop-worn advice. But it's as true today as it was ten or twenty years ago. Insurance firms are competitive; their rates do differ. It's possible that you could knock 10% or 15% off your costs by changing insurance carriers.

But know what you are shopping for. For instance:

• If you have two cars, insure both with one company. Most insurers give a discount for a two-car policy.

• If you have an accident-free driving record, use it to the hilt. Many companies give discounts for this. Deal with one that does.

• Some firms grant lower premiums—or tack on surcharges—for different auto models.

• If your under-age-25 child uses the car, you're in high-premium territory. But many insurers give discounts for:

Good student drivers: Your child's completion of an approved driver training course can lop 5% to 15% off your liability and collision premiums.

Limited teen-age use: If your child is away at college much of the year (and carless), ask your insurer what sort of break you get.

Buying right: Though far less publicized than mileage ratings, *insurance ratings* of car models do exist—and can save you money. An insurance rating is an objective evaluation of how much it costs to repair a particular car.

If your insurer uses ratings for accident costs, it can mean a difference of as much as 40% a year in collision premiums for two similarly priced cars.

▶ **BUYING SMART:** Ask your insurer for a list of accident cost ratings for car models you have in mind. The information on insurance ratings will help you factor in the cost of insurance when you make your car buying decision.

A second way to slash insurance costs is to custom tailor your insurance policy.

▶ **COST-CUTTING TACTIC #2:** Tell your insurer what *you* need and *you* want. The typical car policy consists of several types of coverage. You may cut costs by reducing or deleting coverage you don't need.

To illustrate this tactic, we use a two-car family in the examples below. But the tactic can also be applied if you own only one car.

How to cut the cost of comprehensive insurance: This protects against fire, theft, vandalism and "natural cause" accidents resulting from, say, bad weather. You can lower the comprehensive premium by raising the deductible, i.e., the amount of damage you would pay for if you file a claim.

Key questions: Is your car frequently parked in high-crime areas? Is the car attractive to potential car thieves? Is a "natural cause" accident likely? If your answers are "no" here's—

▶ **WHAT TO DO:** Consider reducing the comprehensive premium by increasing the deductible. If your family owns two cars, you may even want to eliminate comprehensive coverage entirely on the second car—in other words, "self-insure" it.

Example: You live in California and drive a '77 Ford valued at $2,100. Your spouse drives an '81 Olds valued at $7,000. Comprehensive insurance costs $212 a year for both cars—with a $50 deductible on each. Since you park your car on your company's enclosed parking lot located in a good neighborhood, there is slight chance of your car being damaged or stolen. Therefore, you eliminate comprehensive coverage on the Ford entirely. You also raise the deductible on the Olds to $200.

Payoff: You cut your comprehensive insurance premium by 52%! You've saved $80 on the Ford and shaved $30 off the $132 premium for the Olds. Your new annual cost is $102.

How to cut costs on collision coverage: The same moves apply to collision coverage as to comprehensive. But the potential savings are greater because collision is more expensive.

Example: On the same facts as above, collision coverage (with a $200 deductible) for the Ford would cost $264. For the Olds: $340. Your annual cost for coverage on both cars is $604. By self-insuring the Ford against collision and boosting the deductible on the Olds from $200 to $500 you would reduce the annual premium to $276.

Payoff: A 54% cut in premium costs that translates into a dollar saving of $328 a year.

Should you cut your liability coverage? The answer is probably "no." Liability covers personal injury and property damage to others for which you (or another person driving your car) are held liable. Applying your cost pruning shears here, and cutting liability coverage to the minimum required by your state, could be—

▶ **PENNY WISE & DOLLAR DUMB:** Judgments of several hundred thousand dollars are not uncommon in personal injury cases. So it is a reasonable precaution to have substantial liability coverage. Moreover, the top dollars of liability coverage cost little. If $300,000 of coverage costs you $574 a year, cutting it to $100,000 would save only about $60—a little more than 10%.

Can you save on medical payment insurance? The answer here depends on how good your other medical insurance is. Your auto policy medical insurance covers medical and hospital costs incurred by you or your passengers as the result of an accident. This may needlessly duplicate hospitalization insurance you and your family have from another source. So all you may want to cover with this insurance is passengers.

▶ **WHAT TO DO:** If you have two cars, eliminate this coverage for the car that is not used for pleasure driving and/or car pooling.

Example: Again assuming the facts above, let's add that you car-pool to work in your Ford. The Ford is also used by your son and his friends. The annual premiums for medical payment insurance ($50,000 per person) are $90 for the Ford and $70 for your spouse's Olds. Your family has adequate medical insurance from other sources. You drop the medical payment insurance for the car that seldom has non-family passengers—the Olds.

Payoff: Your total insurance premium is cut 44%. The annual cost of the medical payment insurance drops from $160 to $90.

Chapter 10

How To Build Wealth For A Financially Secure Future

Who is Going To Foot The Bill for Your Retirement Income?

If your answer is Social Security, let's be blunt: you're in trouble. Sure, that monthly benefit check will help out (and later on, we'll show you how to get your fair share). But Social Security will not provide you with enough income to maintain your accustomed standard of living during retirement. If you want to live well when you retire, you will have to look elsewhere. That's what this chapter is all about: showing you the best ways to build an adequate retirement nest egg—at minimum trouble and expense.

THE BEST TAX-SHELTERED WAY TO BUILD A RETIREMENT NEST EGG

For the majority of Americans who get paychecks, a good pension or profit-sharing plan is the best source of retirement income. In effect, the company sets aside part of your compensation and invests it—with the aid of competent financial specialists—for your retirement. This part of your compensation is tax-sheltered: The money set aside for you by the company does not appear on your W-2, and is not reported on your tax return. And your retirement account grows free of federal and state tax erosion until you make withdrawals.

"How good is the retirement plan?" That's a critical question to ask about any prospective (or present) employer. *Reason:* An excellent plan can turn what appears to be an "adequate" compensation plan into a real winner. Conversely, a poor plan (or the lack of one) can mean a big salary offer isn't that hot after all. To dramatize this point—and show how to size up a compensation package—let's look at this—

> **Example:** John Archer, a sales executive, is employed by XYZ, Inc., at a salary of $45,000. XYZ has a profit sharing plan that calls for annual contributions equal to 15% of each employee's salary. In Archer's case, that works out to a profit-sharing contribution of $6,750 a year.

ABC Corp. makes a play for Archer by promising him a salary of $54,000—a substantial 20% increase. But ABC does not have a profit sharing plan.

Assuming that the companies have equal non-retirement benefits, and offer Archer equal long-term opportunity, what should Archer do—stay or go?

Answer: On our facts, Archer may well be better off financially staying where he is. *Reason:* That profit-sharing contribution is undiluted, tax-sheltered cash—worth far more in terms of raw, full-taxed dollars.

▶ **HOW TO MAKE A TRUE COMPARISON:** Archer has to compare apples with apples—compare his true net in his present job with what's being offered him.

Let's suppose Archer files a joint return with his spouse, has $3,000 of other income subject to tax (outside work, interest, dividends), and will finish off 1984 with $11,400 in total itemized deductions and exemptions. For simplicity, we'll disregard the tax-deductible IRA contribution that is available to Archer in either situation. Here's how things look. In both situations, the tax is calculated on *taxable* income (income less total itemized deductions and exemptions).

	Present Job	Job Offer
Salary	$45,000	$54,000
Other income	3,000	3,000
	48,000	57,000
Federal income tax ('84 rates)	7,858	10,988
	40,142	46,012
Money out-of-pocket for retirement	-0-	$ 6,750
Net before Personal Expenses	$40,142	$39,262

Bottom line: The "$9,000 higher" job offer boils down to $880 LESS in Archer's pocket than he's getting now. *Reason:* XYZ is providing Archer with $6,750 for retirement at no current tax cost to Archer. On the other hand, if he takes ABC's offer, Archer has to dip into his own pocket—using after-tax dollars—to pay his own way to a secure retirement future.

All other things being equal, Archer shouldn't go with ABC unless it sweetens the compensation package—or he should look for a job that offers retirement benefits comparable to what he's now getting with XYZ, plus a higher salary.

HOW A PENSION PLAN ALLOWS YOU TO FORETELL YOUR RETIREMENT FUTURE

A pension plan gives employees a fixed income when they retire. Each year, the company must set aside enough money in the plan to provide employees with their promised pension income. The company contribution is not tied into profits, and must be made in good years and bad years.

A pension plan can take many forms. Here are three common arrangements:

(1) Fixed benefit plan: Under this plan, you annually receive at retirement a definite percentage of your compensation. For this purpose, your compensation is (1) your average compensation during your entire employment or (2) an average of your compensation during a stated number of years before retirement. Obviously, for employees the second option is better. *Reason:* Your pay during your final work years will be higher than your average pay. So your pension will be based on a higher salary. Your compensation is the primary factor in a fixed benefit plan. The number of years of service doesn't enter into the computation of benefits. However, the plan may require a given number of years of service before an employee becomes eligible to participate.

(2) Unit benefit plan: Under this plan, your years of service do enter the computation of your pension benefit. You receive a unit of pension benefit for each year of credited service. The annual unit benefit can be expressed as a percentage of compensation or as a stated dollar amount.

Percentage of compensation: You earn each year a pension benefit that is a percentage of your compensation. For example, in a one percent unit benefit plan, an employee with 25 years of credited service would be entitled to 25% of his compensation as an annual pension. It is common to apply a certain percentage figure to compensation below a specific amount and then apply a larger percentage figure to compensation in excess of that amount.

Stated dollar amount: The stated dollar amount is multiplied by your credited years of service under the plan. For example, if the annual unit of credit is $200 and you have been an employee for 30 years, you would be entitled to a pension of $6,000 per year.

Example: Your plan provides a pension of 1% of the first $10,000 of annual compensation plus 1 1/4% of any excess. An employee with 40 years of credited service and an annual compensation of $25,000 would be entitled to an annual pension of $11,500 computed as follows:

40% (40 x 1%) x 10,000	= $ 4,000
50% (40 x 1 1/4%) x 15,000	= 7,500
Annual pension	$11,500

(3) Money-purchase benefit plan: A money-purchase plan provides for a stipulated annual contribution by the employer. No specific benefit is formulated in advance as under the fixed or the unit benefit plans. Instead, you will receive whatever retirement benefit the total contributions (plus earnings) will purchase at retirement. A simple money purchase plan, therefore, recognizes no element of past service. The benefits of each employee will vary according to the amounts actuarially required to provide proportionately equal benefits, or units of benefits, for all employees. As a general rule, a money-purchase plan favors younger workers, while a fixed-benefit plan favors older workers.

Under a money purchase arrangement, the employer usually contributes a constant amount or percentage of your compensation. (The amount, however, can also be fixed at a specified dollar amount for each participant.) The money is held either in trust or by an insurer.

> **Example:** In a 15% money purchase plan, the employer annually contributes 15% of your compensation. Assuming your annual compensation is $40,000 and there are 20 years until you retire, the employer would contribute $120,000 for your pension. This amount plus your share of fund earnings would then be available at retirement to provide your pension.

Your pension rights as an employee: At one time, some employees who left a job before retirement lost all their pension benefits. But this can't happen any more since all formal retirement plans must give employees specified vested rights in their benefits. The vested portion of an employee's benefit represents the part he can walk away with even if he quits or is fired before retirement. The nonvested portion is forfeited and left behind by the departed employee and remains in the plan.

A company can choose a vesting schedule from among three that meet Government approval. One example is 5 to 15 year vesting: After five years, an employee is 25% vested, after 6 years, he's 30% vested. The vested portion goes up 5% for each subsequent year until the employee is 100% vested after 15 years.

Summing up: From the employee's standpoint, a pension plan has three positive features:

(1) You know what your pension income will be;

(2) Your right to a pension benefit is safe (most pension plans are insured by a Government agency).

(3) Your employer must put money away from your retirement regardless of the level of its prosperity.

The minuses: Generally speaking, you cannot tap your pension money before retirement, and, generally, you don't have any sort of control over how the pension fund invests its money.

How The Tax Law Treats Your Pension Income

Where your employer funds the entire cost of the retirement plan, your pension checks are fully taxable. However, if the plan required you to make contributions from your own pocket to supplement the company's plan contributions, you can recover your invested dollars without any tax cost. If your pension income for the first three years comes to less than the gross amount you contributed, then your pension checks are all tax free—until you have recovered your contributions. From that point on, all of your pension is taxable. If you don't meet this three-year rule, part of each pension check representing the employer's contribution will be taxable and part representing your own contribution will be tax free (your company will let you know how much of each pension check is taxable).

A new tax complication: Your company is now required to withhold federal income tax on your pension checks (other types of retirement plans are affected as well) UNLESS you—

▶ **"ELECT OUT" OF WITHHOLDING:** You can elect not to have the withholding provision apply to your pension. The company issuing the pension checks must notify you of your right to "elect out" of withholding.

If you do not "elect out" then tax is withheld just as if your pension check were salary. In other words, the amount withheld will depend on the number of exemptions claimed on your withholding certificate.

Should you have the company withhold on your pension checks? There's no set answer. The one thing withholding has going for it is convenience: You may not have to worry about filing estimated tax payments, or coming up with a big sum of cash at tax return time.

HOW PROFIT SHARING PLANS LET YOU CASH IN ON YOUR EMPLOYER'S SUCCESS

In a profit-sharing plan, your employer contributes part of its annual profits for investment, accumulation, and eventual distribution to you and your fellow employees. Since contributions are tied to your company's profits, you have a direct share in its financial success (on the other hand, you may suffer in the years the company doesn't do well).

Tax benefits for employees: You don't pay a cent of current tax on the employer's contribution. In addition, your contributions grow tax-free in your account. These two tax benefits make it possible for rank-and-file employees—as well as executives—to accumulate a tax-sheltered fortune for their retirement.

> **Example:** ABC, Inc. has a profit sharing plan that calls for annual contributions of 20% of profits, but not in excess of 10% of each employee's salary. Assuming sufficient profits, Worker A with a salary of $20,000 gets $2,000 a year, Worker B earning $40,000 gets $4,000, and Worker C earning $60,000, gets $6,000.

Let's assume each worker joins ABC's plan at age 40, and that ABC has enough profits each year to make the full 10% profit-sharing contribution. If the plan's money is invested at an 8% rate, then Worker A will have $157,909 in his account at age-65 retirement, Worker B will have $315,818, and Worker C will have $473,726.

How profits are shared: A company has much leeway in controlling the profits to be shared. For example, it can provide for a flat percentage of pre- or post-tax profits to be contributed to the plan. It may have a sliding scale formula that increases contributions as profits rise, or it may provide that profits are to be shared only if and to the extent that company profits exceed a predetermined level. Generally, a company may deduct contributions equal to 15% of payroll.

Allocation among employees: Usually each contribution is allocated among the accounts of the employees in proportion to their compensation. Thus the basic share of a $30,000 employee would be twice that of a $15,000 employee.

Vesting: An employer setting up a profit-sharing plan must, as a general rule, provide for complete vesting of each year's contribution to an employee's account by the end of the fifth plan year after the year the contribution is made. The simplest vesting method: After six years of employment, the company contribution for the first year of employment is 100% vested; after seven years, the second year's contribution is also 100% vested; after eight years, the third year's contribution is 100% vested; and so forth.

Summing up: From the employee's standpoint, a profit sharing plan has these advantages:

(1) If things go well for your employer, you share in its success;

(2) Your retirement fund is safe. *Reason:* The profit-sharing funds must be held by an independent trustee for your benefit.

(3) You may have some control in how your retirement funds are invested. For example, you may have the choice of receiving annual interest on your account accumulation, or investing your funds in a diversified stock-market portfolio (or dividing your money between the two options).

(4) Many profit-sharing plans allow employees to withdraw all or a portion of their vested units before retirement. So your profit-sharing account is a ready source of funds for family emergencies or major purchases.

Disadvantages: There is the risk that a company won't be able to make profit-sharing contributions in a severe business downturn. And you don't know how much your retirement benefit will be.

HOW TO HANDLE PROFIT SHARING PAYOUTS

As we've seen, it's not uncommon for long-term employees to have hundreds of thousands of dollars in their profit-sharing account when they retire. Basically, there are three ways to tap this cash:

(1) Withdraw the entire account balance in one lump sum;

(2) Take the cash over a period of years (through an annuity for example); or

(3) A combination of (1) and (2). For example, if your profit-sharing account balance is $200,000 at retirement, you can take $70,000 in one lump sum, and use the $130,000 balance to buy an annuity that pays you fixed income for life or for a set period of years.

While your personal needs may dictate how you handle your payout (e.g., you need a large sum of cash to buy a retirement home), taxes will play a big part in the decision. Here's how the tax law affects your profit-sharing payout options, beginning with—

How Lump-Sum Distributions from Retirement Plans Get Favorable Tax Treatment

If you take out your profit-sharing cash in one lump sum at retirement, you qualify for favorable tax treatment. Key condition: Your entire account balance must be distributed to you within one year.

If you became a member of a profit-sharing plan before 1974, you can figure your tax using one of the two options shown below. If you became a member of the plan after 1973, you must use the first option:

Option #1—Ten year averaging: The lump-sum payment is taxed as ordinary income separate and apart from your other income. However, the tax is computed as if the income had been received over ten years. And if the payout is less than $70,000, part of the payout may be tax-free due to a minimum distribution allowance.

> ▶ **HOW AVERAGING WORKS:** You take the entire lump-sum distribution (less any minimum distribution allowance) and divide it by ten. To the result, you add $2,300 and compute tax on the total using the tax rates for single individuals. You multiply the result by ten to arrive at the tax on your profit-sharing payout. This tax is then added to the tax on your other income for the year.

You must have been a plan member for at least five years to qualify for ten-year averaging.

Option #2—Part Capital Gain, Part Ten-Year Averaging: Your payout is divided into two portions. The first portion is composed of profit-sharing accumulations attributable to your years in the plan before 1974. The other portion is made up of accumulations attributable to your plan years after 1973. Each portion is taxed differently.

Pre '74 portion—is taxed as long-term capital gain. That is, only 40% of this amount is taxable. Since it's capital gain, the amount can be offset by capital losses.

Post '73 portion—is taxed under the ten year averaging rules shown under Option #1.

Either option will produce a smaller tax than you'd pay if the distribution were treated as salary income. But the tax bite can still be very substantial.

> *Example:* Let's suppose Mr. Smith entered a profit-sharing plan after 1973 and has a $200,000 profit-sharing account balance at retirement. At 1984 tax rates, ten-year averaging results in a tax of $38,030. Over 19% of the payout is washed away.

If Mr. Smith had joined the plan in, say, 1965, he can use the part capital gain, part ten year averaging option. But if the capital gain portion of the payout is very large, Smith might be subject to another tax—the special alternative minimum tax. (See your tax adviser for more details.)

Why Spreading Out Your Plan Payout Can Leave You Dollars and Cents Ahead

If you don't need a large sum of cash at retirement, and plan to live off your retirement account earnings, then you will probably be better off not using a simple lump-sum distribution. Instead, you should take the profit-sharing cash over a period of years. One way to do this is to use an—

▶ **IRA ROLLOVER ACCOUNT:** An IRA rollover account is basically an Individual Retirement Account set up to receive the payout from your retirement plan. (Regular IRA plans are covered later in this chapter.)

There is no limit on the amount of cash you can put into an IRA roll-over account. Big tax advantage: If you take a lump-sum payout from your profit-sharing plan and roll over the entire sum within 60 days of receipt, you owe no current tax on the payout. The tax is deferred and is payable only as you withdraw cash from the IRA (withdrawals must commence by the time you reach age 70½).

Dollars and cents: Let's go back to our example of Mr. Smith. Without an IRA rollover, his $200,000 profit-sharing withdrawal (using ten year averaging) will dwindle down to $161,970 after taxes (gross distribution less $38,030 tax). Invested at 9%, that sum will earn Smith $14,577 a year.

If he rolls over his account balance into an IRA, the entire $200,000 will be available for investment. If the IRA earns the same 9%, Smith's annual income will be $18,000.

Tax angles: All amounts withdrawn from an IRA are taxed as ordinary income, and aren't eligible for special tax breaks (other than five-year averaging). However, by spreading out his IRA withdrawals over, say, ten years, Smith will in effect be averaging out the tax over ten years. Since the typical retiree's tax rate is low, Smith may not only spread out the tax, but cut it as well.

Still another option: You can have the trust of your profit-sharing plan buy an annuity for you. The full balance in your profit-sharing account is available for investment in the annuity. None of the payout is subject to tax at this point. You pay tax, of course, on the full annuity payment each year as you receive it.

Result: you accomplish essentially the same thing as you do with the IRA rollover. However, there are a few differences: With an annuity, your annual income is fixed and when the annuity stops (when you die, or, in the case of a joint and survivor annuity when you and your spouse are both gone), there's nothing left over for your heirs. On the other hand, with an IRA rollover account, you retain control. You can take advantage of rising interest rates by switching your money around (or lock in high interest with a CD when rates start falling). Finally, if you don't exhaust the rollover account's principal, your heirs will be left the balance when you pass on.

▶ **WATCH THIS PITFALL:** If you want an annuity, be sure the trustee of the profit-sharing plan buys it for you. Don't take a lump sum and then buy the annuity yourself. If you do, you will be taxed on the entire lump-sum distribution, and will have far less to invest in your annuity.

How a Retiring Employee Can Receive a Payout of Cash Plus an Annuity and Still Get a Big Tax Break

Many employees nearing retirement want their profit-sharing account to do two things: Supply a lump sum of cash (to buy a retirement home, take a world tour, etc.) *and* provide them with a source of income during retirement.

▶ **GOOD NEWS:** You can accomplish both goals—and retain tax breaks—by getting part of your profit-sharing payout in cash, and part in an annuity.

Tax break #1: You can use special ten-year averaging on the ordinary income portion of the payout (generally, the payout attributable to post-1973 plan participation). *Reason:* You are considered to have received a lump-sum payment (your entire balance) even though the annuity won't be paid until future years.

Tax break #2: Even though the annuity is considered to be part of a lump-sum distribution, the employee doesn't pay tax on the annuity until he receives the payments.

The tax on the ordinary income portion of the distribution is computed on the cash plus the current actuarial value of the annuity. The amount of tax is then reduced by the portion of the tax attributable to the value of the annuity.

Result: Although the annuity contract is taken into account as part of the lump-sum distribution, it is not currently taxed. You pay tax on the annuity when you receive payouts.

Key point: The annuity contract is disregarded for purposes of computing the tax on any capital gain portion of the payout (i.e., the portion attributable to the pre-1974 plan participation).

Q. What if I take half my $200,000 payout in cash and roll over the $100,000 balance into an IRA?

A. This won't work as well. The $100,000 rolled over to the IRA is tax-free. However, the $100,000 balance is fully taxable and is not eligible for ten-year averaging.

How to Save Tax Dollars by Taking Profit-Sharing Payouts in Company Stock

Another way of saving taxes is to take a profit-sharing payout in company stock. *Reason:* If you take your payout in stock instead of cash, the tax law says you are currently taxed only on the adjusted basis (tax cost) of the stock to the profit-sharing plan. The tax on the stock's paper gain is deferred until you sell the stock, and then it's *all tax-sheltered capital gain*. Let's compare some stock versus cash payouts.

Example (1): Assume that XYZ Corp. set up a profit-sharing plan 20 years ago and Brown, its personnel director, is retiring. Assume that his total profit-sharing payout comes to $100,000, of which $30,000 represents years of plan participation after 1973. Brown takes down a lump-sum cash distribution.

Brown will report as follows: (a) $30,000 ordinary income—the amounts attributable to post-'73 participation—taxed under the special 10-year averaging device provided for this portion of the profit-sharing payout; and (b) $70,000 long-term capital gain.

Example (2): Assume that, instead of taking a full cash distribution, Brown takes all of his payout in his employer's stock which is presently worth $50 per share and has an adjusted basis to the profit-sharing plan of $2. Brown thus will receive 2,000 shares of XYZ stock (total adjusted basis: $4,000).

Brown will report: (a) $1,200 ordinary income—the portion of the stock's basis attributable to years beginning after 1973; and (b) $2,800 long-term gain—the portion attributable to 1973 and earlier years.

How about the $96,000 "paper profit" on the stock? Brown doesn't pay tax on that until he sells the stock. And when he does, it will be long-term capital gain. Brown, by electing to take his profit-sharing payout in stock instead of cash, has succeeded in converting $28,800 ($30,000 − $1,200) of what otherwise would have been ordinary income back into capital gain.

▶ **WHAT TO DO:** Check with your company's profit-sharing adviser and see if a stock payout option is a good idea for you.

HOW TO BUILD A TAX SHELTERED NEST EGG WITH AN IRA

It's no accident that Individual Retirement Accounts are the most popular tax shelter around today. The secret of their success is simple: They work!

▶ **TWO-WAY TAX SHELTER:** (1) You can contribute as much as $2,000 to a regular IRA and *deduct every dollar.* (2) The interest or other income credited to your account is not currently taxed—you have a free and clear compounding of income until you withdraw it from the account.

Q. Who's eligible to set up an IRA?

A. You can set up an IRA and make deductible contributions in any year that you (1) have earnings from employment or self-employment, and (2) have not reached age 70½.

Q. Is there any minimum age at which an IRA can be set up?

A. No. For example, if your child has earnings from a summer job, he or she can set up an IRA and make a deductible contribution.

Q. How can I set up an IRA?

A. You can set up two basic types of IRAs:

Custodial or trust account: Custodial or trusteed IRAs are usually set up at a bank, savings and loan association or credit union. The contributions can be invested in savings accounts, mutual fund shares or any other asset that's an acceptable investment for a qualified retirement plan.

Annuity or endowment contract: You can use your contributions to purchase an annuity directly from an insurance company. And although no assets of an IRA may be invested in life insurance contracts, you are not prevented from purchasing an endowment contract with incidental life insurance features. This type of endowment policy will be treated as a retirement annuity. However, only the premium attributable to the retirement saving portion of the contract is deductible.

Q. How much can I contribute to an IRA each year?

A. Your annual deductible contribution to a regular IRA is limited to the lesser of (1) 100% of your earnings or (2) $2,000 ($2,250 if you set up a spousal IRA—more on this later).

Q. What happens if I contribute more than the allowable limit?

A. To the extent the contribution is not permitted, it's an "excess contribution." That means it's not deductible and is subject to an annual excise tax. But there are two ways to correct an excess contribution.

> ▶ **WHAT TO DO:** (1) If you make an excess contribution in any year, you have until your tax return date (usually April 15 of the following year) or the extension date to withdraw the excess without penalty. (2) You can limit the excise tax to just one year by contributing *less* than the maximum the following year (assuming you're eligible to contribute in that year).

Q. How late in the year can I make my annual IRA contribution?

A. You can make your contribution in the *next* year. Of course, the earlier in the year you make your contribution the better—you put your money to work for you tax-free just that much sooner. But you can wait as late as your tax return date (again, usually April 15 of the following year) to make a contribution for the year. In fact, you can wait as late as the tax return due date to both set up your IRA *and* make a contribution.

Q. What happens to the contribution after I put it in the IRA?

A. The full amount put into an IRA accumulates tax-free until it's withdrawn. So each year you have more dollars earning more dollars. To see what this can mean in dollars-and-cents, let's look at a—

Typical example: Mr. Brown is 40 years old and in the 50% tax bracket. He want to put $2,000 of his *pre-tax* earnings aside each year to supplement other retirement income. Let's see what Brown will have by the time he's 65 if he puts money in a—

Bank account at 10% interest: Each year he will be able to deposit on after-tax net of only $1,000. And his 10% annual return is actually only 5% after he pays the tax collector. *Result:* At age 65, Brown will have about $50,000 in his account.

Individual Retirement Account at 10% interest: Because he gets to deduct his contribution, Brown can put the full $2,000 in his IRA each year. And his 10% annual return is completely sheltered from tax. *Result:* At age 65, Brown will have about *$216,000 in his IRA.* Of course, there is a tax bill to pay on that accumulated amount. But even if half goes to the tax collector, Brown will still be left with over $100,000. And Brown may be able to boost his after-tax take by spreading out his IRA withdrawals over his retirement years.

Q. Must I make IRA contributions each year?

A. No. If you don't want to contribute in a given year, you can skip it. It's all up to you—you can skip, increase or decrease contributions at your option. But if you don't make a contribution—or contribute less than you could have—you can't make it up in a later year.

Q. Must I make contributions each year to the same IRA?

A. No. You can set up as many IRAs as you want. For example, you can put your IRA contributions in a mutual fund IRA one year and in a savings account IRA the next. Or you can split a year's contribution between two or more IRAs. As long as your total contribution doesn't exceed the annual maximum, you're okay.

Q. Can I transfer amounts from one IRA to another?

A. Yes. You can transfer all or part of an IRA deposit to another IRA without any tax consequences if the transfer is completed within 60 days. This is known as a "tax-free rollover." A rollover contribution is, of course, not deductible and you are limited to one rollover a year (unless the transfer is made directly between IRA trustees). If you fail to meet the rollover requirements, the transfer will be taxed to you as a regular IRA withdrawal and what you put in the second IRA may be treated as an excess contribution.

Q. How are regular IRA withdrawals taxed?

A. IRA withdrawals are taxed as ordinary income in the year you make them. If you use an annuity contract as an IRA, each annuity payment is taxable as you receive it. If you hold IRA bonds, you are taxed on each bond as you redeem it (or at the end of the tax year in which you reach age 70½, if that's sooner). IRA distributions, whether received in a lump sum or not, are not eligible for the 10-year-averaging treatment that's available for payouts from corporate or Keogh plans. However, you can use regular 5-year income averaging.

Q. Can I make withdrawals whenever I want?

A. Yes. But if you make a withdrawal too soon—or too late—you may owe a penalty tax in addition to the regular income tax.

If you make a withdrawal before age 59½, it's subject to a 10% excise tax. However, this doesn't apply in cases of death or disability.

You must begin making certain minimum withdrawals at age 70½. To the extent your withdrawals fall short of these minimum amounts, there's a 50% excise tax.

Q. How are death benefits paid?

A. If the owner of an IRA dies before receiving everything in his IRA, the remainder must be paid to his or her beneficiary within five years or must be used to buy an annuity for the beneficiary. Retirement bonds quit paying interest five years after death (or when the decedent would have reached 70½, if that's sooner).

Q. Are death benefits subject to estate taxes?

A. In general, yes. But there's an important exception: The first $100,000 of death benefits are not taxed in a decedent's estate if (1) the beneficiary is someone other than the decedent's estate, and (2) the beneficiary agrees to take the benefits in the form of an annuity or in installments spread over at least 36 months.

Important point to keep in mind: All amounts left to the spouse are protected by the unlimited estate-tax marital deduction.

How Your Spouse Can Help You Make Bigger IRA Contributions

The general rule is that you can't contribute more than $2,000 annually to an Individual Retirement Account (IRA). But if your spouse isn't employed (or self-employed), you may be able to contribute an additional $250—for a combined IRA deduction of $2,250—if you set up a spousal IRA. The annual contribution limit for your IRA and your spousal IRA is the lesser of $2,250 or 100% of your earnings. You get the same tax benefits with a spousal IRA as you do with a regular IRA.

Your contribution is fully deductible and it grows tax-free until withdrawn. It's just that with a spousal IRA you can get a bigger deduction and more tax-free growth. And you have flexibility in allocating deposits. As long as no more than $2,000 is contributed to either IRA, you can divide the contributions as you wish.

Q. My spouse works part-time and makes just a few dollars a year. That's the only work my spouse does outside of our home. Does that mean I can't set up a spousal IRA?

A. That's exactly what it means. If your spouse has one penny of earned income, you cannot set up a spousal IRA. However, there's a—

▶ **BRIGHTER SIDE TO THE PICTURE:** If your spouse works, then your spouse can set up his or her own regular IRA. Your spouse can contribute up to $2,000 or 100% of his or her earnings, whichever is less. In other words, if you and your spouse both contribute to regular IRAs, you can put away as much as $4,000, fully deductible, each year.

Q. Although my spouse doesn't have any earned income, there is a lot of investment income—interest, dividends and so forth. Can I still set up a spousal IRA?

A. You certainly can. There's no restriction on the amount of investment income your spouse can receive.

Q. What happens if I set up a spousal IRA this year and my spouse gets a job next year?

A. No problem. You just make a regular IRA contribution to your IRA next year and your spouse makes one to his or hers. The tax law says that the same IRA can be a spousal IRA one year and a regular IRA the next.

How the Tax Law Lets You Choose the Way to a Secure Retirement Future

The Individual Retirement Account (IRA) was designed for those millions of Americans not covered by a company pension or profit-sharing plan. But now in a turnabout, the tax law says that those millions who are members of company retirement plans can set up their own IRAs, too. Or as an alternative to making contributions to an IRA, you can make deductible voluntary contributions to your company plan, provided the plan permits this. (Previously, only limited, *non-deductible* voluntary contributions, could be made to a company plan.) So you can belong to a regular retirement plan (for example, a pension or profit-sharing plan or Keogh Plan) and set up an IRA or make deductible voluntary contributions to the plan.

An IRA or contributions to the company plan—which is right for you? There are a number of factors to consider before deciding whether to set up and contribute to an IRA or to make voluntary, deductible contributions to the company plan. The plan contribution route has appeal. You are more familiar with the operations of the company plan, and making voluntary contributions is likely to be more convenient than opening your own IRA.

And, from a tax standpoint, there's not much difference between voluntary contributions and IRAs. In general, the maximum deductible contribution an employee can make to either an IRA or as a voluntary contribution to a company plan is $2,000. Contributions to either setup grow tax-free, and you can't make withdrawals before age 59½ without paying a penalty (exceptions: withdrawals for death or disability). When you do withdraw your money at retirement, the payouts qualify for regular 5-year income averaging only.

There are some non-tax differences, however, between an IRA and deductible voluntary contributions made to a company plan. Here's a rundown of some of the more important differences:

- *Contributions for non-working spouse:* If your spouse doesn't work, you can contribute and deduct $2,250 to a spousal IRA. You can divide the contribution as you wish as long as no more than $2,000 is contributed to the account of either spouse. On the other hand, your maximum contribution to a company plan would still be limited to $2,000. The other $250 would have to be contributed to a separate spousal IRA.
- *Tax-free rollover:* Amounts in an IRA generally cannot be rolled over into a company retirement plan. But deductible voluntary contributions to a company plan can be rolled over into another employer's retirement plan. The rollover is permitted, however, only if the second employer's plan (1) permits such rollovers on a nondiscriminatory basis, and (2) continues to treat your rollover as a deductible voluntary contribution.
- *Time for withdrawals:* You must begin withdrawing money from an IRA in the year you reach age 70½ or face a big penalty. But funds from your deductible voluntary contribution account don't have to be withdrawn at any certain time.

The IRA has a critical non-tax advantage over plan contributions.

▶ **INVESTMENT FLEXIBILITY:** You have limited options as to how you invest what you contribute to the company plan. With your own IRA, however, you call the shots. There's a wide variety of ways to invest your IRA contributions, and you can move your funds from one IRA investment to another as the changing economic times dictate.

While the tax law prohibits IRA investments in collectibles (art, coins, gems, etc.), you can still invest in a wide variety of investments, such as: bank certificates of deposit; mutual funds; stocks and annuities.

▶ **WHAT TO DO:** Whichever way you decide to go, you should make your decision as soon as possible. That way, you can make your first contribution early in the year. *Result:* Your contribution will start earning tax-deferred dollars right away.

HOW THE BETTER-THAN-EVER KEOGH PLAN SETUP CAN HELP SELF-EMPLOYEDS BUILD A TAX-SHELTERED RETIREMENT FUND

A Keogh Plan is simply a retirement plan for self-employed business people or professionals. If you run your business or practice as a sole proprietorship or a partnership, or you're an employee with an outside source of income, like consulting, you can set up your own—

> ▶ **TAX-SHELTERED RETIREMENT PLAN:** (1) You get a deduction for what you put into your Keogh retirement fund; (2) the earnings from the fund build up tax-free; and (3) you pay no tax until you retire and withdraw your money.

In the past, self-employeds were at a big disadvantage to incorporated people when it came to retirement plan benefits. *Reason*: The Keogh rules were not as generous as the rules for corporate pension and profit-sharing plans. Beginning in 1984, however, all that is changed. Generally, the Keogh plan offers the same shelter benefits you would get with a corporate retirement plan. That means bigger current deductions for Keogh people, and a bigger tax sheltered retirement fund. Here's a closer look, beginning with—

How to Make the Best Tax-Shelter Use of the Most Popular Type of Keogh Plan

So-called "defined contribution" Keogh plans have always been more popular than pension-type Keogh plans. *Reason*: They are simpler to administer since the contribution is expressed as a percentage of each participant's earned income. Your retirement benefit depends on how well your contributions are invested.

A defined contribution Keogh can be either a profit-sharing type plan or a money-purchase type plan. In a profit-sharing Keogh, you are obligated to contribute a set percentage of profits to participants' accounts (yours and your full-time employees, if any). In a money purchase pension Keogh, you must make a specific contribution to each participant's account each year, regardless of the level of profits.

In 1984, the maximum deduction to a money purchase Keogh is the lesser of $30,000 or 25% of earned income. For profit-sharing Keoghs, the deduction is the lesser of $30,000 or 15% of earned income. (In prior years, the deductible contribution to either type of plan was the lesser of $15,000 or 15% of earned income.) "Earned income" is the net income from a business or professional practice less ALL deductible Keogh contributions (including the self-employed's own contribution). Under pre-1984 rules, the self-employed subtracted only deductible Keogh contributions made on behalf of employees. The self-employed's own Keogh contribution was not figured in.

Here's an example of how a defined contribution Keogh plan allows you to sock away big dollars for a comfortable retirement—and get big current deductions to boot.

Mr. Smith is a 40-year-old self-employed businessman with earned income of $65,000, and taxable income of $50,000 (income after all deductions and exemptions). This year, he sets up a Keogh plan and contributes $7,000 (less than the maximum with either a profit-sharing or a money-purchase Keogh). Let's assume he makes the same contribution each year—and has the same annual income and deductions—until he retires at 65.

Tax shelter result: Smith saves over $2,500 a year in Federal income taxes due to the Keogh contribution. At 1984 tax rates for marrieds filing jointly, here's how this works out:

```
Tax on $50,000 taxable income (without Keogh)............... $11,368
Less tax on $43,000 taxable income
  ($50,000 less $7,000 Keogh contribution).................    8,848
Net annual tax saving ......................................  $ 2,520
```

Wealth-building result: Smith's Keogh contributions grow free of tax erosion until retirement. If the money earns 8% a year, Smith's annual $7,000 contribution will swell to $500,000 *plus* by the time he retires.

Keogh contributions can be invested in a wide variety of ways. For example, you can set up your Keogh plan at a local bank, which acts as trustee and invests the funds for you. You can purchase nontransferrable annuity contracts from an insurance company. Or you can invest your Keogh money in mutual funds or in a wide variety of investment programs offered by brokerage houses.

▶ **BEST APPROACH:** Resist the temptation to use your Keogh money for speculation (e.g., in the stock market). Most of your Keogh retirement nest egg should be invested conservatively, in high-yielding CDs, for example.

Should You Have a Pension-Type Keogh?

Like all pensions, a Keogh pension is more costly to administer than a defined-contribution-type retirement plan. For example, you need the services of an actuary to determine your annual contribution. In the past, the extra expense just wasn't worth it. That's because until 1984, the maximum Keogh retirement benefit was based on a rigid formula set forth in the tax law.

Example: Dr. Smith earns $100,000 a year. He sets up a pension-type Keogh when he is age 50. Under prior law, Smith could accrue an annual retirement benefit of $3,000 (3% allowed by statute applied to a maximum of $100,000 in earned income). *Result:* Smith could make annual deductible contributions necessary to fund an annual retirement benefit of $45,000, beginning at age 65 (15 years times $3,000).

▶ **TAX LAW CHANGE:** Beginning in 1984, the old restrictive formula for pension Keoghs is repealed. The maximum Keogh pension benefit is the lesser of 100% of earned income, or $90,000.

This big change means that self-employeds—particularly those who are middle aged—should take another look at a pension-type Keogh plan. If you can afford to make the contributions, you can set aside enough money each year to fund a retirement pension equal to your three highest years of earned income (up to $90,000).

What's the Price You Pay for Setting up a Keogh Plan?

If you're a self-employed business person or professional with no employees other than family members, there is no price. But if you have full time employees, you will have to lay out cash for their retirement, as well as your own.

Reason: Generally, you must include all full time employees with three or more years of service in your plan. You don't have to include employees who don't put in at least 1,000 hours of service per year. And you must make Keogh contributions in the same proportion for employees as you do for yourself. However, contributions you make for your employees are fully deductible (as are your personal contributions).

▶ **THE GOOD NEWS:** There are ways to cut down the cost of funding a Keogh plan—without reducing your personal Keogh contribution. One simple method: Gear the Keogh contribution level to the maximum amount you will set aside for yourself.

Example: Mr. Jones is a self-employed businessman with $80,000 in earnings. His two employees earn $15,000 each. All told, Jones can afford to put away $7,000 each year for his retirement.

▶ **WHAT TO DO:** Jones should use $2,000 of that $7,000 for an annual IRA contribution. The $5,000 balance is the amount he'll be putting into his own account in the Keogh plan. Since he's limiting his own Keogh contribution to 6¼% of earnings ($5,000 divided by $80,000) he can limit his contributions on behalf of employees to 6¼%.

Result: Jones' annual Keogh contributions for his employees is just $1,875 (6¼% of $30,000 combined salary).

▶ **CAUTION:** Beginning in 1984, all Keogh plans which are "top heavy" (most of the plan benefits are for the top people) must provide minimum benefits for employees. In the case of a defined contribution Keogh, the minimum contribution for employees is 3% of earnings.

How Keogh Plan Payouts Qualify for Generous Tax Treatment

Income tax is payable only when you withdraw cash from your Keogh plan. You can't begin withdrawals before age 59½, and you must commence withdrawals by the time you are age 70½. In general, your withdrawals from a Keogh plan qualify for the same favorable tax treatment available to employees who receive benefits from a corporate profit-sharing or pension plan. For example:

• If you take all your Keogh accumulation in a lump sum you can qualify for favorable ten-year averaging. And if you set up your plan before 1974, you can treat part of your Keogh payout as low-taxed capital gain, and have the balance qualify for ten-year averaging (see p. 1007).

• You can spread out your withdrawals for a period of years and reduce taxes (since you will be in a lower tax bracket when you retire).

WHAT SOCIAL SECURITY RETIREMENT BENEFITS ARE YOU ENTITLED TO?

The Social Security system underwent a massive overhaul in 1983. The new changes mean higher Social Security taxes for everyone in the years to come. Unfortunately, the changes don't create bigger benefits for retired workers and self-employeds. The opposite is true: People will have to work longer to collect full benefits. And beginning in 1984, part of the Social Security check may be subject to federal income taxes.

Despite these major changes, the Social Security check will continue to be an important supplement to other retirement income. Here—in question and answer form—is a look at what the system will give you at retirement.

Q. How do I qualify for Social Security benefits?

A. If you are "fully insured," have reached "retirement age" and have filed an application, you qualify for Social Security benefits.

Q. How do I become "fully insured"?

A. You become "fully insured" when you meet the quarters-of-coverage requirements. Generally, quarters of coverage refers to the length of time (in quarter-year increments) that you have participated in the Social Security System (as an employee or self-employed). The exact number of quarters of coverage needed to be fully insured depends on your age. Generally, you never need more than 40 quarters of coverage (but you must have a minimum of six quarters). "Fully insured" does not mean you get the highest monthly benefit. It means you are eligible for benefits when you retire, or your survivors can get benefits when you die.

Q. What is the minimum retirement age?

A. The minimum—or early—retirement age is 62. The normal retirement age, currently 65, will gradually increase.

▶ **1938 IS THE BREAKPOINT:** You can retire anytime on or after your 65th birthday with full Social Security benefits, if you were born before 1938. If you were born in 1938 or a later year, you will have to wait beyond your 65th birthday to draw 100% of the benefit to which you are entitled.

How it works: The normal retirement age is gradually raised to 67 over a 27-year period. The first two columns in the box on page 1023 display the specific stages of the phase-in as they apply to you and your family. The third column in the box shows how much of your full benefit you will receive at age 62, depending on when you were born.

> **Examples:** If your normal retirement age is 66 (you were born between 1943 and 1954), you will receive 75% of your full benefit if you retire at age 62. If your normal retirement age is 67 (you were born in 1960 or later), you will receive 70% of your full benefit at age 62.

Early retirees in future times will receive a lesser percentage of full benefits than early retirees now receive. However, while the normal retirement age will increase from 65 to 67, the early retirement age will remain at 62. So early retirees will receive benefits for a longer period of time.

> ▶ **IMPACT:** Whether you retire tomorrow or 30 years from tomorrow, if you retire at the normal retirement age it will take approximately 12 years at full benefits to recoup benefits you could have received if you had retired at age 62.

> **Example:** Jane Smith who is now 40 years old can retire at age 66 with 100% benefits—in her case, we'll say $12,000 a year. But she decides to retire at age 62 instead and receives 75% of her normal benefit. Smith gets $9,000 a year in Social Security. This totals $36,000 between ages 62 and 66.

Since her $12,000 annual benefit at age 66 would exceed the $9,000 early retirement benefit by $3,000 a year, it would take 12 years of taking full benefits to recover the benefits she's received before age 66 (12 years × $3,000 = $36,000).

Q. What if I retire after age 62, but before my normal retirement age?

A. If you retire within three years of normal retirement age, you'll be eligible for at least 80% of your full monthly benefit, and possibly more. For instance, if you retire two years before your normal retirement age, you'll be eligible for 86.6%; one year before, 93.3%.

If you retire more than three years before your normal retirement age, you'll be entitled to receive less than 80% of your full monthly benefit, but as we have said, in no case would you receive less than 70%.

Q. How is my retirement benefit figured?

A. If you reach 62 in 1984 or thereafter, retirement benefits are figured under the method known as "indexing." Your actual earnings for past years are adjusted (indexed) to take account of changes in average wages since 1951. These adjusted earnings are averaged together and a formula is applied to the average to get the benefit rate. The indexing method of figuring benefits is intended to insure that benefits will reflect changes in wage levels over a person's working lifetime and will have a relatively constant relationship to pre-retirement earnings.

Individual benefit amounts could vary depending on the earnings covered under Social Security. Your local Social Security Office will figure your exact benefit rate. However, once you are on the the Social Security benefit rolls, your checks will increase automatically to keep pace with increases in the cost-of-living. Under the current system, each year's living costs are compared with those of the year before. For 1984, if living costs have increased 3% or more, benefits will be increased by the same amount.

Q. How do I apply for benefits?

A. You can apply in person or over the telephone. Once you've been interviewed by telephone, the rest can be done by mail.

When applying in person you should have with you; your Social Security card or a record of the number; proof of age (birth or baptismal certificate, military record if any, or passport); your income tax Form W-2 for the last two years (or copies of your last two federal income tax returns if you were self-employed); children's birth certificates, if you're applying for them; if you're applying for benefits under your spouse's earnings record, it would be helpful to bring your marriage certificate. If you're not sure what to bring, telephone any Social Security office for instructions.

Q. How much can my family get when I retire?

A. Monthly Social Security checks are also paid to certain members of your family. They can collect benefits equal to 50% of the amount you'd get if you started collecting benefits at normal retirement age.

Here are the basics for a spouse. Your spouse (or divorced spouse if married to you for at least ten years) will get 50% if: (1) an application for a spouse's benefits is filed; (2) spouse is not entitled to benefits in own right equal to 50% or more of the amount of your benefit; and (3) spouse has reached normal retirement age.

Q. What if I continue working beyond my normal retirement age?

A. You are entitled to increased Social Security benefits. For those born in 1925 and thereafter who delay retirement past their normal retirement age, the percentage of increased benefits they can expect to receive is going to grow. For some employees, the result will be dramatic.

Over time, the present 3% per year increment—for each additional year worked past the normal retirement age—increases to 8%. Column four in our chart on page 1023 shows you the details. For example—

▶ **BORN IN 1935?** For each year you work after the age of 65, you get a scheduled increase in benefits of 6%. And you may do—

Even better: The post-age 65 work improves your earnings record. Your years of high earnings after 65 displace years earlier in your career when you earned less. This boosts the basic benefit you're entitled to when you eventually file for Social Security. And it is to this already expanded benefit that the 6% per-year increment is applied.

▶ **IMPORTANT:** Effective for those who reach age 70 after 1983, the boost for extra years worked is not available for work past age 70.

Q. Can I continue working past retirement age and collect benefits at the same time?

A. Yes, but a penalty is imposed, in the form of a reduction in the benefits you receive.

> ▶ **GOOD NEWS:** Effective for workers who attain age 65 in 1990 or later, this penalty is eased. These people can continue working and collect one-third more in benefits.

Here's why: Under prior law, beneficiaries under age 70 who worked were subject to a $1 reduction in benefits for every $2 they earned over a base amount (in 1983, for example, the base amount is $6,600 for those age 65 or older). But for employees born in 1925 or later, the new formula is: a $1 reduction in benefits for every $3 of earnings over a base amount. In other words, it would take $15,000 of earnings above the base amount to offset $5,000 of annual benefits. Under the old rules, $10,000 of earnings has the same impact on benefits. (The base amount will continue to be adjusted annually to bring it in line with the Consumer Price Index.)

Q. What happens to my family when I die?

A. Your surviving spouse (or divorced spouse) will get 75% if caring for an eligible child (except a child getting student's benefits).

Your surviving spouse (or divorced spouse) will get 100% of your full benefit if he or she is at normal retirement age when applying and your benefits began when you reached normal retirement age.

At-A-Glance Guide to Your Retirement Benefits Under the Social Security Law

A number of important changes in the Social Security Law could have an effect on when you retire and on the amount of benefits you receive upon retirement:

● The Law raises the normal retirement age (currently age 65) to age 67 over a 27-year period;

● Over the same period of time, it also gradually cuts *early* retirement benefits from the current 80% down to 70% of the benefits available at *normal* retirement age; and

● It gradually boosts the percentage by which benefits increase for people who work beyond normal retirement age.

The table on the following page shows how people born in various years will be affected by the phase-ins of later retirement age, lower early retirement benefits, and benefit increases for years worked past normal retirement age.

Born	Retirement with full benefits at age:	Early retirement (age 62) % of full benefit that will be available to retirees	Benefit increase for each year worked after normal retirement age
1924-and before	65 years	80.0%	3.0%
1925-1926	65 years	80.0%	3.5%
1927-1928	65 years	80.0%	4.0%
1929-1930	65 years	80.0%	4.5%
1931-1932	65 years	80.0%	5.0%
1933-1934	65 years	80.0%	5.5%
1935-1936	65 years	80.0%	6.0%
1937	65 years	80.0%	6.5%
1938	65 & 2 months	79.2%	6.5%
1939	65 & 4 months	78.3%	7.0%
1940	65 & 6 months	77.5%	7.0%
1941	65 & 8 months	76.7%	7.5%
1942	65 & 10 months	75.8%	7.5%
1943-1954	66 years	75.0%	8.0%
1955	66 & 2 months	74.2%	8.0%
1956	66 & 4 months	73.3%	8.0%
1957	66 & 6 months	72.5%	8.0%
1958	66 & 8 months	71.7%	8.0%
1959	66 & 10 months	70.8%	8.0%
1960-and after	67 years	70.0%	8.0%

How to Cope With the New Tax on Social Security Benefits

Starting in 1984, a portion of Social Security benefits are subject to Federal income tax. Affluent retirees will pay income tax on one-half of their Social Security benefits. Other retirees will pay tax on a smaller portion of their benefits. Most retirees escape the extra income tax altogether.

How it works: The benefits are subject to tax only if a special gross income base exceeds $25,000 (for single filers) or $32,000 (for joint filers) or zero for marrieds filing separately. The special gross income base consists of: (1) a retiree's adjusted gross income (generally, gross income subject to tax less deductions the typical retiree doesn't take anyway); (2) interest not subject to tax; and (3) one-half of Social Security benefits.

If the total of these items exceeds the $25,000/$32,000 figures, then there is an income tax on the lesser of: (1) one half of Social Security benefits; or (2) one-half of the excess of the special gross income base over the threshold amount.

Example: Mr. and Mrs. Smith are over 65 and have pension income from their employers. In 1984, they have $23,000 in fully taxable pension income, $5,000 in taxable dividends and interest and $2,000 of tax-free municipal bond interest. They receive $10,000 in Social Security benefits.

Here is how the Smiths would calculate the portion of Social Security benefits subject to income tax.

Adjusted gross income	$28,000
Municipal bond interest	2,000
One-half of Social Security benefits	5,000
Special gross income base	35,000
Less threshold amount for joint filers	32,000
Excess	3,000
One-half of excess	1,500

The Smiths' Social Security benefits subject to tax is $1,500 since that figure is less than $5,000 (one half their benefits).

The bottom line: Assuming the Smiths do not itemize deductions, their tax in 1984, with the inclusion of $1,500 in Social Security benefits, is about $3,690. Without the new tax change, their tax would be $3,333.

Result: The Smiths income tax bill for 1984 is $357 more ($3,690 less $3,333). Put another way, the Smiths lose 3.57% of their $10,000 Social Security benefit.

▶ **TAX-SAVING SUGGESTION:** You may want to look into investments that yield tax-free distributions that are not tax-free interest. For example, some stocks pay dividends that are in whole or in part a tax-free return on your capital (see Chapter Three for more details). These return-of-capital dividends are generally exempt from current income tax, and do not expose Social Security benefits to income tax.

Another idea: Long-term capital gains (profit from the sale of stocks, bonds, and real estate held more than one year) become more valuable to the retired person. Sixty percent of long-term gain is tax-free. So, to that extent, capital gains do not jeopardize Social Security benefits. They are not as damaging as interest income (tax-free or not), dividends, or fully taxable pension income.

What You Can Do Now to Make Sure You Get All of Your Social Security

It's important that you make sure your Social Security tax dollars are doing what they're supposed to do—building future Social Security benefits.

▶ **WHAT TO DO:** Check to see if your earnings have been properly credited to your Social Security account. If some haven't—or if they've been recorded incorrectly—you will pay for it in reduced benefits when you retire.

▶ **HOW TO DO IT:** Ask your local Social Security Office for a copy of Form SSA-7004 PC (reproduced below). Fill out the Form, and mail it to Social Security Administration, P.O. Box 57, Baltimore, MD 21203. You will receive a statement of earnings and the number of quarters of coverage with which you have been credited.

Important: There is a time limit involved when it comes to correcting any mistakes you may discover. Generally, an earnings record can't be corrected if the request is made more than 39½ months after the year in which the wages are paid. So a checkup at least once every three years is a good move.

REQUEST FOR SOCIAL SECURITY STATEMENT OF EARNINGS

Your social security number

Date of Birth

Month	Day	Year

Print Name and Address in ink or use typewriter

Please send a statement of my social security earnings to:

Name _____

Number & Street _____

City & State _____ Zip Code _____

Sign Your Name Here _____
(Do Not Print)

I am the individual to whom the record pertains. I understand that if I knowingly and willingly request or receive a record about an individual under false pretenses I would be guilty of a Federal crime and could be fined up to $5,000.

If you ever used a name (such as a maiden name) different from the one above, on a social security card, please print name here: _____

Chapter 11

What You Must Do Right Now To Provide For Your Family's Future

This chapter will NOT give you a "do it yourself" estate plan. *Reason:* The process of providing for your family's future is far too important to be handled by a non-professional. The best advice we can give you is to see a lawyer, one you can trust with your most intimate personal and financial details. The legal fee you will pay will be one of your family's best investments.

What we *will* show you are the preliminary steps to take—and decisions to make—right now, before you see your lawyer:

(1) How to prepare an inventory of assets to be left to the family.

(2) The basics on how to decide the division of your property.

(3) How to prepare your final letter—this tells your family what needs to be done when you die.

(4) How to make the most of today's liberal estate and gift tax rules. Federal estate and gift taxes play an important role in many a family's estate plan. We'll show the basics of today's estate tax setup and explain some tax-saving strategies you and your lawyer may wish to consider.

But before we start, let's address the one topic that comes up again and again in connection with estate planning —

AVOIDING PROBATE

The process of probate—and how to avoid it—is the subject of many books and articles, and the source of much confusion and misunderstanding for a lot of families. What it is: Probate is the name given to a court proceeding that processes a will. The court determines the will's validity, sees that property is distributed according to the decedent's instructions, and settles any controversies surrounding the document (e.g., interpreting ambiguous language, or settling disputes between heirs). A probate court may also step in when a person dies without leaving a will, and does not own most of his or her important assets in joint name with someone else.

The problem: Probate can be costly. It involves attorneys' fees, court costs, and still more costs if the court finds it necessary to appoint an administrator for the estate.

▶ **COMMON SOLUTION:** The "way out" of probate is to own all significant assets (bank accounts, stock, home, etc.) in joint name with either your spouse or your children. "Joint tenants with rights of survivorship"—or JTWROS, for short—is the legal term.

When you die, property held in this form passes automatically to the joint tenant. If you hold title to all your significant assets (other than, say, items of personal property with low value) in this fashion, then the probate process is avoided.

Sounds simple enough—and it is. Unfortunately, JTWROS isn't the right answer for everyone. There are many instances where it is advisable *not* to hold everything in joint name, and to prepare a will. Here's a brief list of such situations:

- Where substantial assets are involved, it may be best not to leave everything to the spouse. There may be big estate tax savings in arranging the disposition of some assets in other ways. And there may be unfavorable income tax consequences to the surviving spouse who sells jointly held property (see page 116).
- Joint tenancy has no solutions for a lot of possible problems. Example: Husband and wife both die in an auto accident, or the wife dies a few weeks after the husband. In such a case, the couple's property may be distributed by the state according to rigid, unalterable rules.

Finally, keep in mind that some property cannot be handled with the JTWROS solution. For example: Husband is a 50-50 partner in a business. Husband must use some other form of conveying the property to his spouse after his death (for example, by trust or by will).

HOW TO PREPARE AN INVENTORY OF ASSETS

You'll need your lawyer's assistance in completing some of the information on the first and second pages of your Confidential Asset Inventory Form (reproduced at pages 1103 to 1110). But before your first estate planning session, it's a good idea to have all the answers to questions in the Asset Inventory. It's a handy guide that gives you an easy way to itemize and locate all your assets. Get the information together on separate sheets of paper. Keep it all in a safe place until you see your lawyer.

HOW IS YOUR PROPERTY GOING TO BE DISTRIBUTED?

One simple way to approach this question is to get out five sheets of paper. Put WHO on the first, WHY on the second, WHEN on the third, HOW on the fourth, and WHAT on the fifth. When you're done with the fourth sheet, you'll have a fairly good idea of what to give each member of your family, and the other objects of your bounty. [Text continues at p. 1111.]

CONFIDENTIAL ASSET INVENTORY FORM
INVENTORY OF

Name _____

Address _____

        as of _____, 19 _____

An estate plan is a living thing, in the sense that changes in your personal situation (or in the law) require changes in the plan. An estate plan should be reviewed periodically. It must be reviewed when a new law or other event specifically indicates a change. Generally, your estate plan should be reviewed at least once a year.

Date last reviewed _____

Location of executed will _____

FAMILY & PERSONAL INFORMATION

Your occupation:

Name and address of employer:

Date of birth; place of birth:

Spouse's name; date of birth; place of birth:

Children's names and dates of birth:

Others mentioned in will:
    Names   Addresses   Relationships

Executor's name and address:

CONFIDENTIAL ASSET INVENTORY FORM

GENERAL OUTLINE OF ESTATE PLAN

Beneficiaries:

Name   Relationship   Property or share of estate—
How given (outright or otherwise)

INCOME TAX INFORMATION FOR YOUR BENEFICIARIES

Marketable bonds and securities: Your income tax basis   Fair market value.
(If property is jointly held)

Other Property: Your income tax basis   **Date of Acquisition**
(If property is jointly held)

Real estate and other investments

Business property

Personal property

Other securities

CONFIDENTIAL ASSET INVENTORY FORM

ASSET INVENTORY

Real Estate; Homes:

Do you own home? Is it owned in your name, as joint tenant with right of survivorship, as tenant in common, as tenant by the entirety, etc? What is name of other owner and relationship to you? Where is the property located?

What is approximate description of property? What is the cost of the property? What is present value of property? What is the amount of mortgage, or mortgages, and other liens on the property? What is value of your equity interest? What is total equity in property?

What other property do you own for your own use, i.e., summer homes, winter homes, hunting lodges, etc?

Fire, title, and other insurance on above property; name and address of insurance company; kind of insurance and coverage; policy number; amount; expiration dates; name and address of broker.

Real Estate; Investments:

Location, description, ownership, cost (including cost of improvements), present value (estimated), and equity in real property owned as an investment. Names and addresses of associates, amounts of mortgages and other liens on property, and by whom held. Addresses of mortgagees and lienors. Fire, title, and other insurance on above property. Include all pertinent information.

CONFIDENTIAL ASSET INVENTORY FORM

Mortgages Owned:

Amount and nature of each mortgage owned; property on which mortgage owned—location, description, ownership, valuation; other liens on said property; names and addresses of associates in ownership of mortgage. Value of your interest in mortgage.

Business Interests:

What is the name of the business? The address?

Is business conducted as a sole proprietorship, partnership, or close corporation?

How many shares of stock (or what percentage of the business) do you own?

What is the estimated value of your interest in the business?

Is there a partnership agreement in writing? A stockholder's agreement? A buy and sell agreement? Stock redemption agreement with corporation?

Employer's Pension, Profit-Sharing, or Stock Bonus Plan:
Where are the copies of plans, certificates of participation, and account books kept?

Other Company Benefit Plans:
Where are the copies of plans, certificates of participation, and account books kept?

Deferred Compensation Agreement with Employer:
Where is agreement kept?

CONFIDENTIAL ASSET INVENTORY FORM

Bank Accounts:

Names and addresses of all banks in which accounts are held; number of each account; names on each account (i.e., joint, tentative trust, etc.); nature of account (i.e., checking, savings and loan, building and loan, etc.); amounts at present in each account.

Where are bank books, certificates of deposit, check books, and bank statements kept?

Safe Deposit Boxes:

Name of safe deposit company, address, box number, names and addresses of other persons having access. Who has keys? Where are keys kept? Rented in more than one name?

Financial Investments; Stocks and Bonds:

Names of brokerage houses where accounts maintained; addresses; names of persons who handle your accounts.

Are stocks owned individually in your name, or jointly with others? Do you own any stock as custodian for a minor?

Where are the stock certificates kept?

What is estimated value of securities owned?

What other property interests do you have in this area, such as stock options, etc? What is estimated value of such interests?

Do you own any U.S. Savings Bonds? Are they in individual, co-owner, or beneficiary form? What are names of co-owners and beneficiaries? What is the face amount of bonds owned? What is their present value?

CONFIDENTIAL ASSET INVENTORY FORM

Life Insurance and Annuity Policies:

Name of insurance company issuing each policy; number of policy; **amount; names,** addresses, and relationships of beneficiaries; any loans under policy. **Participation in life** insurance (group or individual) program of employer?

Other types of personal insurance policies **owned by you (disability income, accident,** sickness, hospitalization, etc.); name of insurance company; **number of policy. Participation** in program of employer?

Policies owned by you on lives of others; name of insurance company; **number of** policy; amount; names, addresses, and relationships of beneficiaries; **cash values; who pays** premiums?

Where are policies and certificates of participation in employer's insurance **plans kept?**

Family or other non-commercial annuities?

Social Security and Veterans Administration Benefits:

Social Security Account No:

If veteran, serial number, branch of service, dates of service?

YOUR FAMILY'S FUTURE 1109

CONFIDENTIAL ASSET INVENTORY FORM

Other Property:
Money owed you personally as distinct from business credits:

Rights under living trusts:

Your rights under testamentary trusts:

Your interest in estates of relatives or others:

General or special powers of appointment held by you:

All facts in connection with jewelry, furs, silverware, art works, books, stamp collections, coin collections, and similar property owned by you:

Value of household furniture owned by you:

Automobiles and boats:

All other property or interests in property not covered previously.

All facts relating to insurance on any of above property.

Cemetery plot; location, custody of deed, owned in what names; perpetual care or not?

CONFIDENTIAL ASSET INVENTORY FORM

DOCUMENTS REQUIRED

Previous will or wills:

Spouse's will:

Ante-nuptial or other property agreement with spouse.

Other instruments as indicated by answers to questions on foregoing pages:

Examples: Partnership or stockholders' agreement; life insurance and annuity policies; employer's pension, profit-sharing and other benefit plans; deferred compensation agreement; deeds of house and business property; leases; tax receipts; maps; surveys; fire and other insurance policies; mortgages and notes owned; copies of trust agreements and wills under which you have power of appointment or other rights; copies of income and gift tax returns; bills of sale and other evidences of ownership.

OTHER INFORMATION ATTORNEY SHOULD HAVE

Example: Ted Smith, a successful executive, has a wife in good health who is capable of handling finances, Son who is successful in his own business, Daughter, married to a mailman with a gambling itch, and two grandsons, ages 6 and 7. He also wants to leave something to his deceased sister's son, a godson who has a long-term chronic illness, and his Alma Mater.

His analysis, in abbreviated form, with some tentative conclusions, would look like this:

WHO	WHY	WHEN	HOW	WHAT
Wife	Income	Starting at my death, lasting for her life.	Outright	
Son	Simple gift	Immediately after my death	Outright	
Daughter	Supplement to Husband's earnings	Starting at my death, for long term	Some form of trusteeship	
Grandson 1	College fund	Starting at 18	In trust.	
Grandson 2		same as above		
Godson	Help with medical bills	For long term	Purchase of annuity?	
Nephew	Simple gift	Immediately after my death	Outright	
Charity	To fund scholarship in my name	Same as above.	Annuity?	

With this basic information, Ted can now go through his Asset Inventory and make some preliminary choices—subject to review by his lawyer—in the WHAT category. For example, if he's got a substantial life insurance policy, maybe the proceeds—together with the family homestead—is enough for the spouse. He can give his son that valuable stamp collection that his dad left him, or, perhaps, leave him the vacation home. Together with his lawyer, Ted must come up with some way of giving income to his daughter without the possibility of his son-in-law's squandering it. As to his grandchildren, Ted ought to think of giving them money in trust now to provide for their education. After he's through providing for his godson and nephew, maybe there won't be enough left over to fund a scholarship—maybe a simple cash gift will have to do.

Overriding considerations: Ted must make sure there will be enough liquid assets to take care of expenses (funeral, plot, debts) when he dies, and to pay any estate taxes— federal and state—that will come due.

Other Choices to Make Before You See Your Lawyer

You should make a preliminary decision on who will be your executor, and, if you have children, who'll take care of their interests. The executor is the one who will carry out the directions in your will and naturally, you don't want your executor to predecease you. So you should select someone who is younger—or at least no older—than yourself. Your executor should also—

• Be willing to spend the time and effort necessary. Locating beneficiaries, rounding up assets, paying debts and making distributions take time and effort. These tasks will be done with the assistance of an attorney. But the executor remains legally responsible for their proper execution. So he or she must be closely involved.

• Have the necessary business know-how. Will the executor be able to evaluate insurance policies on your home or other assets, handle securities, make sound decisions concerning real estate or other property? All this and more may be necessary during the time your estate is being administered.

• Know something of your personal affairs and family relationships. It could be crucial for the executor to know why you distributed property the way you did. So, while an executor shouldn't have a conflicting interest under your will, he or she should be close enough to you to know what's what.

▶ **APPOINT A SUCCESSOR:** You can name a successor executor in your will, or give the executor power to name his or her own successor. This can avoid a court-appointed executor, if your first choice is unable to serve.

NOTE: An executor must furnish a bond. However, in most cases you can save this expense by waiving this requirement in your will. Also, you can provide in the will what commissions, if any, your executor is to receive.

Taking care of the children: If you have minor children, you should make a provision for someone to take care of them in the event you and your spouse both die. This involves appointing a guardian in your will to oversee the upbringing of your children. You can also appoint a trustee to handle property you leave them. The guardian and trustee can be the same or different persons—the trustee can even be a bank.

Banks and individuals have different advantages and drawbacks as trustees. Many banks will not take a trust that's less than $50,000. Smaller banks may, but their expertise in handling investments may be limited. Banks are conservative money managers; their record in getting growth on trust dollars is often poor. Last but not least, a bank may be insensitive to the legitimate needs of your children.

On the other hand, banks usually stay put—a friend, lawyer or relative you've appointed as trustee may not. He or she may fall out of contact with your children and grow callous to their needs. Or an individual trustee may become disabled or die. Finally, even the most conservative banks may do better by the beneficiaries of your trust than a close friend with little financial acumen.

▶ **WHAT TO DO:** Put prospective individual trustees through the tests we outlined above for potential executors. And add one more: Does the trustee share most of your opinions concerning family relationships and acceptable behavior? If you're leaning toward a bank trustee, ask the lawyer who drafts your will for his or her recommendation.

HOW TO PREPARE A LETTER OF INSTRUCTION

One of the best things you can do for your family is to prepare a letter of instruction, explaining what has to be done after you die.

It may be the single most important thing you can do right now to ease the way for your loved ones during a difficult time. Besides directions concerning ceremony and burial, the Letter should contain the following elements:

(1) Whom to Contact and What to Do Immediately

Name and telephone of funeral parlor and lawyer; names and phone numbers of family and friends to contact; name and telephone of your company's benefits officer (for final paycheck, pension/profit sharing benefits, company paid life insurance, etc.); name and telephone of insurance agent (to file insurance claim); contact Social Security (and Veterans Administration, if applicable) for death benefit payable to spouse; obtain multiple copies of death certificate (for filing of claims); begin taking inventory of any expenses associated with death.

(2) Other Matters to Take Care of

All joint property accounts should be transferred to survivor; cancel credit cards or convert to single name; re-register automobile (and contact auto insurance agent); cancel subscriptions to periodicals and cancel special memberships to organizations.

(3) A List of Where Everything Is

Here's a representative list of items you ought to include here:

Birth certificate	Marriage certificate
Divorce decrees	Separation agreements
List of heirs	List of other relatives
Military service record	Social Security card
Medical record	Tax records
Will, original	Will, copy
Life insurance policies	General insurance policies

Stocks	Bonds
Notes receivable and Mortgages	Deeds
Leases	Estate Inventory
Bank books	Financial records
Business agreements	Trust instruments
Cemetery deeds	Employee benefit plan statements
Miscellaneous documents and property	Other

▶ **WHAT TO DO:** After you have prepared this final Letter, sit down and review it with your spouse, or other family members. The time to clear up any questions is now—when you're around to answer them! And it's a good idea to take this letter out and review it every couple of years for any possible changes.

HOW YOU AND YOUR FAMILY CAN TAKE ADVANTAGE OF TODAY'S LIBERAL ESTATE AND GIFT TAX RULES

Due to a number of liberalizations, estate and gift taxes will be less of a problem for most people. Estate and gift taxes are totally eliminated for some, substantially reduced for others. However, you must know what to do and how to do it in order to take maximum advantage of the tax law's breaks. Here's an overview of the estate and gift tax rules.

The Federal Estate Tax

This is a tax on the gross estate, less certain deductions. The gross estate includes all property which the decedent owned, or had an interest in at the time of his death, and lifetime gifts over which he "held the strings" (for example, a trust that can be revoked). The estate tax is computed by applying a uniform rate schedule to the sum of (a) transfers at death, plus (b) lifetime taxable gifts made after 1976 (basically, gifts that exceeded the gift-tax exclusion). The estate tax (less any gift tax paid on post 1976 gifts) is then offset dollar- for-dollar by the unified estate-and-gift tax credit.

The Federal Gift Tax

The first $10,000 of gifts made to any person during the course of a year is not subject to any gift tax. This annual exclusion is doubled to $20,000 if the donor's spouse joins in the gift. Gifts in excess of the exclusion are subject to the gift tax, but are offset by the unified gift-and-estate tax credit. However, any part of the credit used to shelter a lifetime gift from tax reduces the credit available for estate tax.

▶ **FAMILY TAX SAVINGS:** Lifetime gifts which do not exceed the annual exclusion save estate taxes. Such gifts are removed from the estate, with no dilution of the unified estate-and-gift tax credit. There may even be estate tax savings where the gift exceeds the annual exclusion. This is especially true where the gift is likely to grow in value. Reason: For gift tax purposes, the current value of the gift is used. If left to a beneficiary by will, the property is included in the decedent's estate at its value at that time.

Unified Gift-and-Estate-Tax Credit

Simply stated, the unified gift- and estate-tax credit enables a taxpayer to transfer a specified dollar amount of property without paying a gift tax or an estate tax. The unified credit increases each year until it reaches a peak of $192,800 in 1987.

Here is a chart showing the gradual increase in the unified credit, and the amount that can be transferred gift- and estate-tax-free because of the credit.

Year	Unified Gift and Estate Tax Credit	Amount That Can Can Be Transferred Gift- and Estate- Tax-Free
1984	$ 96,300	$325,000
1985	121,800	400,000
1986	155,800	500,000
1987	192,800	600,000

▶ **TAX SAVING RESULT:** By 1987, a taxpayer will be able to transfer up to $600,000 in property totally free of estate and gift taxes. Another break: When the unified credit is fully phased in, a Federal estate tax return will not have to be filed for any estate of $600,000 or less.

▶ **CAUTION:** Tax planning for estates is still necessary. *Reason*: Although the $600,000 exemption may seem high, remember that it is phased in. In addition, with inflation, many taxpayers whose net worth is currently under $600,000 may have assets worth substantially more than $600,000 by 1987.

Unlimited Marital Deduction

An unlimited amount of property can be transferred to a spouse free of estate and gift taxes. Practical impact: By 1987, the unlimited marital deduction and the unified credit will enable a taxpayer to leave up to $1.2 million to the spouse and family without paying an estate tax.

Example: Arthur Johnson dies in 1987 and leaves an estate of $1.2 million. He leaves $600,000 to his children, and the balance to his wife. Arthur's estate pays no tax. The unified credit shelters $600,000 of his estate from tax; and the unlimited marital deduction shelters the other $600,000.

Furthermore, his spouse's estate, assuming it consists of $600,000 in assets, will not pay an estate tax, either. *Reason*: The spouse's estate is entitled to a separate unified credit.

▶ **CAUTION:** Under prior law, the marital deduction was limited to the greater of $250,000 or half the decedent's gross estate. Wills that were executed before September 12, 1981, and contain a maximum marital deduction clause geared to the old limited deduction, should be amended immediately.

Reason: Without an amendment, the property passing to the surviving spouse will be based on the old limited deduction. Without amendment, the taxpayer's estate will not be able to benefit fully from the marital deduction.

Joint Property with Right of Survivorship

Only one half of the value of property held in joint tenancy by a husband and spouse is includable in the gross estate of the first spouse to die. However, note that the half included in the estate is not subject to tax because of the unlimited estate tax marital deduction.

Income tax treatment: Generally, the decedent's surviving spouse has an income tax basis that consists of two elements: (1) One half of the original cost of the property (i.e., the surviving spouse's half), plus (2) half the fair market value of the property at the decedent's death (i.e., the half that is included in the estate).

For example, suppose Mr. and Mrs. Smith bought property as joint tenants years ago. The cost was $10,000, and the fair market value at Mr. Smith's death is $100,000. One half of the property value ($50,000) is included in Smith's estate, but is free of tax because of the unlimited estate tax marital deduction. Mrs. Smith's income tax basis for the property is $55,000— $5,000 (half the original cost), plus $50,000 (half the value at death). If Mrs. Smith were to sell the property for $100,000, she would have a taxable long term capital gain of $45,000.

Possible move: If Mr. Smith were to hold the property in his name only (the change in the form of ownership can be accomplished without a gift tax), the property will be included in full in his estate. The property will still be sheltered by the unlimited estate tax marital deduction. However, when Mrs. Smith inherits it, her income tax basis will be a full $100,000 (its value for estate tax purposes). Thus, Mrs. Smith could sell the property for $100,000 and pay no federal income tax.

Retirement Plan Distributions

The first $100,000 of retirement plan benefits (payable in lump sum at death, or as annuity to survivor) is excluded from the estate. The balance, however, is included in the estate.

▶ **TAX-SAVING MOVE:** If retirement plan distributions are left to the spouse, the proceeds are estate-tax free due to the unlimited marital deduction.

▶ **CAUTION:** We've given you a brief overview of how estate and gift taxes work. There are many complications and special twists and turns that could affect you and your family. Your lawyer will fill you in on the details.

Chapter 12

How To Save Tax Dollars On Your Tax Return

One of the best ways to conserve family cash is to take maximum advantage of all possible deductions and credits on your tax return. These include your dependency deductions, medical deductions, and charitable deductions. Another tested way to slash your taxes is by a shrewd approach to special tax provisions such as income averaging, the child care credit, and deductions for office at home expenses. The techniques we explain in this Chapter can add hundreds—maybe thousands—to your net after-tax income.

DON'T MISS THE EXTRA DEDUCTION FOR YOUR WORKING SPOUSE

The tax law provides a special break to offset the impact of the so-called marriage penalty. The marriage penalty is the extra tax a working couple pays simply because they are married: If their combined income is split more evenly than 80%-20%, they pay more in taxes on a joint return than if they filed as single persons. This happens because the second earner's income is stacked on top of the other spouse's income on a joint return. The second earner's income is therefore taxed at higher marginal rates than if he or she were single.

> ▶ **WORKING COUPLE'S DEDUCTION:** A working couple can deduct 10% of the lesser of $30,000 or the "qualified earned income" of the spouse with the lower earnings. Maximum deduction: $3,000.

Key points: A couple doesn't actually have to be affected by the marriage penalty to be eligible for the deduction. In other words, if the income split is greater than 80%-20%, a couple gets the tax savings of a joint return *and* the new deduction. And the break is not an itemized deduction; it's a deduction for adjusted gross income. So even couples who claim the flat standard deduction can take advantage of it.

What is 'qualified earned income?' Generally speaking, this is earned income (salary, wages or professional fees) less certain deductions—primarily, business and employment-related expenses and contributions to Keogh Plans and Individual Retirement Accounts. Qualified earned income does *not* include tax-free income or any investment income. Nor does it include pensions, annuities, deferred compensation, IRA distributions and unemployment compensation. Wages paid by one working spouse to the other working spouse also do not count.

Important: Wages paid to a spouse working for a corporation owned by one or both spouses *do* qualify for the new deduction.

▶ **BONUS TAX BREAK:** The new marriage penalty deduction may increase a couple's medical deduction. *Reason:* A couple can deduct their medical expenses to the extent that they exceed 5% of the couple's adjusted gross income. Since the working couple's deduction lowers adjusted gross income, it also lowers the "floor" beneath medical expenses.

Result: More of a couple's medical expenses will be in excess of the "floor"—and therefore deductible.

HOW INCOME AVERAGING CAN SAVE YOU BIG TAX DOLLARS ON RISING INCOME

It happens every year. Many astute taxpayers overlook one of Form 1040's most generous and reliable money savers—

▶ **INCOME AVERAGING:** For one reason or another many people simply don't take advantage of the fact that you can often average one year's taxable income over five years. If your taxable income is above average this year (either because your gross income is up or your exemptions or itemized deductions are down), you may be able to spread the part that's higher than average over the last four years so that it's taxed in a lower bracket. The tax savings can come to thousands of dollars.

Why isn't income averaging used at every opportunity? Probably because the phrase, "income averaging," is confusing and because of a few commonly held misconceptions.

"I can use averaging only if my income suddenly zooms into the sky-high tax rates."

Not so. It doesn't take that much of a jump in income.

▶ **TO QUALIFY:** The basic requirement is that your taxable income must be at least $3,000 more than 120% of your average taxable income for the preceding four years. If it is, you can average everything over the 120% figure. So if your four-year average is $30,000, you can average everything over $36,000 (120% of $ 30,000) if your taxable income for the current year is at least $39,000.

"My income just didn't go up that much this year. So income averaging won't do me any good."

Take another look. Remember that averaging involves your *taxable* income (that's after exemptions for spouse and other dependents and after excess itemized deductions). It doesn't refer to your gross income. So your current year's gross income before such adjustments could be the same as or slightly higher than the previous four years, but your current year's *taxable* income may be substantially higher because you have fewer exemptions or itemized deductions. And the jump in taxable income may be enough to qualify you for income averaging.

> **Example:** Your gross income for the last four years averages around $40,000—but after deductions, your average *taxable* income is only $30,000. You need a taxable income of $39,000 in the current year to qualify for income averaging. Let's say your current year's gross income goes up to $45,000. If you have the same deductions this year as in previous years, you would not qualify for averaging.

But suppose you had $5,000 less in deductions this year—perhaps your son got married and is no longer a dependent and your medical expenses are not deductible because they do not exceed 5% of your adjusted gross income. Even though your *gross* income goes up by only $5,000 your taxable income increases by $10,000 to $40,000.

Result: By combining an increase in income with a drop in deductions, you qualify for income averaging. In fact, if your deductions take a nose-dive, it's possible to qualify for averaging even though your gross income stays the same.

"Averaging is great for the overnight success—the state lottery winner, the boxer with the million-dollar gate—that sort of thing."

That's true. But averaging also gives across-the-board relief to executives, professionals and business people like yourself. And it applies to almost any type of income. Actually, it can be your—

▶ **ACE IN THE HOLE:** Suppose your compensation this year is way up, or you sell stock at a big profit. Or say that in some prior year you took a loss on an investment that did not occur again this year. Income averaging can shelter at least some of your dollars in cases like these. And this is true whether the dollars in question are taxed as ordinary income or as capital gains.

"I used averaging last year; I can't use it again this year."

That's not true. As long as you meet the mechanical qualification test, you can average every year. Repetitive averaging is not uncommon at all. It can occur even if your income declines after your first averaging year. *Reason:* Your income in the three years before your first averaging year may still be well below this year's taxable income.

"It's just too darned complicated."

Understanding how it works may be complicated. But the Revenue Service form (Schedule G, Form 1040) really does the job. All you need is a quick look at one line on each of your tax returns for the last four years. Once you have those four taxable incomes, you simply plug in the figures, do the simple arithmetic, and the tax saving is all yours. It's as simple as that.

▶ **HOW TO CHOOSE INCOME AVERAGING:** The income averaging provisions are elective, not mandatory. Hence, you must positively choose to average—it's not given to you automatically. Simply figure your tax for the computation year under the income averaging provisions and attach Schedule G (just one page) to your return.

PLAN YOUR "REFRESHER" COURSES WITH TAX SAVING IN MIND

In the morning's mail, there was notice that caught your eye—a special two-week "refresher" course covering new developments in your profession or your business is being offered by your alma mater. This is just the thing for you. It will give you the chance to brush up on new happenings in a relaxed atmosphere. Of course, it'll cost a few dollars, but it's well worth it, when you consider this—

▶ **TAX BREAK TOO:** You can deduct the cost of education that's undertaken to maintain or improve your skills or to keep your present position. What's more, under the Revenue Service's Regulations, a change of duties after taking such courses will no longer knock out your deduction—as long as your new duties involve the same *general* type of work you're now doing.

Thus, even if your main purpose is to pick up a new specialty or get a promotion, you can still deduct the cost of the courses. So, you decide you'll go. Now let's see how you can make the most of the deductions.

First of all, you can deduct your actual costs, including tuition, books, and the like. In addition, you can deduct the cost of any transportation, plus—if you must travel away from home overnight to take the courses—the cost of meals and lodging while away from home.

Example: Your office is in Chicago. The courses you want to take are being given in Chicago and Philadelphia. If you go to Philadelphia to take the courses, will you forfeit your deduction for travel, meals and lodging? *Answer:* No. You can pick and choose the education center that you prefer.

How about sightseeing? While you're in Philadelphia, you expect to do some sightseeing and some visiting—you have a lot of friends and associates in the area. How will this affect your deduction? *Answer:* As long as your *primary* reason for going is to take the courses, your deductions won't suffer. However, the actual cost of visiting and sightseeing comes out of your own pocket—it's not deductible. But if your *primary* reason for going to Philadelphia is sightseeing and visiting, with a refresher course thrown in, you can deduct only the actual cost of attending the course. Everything else, i.e., travel, meals and lodging, is non-deductible.

Q. What if my company reimburses me for out-of-pocket tuition and textbook costs for a job-related course? How should I treat the reimbursement on my return?

A. The good news is that the Government does not consider education reimbursements for job-related courses to be "wages".

Result: The reimbursements are not subject to withholding or to employment taxes. If you are paid directly by your company, you don't report the payments on your tax return. You simply state that payments didn't exceed expenses. And if the company makes payments directly to the school, you don't even have to do that.

HOW YOUR HOBBY CAN ALLOW YOU TO DEDUCT "NONDEDUCTIBLE" PERSONAL EXPENSES

Years ago, you took up stamp collecting as a hobby (or coins, baseball cards or what have you). You needed something to get your mind off the pressures of your business or practice. Your collection has turned into quite an investment, yet it's still basically a hobby as far as you're concerned. What you may have overlooked during the years is that there are—

Tax savings in hobbies: As a general rule, personal expenses—for example, the expenses connected with a hobby—are not deductible. But if, from time to time, you sell off a piece of your collection—you get an attractive offer that you don't want to pass up—you are entitled to—

▶ **DEDUCT PERSONAL EXPENSES:** In any year you make money selling your stamps, you can deduct such things as insurance premiums, appraisal fees, publications and other expenses connected with your hobby. In other words, the cost of a personal hobby has now become deductible.

There is a limit, however. Your hobby expenses are deductible only up to the amount of your gross income from your hobby, in other words, the profit from any sales you made during the year. Thus, if you sell a stamp for $1,000 that you bought years ago for $100, your gross income is $900. That means you can deduct up to $900-worth of hobby-connected expenses.

▶ **TAX-SHELTER OPPORTUNITY:** On the one hand, your hobby expenses up to $900 are itemized deductions, and thus fully offset $900 of ordinary income. On the other hand, your $900 profit from the sale of the stamp is long-term capital gain. And since it's long-term capital gain, only 40% of the total profit, or $360, is taxable with your other income.

So, your hobby-connected expenses may save you more in taxes than you pay out on the hobby-connected profit. To see exactly how you should handle hobby-connected income and expenses, let's look at this—

Example: Charles Gregory owns and runs a large film processing lab. He is also a collector of antique cameras and photographs. Over the last twenty years, he has built up a collection worth $20,000. This year, he decides to sell a rare turn-of-the-century stereo camera. He bought it for $200 fifteen years ago, and sells it in November of this year for $1,800.

Hobby costs: His annual subscriptions to various magazines devoted to camera collecting come to $60. Since Mr. Gregory stores his collection at home, he carries special insurance which costs $450 a year. he has his collection professionally appraised this year at a cost of $150.

Mr. Gregory is careful to keep all records relating to his purchases, sales, and hobby-connected expenses.

▶ **WHAT TO DO:** Mr. Gregory reports his $1,600 capital gain on the sale of his camera for the year of sale. Mr. Gregory also deducts his hobby-connected expenses in full as itemized deductions for the year of sale. He can deduct all his $660 of expenses since they do not exceed his $1,600 of gross profit from his hobby.

HOW YOU CAN SALVAGE HUNDREDS—MAYBE THOUSANDS—OF TAX DOLLARS OUT OF HOUSEHOLD EXPENSES

The tax law allows someone who conducts business out of a home to deduct home expenses related to that business. In general, you can deduct these expenses only if (1) a room (or rooms) in your home is used regularly and exclusively as (2) a "principal place of business" (it can be a "sideline business") or as a place to meet with customers in the normal course of your business.

Let's say you or your spouse conduct a profit-making enterprise out of your home. Which expenses can you deduct, and how do you figure your deduction? *Answer*: First off, any expenses directly connected with your business—i.e., supplies, telephone, postage—are 100% deductible. In addition, you can also deduct part of home-maintenance and repair expenses that are related to your office at home. Examples: Utilities, insurance, trash removal, even some home repairs (e.g., repairs to the home heating or air conditioning system).

How do you allocate these home expenses to your business? *Answer*: You allocate either on a percentage of area used or on a percentage of rooms used. Thus, if a home is 1,500 square feet, and the office at home is 150 square feet, then you can deduct 10% of home expenses that relate to the business conducted at the home. If your home has eight rooms and one room is used as an office, at home, then ⅛th of the home expenses is deductible.

Example: Robert Tibor is an executive in an electronics company. His wife Alice works in a downtown art gallery and is also a freelance illustrator of children's books. She does her freelance work in a studio that is part of their eight-room residence which they bought six years ago for $150,000. The room is used exclusively as Alice's studio.

This year, Alice grosses $9,000 from her illustrations. Alice's expenses which relate directly to her work are as follows: artist's supplies, $500; postage, $45; telephone calls, $150; and $980 (fares, hotel expenses, meals, etc.) for a trip to a convention of illustrators in San Francisco. Alice attended the convention to keep up with current trends, display her work, and cultivate industry contacts. These expenses are fully deductible. In addition, the Tibors had the following home expenses:

Mortgage interest	$ 4,800
Property taxes	3,000
Utilities (oil heat, electric light)	2,500
Cleaning woman	3,300
Trash removal	380
Home insurance	480
Repairs to roof	500
	$14,960

Of their total $150,000 cost for the home, $125,000 was allocated to the building by an appraiser who also assigned a 30-year useful life to the structure. Using straight line depreciation, the deduction for the whole house is $4,167.

The Tibors use the per-room method of allocation. One-eighth, or 12.5% of all the out-of-pocket home expenses—or $1,870—is deductible. In addition, one-eighth of the total $4,167 in depreciation ($521) is deductible.

Important: The Tibors also deduct separately the *non-business portion* of their bill for home mortgage interest and taxes.

HOW THE CHILD-CARE CREDIT CAN CUT YOUR TAX BILL

The child-care credit is a top-flight tax cutter for many executives, professionals and business people who have children, and whose spouses work. It even helps those taxpayers whose spouses have gone back to school. Here's how the tax credit can cut your tax bill:

You can take a tax credit for the first $2,400 of eligible child care expenses if one child or dependent is involved: or for the first $4,800 of expenses if two or more children or dependents are cared for. The credit depends on the income level. It's a 30% credit for taxpayers with an adjusted gross income of $10,000 or less. For those earning more than $10,000, the credit drops 1% for each additional $2,000 of income. However, the tax credit can't drop below 20%.

In practical terms, this means the tax credit is 20% for taxpayers with an adjusted gross income of $28,000 and up. Maximum credit for these taxpayers is $480 if one dependent is involved (20% of $2,400), and $960 if two or more dependents are involved (20% of $4,800).

Q. Who can take the child-care credit?

A. The tax law grants the credit to a number of categories of taxpayers who spend money on the care of a child under 15, or a spouse or dependent incapable of self-care. Is your family described below?

Families where both spouses work full-time.

Families where one spouse works full-time and the other is either working part-time or is a full-time student (in school full-time for 5 or more calendar months).

A working widow, widower, or a divorced or separated parent who has custody of a child (or children) under 15. Divorced or separated parents can get the credit even though they don't claim the child as a dependent, as long as their custody period runs longer than the other parent's.

Q. Which expenses are eligible?

A. The cost of looking after a dependent under 15 at home and out-of-household expenses such as boarding and nursery school expenses qualify. But the cost of caring for children under age 15 can be incurred far from home and still qualify for the child-care credit.

Business trip: In a recent case an executive's job required him to go to Europe. While he traveled throughout Europe, his children stayed with a French family. The Tax Court implied that the cost of the children's stay with the French family would have been a qualified child-care expense if the exec had documented the cost [Herder, TC Memo 1979-323].

Private school: As a general rule, the direct expense of educating a child doesn't qualify for the child-care credit. But if you send your child away to boarding school, the non-education portion of the school's cost (room, board and supervision before and after the normal school day) does qualify for the credit.

▶ **TAX-SAVING EXCEPTION:** If your child is in nursery school, the entire expense—educational and non-educational—qualifies for the credit.

In addition, a recent Tax Court case liberalized the child-care credit, making it available to more parents of school-aged children. The Tax Court has said that a couple can get the credit even where their primary concern is simply to give their children a good education. As long as *one* of the couple's motives in sending a child to boarding school is employment-related, the couple can get the credit [Brown, 75 TC No. 15].

Summer camp: The cost of having a babysitter look after your children during the summer certainly qualifies for the credit. So the cost of a day camp should also qualify.

Case in point: Mrs. Zoltan, an accountant, was required to spend approximately 55 hours a week away from home at her job. For eight weeks during the summer, she sent her 11-year old son to a summer camp in Canada (the Zoltans lived in Ohio). Cost of the camp: $1,100.

Zoltan sent her son to summer camp so she would be able to work. The Tax Court stated that, for purposes of the tax credit, parents do not have to choose the least expensive way to care for their children. Zoltan's choice in this case was reasonable since the alternatives (a full-time housekeeper or a combination of day camp and babysitters) would cost as much as the summer camp. Result: Credit allowed [Zoltan, 79 TC No. 31].

Q. Must the expense be for a small child?

A. No. You can claim the credit for in-household and personal care expenses for the protection and well-being of a spouse or dependent who, regardless of age, is physically or mentally incapable of self-care.

For example, your spouse may be temporarily laid up with a broken leg. If you hire a housekeeper to look after the house and help your spouse recuperate, her wages and the cost of her meals and any extra lodging costs you incur qualify for the credit.

Q. Exactly what do in-household expenses encompass? Are they restricted to amounts relating only to actual child (or dependent) care?

A. Not at all. They include all household help expenses—maid, cook, housekeeper, or caretaker. The key condition: The household help's presence allows both parents (or a single parent) to go to work.

Q. Do payments made to relatives qualify for the credit?

A. Definitely yes. Payments made to any kind of relative are OK, as long as the person claiming the credit doesn't also claim the relative receiving child-care payments as a dependent and the relative is not less than 19 years old and a child of the taxpayer.

Q. Say a family has their first child in mid-year and spends $2,400 on eligible child-care payments that year. Can they get the full credit?

A. Yes, they can. There's no month-by-month allocation required. The full credit would thus be available also in instances where, for example, the parents were employed for only part of the year.

Q. Do taxpayers have to wait until tax return time to benefit from this child-care credit?

A. Not necessarily. The wage-withholding tables must take the child-care credit into account. Thus, the taxpayer can file a new W-4 withholding form and get a break on the credit before tax-return time.

▶ **KEEP RECORDS:** It's up to you to prove you're entitled to the credit. So keep adequate records. It's the only way to make sure you'll be able to take full advantage of this better-than-ever tax saver.

DON'T MISS OUT ON ANY OF YOUR PERSONAL EXEMPTIONS

Thousands of dollars are sent down the tax drain each year by usually astute taxpayers who fail to claim the exemptions and deductions they're entitled to. To prevent you from adding to this tax waste, let's take a bird's-eye view of the personal exemption and dependency deduction area.

There are two types of personal exemptions: (1) Those for you and your spouse, and (2) Those for your dependents who meet five tests. First, let's look at—

Exemptions For You and Your Spouse

You, as well as every taxpayer, get a $1,000 exemption for yourself. In addition, you get another one for your spouse. However, if your spouse has even a penny of gross income, you must file a joint return with him or her in order to claim the exemption.

Furthermore, you get another exemption when you reach 65, and still another when your spouse arrives at that age. For purposes of the extra exemption for age, you are 65 this year if your 65th birthday occurs on or before January 1 of next year.

Finally, there's still another exemption available if a taxpayer is blind; still another if his or her spouse is blind.

Exemptions For You and Your Dependents

You get an exemption for every person who qualifies as your dependent under the tax law. In order to qualify as your dependent, the person must meet all of the following five tests:

(1) Support test. The rule itself is easy—you must furnish more than one-half the support of your dependent. But the application can be tough. For instance—

What is support? It includes any money you give, directly or indirectly, for the person's food, shelter, clothing, education, medical care, allowance, and the like. It also includes goods furnished, at their fair market value. Lodging is measured by the fair rental value of the room, apartment, or house supplied, including furnishings, heat, and utilities. Fair rental value is what you'd reasonably expect to get from a stranger for the same facilities. If you're a tenant yourself, lodging is a proportionate part of your rent. Support doesn't include income taxes (Federal or local), or life insurance premiums. But support does include capital purchases, such as the cost of buying a car.

There's more: Sunday School money, toys, haircuts, recreation, music, dancing and dramatic lessons, and so on, are also support.

Surprise tax break: The Revenue Service says that "expenditures made by parent for child's wedding apparel and accessories, wedding reception and for flowers for wedding party, church and reception are part of child's support . . . " [Rev. Rul. 76-184, 1976-1 CB 44].

▶ **REMEMBER:** A small amount can tip the scale either way. Make sure of your deduction by keeping accurate, complete records.

(2) Gross income test. Your dependent must have less than $1,000 in gross income. Gross income means all income subject to tax, without taking into account any deductions.

Example: Your mother owns a small building. Rents total $1,500; she has rental expenses of $1,000. Though net rental income is only $500, her gross is still $1,500, and she fails the gross income test.

Tax-exempt income (e.g., municipal bond interest), or non-taxable income, e.g., Social Security payments, are not part of gross income. But, if they're used by the dependent for his or her own support, they may kill your deduction under the support test.

▶ **TWO EXCEPTIONS:** There is no gross income test for your child or stepchild if he or she is (1) under 19, OR (2) a full-time student (no matter what his age) for a part of five calendar months during the tax year at some educational institution maintaining a regular faculty and curriculum.

(3) **Relationship test.** Your dependent must be either (a) A member of your household (but not in an unlawful relationship) who had your home as his or her principal place of abode for the entire taxable year, or (b) Related to you as your child, or adopted child (or a child placed in your home by a legally authorized placement agency for adoption), or such child's descendant; stepchild; son- or daughter-in-law; parent or other ancestor, stepfather or mother; father- or mother-in-law; brother; sister; step-brother or sister; half-brother or sister; brother- or sister-in-law. Also, if related by blood: uncle, aunt, nephew, niece.

Reminder: Even if the marriage that gave rise to the relationship in the first place ends, an in-law is still a relative. Furthermore, if you file a joint return, your spouse's relatives, e.g., his or her uncles, become yours, too. Not so on a separate return.

(4) **Citizen or resident test.** If your dependent is not a U.S. citizen, he must be a resident of the U.S., Canada or Mexico.

(5) **Joint return test.** Your dependent, if married, must not file a joint return with his or her spouse. Otherwise, you'll lose him or her as a dependent.

▶ **IMPORTANT:** You still get a full exemption for a dependent who is born or dies during the year, provided all the tests for claiming the exemption are met for the part of the year the dependent is alive.

HOW TO CLAIM A FULL DEPENDENCY EXEMPTION FOR A RELATIVE YOU SUPPORT ONLY PARTIALLY

You have been successful in your business or profession, and you feel that you have a special obligation to provide for your parents in their old age. Your brothers and sisters feel the same way, so you all chip in to help your parents make ends meet. You're glad to do it. But this sometimes creates a—

Tax problem: Say you and your brothers and sisters together are contributing most of Mother's support. But none of you, individually, contribute more than half. The basic rule is that a taxpayer gets a dependency deduction for a parent only if he or she provides more than half the parent's support. But the tax law provides a way for someone in the family to get the exemption even though none of you meet the more-than-half test.

▶ **TAKE TAX ACTION NOW:** Set things up so that your family can take advantage of a "multiple support agreement." This agreement lets you and your brothers and sisters decide which of you can take the exemption for, say, your mother. And you can trade off the exemption so that over the years everybody gets a chance to claim it.

Here Are the Key Requirements

(1) Mother must have received over half of her support from you and your brothers and sisters;

(2) Each of you must be able—except for contributing half of her support—to claim her as a dependent. (This means that Mother can't have more than $1,000 in gross income.)

(3) No one of you can contribute singly more than half your Mother's support;

(4) If you're the one who's selected to take the exemption, you must contribute more than 10% of support;

(5) Anybody else who gives more than 10% support must agree not to claim an exemption for Mother in the year you claim the exemption. This entails filling out Form 2120 (Multiple Support Declaration), available at any IRS office.

▶ **ADDED TAX BREAK:** The one who claims Mother as an exemption can also treat medical payments made on Mother's behalf as a deductible medical expense on his or her tax return.

Q. Let's say I share the support of my parent, together with my brothers and sisters. But my parent's yearly income from investments is way over the $1,000 limit so she can't be claimed as a dependent. Any tax breaks here?

A. You can still deduct your parent's *medical* expenses on your return. Here's how: Have your brothers and sisters designate you as the one entitled to deduct the medical expenses. The family uses the same multiple support agreements it would use if a dependency exemption were being claimed for the parent.

▶ **TAX ACTION NOW:** If your family chips in to support a family member this year—and a dependency exemption won't be claimed—designate one of the supporting members to pay nothing but medical expenses. You can all share the total costs equally. But if one person pays the medical bills and the others pay non-medical items, that one person gets a bigger medical expense deduction.

HOW TO GET TWO DEPENDENCY DEDUCTIONS FOR THE PRICE OF ONE

If you help support your parents, keep in mind this special tax-saving twist: You may be able to get two dependency deductions for the money you contribute.

Here's why: For dependency purposes, unless you can prove otherwise, both parents are treated "as a unit." Everything Dad and Mother receive—whether from you or elsewhere—is assumed to be received equally by both.

Case in point: The total support of Smith's retired parents came to $4,100. Of this, he paid $2,100, and his parents' Social Security benefits provided the other $2,000. It's assumed that everything Dad and Mom received—both from their son and otherwise—is spent equally on each. Since Smith provided more than half their support together, he gets dependency deductions for both.

But the rule works both ways: Let's say your parents receive $2,520 in Social Security benefits. You give them another $1,300. Under the unit rule, you get no deduction at all because you're not providing more than half of either parent's support. But you can salvage one deduction—for your Mother, for example—by getting around the unit rule.

▶ **WHAT TO DO:** Allocate your support payments solely to Mother and keep careful records proving your allocation. This salvages Mother's exemption. *Reason:* Because you've specifically allocated your support payments, the unit rule does not apply.

The best way for you to handle things is to pay Mother's expenses directly for clothing, medical bills and the like. Ask Mother to obtain bills made out to her for the expenses, and you pay them by check. Make sure you keep both the bills and the remitted canceled checks as proof. *Added benefit:* This way you not only nail down Mother's exemption, but you can add the medical expenses you paid for Mother to your own in computing your medical deduction.

▶ **WATCH THIS:** Meeting the more than half support test may require more cash every year. One reason: Social Security benefits are now geared to the cost-of-living index. And they keep going up. That means you might have to chip in extra cash to hold on to your dependency deductions.

HOW TO BOOST YOUR DEDUCTIONS BY MAKING EVERY YEAR A "RECORD YEAR"

Most of us do not keep records of our "personal" expenses as carefully or completely as we keep our business records. For example, on January 2, if you ask your secretary, bookkeeper or office manager how much was spent on typewriter ribbons or letterheads last year, you'll get the exact answer in a flash. Could you or your spouse give an immediate answer on, say, last year's medical and dental bills—to the penny?

If you're a typical person, you'll have to do some digging, and even some guessing, on many outlays which you itemize on your personal income tax return. Yet, every dollar of deductible expenses which you can *prove* will cut down your tax bill.

Here's a time- and money-saving suggestion: Keep a current log of your at-home expenses. That way, you won't miss any deductions and, come tax-return time, you'll avoid that aspirin and black coffee session, shuttling between a hazy memory and a heap of disorganized papers.

▶ **WHAT'S MORE:** You'll probably come up with many items you never previously dreamed of deducting. You'll be surprised at how these little deductions add up.

To help you save these important tax dollars by getting business-like about your personal expenses, we've prepared a special record-keeping form. You can use this form for noting your daily outlays (we've filled in some sample items to show you how it works):

Daily Personal Expense Record

Date & Check	To Whom Paid and Why	Amount	Contri-butions	Interest	Taxes	Medi-cal & Drugs	Other Deduc-tions
1/5—#12	Dr. Jones eye exam wife	$75.00	—	—	—	$75.00	—
1/5 cash	Cab fare; trip to Dr. Jones	8.50	—	—	—	8.50	—
1/7 cash	Alpha Optical; glasses for wife	65.00	—	—	—	65.00	—
1/9 cash	Boy Scouts of America	25.00	$25.00	—	—	—	—
1/15 #18	Collector of taxes (real property-home)	950.00	—	—	$950.00	—	—
2/15 #30	Smith's Drug Store (prescription)	12.00	—	—	—	$12.00	—

▶ **TAX TIPS:** (1) When you pay cash, get receipts. These can be preserved in manila folders. (2) When you pay by check, make the check out to the one who is being paid. A check made to "cash" doesn't prove the nature or even the amount of an expense. But a check to a physician, dentist, druggist, and the like, is respectable evidence. And keep your canceled checks in the manila folders, too.

The wall-calendar way: The calendar on your kitchen wall can also serve as a record-keeping form. You may choose to use this rather than the other form we've just described. First of all, make sure the calendar is fairly large. All you do is use the date space for the expenses of that day. Naturally, you also put down the why's and wherefore's. Make it a daily habit to transfer all tax information to the calendar. Don't forget—be systematic and do it daily.

HOW TO COPE WITH THE NEW, TOUGHER RULES FOR DEDUCTING MEDICAL EXPENSES

It will be difficult to get any tax relief from your family's 1983 medical bills on the tax return you file in 1984. *Reason:* The rules for deducting medical expenses have undergone major changes. Beginning with the tax return you file this year:

(1) The separate deduction for up to one half of your medical insurance premiums is eliminated. Now, all such premiums are lumped in with your other medical expenses.

(2) You can take a medical deduction only if total medical costs exceed 5% of your adjusted gross income (for 1982 tax returns, it was 3%). Drug costs count only to the extent they exceed 1% of your adjusted gross income.

These two changes mean a much smaller medical deduction—maybe no deduction at all—UNLESS you hunt down and claim the many overlooked but perfectly legitimate medical expenses that a lot of people shell out money for each year.

Let's begin with a look at the—

Nineteen Deductible Medical Expenses You Won't Find In Your Tax Form Instructions

The Government instructions that accompany your tax return are helpful. But they only tell you the bare minimum about medical expense deductions. They list only the best known deductible medical and dental expenses. Over the years, however, Revenue Rulings, court cases and private rulings have added many deductible expenses to this basic list. The following are some of the important items *not* in the instructions. A quick review may save you hundreds of tax dollars at tax return time.

1. *Non-prescription drugs:* The instructions say drugs are deductible. But deductible drugs include more than those your doctor prescribes. For the 1983 return, the cost of everyday items such as aspirin, decongestants, cough syrup and antacids are also deductible [Reg. §1.213-1(e)(2)].

2. *Special diets:* The extra cost of a prescribed special diet is deductible if it is (1) solely for the treatment of a medical problem, and (2) in addition to normal nutritional needs. Examples: organic foods [Randolph, 67 TC 35], and high protein meals for hypoglycemia [Von Kalb, TC Memo 1978-366].

3. *Special mattress:* The Government has approved a medical expense deduction for the extra cost of a special mattress designed to alleviate an arthritic condition [Rev. Rul. 58-280, 1958-1 CB 157].

4. *Cosmetic surgery:* The cost of cosmetic surgery is deductible. Unlike most other medical expenses, the surgery need not be recommended by a doctor. A

face lift is deductible [Rev. Rul. 76-332, 1976-2 CB 81]. Electrolysis is also deductible [Rev. Rul. 82-111, IRB 1982-22].

5. *Acupuncture:* The Government has okayed a deduction for the cost of undergoing acupuncture to alleviate a specific ailment [Rev. Rul. 72-593, 1972-2 CB 180].

6. *Weight reduction:* You can't deduct the cost of a weight reducing program that simply improves your general health and well being [Rev. Rul. 79-151, 1979-CB 116]. But you can deduct the cost of a program that prevents or alleviates a specific ailment or illness. Example: A program prescribed for an individual with hypertension, obesity and hearing problems [Ltr. Rul. 8004111, P-H Ltr. Rul. ¶392(80)].

7. *Hairpiece:* The cost of a hairpiece (or wig) is a deductible medical expense if it is necessary to relieve severe mental distress [Rev. Rul. 62-189, 1962 CB 88].

8. *Nursing home:* You often have to pay a lump sum to get your dependent parent into a nursing home. If part of the prepayment is for future medical care, that portion is deductible [Rev. Rul. 75-302, 1975-2 CB 86].

9. *School tuition:* If part of your child's college tuition is for medical care, that amount is deductible [Rev. Rul. 54-457, 1954-2 CB 100]. The charge for medical care, often a sizable sum, is included in a college's "general fee." If you write to the college treasurer, you usually can find out the amount that's allocated to medical care.

10. *Special schools:* You can deduct the cost of sending your child to a special school if the principal reason for his or her attendance is the treatment of a handicap; educational services must be incidental. The school must have specially trained personnel and special resources [Sims, TC Memo 1979-499], or there's no deduction [Giovengo, TC Memo 1978-375].

11. *Travelling companion:* You can deduct the cost of bringing someone along on a medically-related trip if your condition makes that person's presence necessary [Ltr. Rul. 8024155, P-H Ltr. Rul. ¶2906(80)].

12. *Visitation costs:* If your presence is medically necessary, you can deduct the cost of a visit to see your ailing child or spouse [Rev. Rul. 58-533, 1958-2 CB 157]. For example, one parent deducted the cost of going overseas to accompany his child home after an illness [Ltr. Rul. 7813004, P-H Ltr. Rul. ¶531(80)]. You can also deduct:

13. The cost of a home health spa that alleviates an illness, to the extent it exceeds the increase in the value of your home [Keen, TC Memo 1981-313].

14. Vasectomies and abortions [Rev. Rul. 73-201, 1973-1 CB 140].

15. The cost of computer storage of your medical history [Rev. Rul. 71-282, 1971-2 CB 166].

16. Legal expenses for having a dependent involuntarily committed [Ltr. Rul. 7931059].

17. Additional charges by a restaurant for preparing a salt-free meal [Cohn, 38 TC 387].

18. The installation and monthly cost of a device that adds fluoride into the home water supply on the advice of a dentist [Rev. Rul. 64-267, 1964-2 CB 69].

19. A reclining chair used by a cardiac patient and not otherwise used personally [Rev. Rul. 64-267, 1964-2 CB 69].

▶ **REMINDER:** This list is not all-inclusive by any means. But it does show that you can deduct more than just the ordinary expenses. Of course, when you're doing your tax return, don't forget the obvious expenses either, such as the cost of a visit to a doctor, the hospital, and so forth.

How to Get a Medical Deduction for the Cost of Help Around the House

Many taxpayers employ domestic help. The cost, of course, is not deductible. But suppose that same domestic is helping out while you or another family member recuperates from an illness. And the domestic spends part of his or her time performing nurse-like services. Of course, the cost of nursing services is deductible as medical care. But what if the services aren't performed by a registered or practical nurse?

▶ **DEDUCTIBLE MEDICAL CARE:** It's the nature of the service provided, not the status of "registered" or "practical" nurse, that's important. As long as the expenses are medically related, they're deductible.

Example: Mr. Johnson's daughter, Mary, had surgery this year and was confined to bed at home for two months. The Johnsons' regular live-in housekeeper and maid helped bathe, feed, and care for Mary (they had someone else come in and do the housekeeping and washing). They paid a total of $1,600 in wages to the regular housekeeper during the two months. Sixty percent of her normal week was devoted to helping Mary.
Result: $960 (60% of $1,600) is eligible for the medical deduction.

How You Can Return Home With a Deduction After Long-Distance Medical Travel

A family member may have to travel out of town to get the very best medical care. Tax bonus: The cost of such a trip is a—

▶ **DEDUCTIBLE MEDICAL EXPENSE:** As long as the primary purpose of the trip is for medical treatment of a specific condition, the entire cost of your transportation is eligible for the medical deduction.

Even if similar treatment is closer: You can deduct the cost of long-distance medical travel even though you could have received similar treatment closer to home. In other words, you aren't required to take the least expensive treatment when seeking medical care.

Taxpayer winner: Mr. and Mrs. Armes lived in Memphis, Tennessee, where Mrs. Armes received cancer treatments. After the couple moved to Richmond,

Virginia, Mrs. Armes returned to Memphis four times to visit her doctor there. The Tax Court said Mrs. Armes' air fare was a deductible medical expense [Armes, TC Memo 1978-258].

Even if you're not the patient: Medical expenses you incur on behalf of your spouse or a dependent are deductible on your return. That's basic. What you may not realize is that the deduction can include their medically-related travel costs. What's more, it's even possible to write off the cost of *your* trip if your sick spouse or dependent's physical condition makes your presence necessary.

Recent ruling: Mr. Smith had to travel to another city for surgery at a top-notch medical center. Smith's physician requested that Mrs. Smith accompany her husband on the trip. The Government said Mrs. Smith's trip was a deductible medical expense. *Reason:* Mr. Smith will be unable to speak after the operation and will need the help of Mrs. Smith [Ltr. Rul. 8024155, P-H Ltr. Rul. 2906 (80)].

▶ **KEY TO THE DEDUCTION:** The physician must recommend that you accompany the patient. Your own good intentions won't do. So be sure to get the physician's recommendation in writing. That way, you may avoid problems later on.

What's deductible? As long as the trip is for the cure, prevention, or alleviation of a specific disease, you can definitely deduct your transportation costs for getting there and back. So you can deduct the airfare if you fly, or your gas, oil, tolls and parking if you drive. But what about the cost of your meals and lodging en route to and from your medical care? Are they deductible?

The Government has consistently said that meals and lodging are not deductible. (Exception: A patient's hospital room and meals in the hospital are deductible.) *Reason:* The tax law allows a deduction for "transportation" that's essential for medical care. But transportation is limited to actual movement from one place to another. Some courts, however, have said meals and lodging en route are—

▶ **DEDUCTIBLE MEDICAL EXPENSES:** The expenses required to get a patient to and from medical treatment—including meals and lodging—are deductible. The tax law wants to prevent possible "resort area" deductions—for example, meals and lodging once the patient has arrived at the place of medical care. But the tax law doesn't mean to deny deductions for the full cost of getting to medical treatment [Montgomery, 26 AFTR 2d 70-5001]. Another case allowing big deductions for meals and lodging en route to medical treatment is Pfersching, TC Memo 1983-341.

So there are deductions for the cost of going to and from long-distance medical care. And according to some courts you may even be able to deduct your meals and lodging en route. At the very least, here's—

▶ **WHAT TO DO:** Get your doctor's orders in writing (especially if you're accompanying a member of your family). Then keep track of your expenses. If you keep a detailed diary of your expenses, you're sure to get a top-dollar deduction. But if the situation doesn't lend itself to record-keeping, at least log the miles and destination.

Reason: If you drive the Government will allow an automatic 9¢-a-mile deduction, plus tolls and parking.

How You Can Deduct the Cost of Supporting an Aging Relative

The cost of a stay in the hospital is deductible. There's no doubt about that. But what about the cost of a nursing home for your aged father, mother or other relative? In most cases—

▶ **IT'S DEDUCTIBLE:** The cost is eligible for the medical deduction if (1) the institution provides medical care, and (2) one of the main reasons your relative is in the institution is to receive medical care for a physical condition.

Important: The cost is eligible whether or not you claim the relative as a dependent. The only requirement is that you provide more than half the relative's total support.

The ailment can be one of those commonly associated with aging, such as arthritis, arteriosclerosis, and high blood pressure. The cost is fully deductible as long as medical care is provided. Your relative can have personal reasons for being in the nursing home without jeopardizing the deduction.

Case in point: Mr. Counts provided more than half the support of his father, Homer, who was in a nursing home. Homer had high blood pressure and a gall bladder condition. Because of these ailments and his age, he was confined mostly to bed and required nursing care. Mr. Counts treated the entire cost of Homer's nursing home care, including meals and lodging, as a medical expense.

The Government disallowed the cost of meals and lodging. *Reason:* It claimed that Homer's principal reason for being in the nursing home was personal. He shared a room at the home with his wife who was paralyzed from a stroke.

▶ **TAXPAYER VICTORY:** The Tax Court said Mr. Counts could treat all of Homer's nursing home costs as a deductible medical expense. The tax law requires only that obtaining nursing care for a physical condition be a principal reason for being in the institution. It does not have to be the only reason.

So although one of the reasons Homer was in the nursing home was personal, the other—obtaining medical care—was a principal reason. So Mr. Counts was entitled to deduct the full cost as a medical expense [W.B. Counts, 42 TC 755].

When you can't deduct meals and lodging: If your relative is in a rest home or retirement home which provides no nursing or medical care, you cannot deduct the cost even if the relative has physical ailments.

Example: Mr. Robinson's 90-year-old father was in good health, except for limited vision. He resided in a rest home, which by law could not provide medical care.

Patients were required to be ambulatory. The father, because of his limited vision, required an attendant to help him shave with a straight razor and accompany him on his outside walks.

Result: The court held that the father's cost at the nursing home could not be claimed as a medical expense by Mr. Robinson. *Reason*: Since the rest home did not provide medical care, receiving medical care could not be a principal reason for the father being there. [Robinson, 25 AFTR2d 70-807].

Important: Although your dependent's food and lodging costs in a rest home are not deductible as medical expenses, those expenses which are strictly medical will still qualify.

Example: Mr. and Mrs. James, who are in good health, are residents of a retirement home. Their son pays a monthly life-care fee in return for their being entitled to live in the home and receive lifetime care. A specific portion of the monthly fee has been allocated by the home for the cost of providing medical care. Their son may deduct the medical care portion of the fee as a medical expense [Rev. Rul. 67-185, 1967-1 CB 70].

Are You Passing Up Some Charitable Deductions?

You and your wife are probably dues-paying members of one or more charitable organizations. As you may know, any amount *you pay over regular membership dues*—e.g., for a sustaining, donor or life membership—is generally treated as a contribution.

Result: It's deductible. But what about your regular dues; are they deductible, too? Yes, if you meet this—

▶ **TAX TEST:** If your membership privileges in the charitable organization are *merely nominal*, and you're entitled to no special services, your dues are deductible. And this is so even though you're invited to occasional social functions as an expression of gratitude or for the solicitation of contributions.

Here's another angle: Sometimes, even the dues you pay to a social club may be partly deductible as a charitable contribution. This can come about when part of your dues are earmarked by the club for certain charities. This earmarked portion is deductible in the year your club turns the funds over to the charity. However, if the club treasurer is a collection agent for the charity, you can deduct the charitable portion of your dues when you actually pay them.

▶ **WHAT TO DO:** Always consider the charitable factor in *any* dues you pay. More than likely, you'll find you have a sizable deduction at the end of the year.

How To Deduct the Cost of Going to Church

If you were to take a couple of minutes to figure out the number of evenings, holidays, and weekends you and your family spend at your church or other place of worship, chances are you'd come up with a surprising result—they add up to quite a few. What's more, if you stop to think about it, much of the time is probably spent for a variety of activities other than actual attendance at services.

▶ **TAX BREAK:** You are entitled to deduct the out-of-pocket expenses you incur in performing these volunteer services for your church.

Result: Unless you keep track of the trips you both make to and from your church for volunteer services, you're sending a perfectly good deduction right down the tax drain. To see just how it can all add up in dollars-and-cents, let's take a look at this—

Example: Sanford Adams and his family live in the suburbs, about 12 miles from their church. Both he and his wife are quite active in church activities, making at least 4 round trips between them each week for committee meetings, choir rehearsals and a Brownie Troop meeting.
Also, Adams, as a member of the fund-raising committee, makes 15 extra round trips during the year, while Mrs. Adams makes another 10 in connection with church rummage sales, bazaars, and other volunteer work.

Result: Each year, Adams and his wife chalk up 5,592 miles on charitable travel. Multiplying this by the "automatic" 9¢ per mile allowance for charitable travel gives them a deduction of $503.28—and we haven't even counted a penny of what they contribute to the collection plate or any other charity.

▶ **ADDED TIP:** The cost of buying and cleaning any distinctive uniforms and accessories—such as choir robes and Brownie Troop Leader's uniforms, for example—are also deductible, since they're not suitable for general use.

▶ **REMEMBER:** You still have to prove the deductions! And the only way to do that is to keep records.

INDEX

ERC FAMILY MONEY BOOK

-A-

Accelerated cost recovery system (ACRS):
. equipment leasing, 420
. income property, 239
. shopping centers, 408
. tables, 240
Adjustable rate mortgages, 111
Adult education:
   see "Refresher courses"
Alternative minimum tax, 425
Annual Constant:
   see "Real estate opportunities"
Annuities:
. family corporation, 824
. profit-sharing plans, 1005, 1006, 1007
Apartment houses:
. condo conversions: 213, 214
. cooperative conversions, 214
. Government-insured loans
.. moderate-income housing, 223
.. refinancing, 222
. rehabilitating, 206
Assumable home mortgages, 114
Auto insurance:
. collision, 923
. comprehensive, 923
. cutting cost of, 924
. liability, 922
. medical payments, 923
. no-fault, 922
. uninsured driver, 923
Auto loans, 709

-B-

Balloon mortgages, 226
Better Business Bureau, 615
Billboards:
   see "Tax shelters"
Blanket mortgage, 227
Bonds:
   see "Stocks & bonds"
Bradford Exchange:
   see "Collector's plates"
Brokers:
. residential sales:
.. buyer broker, 104

.. selling home without broker, 131
. stock market:
.. discount brokers, 302
.. how to pick, 301
.. penny-stock dealer, 518
Budgeting:
. college loans, sources, 617
. credit cards, 607
. financial goals, 601
. installment loans, 608
. take-home pay, boosting, 607
Bureau of Land Management (BLM):
   see "Oil lottery"
"Buy-down" plans, 114
Buyer broker, 103

-C-

Cable TV, 415
Call options,
   see "Stocks & bonds"
Cattle raising:
   see "Tax shelters"
Certificates of deposit (CDs):
. advantages, 339
. tax deferral, 339
Charitable contributions:
. deductions, 1220
. travel for, 1221
Child care credit:
. eligibility, 1207
. private school, 1208
. summer camp, 1208
Church-related deductions, 1220
Christie's, 507
"Closed-end" funds:
   see "Mutual Funds"
Collectibles:
. antiques, 503
. baseball cards, 503, 505
. collector's plates, 505
. comic books, 503, 504
. movie posters, 503
. photographic prints, 501
. tax savings from, 1205
. "worthless stocks", 507

1302 INDEX

Collectibles: *(continued)*
Collector's plates:
. Bradford Exchange, 506
. investing in, 505
College education:
. loans, 617, 714
. short-term trust, financing with, 807
. tax scholarships, 804
. tax-free fund, 813
Commercial loan insurance, 220
Comic books:
. collectibles, 503, 504
. "Comic Book Price Guide," 504
Commissions:
. residential:
.. how to negotiate, 132
.. typical charge, 104
. stockbrokers:
.. offsetting cost of, 308
.. how to get bargain rates, 302
.. load fund sales charge, 316
Commodities, 514
Condominiums:
. apartment conversions, 213
. definition, 109
. professional offices, 215
Confidential Asset Inventory Form, 1103-1110
Consumer protection:
. Better Business Bureau, 615
. homebuyer warranties, 107
. product warranties, 611
Convertible bonds, 329
Cooperative apartments:
. buying in bulk, 215
. conversions, 214
. definition, 109
Corporate bonds, 326
Cosmetic surgery, 1216
Credit:
. applying for, 701
. credit bureaus, 701
. credit cards, 607, 704, 709
. buying on, 608
. legislation,
.. Equal Credit Opportunity Act, 703
.. Social Security changes, 1019
.. Truth in Lending Act, 702
. loans
.. auto loans, 709
.. CD, 704
.. collateralized, 704
.. consolidating, 710
.. credit union, 705
.. discount, 711
.. employer, 705, 706

.. interest-free, 706
.. overdraft privilege, 704
.. personal, 703
.. passbook, 704
.. second mortgage, 708
.. refinancing, 707
.. renewing, 713
.. retirement plans, 706, 707
. revolving-charge account, 702
. reports, 701
. tax angles, 712
Credit cards, 607, 704, 709
Custodial accounts, 803

-D-

Daily personal expense record, 1214
Deep discount municipal bonds:
. investment, 331
. tax scholarship, 806
"Denver Business World," 518
Dependents,
. exemptions for, 1210
. partial support of, 1211
. relationship test, 1211
. supporting parents, 1212
. support test, 1210, 1213
Depletion allowance:
. gold, 413
. oil & gas, 412
Depreciation:
. ACRS, 239
. cable TV, 415
. cattle breeding, 419
. equipment leasing, 420
. oil & gas, 413
. shopping centers, 408
Diamonds:
. "diamond trust," 511
. investing in, 510
Discount brokers, 302
Discount loans, 711
Discounting a mortgage, 225
Distributing property to heirs, 1102, 1111
Dollar averaging:
    see "Stocks & bonds"

-E-

Education:
    see "College education"
Energy-saving methods:
. caulking, 122
. insulation, 122
. lighting, 123
. oil burners, 124

. quartz heaters, 124
. tax breaks from, 127
Equal Credit Opportunity Act, 703
Equipment leasing:
    see "Tax shelters"
Equity sharing, 811
Estate planning, 1101
Estate tax, 1114
Estate tax marital deduction, 1115
Exchanges:
. municipal bonds, 333
. tax free, 242
Executor, selection of, 1112

-F-

Family loans:
    see "Income splitting"
Family partnership:
    see "Income splitting"
Farmers Home Adm'n (FmHA):
    see "Government-backed loans"
Federal Housing Adm'n (FHA):
    see "Government-backed mortgages"
Federal National Mortgage Ass'n (FNMA), 114
Financing:
. adjustable rate mortgages, 111
. balloon mortgages, 226
. blanket mortgage, 227
. borrower checklist, 117
. due-on-sale clause, 229
. gap financing, 225
. Government-backed loans, 113
. home loans, 110
. leverage, 201, 219, 403
. "points," 118
. prepayment, 118
. refinancing:
.. apartment houses, 222
.. pyramiding, 230
. second mortgages:
.. investment property, 224
.. discounting, 225
. wraparound mortgages, 228
Flexible rate mortgages, 111

-G-

Gap financing, 225
Gas stations:
    see "Real estate opportunities"
Gift leaseback, 814
Gift taxes:
. family corporation, 822
. how to avoid, 809, 1114
Gift tax marital deduction, 1115

"Ginnie Maes":
    see "Stocks & bonds"
Gold:
. certificates, 508
. investing in, 501, 508
. tax shelters, 413
Government-backed loans:
. FHA investor mortgages:
.. moderate-income multifamily, 223
.. refinancing, 222
. FHA single-family, 113
. FmHA, 114
. VA, 113
Growing equity mortgage, 112
Graduated payment mortgages, 112, 220
Gross Income Multiplier
    see "Real estate opportunities"
Gross income test, 1210
Group Health Insurance:
    see "Health insurance"
Group Term Insurance:
    see "Life insurance"
Growth stocks:
    see "Stocks & bonds"
Guaranteed Student Loan Program, 618

-H-

Health Insurance:
. coordination of benefits, 917
. coverage gap, 921
. duplicate coverage, 917
. disability coverage, 916
. group health insurance, 916
. major medical, 916
. medical reimbursement plans, 917
Historic properties:
    see "Rehabilitation"
"Home Expenditure Record Book," 125
Home improvement:
. medical deduction, 128
. remodeling, 124
. repairs, 121
Home inspection:
. personal, 105
. professional, 107
. investment property, 210
Home ownership:
. borrowing on equity, 708
. buy-down plans, 810
. closing statement, 118
. condominium, 108
. cooperatives, 108
. equity sharing, 811
. financing, 14 ways of, 110

INDEX

Home ownership: *(continued)*
. helping your child buy, 809
. homebuyer checklist:
.. existing home, 105
.. new home, 107
. improvements, 121
. mortgage charts, 103
. new home, 107
. remodeling, 124
. vacation home, 133
Home insurance:
. co-insurance trap, 920
. coverage, types of, 919
. Federal crime insurance, 919
. flood insurance, 920
. umbrella policy, 919
Home remodeling, 124
Household expenses, deducting:
  see "Office at home"
HUD project notes, 338, 341

-I-

Income Averaging,
. definition of, 1202
. election, 1203
. how to figure, 1203
Income splitting:
. custodial accounts, 803
. family corporation:
.. S corporation, 816, 820
.. transferring ownership, 823
. family loans:
.. business, 816
.. buy a home, 810
. family partnership, 819
. gift leaseback, 814
. hiring your family, 812, 813
. property, gift of, 801
. S corporation, 816, 820
. Section 1244 stock, 816
. stock redemption, delayed, 818
. tax losses, 811
. tax scholarships, 804
. trust accounts, 803
. Uniform Gifts to Minors Act, 801, 803
Individual retirement accounts (IRA):
. annuity, 1011
. contributions, 1011
. custodial, 1011
. excise tax on premature withdrawals, 1013
. investment flexibility, 1015
. spousal, 1013
. tax-shelter advantages, 1010
. withdrawals, 1013, 1015

. working couple, 1014
  see "retirement income, tax favored"
Installment plans:
. auto loans, 709
. budgeting, 609
. contracts, how to read, 609
. unsecured personal loan, 702
Installment sales, 242
Insurance:
  see "Life, Health, Home or Auto insurance"
Interest free loan:
. from builder, 116
. from employer, 706
. short-term trust, 807
  see "Zero interest mortgage"
Investment clubs, 311
Investment credit, 402

-J-K-

Joint tenancy:
. income-tax consequences to survivor, 1116
. tool for avoiding probate, 1101-1102
Keogh plans,
. defined contribution, 1016
. how to benefit from, 1016
. pension-type, 1017
. setting up, 1018
. withdrawals from, 1019

-L-

Letter of Instruction, 1113
Leverage:
. multiple tax writeoffs, 403
. real estate, 201, 239
Life Insurance:
. borrowing on, 120, 708
. coverage, how to figure, 901
. estate and gift taxes, 913
. group term, 907
. modified-ten policy, 909
. prepaying a mortgage, using to, 120
. retired lives reserve fund, 908
. settlement options, 912
. split-dollar, 910
. straight life, 904
. tax treatment of, 911
. term insurance:
.. annual term, 903
.. decreasing term, 904
.. deposit term, 904
.. group term: 907, 914
.. level term, 904
. transfer of:
.. to child, 914

.. to spouse, 913
. universal life, 906
. whole life:
.. basic, 904
.. company-paid, 909
.. endowment policies, 906
.. limited-payment life, 906
.. single-payment life, 906
Limited partnerships, 404
"Load" funds
　see "Mutual funds"
"Low-Priced Stock Digest," 518
Lump-sum distribution:
　see "Profit-sharing"

-M-

"Mailbox" centers, 218
Margin, buying on:
. commodities, 514
. stocks & bonds, 317
Marital deduction, 1115
Medical expenses,
. deductible, 128, 1215
. household help, 1217
Medical travel, 1216
Miniwarehouses, 216
Money market funds, 338
Mortgage insurance:
. FHA loans, 113
. investment financing, 220
. VA loans, 113
Motion-picture theaters:
　see "Real estate opportunities"
Multifamily housing:
　see "Apartment houses"
Multiple support agreement, 1211
Municipal buildings:
　see "Real estate opportunities"
Mutual Funds:
. "load" vs "no-load," 316
. "open-end" vs "closed-end," 317
Municipal bonds, 330

-N-O-

National Direct Student Loan Program, 618
Net Multiplier:
　see "Real estate opportunities"
"No-load" funds,
　see "Mutual funds"
Net worth:
. how to determine, 602
. income statement, 605
. statement of, 603

Nursing homes, 1219
Office at home, 1206
Oil & gas:
. drilling, 410, 503
. tax shelters, 409
. wildcat operations, 410
"Oil lottery," 501
"Open-end" funds:
　see "Mutual funds"
"OTC Review," 518
Over-the-counter (OTC) trading, 516

-P-Q-

Parents Loan Program, 620
Penny stocks, 516
"Penny Stock News," 517, 518
Personal exemptions, 1209, 1213
Pension plans:
. introduction, 1002
. employee rights, 1004
. fixed-benefit plans, 1003
. money-purchase benefit plan, 1003
. taxable income, 1004
. unit benefit plan, 1003
. withholding, 1005
Prepaying a mortgage:
. life insurance, borrowing against, 120
. systematic, 118
Private school:
　see "Child care credit"
Probate:
. defined, 1101
. how to avoid, 1101
. joint tenants, 1102
Profit-sharing:
. financial benefits, 1005
. how profits shared, 1005
. IRA rollover, 1008
. lump-sum distribution:
.. capital gain, 1007
.. 10-year averaging, 1007
. payouts, 1006
. payout in stock, 1009
. tax breaks, 1006-1010
. used to buy annuity, 1008, 1009
. vesting, 1006
Precious stones:
　see "Diamonds"
Preliminary Scholarship Aptitude Test (PSAT), 621
Put bonds, 332
Put options,
　see "Stocks & bonds"
Pyramiding, 230
Qualified earned income, 1201
Quartz heater, 124

-R-

Raw land:
. criteria for buying, 203
. farmland, 202, 421
. "hunter's paradise," 206
. opportunities in, 202
. overlooked sites, 205
Real estate opportunities:
. Annual Constant, 231
. apartment houses, 206
. condominiums, conversion to, 213
. condominium offices, 215
. co-op apartments, 214
. depreciation, 239
. farmland, 202, 421
. gas stations, 212
. Government-insured loans, 221, 222, 223
. Gross Income Multiplier, 233
. historic structures, 243
. how to negotiate, 235
. "mailbox" centers, 218
. miniwarehouses, 216
. municipal buildings, 210
. Net Multiplier, 234
. raw land, 202
. safe-deposit centers, 217
. schoolhouses, 211
. single-family homes, 208
. tax-free exchanges, 242
. tax shelter opportunities in, 238
. "white elephant" properties, 210
Refinancing: see "Financing"
Refresher courses, 1204
Rehabilitating:
. apartment houses, 206
. historic structures, 243
Relationship test, 1211
Remodeling, home, 124
Research & development,
   see "Tax shelters"
Retirement income, tax-favored,
. IRA, 1010
. Keogh plans, 1015
. pension plans, 1002
. profit-sharing, 1005
. Social Security, 1019
Retirement plans:
. borrowing from, 706, 707
. distributions from:
.. estate tax exclusion, 1116
.. income tax treatment of 1004
Revolving-charge account, 702
ROTC scholarships, 620

-S-

Safe-deposit centers, 217
Sale and leaseback, 407
Schoolhouses:
   see "Real estate opportunities"
Scholarships:
. National Merit Scholarships, 621
. PSATs, 621
. private, 622
. ROTC, 620
. tax scholarships, 804
S corporation, family style, 816
Second Mortgages
   see "Financing"
Section 1244 stock, 816
Shared-appreciation mortgage, 115
Shared equity plan, 115
Short sales:
. commodities, 515
. stocks & bonds, 319, 325
Shopping centers, 408
Short-term trusts, 807
Social club dues, 1220
Social Security,
. benefits:
.. applying for, 1021
.. indexing, 1021
.. New Law, 1022
.. table of, 1023
.. tax on, 1024
. early retirement, 1020
. law changes, 1019
. statement of earnings, 1025
. surviving spouse, 1022
. working past 65, 1021
. working past 70, 1022
Sotheby's, 507
Stockbrokers,
   see "Stocks & bonds"
Stocks & bonds:
. broker's commission, offsetting, 308
. call options, 320
. convertible bonds, 329
. corporate bonds, 326
. delayed redemption, 818
. discount brokers, 302
. dividends:
.. reinvested, 308
.. tax free, 322
. dollar averaging, 314
. EE bonds, 336
. ex-dividend, 303
. "fingerprinting," 323

. "Ginnie Maes," 338, 340
. glossary, 303
. growth stocks, 307
. HH bonds, 336
. HUD project notes, 338, 341
. income splitting, used for, 807
. inflation hedge, 308
. investment clubs, 311
. key indicators, 305
. market tables, 302
. money market funds, 338
. municipal bonds:
.. deep discount, 331, 806
.. optional tender (put), 332
.. tax-free advantages, 330, 332, 334
.. swapping, 333
. mutual funds, 315
. optional tender bonds, 332
. price-earnings ratio, 304, 306
. Puerto Rican bonds, 334
. put bonds, 332
. put options, 325
. short sales, 319, 325
. stockbroker, selecting, 301
. stock options, 320
. systematic purchase plan, 312
. tax-free bonds:
.. municipals, 330, 332, 334
.. Puerto Rican, 334
.. HUD project notes, 341
.. U.S. government, converting, 336
. tax loss, offsetting, 324, 811
. Treasury bills, 336
. U.S. government bonds, 334
. utilities, 309
. worthless, 507
Stock options,
 see "Stocks & bonds"
Strategic metals:
. investing in, 511
. portfolio funds, 513
Student loans, 617
Subchapter S:
 see "S corporation"
Successor executor, 1112
Summer camp,
 see "Child care credit"
Support test, 1210, 1213
Surgery:
see "Medical expenses, deductible"
Survivorship:
 see "Joint tenants"
Swaps
 see "Exchanges"

-T-

Take-home pay
 see "Budgeting"
Tax-Free Exchanges, 242
Tax preference items, 425
Tax savers:
. accelerated cost recovery (ACRS), 239
. conversion, 403
. dividend reinvestment, 308
. home seller breaks:
.. $125,000 exclusion, 130
.. "rollover," 128
. "like kind" exchanges, 242
.   see also "Income splitting" and "Tax shelter"
Tax scholarship plan, 804
Tax shelter:
. accelerated cost recovery system, 239
. billboards, 417
. cable TV, 415
. cattle raising, 419
. equipment leasing, 420
. farms, 421
. gold, 413
. intangible drilling costs, 403, 411
. investment credit, 402
. limited partnerships, 404
. oil & gas, 409
. real estate, 407
. research & development, 416
. sale and leaseback, 407
. shopping centers, 408
. tax penalties, 425
. timber, 423
Term Insurance
. see "Life Insurance"
Timber:
 see "Tax shelters"
Time-sharing, 629
Treasury bills, 336
Trust accounts, 803
Truth in Lending Act, 702

-U-V-

Unified credit, 1115
Uniform Gifts to Minors Act, 801, 803
Uniforms, medical deduction for, 1221
Universal life insurance,
 see "Life insurance"
U.S. Government bonds, 334
Utility stocks, 309
Vacation home, 133
Vacations,
. airlines, 626

Vacations: *(continued)*
. discounts, 626
. package plans, 627
. offseason, 625
. time-sharing, 629
. vacation home, 133
Variable rate mortgage (VRM), 220
"Value Line" futures, 516
Veterans Adm'n (VA):
   see "Government-backed loans"

-W-Z-

Warranties:
. "full," 611
. homebuyers, 107
. "implied," 612
. "limited," 611, 612
Weight loss,
see "Medical expenses, deductible"
Whole Life Insurance,
see "Life insurance"
Wildcat oil & gas, 410
Working couple:
. child care credit, 1207
. income splitting, 812
. marriage penalty deduction, 1201
Wraparound mortgages, 115, 228
"Zero-interest" mortgage, 116